# Armed Conflict
# and
# Environmental Damage

# Armed Conflict
# and
# Environmental Damage

Wing Commander (Dr) U C Jha

Vij Books India Pvt Ltd
New Delhi (India)

Published by

**Vij Books India Pvt Ltd**
(Publishers, Distributors & Importers)
2/19 (Second Floor), Ansari Road, Darya Ganj
New Delhi - 110002
Phones: 91-11-43596460, 91-9811094883
e-mail : vijbooks@rediffmail.com

Paperback Edition 2015

Aditya & Malini

# Contents

# Preface

History is full of examples of armed conflicts that have plundered the environment. In the third Punic War, Roman legions, salted the ground to prevent the Carthaginians from challenging Rome; during World War I, the British set Romanian oil fields on fire; and during World War II, Germany and the Soviets adopted scorched earth tactics, other than the US dropping two nuclear bombs over Japan. States have continued to deliberately destroy the environment with impunity even in the modern era, i.e., post-World War II. A few examples are the US bombing of Korean dams in the Korean War of 1950–1953 and the extensive use of chemicals and environmental modification techniques during the Vietnam War of 1961-1975; the targeting of Iranian oil installations by Iraqi bombers during the Iraq–Iran war in the 1980s; the detonation of 720 oil wells and pumping of enormous quantities of Kuwaiti oil into the Red Sea by Iraqi soldiers during the Gulf War of 1990–1991; the intensive bombing of petrochemical plants, fertilizer-processing factories, and oil refineries in Kosovo by NATO's in 1999, resulting in the drainage of large quantities of toxic chemicals into the Danube; the catastrophic environmental damage wreaked in Afghanistan and Iraq during a decade of military operations by the US and allied forces since 2001; the extensive damage inflicted on infrastructure in Lebanon in the conflict of 2006; the targeting of fuel stations and tanks during Israel's military operations in Gaza in December 2008–January 2009, which severely contaminated soil and groundwater; and the use of chemical weapons in Syria in 2013.

The use of chemical weapons in Syria in August 2013 has reportedly caused nearly 2000 casualties. The use of explosive weapons in populated areas has been identified as a major factor responsible for the forced displacement of population in the country. Since March 2011, the bloody and complex civil war has driven nearly three million Syrians into neighbouring countries as refugees. Many more have been internally displaced and are in need of humanitarian assistance. The extensive use of cluster munitions, white phosphorus, high-explosive devices, depleted uranium (DU), landmines, and the use of an excessively large quantity of conventional weapons in international armed conflict (IAC) have made recovery more or less impossible. Evidence gathered by some scientists after the Gulf War, linked DU to birth defects and long-term illnesses, including cancer, in Iraq.

The scenario is equally grim in the sphere of non-international armed conflict (NIAC). Conflicts have affected important wildlife habitats in numerous countries since 1990. NIACs often take place in areas where there is little governmental control. Few public services are available to the hundreds of millions of people inhabiting these remote areas. In these conflicts, the military and the non-state actors deliberately and indiscriminately target the environment in order to deprive the opposing troops of cover, food and water. NIACs are marked by the use of landmines, violation of protected areas due to troop movements, poaching for food and scorched earth practices. The government forces as well as non-state actors are increasingly plundering natural resources to finance their operations. The refugees and internally displaced persons, who require shelter, food, water and cooking fuel, also damage the environment.

The destruction of habitats and the resultant loss of wildlife have been the most common and far-reaching impacts of NIACs on the environment. When large numbers of displaced people are temporarily resettled, they often clear the vegetation to farm and to obtain firewood—practices that swiftly lead to deforestation and erosion. Since internally displaced people are often located in ecologically marginal and vulnerable areas, the ability of the environment to recover subsequently may be limited. With the destruction of the habitat, certain plant and animal species may become threatened locally, or even extinct. In areas of conflict, troops often hunt large mammals in great numbers to obtain food. Further, during an armed conflict, those in power may be in need of immediate revenue. To fund their military activities, they may turn to commercial-scale extraction of natural resources such as timber, ivory and diamonds.

Military forces all over the world are also responsible for damaging the environment during their peacetime activities and in the post-conflict period. There are reports that presence of the Indian and Pakistani military in Siachen is taking a toll on the ecologically fragile environment. The global consumption of petroleum for military purposes is about six per cent of the total world consumption, or almost one-half of the total consumption of all developing countries combined.[1] Together with developmental issues,

---

1   Tolba, MK and OA El-Kholy, *The world environment 1972-1992: Two decades of challenge,* London: Chapman and Hall, 1992.

all these factors contribute to global warming. It has been predicted that global warming will have a severe impact on food and grain production, water resources and human settlements. It will give rise to mass movement and increase the risk of violent conflict, and is likely to cost the world trillions of dollars. The majority of those affected will be from East Asia, South East Asia and South Asia. With the world's population set to rise from six billion to nine billion people in the next half-century, there is a need to improve the management of our atmosphere, air, lands, soil, and oceans.[2]

Although armed conflict is a recurring feature, little effort has been made to limit the environmental effects of war. Today, there are a number of laws and regulations that are meant to restrict armed conflict in various ways. This legal framework consists of a body of declarations, conventions and treaties aimed at regulating the various aspects of warfare. However, the standards set by most conventions and protocols have proved inadequate in terms of preventing and redressing environmental degradation caused by armed conflict. International law has serious drawbacks and it seems impossible to prosecute an individual for environmental crimes arising from IACs or NIACs. Domestically, offences against the environment are generally dealt with as regulatory violations that fall under discrete parts of environmental statutes rather than as offences covered by central pieces of criminal codes. A number of environmental offences have been recognised as such following a public outcry over specific incidents.[3]

---

2   For instance desalination has become a necessity to meet increasing freshwater demand in the Gulf region. The energy intensive nature of this operation presents alarming projections: by 2035, Kuwait, for example, may have to allocate as much as 2.5 million barrels of oil per day for water desalination, equal to the country's entire 2011–2012 oil production. *The United Nations World Water Development Report 2014: Water and Energy*, Volume 2, Paris, The United Nations Educational, Scientific and Cultural Organization (UNESCO), 2014, p. 137.

3   The explosion at the Union Carbide chemical plant at Bhopal in December 1984 was the world's worst environmental accident so far. The plant used highly toxic chemicals in its production process; when water somehow mixed with these, the resulting explosion was catastrophic. Estimates of fatalities and of those seriously affected in the immediate aftermath and subsequently have varied, with official, academic and media reports suggesting around 6,000 or more fatalities, plus 60,000 people seriously affected by the toxic gases and over 20,000 permanently injured as a result of exposure. The ultimate impact of the event on the local natural environment and wildlife is still not clear. The result of this accident was that the Government of India made the amendments to the Factories Act in 1987 and introduced special provisions on hazardous industrial activities. It empowered the State to appoint site appraisal committee to advise on the initial location of the factories using hazardous processes. The Government also enacted, the Environment (Protection) Act, 1986. Besides

Because of these shortcomings, efforts have been made by activists and academics to draw the attention of the international community to the protection of the environment during armed conflict. This book attempts to highlight instances of the environmental devastation caused by armed conflict and arrive at a possible solution to overcome the lacunae in the field of international humanitarian law. The first chapter is introductory; besides defining the term 'environment', it surveys the literature relating to environmental damage during armed conflict. The second chapter discusses environmental devastation caused by international armed conflict, taking up examples spanning from World War I to the Israel-Palestine conflict of 2009. Environmental damage by NIACs is covered in the third chapter, which covers 16 such situations. Militaries are the prime users of sources of energy, especially oil, and besides being 'normal' polluter are also and 'special' polluters, producing toxic and radioactive wastes. The environmental damage caused by armed forces, primarily during training, garrison duty and weapon-testing have been discussed in the fourth chapter. The fifth chapter of the book reviews the treaty regime and the provisions of customary international law with respect to the protection of the environment and assesses their effectiveness. The last chapter, chapter 6, presents various options that could help to overcome the legal vacuum with respect to the protection of the natural environment during armed conflict, and also contains recommendations aimed at the United Nations, governments and the armed forces.

I am obliged to the UN Environmental Progamme (UNEP), as this work would not have been possible without consulting several of its reports. I express gratitude to my wife, Ratna, for all her support and to Ms Medha and Ms Chandana for the editorial assistance provided by them. My son, Aditya, contributed valuable comments on certain aspects of the book. Finally, I thank Vij Books India Pvt Ltd, New Delhi for their cooperation in bringing out this edition.

---

introducing provisions relating to the environmental offences, the Act empowers the Central Government to take all such measures as it considers necessary or expedient for the purpose of protecting and improving the quality of the environment and preventing, controlling and abating environmental pollution.

# CHAPTER 1

# Introduction

Throughout history, the environment has remained a mute victim of armed conflict. Militaries, in order to gain advantage over adversaries, have burned crops and fields, sprayed large quantities of chemicals on forests, destroyed dams and dykes and poisoned water supplies. Even in modern times, military commanders place a lot of emphasis on weather and terrain while planning campaigns. They manipulate natural resources for their strategic purposes, and even use natural processes as weapons. In the wake of armed conflict, the focus has always been on the loss of human life and destruction of property. Analysts have never calculated the ecological consequence of such conflicts. The destruction of the environment, depletion of natural resources, and death of flora and fauna has always been overlooked. In many places of the world today the environment is under heavy pressure, affecting the security of man and the community of life. In some places, armed conflicts have caused environmental degradation, while in others environmental degradation has been a factor causing violent conflict. Environmental degradation is increasingly threatening the natural resource base and processes upon which all life on earth depends. Species are becoming extinct at an unprecedented rate, taking with them yet unknown sources of medicines, nutrition and other benefits.

A number of analysts have predicted that environmental change in general and climate change in particular will have enormous impacts on humanity. In April 2007, the United Nations Security Council debated the link between climate change and conflict. The argument was that climate change would aggravate traditional and long-standing security issues, and six areas of linkage were identified: border disputes, migration, energy supplies, resource shortage, societal stress, and humanitarian crises. Christian Aid claims that an estimated 1 billion people will be forced to leave their homes between now and 2050, which might destabilize whole regions where increasingly desperate populations compete for dwindling food and water.[1] Homer-Dixon is of the view that climate change will catalyze insurgencies, genocide, guerrilla attacks, gang warfare, and global terrorism.[2] It has been reported that the future impacts of climate change will be more than threat multipliers; they will serve as catalysts for instability and conflict. The impacts of extreme weather in Africa, Asia, and the Middle East, such as prolonged drought, flooding, and resulting food shortages, desertification, population dislocation and mass migration, and sea level rise would pose serious security challenges to the governments.[3]

## Environment

The word 'environment' is derived from the French word *environner,* meaning to encircle. By broadly applying to surroundings, the environment can include the aggregate of natural, social and cultural conditions that influence the life of an individual or community.[4] Geographically, the environment can refer to a limited area or encompass the entire planet, including the atmosphere and stratosphere. The term 'environment', according to Article 2 of the UN Convention on Civil Liability for Damage Resulting from Activities Dangerous to the Environment,[5] includes: (i) natural resources both biotic and abiotic, such as air, water, soil, fauna and flora and the interactions between the same factors; (ii) property which forms part of the cultural heritage; and (iii) the characteristic aspects of landscape.

A look at national laws shows that there is no general agreement on the definition of the term 'environment'. The Environmental Protection Act of

---

1   *Human Tide: the Real Migration Crisis,* Christian Aid, 2007. Available at: http://www.christianaid.org.uk/Images/human_tide3__tcm15–23335.pdf, accessed 12 July 2013.

2   Homer-Dixon, Thomas, 'Terror in the Weather Forecast', *New York Times,* 24 April, 2007. Available at: www.nytimes.com/2007/04/24/opinion/24homer-dixon.html?_r=1&oref=slogin, accessed 31 January 2014.

3   As the world's population and living standards continue to grow, the projected climate impacts on the nexus of water, food, and energy security will become more profound. Fresh water, food, and energy are inextricably linked, and the choices made over how these finite resources will be produced, distributed, and used will have increasing security implications. *National Security and the Accelerating Risks of Climate Change,* The CNA Military Advisory Board, CNA Corporation, USA, 2014, p. 2-3.

4   Broadly, "environment" refers to the surroundings or conditions in which any person, animal or plant lives or operates. *The New Oxford English Dictionary,* 2000, p. 617.

5   Article 2(1), UN Convention on Civil Liability for Damage Resulting from Activities Dangerous to the Environment, Lugano, 21 June 1993.

Bulgaria defines environment as a complex of natural and anthropogenic factors and elements that are mutually interrelated and affect the ecological equilibrium and the quality of life, human health, the cultural and historical heritage and the landscape. [6] The Environment Act of India----includes water, air and land and the interrelationship which exists among and between water, air and land, and human beings, other living creatures, plants, micro-organism and property in its definition of the environment.[7] According to the British Act, the environment consists of all, or any, of the following media, namely, the air, water and land; and the medium of air includes the air within buildings and the air within other natural or man-made structures above or below ground.[8] The United States Council on Environment Quality defines the term environment as man's total environmental system including not only the biosphere but also his interactions with his natural and manmade surroundings. These definitions, however, exhibit one common aspect that the environment is not confined to national boundaries and it embraces all forms of life on this planet.

Despite the inability of the international legal community to agree on a useful definition of environment, it is clear that the trend is to view the environment as a very broad and inclusive entity.[9] The 1972 United Nations Conference on the Human Environment in Stockholm represented a first taking stock of the global human impact on the environment, and attempted to forge a common outlook on how to address the challenge of preserving and enhancing the human environment. It proclaimed that:

> Man is both creature and moulder of his environment, which gives him physical sustenance and affords him the opportunity for intellectual, moral, social and spiritual growth. In the long and tortuous evolution of the human race on this planet a stage has been reached when, through the rapid acceleration of science and technology, man has acquired the power to transform his environment in countless ways and on an unprecedented scale. Both aspects of man's environment, the natural and the man-

---

6 Section 1(1), The Environmental Protection Act (Supp.) 1991, Bulgaria.

7 Section 2 (a), The Environment (Protection) Act, 1986.

8 Section 1 (2), The Environmental Protection Act, 1990.

9 Jensen, Eric Talbot, The International Law of Environmental Warfare: Active and Passive Damage During Armed Conflict, Vol. 38 (1), *Vanderbilt Journal of Transnational Law* (2005), p. 152.

made, are essential to his well-being and to the enjoyment of basic human rights the right to life itself.

The protection and improvement of the human environment is a major issue which affects the well-being of peoples and economic development throughout the world; it is the urgent desire of the peoples of the whole world and the duty of all Governments.

Unfortunately, the damage and destruction of the environment has remained unchecked for the last five decades, not only because of its exploitation and haphazard economic development, but also due to armed conflict. Armed conflict has a direct impact on the environment through toxic hazards from the bombardment of industrial sites and urban infrastructure; landmines, unexploded ordnance and munitions including depleted uranium; use of hazardous chemicals; environmental damage caused by human displacement; use of extractive industry to fund conflicts; loss of infrastructure for water supply, sanitation and waste disposal; and scorched-earth tactics that directly affect the resources necessary for the livelihood.

## War or Armed Conflict

The terms 'war' and 'armed conflict' have been used interchangeably by historians. After the adoption of the United Nations Charter, the use of the term 'armed conflict'[10] has been preferred over 'war'.[11] The use of the term 'armed conflict' is not entirely new in international law. It has always been seen as the manifestation or expression of the concept of war. The Hague Convention IV of 1907 stressed that parties should make an effort to find means of preserving peace and preventing "armed conflict" between nations. As a rule, armed conflicts are generally defined as the

---

10 An armed conflict is a contested incompatibility which concerns government and/or territory where the use of armed force between two parties, of which at least one is the government of a state, results in at least 25 battle-related deaths. Wallensteen, Peter and Margareta Sollenberg, Armed Conflict 1989–2000, *Journal of Peace Research*, Vol. 38(5), 2001, p. 629–644.

11 The 1949 Geneva Conventions and their Additional Protocols use the terminology of 'armed conflict' instead of 'war'. There are two main reasons to introduce the concept of 'armed conflict' and to prefer it above the notion of 'war'. First the concept of 'armed conflict' more aptly captures the spectrum of violent clashes between organized groups; and second, the notion of armed conflict is a more legal one. The concept of 'armed conflict' allows for a better protection of victims regardless of formalism. After the notion of armed conflict was introduced, it was quickly adopted in other IHL documents and in resolutions of the UN General Assembly.

use of armed forces by one or more states against another state or several states (international armed conflict or IAC), or between one or more armed groups against their own government or between armed groups themselves (non-international armed conflict or NIAC).

The modern international law of war is now called the 'law of armed conflicts' or 'international humanitarian law (IHL)'. Sometimes the terms are used interchangeably. IHL has been defined as "international rules, established by treaties and customs, which are specifically intended to solve humanitarian problems directly arising from international or non-international armed conflicts and which, for humanitarian reasons, limit the rights of the parties to a conflict to use the methods and means of warfare of their choice or protect persons and property that are, or may be, affected by conflict."[12]

IHL distinguishes two types of armed conflicts: (a) IAC, involving two or more opposing states; and (b) NIAC, between governmental forces and non-governmental armed groups, or between such groups only.[13] An IAC occurs when one or more states take recourse to armed force against another state, regardless of the reasons or the intensity of the conflict.[14] The provisions of IHL may be applicable even in the absence of open hostilities. Moreover, no formal declaration of war or recognition of the situation is required.[15] The existence of an IAC, and as a consequence, the possibility

---

12  Y Sandoz, *Commentary on the Additional Protocols of 8 June 1977 to the Geneva Conventions of 12 August 1949*, Geneva: ICRC, p. xxvii..

13  The 'distinction' between international wars and internal conflicts is no longer factually tenable or compatible with the thrust of humanitarian law, as the contemporary law of armed conflict has come to be known. One of the consequences of the nuclear stalemate is that most international conflict now takes the guise of internal conflict, much of it conducted covertly or at a level of low intensity. Paying lip service to the alleged distinction simply frustrates the humanitarian purpose of the law of war in most of the instances in which war now occurs. W. Michael Reisman and J. Silk, Which law applies to the Afghan conflict? *American Journal of International Law*, Vol. 82, 1988, p. 465.

14  How is the Term 'Armed Conflict' defined in International Humanitarian Law? International Committee of the Red Cross (ICRC) Opinion Paper, March 2008. Available at: http://www.icrc.org/eng/assets/files/other/opinion-paper-armed-conflict.pdf, accessed 12 June 2014.

15  The International Criminal Tribunal for the former Yugoslavia (ICTY) proposed a general definition of international armed conflict. In the *Tadic* case, the Tribunal stated that "*an armed conflict exists whenever there is a resort to armed force between States.*" This definition has been adopted by other international bodies since then. ICTY, *The Prosecutor v. Dusko Tadic*, Decision on the Defence Motion for Interlocutory Appeal on Jurisdiction, IT-94-1-A, 2 October 1995, paragraph 70.

of applying IHL to the situation, depends on what actually happens on the ground. It is based on factual conditions. For example, there may be an IAC, even though one of the belligerents does not recognize the government of the adversary.[16]

NIACs are armed confrontations occurring within the territory of a single State and in which the armed forces of no other State are engaged against the central government.[17] IHL treaty law makes a distinction between two types of NIACs, as se out in common Article 3 of the Geneva Conventions of 1949 and the definition provided in Article 1 of the 1977 Additional Protocol II.[18] Internal disturbances and tensions (such as riots, isolated and sporadic acts of violence, or other acts of a similar nature) do not amount to a NIAC. They also do not encompass conflicts extending to the territory of two or more States. When a foreign State extends its military support to the government of a State within which a NIAC is taking place, the conflict remains non-international in character. Conversely, if a foreign State extends military support to an armed group acting against the government, the conflict becomes international in character.

Today, no one would deny that the nature of armed conflict is changing. The distinction between the two kinds of armed conflict--IAC and NIAC--is becoming less relevant and is gradually disappearing.[19] In reality NIAC

---

16  Dieter Fleck. 2008. *The Handbook of Humanitarian Law in Armed Conflicts*, Oxford: Oxford University Press, p. 45-57.

17  The San Remo Manual relating to the Law of Non-International Armed Conflict (2006). The International Committee of the Red Cross (ICRC) has proposed the following definition for NIAC: "NIAC are *protracted armed confrontations* occurring between governmental armed forces and the forces of one or more armed groups, or between such groups arising on the territory of a State [party to the Geneva Conventions]." The armed confrontation must reach *a minimum level of intensity* and the parties involved in the conflict must show *a minimum of organization*. ICRC Opinion paper, March 2008.

18  The treaty law governing NIAC is rather limited. It includes Common Article 3 of the 1949 Geneva Conventions for the Protection of War Victims; the 1977 Protocol Additional (II) to the Geneva Conventions of August 12, 1949, and Relating to the Protection of Victims of NIAC; the 1980 Convention on Certain Conventional Weapons, as amended, and its Protocols; the 1998 Statute of the International Criminal Court; the 1997 Ottawa Convention banning anti-personnel land mines; the 1993 Chemical Weapons Convention; and the 1954 Hague Convention for the Protection of Cultural Property and its 1999 Second Protocol. In addition to treaty law, there is a growing body of customary law applicable in NIAC. The International Court of Justice has recognized Common Article 3 as customary international law.

19  For further study on the issue see: Elizabeth Wilmshurst (ed.), *International Law and the Classification of Conflicts*, Oxford: Oxford University Press, 2012; James G. Stewart, Towards a single definition of armed conflict in international humanitarian

are often 'mixed' conflicts, that is, they take place largely within the territory of one State, but take place in an internationalized setting with a high level of foreign intervention involving both State and non-State actors. These conflicts both affect and are affected by the actions of neighbouring states and the international community at large. Thus, it is becoming increasingly difficult to categorize these conflicts as either IAC or NIAC. The changing tactics used in armed conflict have resulted in a shift in the casualties of war from combatant soldiers to innocent civilians, with an estimated nine civilian deaths for every death of a soldier. Armed conflict has moved from conventional battlefields to urban and rural centres, causing massive numbers of residents to flee to regions which lack adequate resources and infrastructure. This gives rise to not only economic, social and moral crises, but also massive pressure on the environment. The one thing common to these conflicts is that the environment is a constant victim, and the scale of destruction has increased over time.

The Stockholm International Peace Research Institute (SIPRI) has concluded that as the technology of weapons has increased, the number of munitions used to kill an enemy soldier has increased correspondingly. Thus, the amount of environmental damage resulting from warfare is also escalating.[20] The IHL instruments discourage the excesses of armed conflict, including the targeting of non-combatants, ill-treatment of prisoners of war, and destruction of dams and nuclear power stations. However, with the increasingly devastating potential of modern weapons and warfare, it has become apparent that the existing provisions of IHL do

---

law: A critique of internationalized armed conflict, *International Review of the Red Cross*, Volume 85, Number 850, June 2003, p. 313-348; Dwidre Willmott, Removing the Distinction between International and Non-international Armed Conflict in the Rome Statute of the International Criminal Court, *Melbourne Journal of International Law*, Volume 5, 2004; David E. Graham, Defining Non-International Armed Conflict: A Historically Difficult Task, in Kenneth Watkin and Andrew J. Norris (ed.), *Non-International Armed Conflict in the Twenty-first Century*, International Law Studies, Volume 88, Naval War College, p. 43-56; Sylvain Vite, Typology of armed conflicts in international humanitarian law: legal concepts and actual situations, *International Review of the Red Cross*, Volume 91, Number 873, March 2009, p. 69-94; Derek Jinks, The Temporal Scope of application of IHL in Contemporary Conflicts, Background Paper, Program on Humanitarian Policy and Conflict Research at Harvard University, 2003; and M E O'Connell, Defining Armed Conflict, Volume 13, *Journal of Conflict & Security Law*, Winter 2008, p. 393.

20 *Warfare in a Fragile World: Military Impact on the Human Environment*, 1980, Stockholm International Peace Research Institute (SIPRI), (hypothesizing an increase in environmental harm caused by an apparent shift in military targets from concentrated target bombing to less defined area bombing).

not fully address the danger that armed conflict poses to the environment. The danger may take the form of the indiscriminate use of landmines, the explosive remnants of war, radioactive hazardous wastes, damaged military machinery, or environmental destruction caused by mass movements of displaced persons. While there are relatively few instances of the deliberate targeting of the environment during IAC, there are a large number of NIACs, in which the environment is deliberately targeted, both by the government as well as the opposing forces.

Armed conflict was common in many parts of the world during the period of the Cold War, but today, almost all NIACs are concentrated in the poorest and most vulnerable areas of the world, i.e. Africa and Asia. According to the United Nations Environmental Programme, 40 per cent of all the intra-state conflicts since 1960 have had a link to natural resources, and these conflicts are twice as likely as IACs to recur within five years. The damage to the environment caused by these conflicts is not only deplorable in itself, but may increase the vulnerability of affected populations as well. For example, it may lead to the displacement of the population and the fleeing of increasing numbers of refugees to other countries. When civilian populations are displaced by armed conflict, the effects on the environment can be as great as those of direct military activities.[21] Once damaged, degraded or destroyed in armed conflict, the natural resources become future causes of conflict.[22]

## Armed Conflict and the Environment

Environmental degradation and armed conflict are interconnected

---

21 Negative impacts of refugees and internally displaced person on environment are: (i) clearing of large tracts of land for settlement causing a decrease in forested area and particular species (e.g. for timber and oil palm) causing and degradation of soil, (ii) pollution of water resources, (iii) dumping of waste, mineral extraction and sand mining, (iv) pit sawing and hunting, (v) decline in agricultural production hence food shortages and poor nutrition, (vi) decrease in the quantity of timber, and (vii) loss of biodiversity. Jojn O. Oucho, Environmental Impact of Refugees and Internally Displaced Persons in Sub-Saharan Africa, Keynote Address to the African Migration Alliance Biennial Workshop on Climate Change, Environment and Migration, East London, 15-16 November 2007.

22 Environmental degradation may become a cause of armed struggle, as history provides numerous examples how states and nations were destabilized by environmental collapse leading to famine, migration and rebellion. In addition environmental degradation may be viewed as contribution to armed conflict in the sense of exacerbating conflicts or adding new dimensions. Holst, Johan Jorgen, Security and the Environment: A Preliminary Exploration, Vol. 20 (2), *Bulletin of Peace Proposal*, 1989.

issues.[23] Throughout history, armed conflict has always left its mark on the environment.[24] Until the late seventeenth century, the environmental impacts of war were largely limited to the areas of conflict and the source locations for metal and wood. The damage to the environment became more severe with advances in technology.[25] Warfare and together with it, environmental damage, took a new dimensions in Europe in the 1790s, when under Napoleon, France increased the intensity of warfare and expanded its reach. By the late 1800s, accurate rifles and machine guns transformed the battlefield, and more powerful explosives were invented to damage both urban and rural targets. World War I saw a new level of environmental destruction as new weapons capable of producing terrifying results were unleashed. In the battle of Somme, 250,000 acres of farmland was destroyed and became unfit for agriculture. As a direct impact of war, almost 500,000 acres of French forests were destroyed. According to Lanier-Graham, in order to keep the Allied war effort going, over 20 billion board feet of timber was harvested.[26] In all, the effects of World War I on the environment were far-reaching, spreading across the globe.

The level of environmental devastation reached a new high in World War II. The nuclear bombs dropped on Hiroshima and Nagasaki were the two single most destructive events in human history. The massive amounts of radiation released made soil and water, inhospitable to both plants and animals. A few battlefields of WW I and II still remain unfit for cultivation

---

23 Since the start of the new millennium, 40 major conflicts and some 2500 disasters have affected billions of people –causing millions of deaths, destroying infrastructure, displacing vast numbers of those affected, and negatively impacting the ecosystems on which people's lives depend. *Programme Performance Report 2012-2013*, United Nations Environment Programme, p. 21.

24 The Roman army, known for their pragmatic combat engineering skills, sometimes diverted the course of streams either to cut an army off from its water supply or to redirect the stream through an enemy encampment. In some cases the Romans deliberately destroyed the dam to create a catastrophic flood designed to wipe out the camp of the opposing army. During the American Revolution war, General Washington ordered the fields of the Iroquois Indians, who were allied with the British, razed so only bare earth was left exposed.

25 Every year from 1814 to 2014, there was at least one interstate or civil war. Since World War II, there have been more than 236 wars in 150 locations. In 1999, more than two thirds of armed conflicts had lasted more than five years and about one third had lasted more than 20 years. People and the environment suffered the consequences for years after the armed conflict ended. Most current conflicts are fought within national borders, not between nations, but the effects often spill over to neighbouring countries.

26 Lanier-Graham, Susan D. 1993. *The Ecology of War: Environmental Impacts of Weaponry and Warfare*, New York: Walker and Company, p.19.

or dangerous to population because of unexploded devices (especially mines) and projectiles embedded in the soil.[27]

The post-World War II period saw an escalation with competition between the superpowers for developing military technology of increasing sophistication. The developed countries competed to build successive generations of ships, aircraft, missiles and fighting machines. The existing weapons, including chemical arsenal grew larger and more lethal.[28] The Vietnam War witnessed large-scale use of chemicals defoliants and destruction of forests, and attempts at rain-making by the US. In addition 14 million tons of bombs and shells, American planes sprayed 44 million litres of Agent Orange and 28 million litres of other defoliants over Vietnam. Nearly three million tons of bombs were dropped creating millions of craters. Many of these craters still exist 45 years after the end of the conflict. The result was serious damage to 1.7 million hectares of upland forest and mangrove marshes, widespread soil poisoning or loss of soil, and destruction of wildlife and fish habitat. These were widely criticized and resulted in international efforts to tackle the environmental consequences of warfare.

Destruction of the environment during Operation Desert Storm is a recent reminder of the military's destructive capability. The major factors that led to environmental destruction were: the explosive remnants of war left by the coalitions forces; and the deliberate destruction of oil wells by the Iraqi force. The daily release of heat from Kuwait's 950 oil wells was estimated to be about 86 billion watts, equivalent to that of a 500 acre forest fire. The fires burned nearly 5,000,000 barrels of oil daily and smoke spread as far as 800 miles south of Kuwait. During the Persian Gulf War, the plumes of burning oil wells darkened skies for months far downwind causing heavy pollution on nearby deserts, farmlands, and the Gulf's waters.

The destruction caused by the US and coalition forces was also significant and lasting.[29] While the UN (or the US) devised a means to punish Iraq by

---

27  Bouvier Antoine, Protection of the natural environment in time of armed conflict, No. 285, *International Review of the Red Cross*, December 1991, p. 567-578.

28  Creveld Martin Van, War in Complex Environments: The Technological Dimension, Prism 1, No. 3, p.119-20. Available at: http://ndupress.ndu.edu/lib/images/prism1-3/Prism_115-128_vanCreveld.pdf, accessed 29 May 2014.

29  Major General Robert E. Linhard, Protection of the Environment During Armed Conflict and Other Military Operations, in Grunawalt, Richard J., John E. King and Ronald S. McClain (ed.), *Protection of Environment during Armed Conflict* , International Law Studies, Volume 69, Naval War College, Newport, p. 59.

imposing sanctions and constituting a compensation commission under international law, no action was taken to fix the responsibility for the environmental harm caused by the coalition forces.[30] Several authors have justified the acts of the US and the coalition forces and the environmental degradation as 'collateral damage'. Though some of the coalition countries helped Kuwait to clean up the residue and ravages of armed conflict,[31] no such action was taken for the rehabilitation of the Iraqi natural environment.[32]

During the Gulf War, the US and its allies used depleted uranium (DU) weapons and large-scale mining both on land and at sea. This created a massive battlefield remnants problem. Although the radioactive levels of DU weapons are considered too low to be a general environmental threat, special handling is required to avoid contamination. It was reported by Iraqi doctors that the DU left behind by the US military had contributed to a spike in cancer rates and birth defects among Iraqi civilians. Recent studies have found that DU particles can persist in the environment for 30 years and that short-term studies cannot accurately predict the corrosion of penetrators.[33]

---

30 The 1991 Gulf War posed a significant hazard to not only the environment of the theatre of operations but to the global environment as well. Incidentally, during the 1991 Persian Gulf War the environmental protection regulations with respect to assessment of the impact of Pentagon projects on the environment were waived in the US. The agreement to waive the requirements was reached to allow the Pentagon to expedite several projects considered vital to the war effort including an increase in the number of flights from Westover Air Force Base in Massachusetts and the testing of new land mine detection and detonation techniques at a base located in the west. Keith Schneider, "Environmental Rule is Waived for Pentagon", *The New York Times*, 30 January 1991.

31 Lanier-Graham, Susan D. 1993. *The Ecology of War: Environmental Impacts of Weaponry and Warfare*, New York: Walker and Company, p. 63-64.

32 During Operation Desert Shield and Desert Storm, US military forces consumed about as much fuel as the seven Persian Gulf countries that assisted them. This US fuel use was equal to one-fifth of all energy consumed by the entire US Department of Defence during 1991. Military consumption of oil in the form of fuel during the war was far exceeded by losses resulting from Iraqi sabotage of Kuwaiti oil fields and terminals. The amount of oil lost from Iraqi sabotage was not trivial; the greater impact was from the resulting economic and ecological effects. Ecological effects of oil spills in the Persian Gulf were magnified by the fact that it took five years to flush contaminated water through the narrow Strait of Hormuz into the Arabian Sea. Martin H. Bender, 'Military Energy Consumption and Environmental Losses of Oil during the 1991 Persian Gulf War', The Land Institute, 2 June 2003. Available at: http://www.envirosagainstwar.org/know/read.php?itemid=230, accessed 20 May 2014.

33 Two new studies from the UK have now shed more light on the processes that impact on

While the Iraqi use of mines and burning of oil wells received a lot of attention, the uses of cluster bombs and depleted uranium by the US and its allies the received must less attention. For instance, the US and allied forces used nearly 61,800 cluster bombs, containing some 20 million bomblets. By a rough estimate, if 10 per cent of these bomblets were duds, they would have left about 2 million unexploded mines.[34]

Operation Allied Force, the United States-led NATO bombing campaign against the Former Republic of Yugoslavia (FRY) on behalf of Kosovo, was initiated on 24 March 1999. The NATO forces targeted an aircraft production factory, fuel storage facilities, oil refineries, pharmaceutical plants, fertilizer production facilities, and petrochemical plants. These airstrikes caused the release of 2,100 metric tons of ethylene dichloride (EDC) and 200 kg of metallic mercury into an adjacent wastewater canal leading to the Danube River. They also resulted in the burning of hundreds of tons of oil products and chemicals releasing highly toxic dioxins, hydrochloric acid, carbon monoxide, polyaromatic hydrocarbons, sulphur dioxide, nitrogen dioxide, and carbon monoxide into the air. The impact of the release of these chemicals into the environment was devastating to humans and the ecosystem.

During the war in the Balkans, NATO forces bombed petro-chemical plants in the suburbs of Belgrade. These air raids destroyed a plastics factory and an ammonia production unit within the complexes, releasing toxins such as chlorine, ethylene dichloride, and vinyl chloride monomer into the atmosphere. These chemicals not only have an immediate and life-threatening effect on humans but also have a residual effect on the environment. Similarly, during the armed conflict in Lebanon in 2006,

---

DU's environmental persistence. The studies were undertaken at two DU firing ranges at Kircudbright in Scotland, where DU rounds are fired into the sea, and Eskmeals in England, where DU was fired into hard targets to examine its effectiveness against different types of armour. Researchers took samples of DU particles from the site and subjected them to analysis to assess how they had changed over the 30 years since they were produced and the uranium oxides particles that had been produced were highly resistant to corrosion and as a result, 30 years after firing the particles would still present an inhalational hazard if resuspended. International Coalition to Ban Uranium Weapons, 30 January 2014. Available at: http://www.bandepleteduranium.org/en/new-studies-on-du-environment, accessed 2 February 2014.

34   William M. Arkin, The Environmental Threats of Military Operations, in Grunawalt, Richard J., John E. King and Ronald S. McClain (ed.), *Protection of Environment during Armed Conflict* , International Law Studies, Volume 69, Naval War College, Newport, p. 125.

the bombing of the Jiyeh power station led to the release of approximately 10,000 to 15,000 tons of fuel oil into the Mediterranean Sea. This resulted in significant contamination of the shoreline, including protected ecological reserve.[35] The consequences of this attack were such that clean-up activities exceeded local capacities and thus required intensive international assistance.[36]

Damage to the environment is not confined to IAC. During the past four decades, NIAC have far outnumbered IAC and the environmental damage caused by these has been a matter of concern for the international community. A partial list of the countries affected by NIACs includes Afghanistan, Angola, Bosnia, the Democratic Republic of Congo, Cambodia, Central African Republic, Colombia, Guatemala, India, Indonesia, Liberia, Mexico, Myanmar, Nepal, Pakistan, Peru, the Philippines, Sierra Leone, Senegal, Sri Lanka, the Solomon Islands, Sudan, South-Sudan and Syria. By definition, an NIAC is a conflict taking place within the borders of a single State, however, in most cases, the environmental impact of such conflict spill over to the neighbouring states, as happened in the Great Lakes region of Africa. During the past 50 years, Africa has been plagued by a large number of armed conflicts. Most of these have been NIACs and many have occurred in countries with a rich biodiversity and over 80 percent have occurred fully or partially in biodiversity hotspots. At least half of the conflict zones included forests and in Africa, such conflicts have affected up to two thirds of forested lands.

After the first Gulf War, the Iraqi Government was responsible for the systematic destruction of the Mesopotamian Marshes, the largest wetlands in Southwest Asia, extending along the Tigris, the Euphrates and the Shatt-el-Arab. They had been occupied by the descendents of the Sumerian and Babylonian people. Reeds were their main building material, while rice, fish, water buffaloes and birds were their main source of food. In 1991, after the Maadan and other Shia tribes revolted against the Iraqi regime, the

---

35   In a research paper of May 1993, titled, "The Impact of Environmental Protection on the Operational Commander's War-fighting Decisions", Commander Shawn B. Morrissey of the US Navy put forth a question: "Imagine the public relations impact of an attack on a suspected chemical plant which causes the release of chemicals into a nearby river causing significant contamination and death of wildlife. What if the target had been a petroleum plant and the oil spill had not only contaminated the target country but other countries downriver?" Paper submitted to the Faculty of the Naval War College. Available at: http://www.dtic.mil/dtic/tr/fulltext/u2/a266558.pdf, accessed 21 January 2014.

36   *Lebanon: Post-Conflict Environmental Assessment*, 2007, UNEP, p. 42-49.

government responded with an attack on the environment that supported them. It built a system of draining canals that reduced the marshes to 7 per cent of their initial 15,000 sq km. The wetlands turned into a salt crust, and the vegetation and wildlife disappeared.

In the ongoing conflict in Damascus, Syria, the use of chemical weapons— most probably a nerve agent--in August 2013, caused nearly 2000 casualties.[37] Even those who survived the suspected chemical weapons attack may have life-long disabilities and health problems for which there are few effective treatments. The use of explosive weapons in populated areas has been identified as a major driver of forced population displacements. Since March 2011, the conflict has driven more than 2.8 million Syrians into neighbouring countries as refugees,[38] while 6.5 millions are internally displaced and in need of humanitarian assistance.[39] These factors will have a tremendous impact on the natural environment in Syria as well as the neighbouring countries. In a country torn apart by conflict, agencies

---

37  Syria has long been equipped with a massive chemical arsenal, together with many related delivery systems. Syria is believed to have more than 1,000 metric tons of chemical warfare agents and precursor chemicals. The Syrian chemical programme started in the 1970's by the import of chemical munitions. In the 1980's, Damascus started acquiring the materials, products and knowledge necessary to set up an autonomous and massive production capacity in that field. The Syrian regime acknowledged on July 23, 2012 that chemical and non-conventional weapons are stockpiled and secured under the supervision of the armed forces. The Syrian arsenal has been massive and its stockpile included sulfur mustard, VX and sarin. The Syrian government, which had not signed the Chemical Weapons Convention (CWC), submitted its instrument of accession on September 14, 2013; the Convention entered into force for Syria on October 14, 2013. As a party to the CWC, Syria is required to declare all of its stocks and destroy its chemical weapon stocks, munitions, precursor chemicals, and related production and storage facilities under international supervision. Based on a joint US-Russian proposal, the Executive Council of the Organization for the Prohibition of Chemical Weapons (OPCW), an intergovernmental body tasked with implementation of the CWC, adopted a chemical weapons destruction plan for Syria on September 27, 2013. The Security Council Resolution 2118 (adopted 27 September 2013), required Syria to comply with 'all aspects' of the OPCW decision. The OPCW executive decision requires Syria to complete the elimination of all chemical weapons material and equipment by 30 June 2014. A joint mission of UN and OPCW staff has been created to monitor and facilitate Syrian chemical weapons disarmament.

38  More than 2.8 million Syrian refugees have sought protection in the region. The average rate of monthly registrations continues to exceed 100,000 so far in 2014. Total persons of concern to the UN refugee agency, the UNHCR are 2,855,089 (registered refugees 2,788,863; and persons awaiting registration 66,226). Available at: http://data. unhcr.org/syrianrefugees/regional.php, accessed 14 June 2014.

39  Syria: The Chaos of War, Journey Without End, *National Geographic Magazine*, March 2014, p. 52.

charged with protecting the environment are usually weak, and the government is consumed with restoring its security from civil uprising. According to the World Resource Institute; "Amid war's brutality, death, and deprivation, the environment may seem a minor casualty. Yet, the destruction of the environment, along with the demolition of democratic, informed decision-making, can prolong human suffering for decades, undermining the foundation for social progress and economic security."[40]

A study of post-World War II armed conflicts in Vietnam, Korea, the Gulf region, former Yugoslavia, Iraq, Afghanistan, Lebanon and Syria manifest that no considerations have been given by the military commanders to the environmental damage during military operations undertaken in support of the war effort. The focus has been on the defeat of the adversary and environmental damage has been considered an unavoidable side-effect of the armed conflict. No military commander has ever been prosecuted by his government for causing serious unwarranted damage to opponent's natural environment.

The UN General Assembly, in recognition of the threat war poses to the environment, established the Post Conflict Management Branch (PCMB) of the UN Environmental Progamme (UNEP) in 2001. Creating the link between the protection of the environment and armed conflicts, the UN General Assembly proclaimed on 5 November 2001, that November 6 of each year would be named International Day for Preventing the Exploitation of the Environment in War and Armed Conflicts. Through its Disasters and Conflicts Sub-programme, the PCMB assesses the effect of armed conflict on the environment, provides measures for environmental recovery, and works on building environmental cooperation. Among the countries in which the PCMB has worked are Afghanistan, Sudan, South Sudan, Iraq, Lebanon, Pakistan, Indonesia and Sri Lanka. Armed conflict affects the environment in six ways.

First, toxic hazards from conventional bombardment, oil fires, and conflict in industrial areas create areas of contamination. During the war in Kosovo, for example, NATO bombed oil refineries in the Serbian cities of Pancevo and Novi Sad. This caused toxic chemicals to leak into the Danube and affected water and soil in Serbia and its neighbours. During the first Gulf War in 1991, Iraqi forces ignited a large number of oil wells. The oil from

---

40 World Resources Institute, *World Resources 2002–2004: Decisions for the Earth: Balance, Voice, and Power*, p. 27. Available at: http://www.wri.org/publication/world-resources-2002-2004, accessed 5 February 2014.

the fires spewed into the Persian Gulf and killed more than 25,000 birds.

Second, refugees escaping armed conflict cause the depletion of natural resources. Often forced to settle in resource-scarce areas, they put further pressure on forests, land, water, and wildlife. They also put an extra burden on existing infrastructure, e.g., living quarters, water supplies, and waste systems. The UN refugee agency, UNHCR has reported that in 2012, 45.2 million people worldwide lived away from their homes due to forcible displacement. Most were in the developing world, which hosts four-fifths of the world's refugees. In Jordan alone, it has been estimated that the number of Syrian refugees reached 1.2 million by the end of 2013.

Third, the armed conflict often causes deforestation, either as an unintended side-effect of combat operations or as an intended effect. One example of direct deforestation is the use of chemicals by the US in the Vietnam War. On the other hand, the conflict in Rwanda led to indirect deforestation, as displaced people felled large sections of forests for survival and the Rwandan army cleared a swath of vegetation up to 100 meters wide along a key trail to reduce the threat of ambush. Similarly the Congolese army in 1999, created a corridor that ran through a national park to prevent insurgent factions from advancing unseen.

Fourth, landmines, cluster munitions, unexploded ordnance, and weapons made of depleted uranium disseminate toxic materials, displace people to more fragile ecosystems, and disrupt resource management and ecotourism. According to the UN, in 2003, there were more than 100 million unexploded landmines in more than 60 countries. Over the past decade, States have removed just 3 million of them. Addressing this problem is costly and time consuming: while it takes just three US dollars to make a landmine, it takes several hundred dollars to dismantle one. In Sudan, direct damage from military attacks, such as bombings, has been negligible, but unexploded landmines have endangered wildlife.

Fifth, armed conflict leads to pollution of air, water and soil. For example, the US and coalition forces left thousands of tons of waste in Afghanistan and Iraq, which will affect the local population for decades to come. The conflict continues to pose dangerous risks to human health and the surrounding environment. According to the Science for Peace Institute, University of Toronto, 10 to 30 per cent of all environmental degradation in the world is a direct result of the various militaries.[41]

---

41 Lanier-Graham, Suzan D. 1993. *The Ecology of War: Environmental Impacts of*

Sixth, armed conflict can wreak havoc on government conservation efforts, especially in protected areas. For example, during the Ethiopian-Eritrean war, parks and reserves lacked funds for staff, infrastructure, research, and management training. In countries where nature tourism provides a major source of income for biodiversity protection, that source quickly evaporates when conflict begins. Armed Conflict often leads to the breakdown of law and order, leaving protected areas and species vulnerable to exploitation. For example, during the Maoist insurgency in Nepal and Sierra Leone's civil war in the 1990s, regional forestry officers, foresters, rangers, and guards went unpaid for long periods, and illegal mining and logging, killing of protected species and massive deforestation occurred in forest reserves. In the Central African Republic, hunting and poaching in war-torn provinces reduced the country's elephant numbers by 90 per cent and led to the disappearance of the rhinoceros. In Cambodia, the Khmer Rouge's trade in timber brought US$10–20 million a month in funds for its civil war effort. This has continued in the Congo, where reports from 2013 reveal that the Lord's Resistance Army has poached elephants to collect and sell ivory in an effort to garner monetary support for its efforts. Even after armed conflicts end, weak political institutions may not have the authority, ability, or funds to effectively manage their country's natural resources. In addition, the military establishments consume great amounts of fossil fuels, causing negative impact on land, air, wildlife and water resources.

## Ecocide

The term ecocide was used for the first time in 1970 at the Conference on War and National Responsibility in Washington, with reference to deliberate destruction of environment. In 1972, at the UN's Stockholm Conference on the Human Environment, then Prime Minister of Sweden referred explicitly to the Vietnam War as an 'ecocide'.[42] However, there was no reference to ecocide in the official documents of the Stockholm conference. Later, Dai Dong, a branch of the International Fellowship

---

*Weaponry and Warfare*, Walker & Company (1993), p. xxix.

42 Many governments were reluctant to protest against what the US has done in Vietnam and thus avoided a concern with environmental warfare. Mrs Indira Gandhi, the then Prime Minister of India and the leader of the Chinese delegation, Mr Tang Ke, also denounced the Vietnam War on human and environmental terms. Bjork, Tord, *The emergence of popular participation in world politics: United Nations Conference on Human Environment 1972*, Department of Political Science, University of Stockholm, 1996, p. 15. Available at: http://www.folkrorelser.org/johannesburg/stockholm72.pdf, accessed 16 March 2014.

of Reconciliation, sponsored a Convention on Ecocidal War (CEW) in Stockholm. The CEW called for a UN convention on ecocidal warfare, to define the term and condemn it as an international crime of war. A draft International Convention on ecocide was also prepared.[43]

Ecocide refers to the process whereby an organism destroys its ecosystem through its own intentional or unintentional actions. While the term can apply to biological processes, increasingly it is used to describe human activities and practices that cause widespread damage to habitats and environments. A proposed definition of ecocide is: "The extensive damage to, destruction of or loss of ecosystem(s) of a given territory, whether by human agency or by other causes, to such an extent that peaceful enjoyment by the inhabitants of that territory has been or will be severely diminished." [44] According to Broswimmer (2002:109), ecocide includes the use of weapons of mass destruction, whether nuclear, bacteriological, or chemical; attempts to provoke natural disasters such as eruption of volcanoes, earthquakes, or floods; the military use of defoliants; the use of bombs to impair soil quality or to enhance the prospect of disease; the bulldozing of forests or croplands for military purposes; the attempt to modify weather or climate as a hostile act; and, finally, the forcible and permanent removal of humans or animals from their habitual place of habitation on a large scale to expedite the pursuit of military or other objectives.[45]

The term 'ecocide' or 'eco-war' has also been used for the extensive destruction of ecosystem associated with military conflicts.[46] Ecocide can and often does lead to cultural damage and destruction; and the direct destruction of a territory can lead to cultural genocide. For example, destroying an indigenous peoples' territory can critically undermine its culture, identity and way of life.[47] Environmental devastation, particularly

---

43 Falk, Richard A., 'Environmental Warfare and Ecocide – Facts, Appraisal, and Proposals', in Thee, Marek (ed.), *Bulletin of Peace Proposals*, Volume 1, 1973, p. 80–96.

44 Eradicating Ecocide, available at:http://eradicatingecocide.com/wp-content/uploads/2012/06/faqs-on-ecocide-law.pdf, accessed 21 March 2014.

45 Broswimmer, F J, Ecocide, *A Short history of Mass Extinction of Species*, 2002, London: Pluto Press.

46 Brisman Avi, Crime-Environment Relationship and Environmental Justice, Vol. 6, Issue 2, *Seattle Journal for Social Justice*, 2008, p.727-817.

47 Anja Gauger, Mai Pouye Rabatel-Fernel, Louise Kulbicki, Damien Short and Polly Higgins, *Ecocide is the missing 5th Crime Against Peace*, London, Human Rights

directed at areas on which indigenous peoples depend for their survival, could be tantamount to genocide or 'ethnocide'.[48]

Since the 1970s many scholars and legal analysts have argued for the criminalization of ecocide. The Sub-Commission on Prevention of Discrimination and Protection of Minorities in its study of the genocide Convention for the UN's Human Rights Commission, proposed the addition of ecocide, as well as reintroduction of cultural genocide, to the list of crimes.[49] The UN International Law Commission (ILC) had also unsuccessfully considered the inclusion of ecocide in the Code of Crimes Against the Peace and Security of Mankind, which later became the Rome Statute of the international Criminal Court (ICC).[50] The proposed Article 26 on crime of damage to the environment during peacetime was removed mysteriously from the Code.[51] In the final version adopted by the ILC, after further amendments by the Drafting Committee, Article 8 (2)(b)(iv) on war crimes referred only to the intentional creation of 'widespread, long-term and severe damage to the natural environment' in the context of war. At present, this is the only provision in international law to hold a perpetrator responsible for environmental damage; albiet, limited to wartime situations and intentional damage. However, it has not been used by the ICC, and nor have comparable articles been used by the *ad hoc* courts. Environmental crimes, such as the pollution of water wells and destruction of ecosystems, can also be seen in the lights of crime against humanity. This interpretation was used in the original prosecution of President Bashir of Sudan who destroyed the water wells and environmental bases of the population in Darfur, thus forcing them to migrate. This charge was not accepted by the ICC as it was not considered to be a core feature of the attacks.

The term ecocide has appeared in a number of national penal legislations.[52]

---

Consortium, 2013, p. 6.

48 Bruch Carl E., All's Not Fair in (Civil) War: Criminal Liability for Environmental Damage in Internal Armed Conflict, Vol. 25, No. 3, *Vermont Law Review*, (2000-2001), p. 695-752, at p. 727.

49 E/CN.4/Sub.2/416, 4 July 1978, p.128-134.

50 Rome Statute of the International Criminal Court 17 July 1998.

51 Anja Gauger, Mai Pouye Rabatel-Fernel, Louise Kulbicki, Damien Short and Polly Higgins, *Ecocide is the missing 5th Crime Against Peace*, London, Human Rights Consortium, 2013, p. 6.

52 Several States have made ecocide during peacetime a national crime. In these countries' penal codes, the crime of ecocide stands alongside the other four international Crimes Against Peace; Crimes Against Humanity, Genocide, War Crimes and Crimes of

Vietnam, as a consequence of its experiences during the long Vietnam War, was the first county to include the crime of ecocide in its domestic law,[53] followed by Russia in 1996. Other countries which have included ecocide in their national penal codes are Kazakhstan, Kyrgyzstan and Tajikistan. Some like Armenia, Belarus, Republic of Moldova, Ukraine and Georgia have included ecocide as a Crime Against Peace. In Georgia, the crime of ecocide is punishable by imprisonment extending from eight to twenty years.[54]

## Environmental Terrorism

Schwartz (1998), who put forth the concept of 'environmental terrorism', says that environmental destruction or the threat of destruction can be labelled 'terrorism' when: (i) the act or threat breaches national and/or international law governing the disruption of the environment during peacetime or wartime; and (ii) the act or threat exhibits the fundamental characteristics of terrorism (i.e., the act or threat of violence has specific objectives, and the violence is aimed at a symbolic target). To be classified as environmental, an act must meet these two criteria and the perpetrator must use the environment as an authentic symbol to instil fear in the larger population over the ecological consequences of the act.[55] Saddam Hussein's action of ordering the detonation of a large number of oil wells in the 1991 Gulf War amounted to environmental terrorism.[56]

---

Aggression. These four core crimes are set out as international crimes in the Rome Statute.

53 Article 278, Penal Code Vietnam 1990 Article 278: 'Ecocide, destroying the natural environment', whether committed in time of peace or war, constitutes a crime against humanity.

54 Criminal Code of the Republic of Armenia 2003, Article 394; Criminal Code Belarus 1999, Article 131; Penal Code Republic of Moldova 2002, Article 136; Criminal Code of Ukraine 2001, Article 441; Criminal Code of Georgia 1999, Article 409; Penal Code Kazakhstan 1997, Article 161; Criminal Code Kyrgyzstan 1997, Article 374; Criminal Code Tajikistan 1998, Article 400.

55 For general discussion on nuclear and bioterrorism see: Zirojevic Mina, Markovic Milos and Pocuca Milan, Nuclear and Biological terrorism Implication on Environment, Vol. LXII, No. 1144, *The Review of International Affairs*, 2011, p. 97-108.

56 Lanier-Graham, Susan D. 1993. *The Ecology of War: Environmental Effects of Weaponry and Warfare*, New York: Walker and Company; Winnefeld, James A. and Mary E. Morris. 1994. *Where Environmental Concerns and Security Strategies Meet: Green Conflict in Asia and the Middle East*, Santa Monica, CA: RAND; Schwartz Daniel M., Environmental Terrorism: Analyzing the Concept, Vol. 35, No. 4, *Journal of Peace Research*, 1998, p. 484.

## Conflict Timber

Timber is an easily exploitable, valuable and readily marketable commodity, and has been the resource of choice in several recent IACs and NIACs.[57] For example large areas of forests in the Philippines were cleared, leading to erosion.[58] In 2001, a UN panel of experts investigating the illegal exploitation of natural resources in the Democratic Republic of Congo (DRC) coined the term 'conflict timber'. It is defined as wood that has been traded or taxed at some point in the chain of custody by armed groups, be they rebel factions or state militaries, or by a civilian administration involved in armed conflict to finance hostilities or otherwise perpetuate conflict. It is closely linked to illegal logging by rebel factions or regular soldiers, either to perpetuate conflict or take advantage of conflict situations for personal gain. The term conflict timber may also be used when timber harvesting leads to competition among forest user groups over remaining forest resources, which ends in conflict (conflict over forest resources). In such cases timber can be viewed as a conflict commodity, comparable to gold, diamonds and other commodities that lead to conflicts.[59]

Conflict timber helped the Khmer Rouge and other factions during the civil war in Cambodia; it helped sustain Liberia's support for the RUK rebels in neighbouring Sierra Leone; and helped fuel a civil war in the Democratic Republic of Congo. The timber trade in Afghanistan and neighbouring Pakistan resulted in significant forest reduction in the eastern provinces of Afghanistan.[60] Local communities lost control over the resources on which they depended for their survival, and forest resources were largely used for immediate profit by organized crime syndicates and traders. In almost every case where conflict timber has been used to finance a State's war fighting capacity, governments or individuals within them have used war

---

57 The Logs of War, The Timber Trade and Armed Conflict, Fafo Institute of Applied Science and Global Witness, London, March 2002, p.7.

58 Greg Bankoff, 'Wood for War: The Legacy of Human Conflict on the Forests of the Philippines', in Charles E. Closmann (ed.), *War and the Environment: Military Destruction in the Modern Age*, USA: Texas A&M University Press, 2009, p. 32-48.

59 Murl Baker and Robert Clausen, *Conflict Timber: Dimensions of the Problem in Asia and Africa, Volume III: African Cases*, US Agency for International Development, p. 12.

60 Illegal logging and forest crime has an estimated worth of $30 to $100 billion annually, or 10 to 30 percent of the total global timber trade. An estimated 50 to 90 percent of the wood in some individual tropical countries is suspected to come from illegal sources or has been logged illegally. Nellemann, C., et al., (eds). 2014. *The Environmental Crime Crisis – Threats to Sustainable Development from Illegal Exploitation and Trade in Wildlife and Forest Resources*, UNEP and GRID-Arendal, Nairobi and Arendal.

as a cover to loot the state's natural resources, using the revenue to further personal political aims or to accrue personal fortunes.[61]

## Environmental Benefits of Armed Conflict

Sometimes military conflicts may prove to be positive for the environment, at least in the short-term and under certain conditions. During WW II, for example, the grey wolf population in Russia grew significantly. During the German occupation of Norway, local citizens were not allowed to hunt. This led to a surge in the population of bears, foxes and wolverines.[62] Demilitarized zones (DMZs) are often beneficial for biodiversity. For instance, the DMZ of the Korean Peninsula (a 5.4-km wide strip of mountainside, stretching about 250 km across Korea) became a haven for rare and endangered flora and fauna and now constitutes a unique wildlife zone.[63] Similarly, the demilitarized zone between the Eastern Block and Western Europe (from the WW II till early 1990's) functioned as a refuge for fauna and flora that was under increasing pressure at other places.

Other examples of the positive impacts of war are to be found among those species that feed on battlefield casualties. It was reported that the tiger population increased in the jungles of Southeast Asia during the Vietnam War. During the Iran-Iraq War, sharks entered the rivers---unusual territory for them---to feed on dead soldiers. When the German Navy forced the closure of the North Atlantic fisheries during WW II, fish stocks recovered dramatically and the catches after the war were larger than ever before. During the Central American wars of the 1980s, trade in mahogany, cedar, animal skins, sea turtles, shrimp, and lobsters nearly stopped. Hunting decreased, and the populations of several endangered species increased dramatically. There was a limited resurgence of even

---

61  The Logs of War, The Timber Trade and Armed Conflict, Fafo Institute of Applied Science and Global Witness, London, March 2002, p.13.

62  Lanier-Graham Susan D. 1993. *The Ecology of War: Environmental Impacts of Weaponry and Warfare*, New York: Walker and Company, p. 73.

63  This area containing marshes, meadows, oak, pine and maple forests, is a habitat of lynx and numerous previously endangered animals. The area today is home to nearly the entire world population of red-crowned cranes—plus mallards, geese, golden eagles, and white-tailed eagles. McNeely, J.A. 2000. War and biodiversity: an assessment of impacts, In: Austin, J.E. and Bruch, C.E. (eds.), *The Environmental Consequences of War: Legal, Economic, and Scientific Perspectives*, Cambridge: Cambridge University Press. Also see: Kim, Ke Chung, Preserving Biodiversity in Korea's Demilitarized Zone, *Science* Vol. 278 (10 October 1997), pp. 242-243; Wildlife Conservation Society, Amid Land Mines and Barbed Wire, Rare Species Abound. Available at: http://www.wcs.org/news/breakingnews/international/990323.dmz.html, accessed 26 June 2014.

populations of jaguars, ocelots, margays, manatees, and river otters.[64] Sea battles have left remains of vessels scattered throughout the world's seas. Notwithstanding the serious adverse environmental effects of these vessels, they have become habitats for colonies of marine plants and animals.[65]

NIACs too can occasionally benefit the environment. For instance, during the Nicaraguan civil war of the 1980s, timber felling ceased; conversion of forests to agricultural land slowed and stopped; animal trafficking largely halted; and fishing declined as fishermen, fearing naval mines stayed ashore, allowing depleted stocks to be restored. McNeely has listed the negative and positive impacts of armed conflict on biodiversity.[66] The negative impacts include desertification, increase in wildlife poaching, destruction of habitat, pollution of land and water, and the forced movement of displaced persons into marginal land. The benefits of armed conflict to environment are, however, incidental, inadvertent and accidental, rather than planned side-effects.

## Literature Survey

The literature on environmental damage during armed conflict is scanty and lacks scientific evaluation. Only two international armed conflicts, *viz*, the Vietnam War[67] and the 1990-1991 Gulf War,[68] have been evaluated in the context of environmental damage. However, the Vietnam War studies are not always supported by scientific evidence. Only a few studies have established birth-defects in Vietnam due to the high concentrations of

---

64  Lanier-Graham, Susan D. 1993. *The Ecology of War: Environmental Impacts of Weaponry and Warfare*. New York: Walker and Company, 1993, p. 42.

65  It was reported that marine world survived amid the wreckage of war; and planes and ships became reefs, housing many specimens of marine life. Even amid the rifles, gas masks, helmets, and boots of nearly half a century ago, life remains a vital force, and nature seems somehow stronger than humans could ever comprehend. Benchley Peter, Ghosts of War in the South Pacific, *National Geographic*, April 1988, p. 424-457.

66  McNeely Jeffery A. 2000. 'War and Biodiversity: An Assessment of Impacts, In Austin, Jay E., and Bruch, Carl E., (ed.), *The Environmental Consequences of War: Legal, Economic and Scientific Perspectives*, Cambridge: Cambridge University Press, p. 365-366.

67  Westing Arthur H. 1984. *Herbicides in War: The Long-term Ecological and Human Consequences*, London: Taylor & Francis; Westing Arthur H. (ed.). 1984. *Environmental Warfare: A Technical, Legal and Policy Appraisal*, SIPRI, London: Taylor & Francis.

68  El-Baz Faronk and R M Makharita. 1994. *The Gulf War and Environment*, USA: Gordon & Breach Science Publishers.

defoliants used by the US forces,[69] and the American government has always been in a denial mode.[70]

The authors who have discussed the issue of environmental protection during armed conflict have broadly concerned themselves with the environmental consequences of war and militarization; and the conclusions they have drawn, both theoretical and empirical, stretch across a great intellectual spectrum.[71] Many who have assessed the consequences of war and militarization on natural habitats, wildlife, and the human environment have concluded that the environmental degradation resulting from warfare has been great in the recent past and is becoming increasingly worse with the use of modern weapons.[72] However, some have concluded that war

---

69  During the Vietnam War, in an attempt to deprive the vegetation cover used by North Vietnamese forces for concealment, the US Air Force initiated a military campaign named the 'Operation Ranch Hand', in which about 77 million litres of herbicides, including 49.3 million litres of Agent Orange containing more than 360 kg of dioxin-contaminated defoliants was sprayed multiple times over 2.6 million acres. In Vietnam, the number of individuals exposed or potentially exposed to Agent Orange was estimated to be 4.8 million. A number of studies have been conducted to determine whether exposure to Agent Orange/dioxin in Vietnam may have increased the risk of having children with birth defects. It has been found that parental exposure to Agent Orange appears to be associated with an increased risk of birth defects. Ngo Anh D., Richard Taylor, Christine L Roberts and Tuan V Nguyen, Association between Agent Orange and birth defects: systematic review and meta-analysis, Vol. 35, *International Journal of Epidemiology*, (2006), p. 1220-1230. Also see: Friedman J., Does Agent Orange cause birth defects? Vol. 29, *Teratology*, (1984), p. 193–221.

70  Virtually every aspect of the effects of Agent Orange on Vietnam is infused with uncertainty and/or controversy. There is some question about the amount of Agent Orange and other herbicides sprayed in Vietnam, as well as the amount of dioxin contained in the Agent Orange used. It is also unclear exactly where the herbicides were sprayed and the amount sprayed at each location. Nor is it known who was exposed to Agent Orange and its dioxin, and for what duration they were exposed. Finally, there is limited information about the long-term effects of Agent Orange on the environment and people of Vietnam. Martin Michael F., *Vietnamese Victims of Agent Orange and US-Vietnam Relations*, 28 May 2009, Congressional Research Service, Document-RL34761.

71  For instance see: Austin, Jay E., and Bruch, Carl E., (ed.). 2000. *The Environmental Consequences of War: Legal, Economic and Scientific Perspectives*, Cambridge: Cambridge University Press. This volume contains 25 articles on various aspects of environment consequences of armed conflict.

72  Bloom, Saul, John M. Miller, James Warner and Philippa Winkler. 1994. *Hidden Casualties: Environmental, Health and Political Consequences of the Persian Gulf War*. Berkeley: North Atlantic Books, p 294; Falk, Richard. 1984. Environmental disruption by military means and international law in Westing, Arthur (ed.), *Environmental Warfare: A Technical, Legal, and Policy Appraisal* London, Philadelphia: Taylor & Francis; Falk, Richard. 1988. 'Nuclear Weapons' in *Arms Control, Disarmament and International Security,* Claremont, Ca: Regina Books.

zones[73] and military training grounds[74] provide valuable wildlife habitat, and that defence institutions are the best situated to protect environmental services and amenities.[75] Still others have concluded that the military appropriation of the environment as a security concern threatens not only the environment[76] but also poor people in the global South.[77]

There are certain deficiencies in the literature relating to environmental damage in armed conflict. The title of a new volume (2009) *War and the Environment: Military Destruction in the Modern Age*, suggests that it would contain an analysis of recent armed conflicts, however, all the nine articles in this volume edited by Charles E. Closmann deal with historical aspects of environmental destruction, some dating back to 1864 and 1565. Also rather than discussing environmental damage, it provides detailed accounts of damage to humans.[78] For instance, an article by Jody Williams (1997), entitled "Landmines: Dealing with the Environmental Impact,"[79] is completely devoid of information on the environmental impact of

---

73  Martin, Paul S. and Christine R. Szuter, War Zones and Game Sinks, Vol. 13(1), *Conservation Biology*, (1991), p. 36; Keely, Lawrence H. 1996. *War before civilization.* New York: Oxford University Press.

74  Butts, Kent Hughes. 1994. Why the military is good for the environment, in Kakonen, Jyrki (ed.), *Green Security or Militarized Environment.* Aldershot, England and Brookfield, Vermont: Dartmouth Publishing Company Limited. Also: Woodward, Rachel., Khaki conservation: an examination of military environmentalist discoursed in the British Army, Vol. 17, *Journal of Rural Studies*, (2001), p. 201-217.

75  Butts, Kent Hughes. 1999. The Case for DOD Involvement in Environmental Security, in Deudney, Daniel H. and Richard A. Matthew, *Contested Grounds: Security and Conflict in the New Environmental Politics*, Albany: State University of New York Press.

76  Woodward, Rachel, Khaki conservation: an examination of military environmentalist discoursed in the British Army, Vol. 17, *Journal of Rural Studies*, (2001), p. 201-217; Peluso, Nancy Lee. 1993. Coercing Conservation: the Politics of State Resource Control, in Lipschutz, Ronnie L. and Ken Conca (eds.), *The State and Social Power in Global Environmental Politics,* New York: Columbia University Press.

77  Deudney, Daniel H, Environment and Security: Muddled Thinking, Vol. 47 (3), *Bulletin of the Atomic Scientists,* 1991. Also see: Peluso, Nancy Lee and Michael Watts, (eds.). 2001. *Violent Environments.* Ithaca, London: Cornell University Press; Timura, Christopher T., Environmental Conflict and the social life of environmental security discourse, Vol. 74 (3), *Anthropological Quarterly*, (2001), p.104-113.

78  Larsson Marie-Louise, Legal Definitions of the Environment and of Environmental Damage, Stockholm Institute for Scandianvian Law, Available at: http://www. scandinavianlaw.se/pdf/38-7.pdf, accessed 20 May 2011. This research paper does not contain any information on environmental damage in armed conflict.

79  Williams, Jody, Landmines: Dealing with the Environmental Impact, Vol. 1, No. 2, *Environment and Security*, (1997), pp. 107-124.

landmines. Westing's "The Environmental Aftermath of Warfare in Viet Nam" (1983)[80] similarly deals exclusively with the impact on humans or on cultivated environments. An article by Barnaby (1991), "The Environmental Impact of the Gulf War"[81] is also almost completely devoid of actual scientific data on environmental damage assessment. Instead, the article brims with what *could* happen and what *may* happen and what is *likely* to happen and what *will* happen to the environment – once the data are in. For example, there is information on the number of oil-well fires and how much smoke and sulphur dioxide and carbon monoxide were released into the atmosphere, but there is no discussion whatsoever on the actual environmental damage this caused. Similarly, Homer-Dixon's article "Environmental Scarcities and Violent Conflict" lacks clarity on what exactly is meant by environmental conflict and fails to distinguish between domestic and foreign conflict.[82] In a recent article, "Nuclear and Bioterrorism: Implication on Environment", the authors make only obscure references to the environment.[83]

Literature relating to environmental damage in NIAC is even more inadequate. Other than the UNEP studies on conflict-prone areas (especially Africa), information is scanty and in some cases, confined to that available in the media.[84] The environmental effects of the long-term presence of the

---

80  Westing, Arthur H, The Environmental Aftermath of Warfare in Viet Nam, Vol. 23, *Natural Resources Journal*, April 1983, p. 365-389.

81  Barnaby, Frank, The Environmental Impact of the Gulf War, *The Ecologist*, Vol. 21, No. 4 (July/August 1991), p. 166-172.

82  Homer-Dixon, Thomas F., Environmental Scarcities and Violent Conflict, Vol. 19, No. 1, *International Security*, summer 1994, p. 5-40. According to Gleditsch, the work of Homer-Dixon (1994) suffers from following problems: (1) lack of clarity over what exactly is meant by 'environmental conflict'; (2) researchers engage in polemics and definitional exercises instead of conducting analysis; (3) important variables are omitted from analysis, especially political and economic variables that, in turn, could explain resources pressure; (4) some models cannot be put to test due to their unwieldy size; (5) case studies are selected on the dependent variable; (6) the causality of the relation between environment and violent conflict is reversed; (7) postulated future events are cited as evidence; (8) studies fail to distinguish between domestic and foreign conflict; and (9) studies are not always conducted at the proper level of analysis. Gledisch, N., Armed Conflict and the Environment: A Critique of the Literature, Vol. 35, No. 4, *Journal of Peace Research* , May 1998, p. 381-400.

83  Zirojevic Mina, Markovic Milos and Pocuca Milan, Nuclear and Biological Terrorism: Implication on Environment, Vol. LXII, No. 1144, *The Review of International Affairs*, 2011, p. 97-108.

84  Insurgents don't spare endangered tigers too, *The Times of India*, New Delhi, 01 June 2010; Step out of dangerous terrain: victims of landmines, *The Hindustan Times*, 19 May

armed forces in ecologically fragile areas, for instance Siachen, are not well studied.[85] This region has been under the control of the armed forces of India and Pakistan, and is not open to civilian researchers.

In this book, the environmental damage in IAC and NIAC has been discussed in two separate chapters.

---

2003; Santiapillai Charles and S. Wijeyamohan, The Impact of Civil War on Wildlife in Sri Lanka, *Current Science*, Vol. 84, No. 9, 10 May 2003; Adhikari Jay Ram and Bhim Adhikari, Political Conflicts and Community Forestry: Understanding the Impact of the Decade-Long Armed Conflicts on Environment and Livelihood Security in Rural Nepal, 2010, available at: http://www.capri.cgiar.org/pdf/CAPRi_Conflict_Adhikari.pdf; and Baral, N. and J. T. Heinen, The Maoist People's War and Conservation in Nepal, Vol. 24, Issue 1-2, *Politics and the Life Sciences*, (2006), p. 2-11; and Nasr, D, et. al., Environmental Impacts of Reconstruction Activities: A Case of Lebanon, Vol. 3, No. 2, *Int. J. Environ. Res.,* Spring 2009, p.301-308.

85 Asthana Vandana and Shukla AC, Environmental Consequences of Armed Conflict in South Asia, *South Asian Journal*, October-December 2008 Issue, p. 79-91. This article discusses more about the terrorism, insurgency and militancy in South Asia and is devoid of scientific evaluation of environmental damage in Siachin and Sri Lanka. Nair Pavan, The Siachin War: Twenty-five Years On, *Economic & Political Weekly*, March 14, 2009, Vol XLIV, No. 11, p. 35-40.

# CHAPTER 2

# Environmental Damage in International Armed Conflict

## I. Historical

Wartime environmental damage is as ancient as war itself. Warfare and the physical environment have always shared a close and interconnected relationship. Literature concerning the philosophy of warfare, such as Sun Tzu's *The Art of War* and Clauswitz's *On War*, attests to the importance of terrain, weather and climate to the waging of war. There is evidence that even in pre-historic times, people used land features for cover and concealment and used products of land such as stone, wood, fire and even animals for military advantage. In ancient India, as early as 2000 BC, combatants polluted the air by causing fumes that caused slumber and yawning.[1] Two of the earliest recorded instances of a direct attack on the environment are in the Bible. Judges 15:4-5 relates the story of how Samson burned corm crops, vineyards, and olive trees belonging to the Philistines. Judges 9:45 recounts the story of Abimelech conquering Schechem. Upon entering the city and killing all the people, Abimelech sowed the ground with salt to make it infertile.[2]

For centuries, military commanders have deliberately targeted the environment, seeking to obtain any possible advantage over their adversaries. The armies of ancient Rome and Assyria reportedly sowed salt into the cropland of their foes --an early use of herbicide, one of

---

1   Jeffery G. Hale. 1999. *The Evolvement of the Chemical Weapons Convention and Applicability of its Verification Framework to other Arms Control Agreements*, The George Washington University: Jacob Burns Law Library, p. 25.

2   Lanier-Graham Susan D. 1993. *The Ecology of War: Environmental Impacts of Weaponry and Warfare*, New York: Walker and Company, p. 3-4.

most devastating environmental effects of war. In the battle of Delium, in 424 BC, the Athenians were at war with the Theban Confederacy. It was a custom at that time not to damage sacred areas, such as the waters at the Delium temple. However, in this operation, short-term military gain took precedence over custom. The Athenians fouled the temple waters and destroyed local vineyards and agricultural fields.[3]

One of the earliest examples of strategic military destruction of the environment occurred during the Punic Wars of the third century BC, when both sides poisoned wells, ruined crops, and destroyed arable land with salt. Southern Italy suffered extensive damage to its agricultural lands, when the Carthaginian general Hannibal invaded the Roman Republic in the Second Punic War (219–01 BC). In a long military stalemate, thirteen years of annual summertime fighting impoverished the land in southern Italy, as both armies attempted to deprive each other of provisions. Tilled land was neglected, forests in hill regions and around watersheds depleted, soil erosion into streams and rivers caused floods. In the Third Punic War in 146 BC, Rome salted the ground around Carthage to prevent Carthage from recovering and challenging Rome.

During the Peloponnesian War, 429 BC, King Archidamus led the Peloponnesians against the town of Plataea. He began his attack by cutting down all the fruit trees around the town to form a palisade. After more than two months of trying to make the city walls collapse by piling dirt, rock, and even more chopped trees against them, Archidamus turned to fire and chemicals to create a deadly weapon. His man covered wood with sulphur and pitch, set it afire and throw it over the walls. According to Thucydides's account, it was a fire unlike ever set by human beings. Luckily for the Plataneans, nature sided with them and a rainstorm put out the fire and saved the city.[4] These campaigns were the grim precursors of modern 'total war', obliterating the distinction between civilian and military targets. The concept of 'total war' was developed by Karl von Clausewitz in 1830, which involved the destruction of crops, food and actual property.

In 674, the Byzantines used chemical warfare to end a seven-year siege on Constantinople. A flammable mixture of sulphur, nitre, and naphtha was loaded into flame throwers and used against Arab ships. The "Greek fire" terrified the Muslim troops, destroyed many of their ships, and ended the

---

3    Hanson, Delium, Vol. 8, *Q.J. of Mil. Hist.*, (1955), p. 29.

4    Lanier-Graham Susan D. 1993. *The Ecology of War: Environmental Impacts of Weaponry and Warfare*, New York: Walker and Company, p. 4.

stalemate at Constantinople.

In the early 1200, during the Mongol invasions of Asia and Eastern Europe under Genghis Khan, all livestock and crops not taken by the enemy were ravaged. The most ruinous act was the destruction of irrigation works near Baghdad. The two-thousand-year-old irrigation system on the Tigris River that had been supplying water to one of the most developed areas of the world was damaged and led to the destruction of entire civilization. Genghis Khan went on to conquer Baghdad and left the city in ruins.

In the 1300s, Kaffa was a major port on the Black Sea. For more than three years, the city withstood an invasion by the Mongol Tartars. Then in 1346 the Tartars launched an early form of biological warfare by catapulting plagued-infested into the city. The resulting epidemic caused the downfall of Kaffa. The few survivors among the Genoese who were defending the walled city eventually fled to Italy and took the 'black death' with them. This may have led to the spread of the Black Plague in Europe.[5]

The destructive power of weapons reached new heights with the introduction of gunpowder into Europe in the 1300s, and the development of more powerful cannons in its wake. Many campaigns were carried on for years, devouring both woods and croplands in the process.[6] The Hundred Years War in France (1337–1453) was a major example of undisciplined armies ravaging crop lands, marshlands and woodlands. In the Thirty Years War (1618–48), northern Europe degenerated into chaos, as anarchic military bands repeatedly pillaged the land until the region reached a point of general exhaustion.[7] The Indian subcontinent saw similar impacts of military movements. In the upper Indus and Ganges river basins, the Mughal armies (1524–1707) led by elephant corps and cavalry devoured the food and fodder resources of the land. The imperial army was a mobile city of nearly a million fighters, camp followers and suppliers, who stripped wide areas of everything useful as they moved. Cavalry swept the countryside, depopulating villages; rural society and its biological base often took decades to recover from the disruption.[8]

5   Hersh, Seymour M. 1968. *Chemical and Biological Warfare; America's Hidden Arsenal*, Bobbs-Merrill Co., p. 3.

6   Maurice Keen. 1999. *Medieval Warfare*, Oxford: Oxford University Press; Also see; John Landers. 2003. *The Field and the Forge*, Oxford: Oxford University Press.

7   Tucker Richard, P., War and the Environment. Available at: http://worldhistoryconnected. press.illinois.edu/8.2/forum_tucker.html, accessed 10 June 2014.

8   Jos Gommens, *Mughal Warfare*, Chapter 4, London: Routledge; Simon Digby. 1971.

Setting fire and causing floods are two war strategies that have inflicted great damage to the environmental. During the Franco-Dutch War (1672-1678), the Dutch destroyed their own dikes to prevent the French army from conquering the Netherlands. During the Napoleonic wars (1796 to 1815), while the French advanced through Russia in the summer of 1812, the Russians practiced a self-inflicted scorched earth policy to impede Napoleon's progress. During the American Civil War, General Sherman's march through Georgia and Sheridan's campaign in Virginia's Shenandoah Valley involved acts of deliberate environmental destruction. In November 1864, General Sherman and 62,000 Union troops set fire to Atlanta and commenced their infamous 'march to the sea'. They burned more than 4000 houses, stores, and other structures, military and civilian alike.[9] They cut a sixty-mile swath across Georgia, burning farms and towns on their march to the coast. About 10 million acres of land was destroyed. All crops and livestock between Atlanta and the savannah were either destroyed or confiscated.[10] The express purpose of this campaign was to cripple the Confederacy's economy and prevent Georgia from supporting military operations. General Sherman accomplished his goal at a high cost to civilians. The damage was as much as $100 million.[11] General Sherman,

---

*Warhorse and Elephant in the Delhi Sultanate*, Oxford: Orient Monographs; Stewart Gordon. 2004. 'War, the Military, and the Environment: Central India, 1560–1820', in Richard P. Tucker and Edmund Russell, (eds.), *Natural Enemy, Natural Ally: Toward an Environmental History of War*, Corvallis: Oregon State University Press, p. 42–64.

9   Thomas G. Robisch, General William T. Sherman: Would the Georgia Campaign of the First Commander of the Modern Era Comply with Current Law of War Standards? Vol. 9, *Emory International Law Review*, (1995), p. 459-473.

10  Virginia's Shenandoah Valley was one of the areas hardest hit during the American Civil War. Sheridan's Shenandoah Valley campaign of 1864 caused massive destruction. In a personal letter to General Sheridan at the beginning of this campaign, General Grant ordered Sheridan to turn the valley into a barren wasteland, "so that crown flying over it for the balance of this season will have to carry their provender with them." Sheridan responded with a promise to grant that when his troops were finished, there would be little left "for man or beast". Lanier-Graham Susan D. 1993. *The Ecology of War: Environmental Impacts of Weaponry and Warfare*, New York: Walker and Company, p. 15.

11  These campaigns took place after the promulgation of General Order No. 100, commonly known as Leiber Code. The Code imposed basic restrictions on the wartime conduct of Union troops, specially protecting non-combatants. While the code did not specifically address environmental damage, it prohibited the wanton destruction of a district and the use of poison, protected private citizens and cultural heritage and provided severe penalties, including death for "wanton violence". There is no evidence that the intentional destruction of civilian property was ever punished. Leiber Code, Articles: 16, 22, 35, 36, 44, 47 and 70; Also see: Bruch Carl E., All's Not Fair in (Civil) War: Criminal Liability for Environmental Damage in Internal Armed Conflict, Vol.

in a report to General Grant had indicated that the land was so wasted that it could no longer support human life. Numerous other attacks on the environment occurred throughout the Civil War, in addition to the incidental and indirect environmental damage.

The United States has its own history of environmental damage in other wars as well. In the US-Navaho Wars of 1860-1864, it deliberately destroyed sheep and other livestock, as well as fruit orchards and crops, as part of its successful strategy of subjugation. A more recent example is the near-extermination of the bison during the 19th century. A critical resource for the indigenous peoples of the North American plains, the bison was hunted to near-extinction by immigrants from the eastern parts of the US. The elimination of baison helped the US government's campaign to extinguish the native's land rights and remove them to reservation. Many natives were forced to choose between capitulation and starvation and freezing.

## II. World War I

The most damaging environmental impact of World War I[12] was the landscape changes caused by trench warfare. Digging trenches caused the trampling of grassland, crushing of plants and animals, and churning of soil. Forest logging led to soil erosion and soil structures were altered severely. If the war was never fought, in all likelihood, the landscape would have looked very different today. The war also presented a new destructive technology: aerial bombardment, which made it possible for civilian populations and industrial facilities to become targets on an unprecedented scale.

Perhaps, the most extensive environmental damage was caused in Thiepval Ridge, France, where close to 250,000 acres of farmland was devastated so severely that it was determined that area could no longer serve any agricultural purpose.[13] In addition, an estimated 494,000 acres of French

---

25, No. 3, *Vermont Law Review*, (2000-2001), p. 695-752.

12  The war was mostly in Europe, between the Allies and the Central Powers. It was fought from trenches, dug from the North Sea to the borders of Switzerland. In 1918 when the war was over, empires disintegrated into smaller countries, marking the division of Europe. Over 9 million people died, most of whom perished from influenza after the outbreak of the Spanish Flu. The war did not directly cause the influenza outbreak, but it was amplified. Mass movement of troops and close quarters caused the Spanish Flu to spread quickly. Furthermore, stresses of war may have increased the susceptibility of soldiers to the disease.

13  The explosive remnants of a conflict can remain in the environment for several

forest was levelled. Besides battle damage, an enormous amount of lumber (some 20 billion board feet), was harvested for the war effort by the Allies. Animal populations were also severely hit by the widespread fighting. The European buffalo, or wisent, which was endangered before the start of the war, lost its habitat when the German occupation forces, cut down Polish forests to obtain lumber needed for military operations. With no place to hide, the wisent was easy prey for the German forces.

The war also saw the first large-scale use of chemical weapon. Germany, France and Britain all attempted to develop chemical weapons before 1914. Germany's chemical industry, the world leader at that time, forged a close link with the military, enabling the German army to use massive amounts of chlorine and mustard gas on Allied troops. By the end of the war chemical warfare had caused 1.3 million casualties, including 100,000 deaths; and temporarily poisoned land in and around the battlefields. It is difficult to assess the immediate environmental impact, because no one measured it. However, its carryover effect was massive as unexploded ammunition caused major problems in former battle areas. Deliberate damage to the environment was also used by both sides in the war. As the Germans withdrew from the Somme battlefields, they systematically destroyed nearly every building, fence, well, bridge, and tree over a sixty-five by twenty mile area to deprive the advancing enemy of sustenance and cover. In the autumn of 1916, the British blew up Romanian oil fields to prevent the Central Powers from capturing them. About seventy oil wells and refineries were set on fire and an estimated 800,000 tonnes of oil was lost. It took the Germans five months to extinguish the fires.

## III. World War II

Lasting from 1939 to 1945, WWII was one of the most destructive and violent events in the history of mankind. In early 1942, immediately after the Pearl Harbour attack, Japan's war machine continued down the Pacific, quickly seizing the strategic forest and rubber resources of the Philippines, Indonesia and mainland Southeast Asia. For roughly three years, until they were beaten back, the occupying Japanese forces brutalized forests and plantations, leaving a seriously compromised environmental legacy.

---

generations after it has ended, posing a threat to the civilian population. An example is in Northern France, where more than 90 years since the end of the First World War unexploded bombs are still being discovered in farmers' fields. Breau Susan, 'Protection of Environment during Armed Conflict', in Shawkat Alam (ed). 2013. *Routledge Handbook of International Environmental Law*, London: Ruotledge, p. 617-632.

The destruction of dams was a common tactics in WW II. In May 1943, the Allies bombed two large dams in the Ruhr Valley in Germany in an attempt to destroy Germany's industrial economic base and to make it impossible for Hitler to produce any additional equipment. The destruction of the dams released an enormous amount of water resulting in the deaths of approximately 1,200 German civilians and over 6,500 cattle and the destruction of nearly 7,500 acres of agricultural land.

The Soviets used scorched earth tactics on their own territory to deny Germany the resources it needed to continue its offensive. Throughout the war, France's forests suffered badly. Over 100 million acres were directly destroyed through combative activities. The Germans, while retreating from Norway, destroyed everything in an area close to 15 million acres. Property, crops, and forests were destroyed, along with wildlife. The reindeer population of 95,000 was reduced to half during that period.

Another area that was severely affected during the war was the Netherlands. The Dutch resorted to large-scale flooding to impede the German forces, but could not stop the German advance. After the German forces broke through into the Netherlands, they ruined an estimated 17 per cent of the productive farmland by flooding the area with saltwater, in an attempt to starve out the enemy.

The bombardment of cities and the destruction of forests, farms, transport systems and irrigation networks produced devastating environmental consequences, and by the end of the war there were almost 50 million refugees and displaced people. Air power was deployed as the pivotal military technology for the first time and resulted in the death of hundreds of thousands of people. In the aerial bombardments of Tokyo in March 1945, about 100,000 to 200,000 people were killed. In the fire bombings of 70 German cities, including Hamburg in 1943 and Dresden in 1945, an estimated that 500,000 to 800,000 people died.[14] In the last year of the war, coastal and northern France was torn up, Holland south of the Zuyder Sea was flooded with the destruction of dikes, and many ports were clogged with unexploded ordnance and sunken ships. The cities including Warsaw, Berlin, Hamburg, Dresden, Dusseldorf, Boulogne, Le Havre, Rouen, Brest, Pisa, Verona, Lyons, Budapest, Leningrad, Kiev and Cracow suffered extensive damage.

---

14 Westing, A. H. 1980. *Warfare in a Fragile World: Military Impacts on the Human Environment.* London: Taylor and Francis.

The war in the Pacific had impacts on island biota, coastal ecosystems and the aquatic environment. Besides the uprooting of trees and burning and destruction of forests, another disastrous consequence of the war was the destruction of coral reefs. When troops landed on a new island, one of the first requirements of war was to build a runway. Bulldozers were brought in to level the land and uproot any remaining trees. Live coral rocks were crushed and used as a base for the runway. Marine life was also endangered. Whales were evidently mistaken for submarines by gunners and oil spills from an estimated 300 tankers were responsible for marine pollution and loss of life.

The United States, the United Kingdom, Japan, Germany, and Italy all carried out campaigns in which civilian populations were targets. They also attacked industrial facilities which led to massive environmental damage.[15] One of the most devastating attacks with perhaps the longest-lasting effects on the environment was the detonation of two nuclear bombs over Hiroshima and Nagasaki, Japan. On 6 August 1945, a uranium bomb by the name of Little Boy was dropped on Hiroshima, and on August 9, a plutonium bomb by the name of Fat Man devastated Nagasaki.

The first impact of the atomic bombings was a blinding light, accompanied by a giant wave of heat. Dry flammable materials caught fire, and all men and animals within half a mile from the explosion sites died instantly. Many structures collapsed in Nagasaki, even the structures designed to survive earthquakes were blasted away. Water lines broke and fires could not be extinguished because of the water shortage, and six weeks after the blast the city still suffered from a lack of water. In Hiroshima, a number of small fires combined with the wind to form a firestorm, killing those who had not died in the blast but were left immobilized. The blasts caused air pollution from dust particles and radioactive debris flying around, and from the fires burning everywhere. Radioactive sand clogged wells used for drinking water, thereby causing a drinking water problem that could not be solved easily. Surface water sources were polluted, particularly by radioactive waste. Agricultural production was damaged; dead stalks of rice could be found up to seven miles from ground zero.[16]

---

15  All of these attacks were carried out in violation of the spirit of the 1868 St. Petersburg Declaration and the 1899 and 1907 Hague Conventions, prohibiting launching projectiles or explosives from the air; and prohibiting attacking or bombarding towns, villages, or dwellings which are undefended.

16  The reason Hiroshima was picked was that it was a major military centre. The bomb detonated at 8.15 pm over a Japanese Army parade field, where soldiers were already

In Hiroshima, 100,000 were killed instantly, and between 100,000 and 200,000 died eventually. In Nagasaki, about 40,000 were killed instantly, and between 70,000 and 150,000 died eventually. In addition to the immediate loss of life and damage from the bombs upon impact, there were further damages caused by massive fires, 'black-rain' that fell over a period of several days, radiation in the soil and water for a long period of time, and destruction of plant and animal life by the explosions and the resulting radiation.

Towards the end of the war, the retreating Japanese army left millions of chemical weapons scattered across northeastern China. To prevent the Allies from capturing them, units buried the shells—containing chemicals including mustard gas, phosgene, and lewisite—in fields, lakes, and streams. The result has been a slow-motion public health disaster: according to Chinese officials, in the last sixty years more than 2,000 people have died from toxins leaking from the weapons and countless more have been sickened and permanently injured by them.[17]

The Nuremberg trials after World War II was the first time that a purely environmental war crime was given recognition. Nine German civilian officials in occupied Poland were charged with the "ruthless exploitation of Polish forestry" including "the wholesale cutting of Polish timber to an extent far in excess of what was necessary to preserve the timber resources of the country".[18]

## Explosive Remnants of WW II

At the height of the war, from 1941 to 1945, military forces from the USA, Japan, Australia and New Zealand clashed in a series of battles in the Pacific region. Large stocks of munitions (predominantly from USA and Japan) were shipped to support ongoing military operations. In addition to the ordnance used in numerous sea engagements between naval warships, high explosive bombs and artillery rounds were fired or dropped

---

present. Nagasaki was picked because it was an industrial centre. The bomb, which was much larger than that used on Hiroshima, was exploded at 11.02 am at an industrial site. In Hiroshima the impact of the bombing was noticeable within a 10-km radius around the city, and in Nagasaki within a 1-km radius.

17 Risen Clay, The Environmental Consequences of War: Why militaries almost never clean up the messes they leave behind. Available at:http://www.washingtonmonthly. com/features/2010/1001.risen.html, accessed 12 June 2014.

18 The UN War Crimes Commission, Case No 7150 496 (1948); this exploitation violated Germany's duty as occupier to safeguard Poland's property.

in large quantities onto small areas of land occupied by enemy forces. A large part of the munitions did not detonate and were left either strewn across the islands and atolls, buried in the soil or sand, or submerged in the surrounding lagoons. At the conclusion of the war, a large amount of ordnance remained on the islands, posing a significant threat to local communities. Nearly seven decades later, the presence of the unexploded or abandoned ordnance continues to plague a number of countries such as the Federated States of Micronesia, Kiribati, Nauru, Palau, Papua New Guinea, Republic of the Marshall Islands, Solomon Islands, Tuvalu, and Vanuatu. Technically, the ordnance found in these islands can be defined as either unexploded (UXO) or abandoned (AXO).[19]

Several islands and atolls across the region, such as Chuuk, Funafuti, Nanumea, Betio, Guadal canal, Tulagi, Gavutu and New Britain were used as military bases and ammunition depots for the storage of ordnance to supply naval vessels, aircraft and infantry. Land mines, grenades, flame throwers, ammunition and in some cases chemical weapons were shipped into the areas of conflict for storage and eventual use. In addition to bombs and artillery used to defend the beaches, Japanese forces, in anticipation of assault landings, often prepared defensive positions using land mines and aerial bombs converted to act as land mines. Much of this ordnance was never used and many failed to detonate. Many areas which had seen fierce fighting were littered with abandoned machinery of war, including tanks, abandoned weapons, unexploded ordnance, pill boxes, fortified gun emplacements, abandoned fuel, hazardous materials, and wrecks and cargoes of sunken vessels.

Nearly seven decades after the war UXO items are present in varying levels---on the ground, sub-surface or underwater in both rural and urban areas. UXO has the potential to cause significant impacts on local communities through (i) safety issues resulting in possible loss of life or injuries; (ii) environmental impacts resulting from the leaching of harmful

---

19 Explosive remnants of war (ERW), as a term, is now formalized in 2003 Protocol V of the UN Convention on Certain Conventional Weapons (CCW) as 'unexploded ordnance and abandoned explosive ordnance' where these in turn are defined as follows: Unexploded Ordnance (UXO) is explosive ordnance that has been primed, fused, armed, or otherwise prepared for use and used in an armed conflict and that may have been fired, dropped, launched or projected and should have exploded but failed to do so. Abandoned Explosive Ordnance (AXO) is explosive ordnance that has not been used during a conflict, and has been left behind unprotected or dumped by a party to an armed conflict, and which is no longer under control of the party that left it behind or dumped it. Abandoned explosive ordnance may or may not have been primed, fused, armed or otherwise prepared for use.

chemicals or from the links of UXO to dynamite fishing which damages reefs and lagoon ecological systems; (iii) impeding development activities especially those linked to excavation; and (iv) impeding the ability of local communities to utilize land for economic activities such as those related to tourism and subsistence agriculture.[20]

It is generally held that chemical leakage from UXO contaminates land and marine environments and lead to health and safety problems. Chemicals in UXO include (i) heavy metals such as lead, zinc, copper; (ii) explosives such as TNT and nitro-glycerine; and (iii) components from propellants such as dinitritoluene and dibutylphtalate. UXO continue to be used as a source for obtaining explosive material to undertake dynamite fishing which causes environmental damage to lagoons and reefs. [21] Under international law, no treaty or agreement specifically regulates the clearance of WWII UXO.

## Dumping of Chemical and Conventional Munitions at Sea

During WW I, there was large-scale production of mustard gas, lewisite, and other chemical agents specially designed and packaged for use in armed conflict.  While chemical weapons were not widely used during World War II, large quantities were produced and stockpiled. At the end of the war, large quantities of these hazardous chemicals were left with no place to go. The technology to destroy these weapons safely did not exist and there was no public concern over their existence. This resulted in extensive dumping of both chemical and conventional munitions at sea.[22] In some cases, the location and type of conventional and chemical munitions is well known. In other cases, both locations and types are not clearly known due to insufficient record keeping, dumping of material outside agreed official dumping areas and the movement of munitions, once dumped, to areas

---

20  WW II Unexploded Ordnance: A Study of UXO in Four Pacific Island Countries, July 2011, The Pacific Islands Forum Secretariat, p. 26.

21  *Best Practice Guide on the Destruction of Conventional Ammunition*, 2008, Organization for Security and Co-operation in Europe, Vienna.

22  One of the earliest methods of disposing of chemical weapons was by dumping them at sea. At the end of both world wars, Germany was ordered to dump stockpiles of chemical agents into the Baltic Sea. There was mustard gas at the end of WW I and various other chemical agents, including nerve gas, at the end of WW II. These canisters of chemical agents continue to contaminate waters, plant life, and fish in addition to killing humans coming in contact with the agents. Lanier-Graham Susan D. 1993. *The Ecology of War: Environmental Impacts of Weaponry and Warfare*, New York: Walker and Company, p. 98-99.

outside the dump locations.[23]

From 1918 to 1970, the US was responsible for dumping more than 350,000 tons of surpluses, and captured chemical warfare (CW) material.[24] Other countries also participated in sea dumping, especially after the WW II, when CW material was confiscated from Germany by France, the Soviet Union, the United Kingdom and the United States. By an estimate, in the aftermath of two world wars, more than one million tons of CW material came to rest on sea-bottoms throughout the world.[25] Each country bore responsibility for disposing of the material found in its respective zone. After WW II, under orders of the United States occupation authority, Japan also dumped CW material off its coast. Obsolete, damaged or malfunctioning conventional weaponry was also dumped.[26]

The US Army has acknowledged that in some instances, conventional explosives and radiological waste were dumped along with chemical weapons. According to its own admission, some of these weapons were damaged or leaking at the time of disposal.[27] The types of chemical

---

23  Thomas Stock and Karlheinz Lohs (eds). 1997. *The Challenge of Old Chemical Munitions and Toxic Armament Wastes,* Oxford: Oxford University Press.

24  The US Armed Forces have routinely disposed of chemical weapons in the ocean from World War I through 1970. The US Army has catalogued 74 instances of disposal in the ocean, of which 32 were off US shores and 42 were off foreign shores. Bearden, David M. 2007. US Disposal of Chemical Weapons in the Ocean: Background and Issues for Congress, CSR Report for Congress. Available at: http://www.fas.org/sgp/crs/natsec/RL33432.pdf, accessed 25 January 2012. It was thought that the vastness of ocean waters would absorb chemical agents that may leak from these weapons. However, public concerns about human health and environmental risks, and the economic effects of potential damage to marine resources, led to a statutory prohibition on the disposal of chemical weapons in the ocean. In 1972, Congress enacted the Ocean Dumping Act to prohibit the disposal of wastes into the ocean waters of the United States, extending to the contiguous zone. Consistent with the decision of the executive branch in 1970 to cease the disposal of chemical weapons in the ocean, Congress included provisions in the Ocean Dumping Act that explicitly prohibited the offshore disposal of chemical warfare agents. Bearden, David M. 2007. *US Disposal of Chemical Weapons in the Ocean: Background and Issues for Congress,* CSR Report for Congress.

25  *Off-Shore Disposal of Chemical Agents and Weapons Conducted by the United States,* 2001, US Department of Defence, Historical Research and Response Team.

26  Emily E. Baine and Margaret P. Simmons, 2005, *Mitigating the Possible Damaging Effects of Twentieth-Century Ocean Dumping of Chemical Munitions,* Huntsville, AL, US Army Engineering & Support Centre.

27  It was thought that the vastness of ocean waters would absorb chemical agents that may leak from these weapons. However, public concerns about human health and environmental risks, and the economic effects of potential damage to marine resources, led to a statutory prohibition on the disposal of chemical weapons in the ocean. In 1972,

weapons commonly included sulphur mustard and nerve agents. The reasons for ocean disposal also varied. Some weapons were deemed surplus, while others were damaged and leaking, presenting an immediate risk to the military personnel who managed them. Certain weapons were not produced by the US, but were captured from foreign nations and were disposed of to prevent their use.

According to Beddington and Kinloch (2005), munitions dumped at sea can cause three types of hazards. (i) Direct physical contact with either chemical or conventional munitions may be hazardous for human health. (ii) Leaking chemicals may contaminate marine organisms and the environment in the vicinity of the dumped munitions and may enter the wildlife and human food chains. (iii) There may be spontaneous explosions which can be directly life threatening, and also have the potential to spread material away from the dump sites thereby increasing the potential for more of it to come into direct physical contact with individuals.[28]

The ecological problems posed by chemical weapons to environment and human beings are impossible to quantify, even though they are very real.[29] The leaked chemical agents may affect fish stocks and other marine life.[30]

---

Congress enacted the Ocean Dumping Act to prohibit the disposal of wastes into the ocean waters of the United States, extending to the contiguous zone. Consistent with the decision of the executive branch in 1970 to cease the disposal of chemical weapons in the ocean, Congress included provisions in the Ocean Dumping Act that explicitly prohibited the offshore disposal of chemical warfare agents. Bearden, David M. 2007. *US Disposal of Chemical Weapons in the Ocean: Background and Issues for Congress*, CSR Report for Congress.

28  Beddington, J. and Kinloch, A.J., 2005. *Munitions Dumped at Sea: A literature review*, IC Consultants Ltd., Imperial College London, 2005. Available at: http://www.mod. uk/NR/rdonlyres/77CEDBCA-813A-4A6C-8E59-16B9E260E27A/0/ic_munitions_ seabed_rep.pdf, accessed 21 March 2014.

29  Chemical weapons agents that are denser than seawater tend to remain on the ocean floor, rather than float to shallower waters where they may present greater risk. For example, encrusted sulphur mustard is denser than seawater, making it unlikely to migrate off the ocean floor. However, ocean currents can disperse such substances along the seabed, spreading contamination beyond the location where the release occurred. Colder temperatures can slow down the process of degradation and allow contamination along the seabed to persist in harmful concentrations and forms for longer periods.

30  There is a possibility that hazardous substances, released from both chemical and conventional munitions, may have negative effects on the marine environment and enter the food chain. Increasing corrosion rate of metal casings may possibly lead to serious impacts in future. Explosions associated with dumped munitions may affect marine species. Marine mammals or fish can be hurt or even killed by the shock wave and the high sound pressure following an explosion. Harbour porpoises may be killed

The weapons themselves could wash ashore or be accidentally retrieved during activities that disturb the seabed, such as dredging and trawl fishing. As we increasingly engage in subsea activities, both commercially and recreationally, the likelihood of coming into contact with long-discarded chemical weapons can only increase.[31] Exposure to chemical weapons can have numerous harmful effects on human beings. Depending on the chemical agent, these effects can include burns and sores on the skin, vomiting, respiratory disorders, damage to the immune system, and loss of life. Chemical agents could also be extremely toxic to the marine organism.[32]

The International Convention on the Prevention of Marine Pollution by Dumping of Wastes and Other Matter (London Convention) entered into force in 1975 and currently there are 86 States parties to the Convention. It prohibits the sea disposal of certain types of hazardous waste. In the countries possessing a chemical warfare (CW) material stockpile, more acceptable land-based chemical disposal and destruction methods have replaced sea-dumping. The 1993 Chemical Weapons Convention (CWC) contains guidelines how to destroy CW and related production facilities. Parties to the CWC are prohibited to eliminate CW stockpile through open-pit burning, land burial or dumping in any body of water.

## Shipwreck

Over 9,000 military, auxiliary, and merchant marine vessels were sunk during WW II. The hazards related to these shipwrecks include oil spills, chemical releases, unexploded ordnance, coral-reef degradation,

---

within four kilometres of large explosions and their hearing can suffer permanent damage as far away as 30 kilometres. Nixon Eugene, Assessment of the impact of dumped conventional and chemical munitions (update 2009), OPSAR Commission, Marine Institute, Ireland.

31 Bryant, Dennis L. Disposal of Chemical Weapons at Sea, available at: http://www.marinelink.com/news/disposal-chemical-weapons338131.aspx, accessed 25 January 2014.

32 However, the degree of risk from weapons leaking chemical agents into seawater depends on factors like the extent to which an agent is diluted and the duration of exposure. Colder water temperatures can also slow degradation and allow contamination along the seabed to persist in harmful concentrations and for longer periods. Bearden, David M., US Disposal of Chemical Weapons in the Ocean: Background and Issues for Congress, CSR Report for Congress, January 2007, available at: http://fas.org/sgp/crs/natsec/RL33432.pdf, accessed 30 June 2014.

altering the feeding grounds of marine life.[33] World War II shipwrecks are deteriorating at an alarming rate. The rate of deterioration depends upon the type and construction of the vessel; the depth of water; temperature; and the chemical, physical, and biological factors associated with salt-water corrosion. Other factors include shifting sea-bottom sediments, marine bacteria and other organisms, storms and currents. Over time, a vessel is reduced to its natural elements. Along the way, it releases some or all of its cargo, fuel, lubricants and other hazardous chemicals,[34] which poses devastating threats to the coastal environment and the safety of human and marine life.

World War II wrecks have significantly affected the waterways, shores, and submerged landmasses of the maritime nations of the world. Every ocean and sea bears the effect of these wrecks.[35] The international governing bodies have turned a blind eye to the inherently devastating hazards of these wrecks. "Out of sight, out of mind" appears to be the policy.[36]

---

33  It has been estimated that about 3,100 ships were sunk in the Pacific region. Wrecks comprised dozens of different classes of cargo and transport vessels, tankers, destroyers, submarines and chasers, gun boats and landing craft, mine craft and aircraft carriers and suppliers), and ranged from 24-ton patrol vessels to the immense Yamato and Musashi battleships, which displaced more than 60,000 tons of water. The majority of the wrecks were conscripted merchant ships from Japan serving as cargo vessels. Approximately ten percent of all lost wrecks were oil tankers. Gilbert, Trevor, WWII Shipwrecks—A Pollution Threat to the Fisheries, Marine and Coastal Environments of the Pacific, Vol. 9 (1), *Waves*, 2002, p. 10. Also see: Christie, Michael. 2002. World War Two Wrecks Haunt Pacific With Oil Spills. *Planet Ark World Environmental News*. Available at: http://www.planetark.org/avantgo/dailynewsstory.cfm?newsid=18431, accessed 30 September 2013.

34  Monfils, Rean. 2005. The Global Risk of Marine Pollution from WWII Shipwrecks: Examples from the Seven Seas. Available at: http://www.seaaustralia.com/publications. htm, accessed April 7, 2013.

35  In the Pacific Ocean, amid a chain of tiny islands that make up the Federated States of Micronesia, more than 50 World War II shipwrecks lie below the placid surface of the 40-mile-wide Chuuk (Truk) Lagoon. Encased in coral, host to abundant sea life, these tankers, destroyers, and other vessels also contain noxious cargo: thousands of barrels of oil and other fuels, and sometimes chemicals and unexploded ordnance. For decades, scientists and governments have said it was best to leave these shipwrecks alone. Woodward, T., Pacific World War II wrecks pose risk of toxic leaks, *National Geographic Magazine*, 10 December 2008. Available at: http://news. nationalgeographic.com/news/2008/12/081210-pacific-shipwrecks-missions.html.

36  WW II wrecks are still considered sovereign property as well as war graves. At present, there is no international treaty to manage the potential threats from these wrecks. A new treaty, the Nairobi International Convention on the Removal of Wrecks, 2007, was adopted by a diplomatic conference held in Kenya on 18 May 2007. The Convention will provide the legal basis for States to remove, or have removed, shipwrecks that may

## IV. Korean War

The Korean War (1950-1953) between South Korea, supported by 16 allied countries led by the United States, and North Korea, supported by China and the Soviet Union,[37] resulted in nearly 2 million civilians being wounded or killed. Approximately 22,000 km or 63 per cent of the landline communication system was destroyed; some 1.2 million war refugees had to temporarily leave their homes in South Korea; and more than 4,000 schools were completely destroyed.[38] Military casualties were also heavy. An estimated 36,940 US servicemen and 245,000 to 415,000 South Korean soldiers were killed in the war.

One of the favourite American strategies in Korea was to bombard North Korea's irrigation dams. The bombardment destroyed the dams, played havoc with agricultural water supply and disrupted the supply of rice to its citizens. The US military relied heavily on destroying the country's food supply. Land became a military target of the war against an agrarian economy.[39] Chemical weapons in the form of defoliants were used by the US forces which were also accused of using biological weapons. The accusations have not been verified, however.[40]

In addition, joint military exercises with the US military also destructed natural habitats. The ecological damage caused by the presence of US military bases has been ignored because the government sees the military alliance with the US as of the utmost priority. Many environmental concerns rising from the presence of the US military include oil leaks contaminating groundwater, illegal dumping of toxic chemicals into the Han River and

---

have the potential to affect adversely the safety of lives, goods and property at sea, as well as the marine environment. However, this treaty does not address World War II wrecks.

37 The Korean War began with North Korea's surprise invasion of South Korea on 25 June 1950, and lasted three years until an armistice agreement was signed on 27 July 1953. Vastly unprepared in terms of equipment and training, South Korean troops were repeatedly defeated and forced to retreat southward. The South Korean capital, Seoul, was captured by North Korean forces in only three days. The United Nations troops arrived in the south upon the UN Security Council's resolution recommending military assistance to South Korea.

38 Kim, W. 1996. *Korean War Damage Statistics*, Seoul: Defence and Military Research Institute.

39 Lanier-Graham Susan D. 1993. *The Ecology of War: Environmental Impacts of Weaponry and Warfare*, New York: Walker and Company, p. 30.

40 Ibid, p. 95.

asbestos contamination.[41]

Despite its historical significance, the Korean War has drawn considerably less attention than the Vietnam War. Though military actions are reasonably well documented, the social and economic aspects of the conflict remain poorly understood. In particular, the effects of the war on the lives of civilians, and its impact on the health and socioeconomic performance of survivors over their life course are inadequately documented.[42]

## V. The Vietnam War

The Vietnam War was a testing ground for new types of weaponry and warfare.[43] The American destruction of this region of Southeast Asia represented a new and unprecedented strategy, aimed not at the destruction of an enemy, a territory, a food crop, a culture but of an entire ecosystem that has been termed 'ecocide'.[44] Chemicals (herbicides), free fire zones, anti-personnel and fragmentation bombs, napalm, food-denial programmes, all formed an unprecedented strategy of counterinsurgency. Never before in the history of mankind was such a magnitude of destruction wrought upon any people in a single place.

In 1961 the US began the 'experimental' spraying of herbicides as a weapon to exterminate forests and crops in South Vietnam. The initial object was to undermine the economic resources of the National Liberation Front (NLF)

---

41  Jeong Ho-Won, Ingyu Oh and SangKee Peter Lee, Human Security, Promotion of Peace and Justice: The Case of Korea, Available at: http://www.tisanet.org/quarterly/v1-4-8.pdf, accessed 29 April 2014.

42  Lee Chulhee, *In-Utero* Exposure to the Korean War and Its Long-Term Effects on Economic and Health Outcomes, available at: http://cliometrics.org/assapapers/Lee.pdf, accessed 29 April 2014.

43  Since 1884, Vietnam was a French colony. An anti-colonial war of independence was led by Ho Chi Minh after the WW II. It concluded with the French defeat in May 1954 and Vietnam became an independent state in July 1954. The first Indochina (or Vietnam) war dates to 1946-1954. The second Indochina war was a direct continuation of the first, lasting until 1975. The second Indochina war is now entitled a 'proxy war', fought during the Cold War between the United States and the Soviet Union to prevent the necessity for the nations to fight each other directly. North Vietnam fought side by side with the Soviet Union and China, and South Vietnam with the United States, New Zealand and South Korea.

44  Ecocide is the premeditated assault of a nation and its resources against the individuals, culture and biological fabrics of another country and its environs. *Scientific American* in January of 1968 described American activities in Southeast Asia as "ecological warfare". The first public recognition of the term 'ecocide' occurred in an editorial of the *New York Times* on 26 February 1970.

movement,[45] but it expanded into a critical aspect of the shift from ground to air power. Besides destroying crops, defoliants were used to destroy the forest canopy that protected NLF forces from detection by air.

Official American reports stated that five million acres of land or 12 per cent of South Vietnam was 'sterilized'. In the first two months of 1969 alone some 37 of the 44 provinces of South Vietnam were sprayed, contaminating 285,000 people of which at least 500 died. According to Vietnamese estimates between late 1961 and October 1969, 43 per cent of the arable land and 44 per cent of the total forested area of South Vietnam were sprayed at least once and in many cases twice or three times with herbicides.[46] Besides forest and mountains, large populated areas in the delta were sprayed as well, including the outskirts of Saigon itself. Approximately 70 million litres of herbicides were sprayed over the country's forests between 1962 and 1971, dousing 1.7 million hectares often several times over.[47] Over 1,293,000 people were directly contaminated.[48]

Mangrove forests, a vital part of the tropical ecosystem, were decimated in

---

45  In 1962 defoliants became 'a central weapon' in the overall chemical and biological warfare strategy of the United States throughout Southeast Asia. Known as 'Operation Ranch Hand', some of the converted C-123 cargo planes used to spray the herbicides were inscribed with the motto "Only we can prevent forests".

46  The actual environmental impact is difficult to decipher though it is consistently reported that mangrove forests were most sensitive to the dioxin (Agent Orange) with irreversible consequences for up to 40 per cent of the population. The Vietnamese government, in cooperation with other governments and international organizations, has begun the process of inland and mangrove afforestation, though in 1993, it was estimated that it would take many more decades of industrious labour and a steady supply of international funding to recover the total area destroyed by herbicides. Jha Pankaj, Agent Orange: resonance on Vietnam-US, *Journal of Chemical and Biological Weapons*, October- December 2009, p. 5.

47  The agents used consists of "Orange" (50:50 mixture of 2,4-D and 2,4,5-T), used on general crops and recorded as amounting to 50 per cent of the defoliation programme; "White" 20 per cent picloram and 80 per cent isoprophalmin salt from 2,4-D, used for 35 per cent of missions; and "Blue" (a form of arsenic) for 15 per cent of the missions; as well as the host of other agents including Phenal compounds of the type DNOC, arsenates and arsenates, and earth sterilizing compounds", such as Bromacil and Urox. Westing Arthur H. 1984. *Herbicides in War: The Long-term Ecological and Human Consequences*, London: Taylor & Francis, p. 6-7.

48  The United States Department of Defence had admitted that four and a half million acres of forest and one-half million acres of cropland were sprayed through July 1969—about 12 per cent land area of South Vietnam. The inadvertent spraying of unintended areas was also a common occurrence because of mistaken target identification, navigational errors, and wind-caused drifting of spray. Westing Arthur H., Poisoning Plants for Peace, *Friends Journal*, 1 April 1970.

the war. It has been estimated that more than 300,000 acres of mangrove forests were lost. This led to erosion and a gradual wearing away of the shoreline. In addition to forests, crop destruction was practised to break the will of the people. The US military often deliberately ravaged farmland, crops, stores of harvested crops, garden plots, and fruit trees. The application of 72 million litres of chemical spray resulted in the death of many animals, and caused health effects with humans. Livestock was often shot, to deprive peasant of their entire food supply. By an estimate over 13,000 livestock were killed during the war.

Herbicides directly damage the soil by destroying the microorganisms needed to maintain soil quality and protect erosion, and removing humus (decomposing vegetation on the forest floor), and turning the soil into a hard rock-like substance. Chemicals entering the Mekong River severely damaged aquatic life. Livestock and wildlife suffered through the interruption of food chains and the near extinction of several rare species. Birds, bats and insects which play a crucial role in pollination and dispersal of seeds in tropical forests lost their habitat and food supply and this endangered forest plants, which, in turn, reduced soil fertility.

Herbicides can enter the human system through contaminated food, water and air or by direct skin contact. The effects were described by a Vietnamese: "Those who were in the sprayed areas found it difficult to breathe, difficult to stay awake, got fever and were thirsty. These symptoms hit mainly the older people, children, and pregnant women. Many vomited and had colic type pains. Others got muscle paralysis and became numb around the hands and feet. Other reported symptoms were loss of hair, pain in the chest, pain in the back, and bleeding in the oesophagus."[49] Women often suffered disturbances in the menstrual cycle and many cases of miscarriage were reported. [50] The operation was condemned in 1964 by

---

49 In the wake of Vietnam War, there was worldwide concern about the environmental damage caused by US military operations in Southeast Asia. Shortly after the end of the Vietnam War, in 1975, it began to become clear that a disproportionate number of Vietnam veterans were coming down with non-Hogkins lymphoma and skin sarcomas. The Centers for Disease Control later determined that the cause of these cancers was the dioxins contained in Agent Orange. The extent of the damage to the natural environment of Vietnam as a result of the spraying was also becoming apparent. While no systematic survey of defoliated areas of Southeast Asia has been conducted, the anecdotal evidence is enormous. Pery Mark & Ed Miles, Environmental Warfare, available at: http://www.crimesofwar.org/a-z-guide/environmental-warfare/, accessed 13 December 2013.

50 Weisberg Barry. 1970. *Ecocide in Indochina: The Ecology of War*, San Francisco: Canfield Press, p. 20.

the Federation of American Scientists as "an unwarranted experiment in chemical warfare" nevertheless, it continued until the early 1970s, when it was revealed in reports that herbicide 'Agent Orange' was causing birth defects.[51] Children fathered by men exposed to Agent Orange during the Vietnam War often have congenital abnormalities. An estimated half a million children were born with dioxin-related abnormalities. Agent Orange continues to threaten the health of the Vietnamese today.[52] Table 1 summarizes major chemical agents sprayed from air in the Vietnam War.

Besides defoliants, more than 7,000 tons of other poisonous gas was used between 1964 and 1969.[53] The most common were CS-1 and CS-2. Other gases affecting the central nervous system were also used. From 1964 to 1973, the US Air Force dropped a total of 6,162,000 tons of bombs and other ordnance over Vietnam. The US Navy and Marine Corps expended another 1,500,000 tons.[54]

---

51  One of the chemicals, picloram, does not decompose readily and may remain active in the environment for several years. Westing, Arthur H., Poisoning Plants for Peace, *Friends Journal*, 1 April 1970.

52  On 9 August 2012, the US and Vietnam began a long-awaited joint cleanup effort at Vietnam's Danang Airbase-- using technology which will heat the contaminated soil to temperatures high enough to break dioxin down into harmless compounds. The base was a key site in the US defoliant program during the Vietnam War, and much of the 80 million litres (21 million gallons) of Agent Orange used during "Operation Ranch Hand" was mixed, stored and loaded onto planes there. The US government is providing $41 million to the project which will reduce the contamination level in 73,000 cubic meters of soil by late 2016. The Danang Airbase is one of three "dioxin hotspots" -- alongside Bien Hoa and Phu Cat airbases -- where concentrations of extremely toxic contaminants from Agent Orange are nearly 400 times the globally accepted maximum standard. According to an estimate, the eventual price tag for cleaning all the country's hotspots and supporting victims could run to US$ 450 million. *Vietnam, US begin historic Agent Orange cleanup,* Available at: http://www.globalpost.com/dispatch/news/regions/asia-pacific/vietnam/120808/agent-orange-cleanup-begins-vietnam, accessed 10 August 2013.

53  *Associated Press*, 3 January 1970.

54  This tonnage far exceeded that expended in World War II and in the Korean War. The US Air Force consumed 2,150,000 tons of munitions in World War II – 1,613,000 tons in the European Theater and 537,000 tons in the Pacific Theater – and 454,000 tons in the Korean War. Vietnam War bombing thus represented at least three times as much (by weight) as both European and Pacific theater World War II bombing combined and about fifteen times total tonnage in the Korean War. Clodfelter, Michael. 1995. *Vietnam in Military Statistics: A History of the Indochina Wars:1772-1991.* Jefferson, NC: McFarland.

| Agent | Spray Period (approximate) | Amount sprayed (10$^6$kg) | Area sprayed (10$^6$ ha) | Area sprayed (per cent) |
|---|---|---|---|---|
| Orange | 1962-1970 | 57.0 | 1.6 | 12 |
| White | 1966-1971 | 22.8 | 0.6 | 5 |
| Blue | 1962-1970 | 10.7 | 0.3 | 2 |
| CS | 1964-1970 | 9.0 | 5.0 | 37 |
| Malathion | 1967-1972 | 3.0 | 6.0 | 44 |
| Total | 1962-1972 | 102.5 | 13.5 | 100 |

*Table 1: Major Chemical agents sprayed from air in the second Indochina war: approximate gross areal coverage*[55]

The use of Rome plows[56] or tractors with cutting blades was another source of great environmental damage. These tractors were used to clear vast tracts of land to build runways and military bases or to deny forest cover to the enemy. Each tractor could clear one acre of land per hour, and more than 150 tractors operated daily. It is estimated that Rome plows cleared 750,000 acres of land between 1967 and the end of the war. In addition to the damage done to vegetation and animal habitat, the Rome plows caused severe erosion, and consequently increased the threat of floods.

The US also deployed 'Daisy Cutter' bombs for clearing large tracts of land in the thick forests of Vietnam. Each bomb was about the size of a Volkswagen car and was dropped from a C-47 transport plane to drift to the ground with the help of a parachute. A long detonation probe attached to the tip of the bomb causes detonation immediately upon contact with the ground. The parachute was employed to reduce air speed so that when the bomb probe touched the ground, the bomb detonated above the surface, thereby directing the blast outwards instead of into the ground. In

---

55  Westing Arthur H. 1984. *Herbicides in War: The Long-term Ecological and Human Consequences*, London: Taylor & Francis, p. 15.

56  A Rome plow is an 11-foot-wide, 2.5-ton blade fitted with a 3-foot splitting lance attached to the front of a 20-ton tractor. The Rome plow operators dubbed themselves Rome Runners and Jungle Eaters, a symbol of the damage they could do. Lanier-Graham Susan D. 1993. *The Ecology of War: Environmental Impacts of Weaponry and Warfare*, New York: Walker and Company, p. 32-33.

this manner, an area of about the size of a football field was carved out of the forest without producing a crater. The cleared area would then be used for troop implant and extraction purposes.

The US tested an unusual tactic of weather modification. The US seeded clouds in an effort to increase rainfall, rendering Vietnam's unpaved roads and trails hard to travel, to disturb radar readings, and to cause floods and landslides. The US military also used forest fire as a weapon of warfare. Large areas of forest were destroyed by Napalm bombing. Beside the loss of valuable cropland, several animal species were threatened or endangered.[57]

The Vietnam War was different from previous wars because in this war, the destruction of key components of the country's physical environment became a deliberate military strategy. The physical landscape was intentionally disturbed by: (i) explosive munitions, (ii) chemicals or herbicides, and (iii) land clearing operations by specialized bulldozers. Aerial bombardment inflicted damage to forests on a scale never before accomplished. The US Air Force widely practiced 'carpet bombing', in which B-52 bombers would fly over and lay down a blanket of bombs into an area thought to be occupied by enemy forces. Typically, these bombing runs consisted of 3 to 12 aircraft, each carrying 108 500lb of bombs. These missions saturated an area of approximately 500 metres by 1000 metres with bombs. Conservative estimates place the number of craters left behind by these missions at around 26 million.[58] For a comparison, during WW II, a total of 2,000,000 tons were dropped in all theatres of war, while in Korea, the total ammunition dropped amounted to 1,000,000 tons. In Vietnam between 1965 and 1971 the US dropped over 14,000,000 tons of ammunition. The effects of these bombing runs can still be seen today.[59]

By the end of the war, a fifth of South Vietnam's forests had been chemically annihilated and more than a third of its mangrove forests had been destroyed. Some forests have recovered, but much of the land has become permanent scrubby grassland. The Vietnam War era also saw a growth in environmental awareness and considerable new activity in the area of international environmental law. The worldwide reaction to the

---

57  *Ecological Consequences of the Second Indochina War*, Stockholm International Peace Research Institute (SIPRI), Stockholm, 1976, p. 58-72.

58  G.H. Orians and E.W. Pfeiffer, Ecological Effects of the War in Vietnam, Vol. 168, *Science*, (1970), p. 544-554.

59  Hupy, Joseph, The Environmental Footprint of War, Vol. 14 (3), *Environment and History*, August 2008, p. 415.

attack on Vietnam's environment led to the adoption of two international conventions: ENMOD and Protocols I and II to the Geneva Conventions of 1949.[60]

## VI. Iraq-Iran War

The Arab world's longest war in the 20th century was Iraq's eight-year war with Iran (1980-1988). Marked by trench warfare and chemical weapons, it was reminiscent of World War I.[61] The heaviest fighting took place around the Shatt al-Arab estuary and the Mesopotamian marshlands. The 1,500-km Iran-Iraq border, which remains heavily mined to this day, was an active front in which chemical weapons were deployed by Iraq.[62] A vesicant or blister agent (mustard) and a nerve agent (tabun) were used against Iranian soldiers and Kurdish citizens of Iraq.[63] Except for occasional raids on cities, the rest of the country was largely spared from military action and hence direct environmental impacts. The heavily-scarred landscape of the Iran-

---

60 The 1976 UN Convention on the Prohibition of Military or Any Other Hostile use of Environmental Modification Techniques (ENMOD); and 1977 Protocols additional to the four Geneva Conventions of 1949, which strengthen the protection of victims of international (Protocol I) and non-international (Protocol II) armed conflicts.

61 The Iraq-Iran War began in September 1980. Iraq commenced a ground assault on Iran, and launched air strikes on strategic targets. However, Iranian resistance proved strong, and all Iraqi troops had withdrawn from the occupied portions of Iran by early 1982. Iran then initiated a series of offensives that Iraq responded to with the deployment of chemical weapons in 1983. Iran accepted the cease-fire agreement in July 1988. *Desk Study on the Environment in Iraq,* 2003, UNEP, p. 52.

62 The Organization for the Prohibition of Chemical Weapons (OPCW) stated that during the Iran-Iraq war, there were various unconfirmed reports that Iraq had used chemical weapons, but the international community was slow to react at first. However, the UN fact finding teams confirmed that Iraq was indeed using chemical weapons on a massive scale and that Iran had suffered thousands of casualties as a result of these attacks". Clinical evidence and soil samples confirmed the use of mustard gas and the nerve agent tabun against the Kurdish population in 1987. The most infamous attack occurred on 16 March 1988 in the town of Halabja, where up to 5,000 Kurdish civilians and Iranian soldiers died from the effects of sarin nerve gas and mustard gas. See: http://www.opcw.org/html/global/search.html, accessed 23 November 2013. At the time of the attacks, both countries were parties to the 1925 Geneva Protocol, a treaty banning the use of chemical weapons against another contracting party (Protocol for the Prohibition of the Use in War of Asphyxiating, Poisonous, or other Gases, and of Bacteriological Methods of Warfare, 19 June 1925).

63 On March 19, 1988, Iraqi airplanes bombed the village of Halabja, in Iraq. The inhabitants were Kurdish Iraqi citizens, a tribes-people who live in the region where the borders of Turkey, Iran, and Iraq meet. The casualties from this raid received worldwide media attention. The chemical weapons allegedly used were nerve agents, cyanide, and mustard.

Iraq border, with its trenches, bunkers, weapon pits, moats and mine fields, is reminiscent of a cratered lunar landscape. The physical disturbance of the landscape (wetland and semi-desert) by major earthworks has been so severe that old topographic maps are no longer valid.

The construction of defensive works and military causeways inside the marshlands contributed to their desiccation, and reduced their surface area by 20-25 percent. The extensive date palm plantations fringing the Shatt al-Arab estuary were devastated, with millions of trees destroyed by shelling, fire and deliberate clearance. The marine environment of the Gulf suffered considerable damage during the so-called 'tanker war' in which over 500 commercial vessels were destroyed and major oil installations targeted; the worst incident being the bombing of the Iranian Nowruz platform where almost 2 million barrels of oil was spilled. The conflict's shipwreck legacy remains an important problem to this day with potentially significant environmental implications that need to be considered in future salvage operations. During the last stages of the war, an estimated 4,000 Kurdish villages were destroyed with evident environmental impacts ranging from large-scale population displacement to the destruction of orchards, cropland and pastures.

Overall, the eight-year war resulted in heavy losses to both sides, with an estimated 600,000 Iranian and 400,000 Iraqis dead, over one million refugees and a total cost running into billions of dollars. However, no formal independent studies have been conducted to determine the long-term environmental impacts and risks to human health from the war.[64]

## VII. The First Gulf War

On 2 August 1990, Iraq invaded and conquered its neighbour, Kuwait.[65] On 29 November 1990, the UN Security Council adopted resolution 678 authorizing the use of "all necessary means" unless Iraq withdrew from Kuwait by 15 January 1991. On 17 January, a US-led coalition of 26 nations, with a combined military force of more than 600,000 troops, initiated

---

64  *Desk Study on the Environment in Iraq*. 2003. United Nations Environment Programme (UNEP), p. 52.

65  The military action by Iraq culminated a longstanding series of disputes between the two states, including contests concerning territorial claims, oil drilling practices, and economic competition over oil pricing practices. Joyner Christopher C. and James T. Kirkhope, The Persian Gulf War Oil Spill: Reassessing the Law of Environmental Protection and the Law of Armed Conflict, Vol. 24, No. 1, *Case Western Reserve Journal of International Law*, Winter 1992, p. 29-62.

Operation Desert Storm against Iraq. A massive air campaign targeted Iraqi military forces and infrastructure, including nuclear, biological and chemical weapons facilities, as well as numerous other sites including oil refineries, electrical power stations, and petrochemical facilities. The coalition declared a ceasefire on 28 February and on 3 April 1991, the UN Security Council adopted resolution 687 setting out provisions for the ceasefire, including neutralization of Iraqi weapons of mass destruction through the creation of a Special Commission (UNSCOM).[66]

## A. Environmental Damage in Kuwait

The UN coalition forces attacked Iraqi military targets in Kuwait more than six months after Iraq's occupation of Kuwait and Saddam Hussein's refusal to remove Iraqi forces from Kuwait. Two days after the Coalition forces launch of the air campaign against Iraq, Iraqi forces deliberately opened valves at Sea Island, an offshore oil trans-shipment terminal, and offloaded crude oil from moored tankers, creating a huge oil spill in the Gulf.[67] The possible motives for the deliberate spillage could have been discouraging the landing of an amphibious vehicle and creating a potential for lighting beaches afire in the event of an invasion; damaging steam turbines of offshore naval vessels; fouling desalination plants in Saudi Arabia, thus depriving civilians and soldiers of drinking water, and also possibly affecting generation of electricity.[68] While these tactical motives for the spillage were largely unsuccessful, the environmental effects have been significant. Since the spillage occurred within the war zone, artillery fire and floating mines severely hindered both the evaluation of the impact

---

66  *Desk Study on the Environment in Iraq*. 2003. United Nations Environment Programme (UNEP), p. 56.

67  This oil slick was for the first time detected by AVHRR imagery, 60 kms south of Sea Island on 23 January 1991. Estimates of the size of the oil spills ranged from 24 to 600 million gallons of oil. Oily sediments were to be found not only on the Gulf's water surface, but also on the seafloor and along its shores, endangering the fragile Gulf ecology and the inlets of desalination plants. El-Baz, F. and R.M. Makharita (ed.). 1994. *The Gulf War and the Environment*. Lausanne: Gordon and Breach Science Publishers S.A., p. 116.

68  During the week of January 20, 1991, about 1.5 million barrels of oil (63 million gallons) were spilled in the Persian Gulf offshore of Kuwait. The spill was more than five times larger than 11 million gallon Exxon Valdez spill of 1989. The 1991 Persian Gulf originated from at least two resources. The major source was a pipeline leading from Port at Ahmari, Kuwait, to the Sea Island filling station 10 miles offshore. The other, lesser source of spilled oil was 5 leaking super-tankers off the coast of Kuwait. Oil from super-tankers may have been due to damage from Coalition force attack, while oil from pipelines was believed to have been deliberately spilled by Iraq.

and remediation efforts.

At the time of the Iraqi invasion, some 900 Kuwaiti wells were capable of oil production.[69] When the Iraqi's retreated, they demolished about 800 of these, carrying out Saddam's long-threatened retaliation against Kuwait's oil-producing infrastructure. Of these, 656 wells were ablaze for several months and the last oil-well fire was extinguished only on 6 November 1991. The fires consumed over 6 million barrels of crude oil and 70 million cubic metres of associated gases daily. Estimates of the amount of oil burning in Kuwait ranged from 1.5 to 6 million barrels per day. The cost of the fires on oil loss exceeded 10 billion dollars, assuming 1991 oil values.

The oil-well fires released large amount of hydrocarbons and particulates which affected the neighbouring areas.[70] It was common to see pitch black skies over large areas of Kuwait. Since smoke particulates absorb and reflect much of the sun's radiation to outer space, the average temperatures dropped by as much as 10°C in several areas of Kuwait and Iraq. For example, in Baharain, 400 km from the fires, the average temperature in May 1991 was 7.5° below normal, making it the coldest May in 35 years. Smoke clouds were visible over a 42,000 km² area, including parts of Iraq, Iran, Qatar, Pakistan, Turkey, Sri Lanka, India, Bulgaria and even the Soviet Union. While no serious global effect was caused, local and regional effects were severe.[71] Black snow was observed as far away as Jammu & Kashmir,

---

69 El-Baz, F., Preliminary observations of environmental damage due to the Gulf War, Vol. 16 (1), *Natural Resources Forum*, (1992), p. 71-75.

70 Environmental impacts of oil fires: Crude oil is a mixture of about one thousand different hydrocarbons, with exact composition varying from one reserve to another. The products of uncontrolled oil fires, whether at a wellhead, a storage area or in trenches, will depend on the type of crude oil, local climate conditions, the content of hydrogen sulphide ($H_2S$), water and/or natural gas, and the presence of naturally occurring radioactivity, especially dissolved radon isotopes as products of the natural uranium decay series. The broad categories of contaminants from oil fires are: extreme heat, carbon monoxide, unburned hydrocarbons, poly aromatic hydrocarbons (PAHs), polychlorinated-dibenzo-dioxins and furans, carbon soot, oxides of sulphur, oxides of nitrogen, carbon dioxide, and radon. Of these, the first two are lethal, capable of causing immediate death upon exposure, even for a short duration. However, this would happen only within the immediate vicinity of the fire. The other pollutants have more chronic effects and some (PAHs, carbon soot) are carcinogenic. Other than potential impacts on human and animal health, the contaminants from oil fires may also damage vegetation (including crops), landscapes, and human artefacts (including buildings and archaeological sites). *Desk Study on Environment in Iraq: 2003*, United Nations Environment Programme (UNEP), p.73-74.

71 The Kuwait oil fires and military operations associated with the 1991 Gulf War resulted in substantially increased levels of airborne particulate matter (PM) in the Kingdom of

India, 2,600 km east of Kuwait.

The vegetation in the Gulf region suffered as the soot and oil covered the leaves and reduced photosynthesis. Black oily rain doubled the amount of oil spilled directly and oil wells which did not catch fire flowed uncontrollably forming stagnant pools of oil several kilometres long and more than a meter deep, endangering the potability of the alluvial groundwater reserves.

The Iraqi armed forces adopted a new kind of scorched earth strategy. They took about five months to build ditches above the soil surface and filled them with oil to prevent ground assaults. These ditches extended about 200 km along the southern border of Kuwait. There were 120 ditches, each about 2.5-3 metres in width and 1.5-2 metres in depth. The crude oil filled in the ditches was estimated at about 3.5 million barrels. The purpose behind Iraq's releasing of oil and destroying oilfields was probably less tactical than punitive and destructive: to show that a country losing a war can still do damage, hurt its adversaries and neighbours, and diminish the value of the prize for which the war is being fought. The fact that only Kuwaiti wells were set alight, and not those on the Iraqi side of the border, confirms this, as does the fact that explosive charges were used, rather than simple ignition with opened valves.[72] The burning oil-wells caused acid rain across large parts of the Middle East and South Asia and contaminated water and food resources and damaged ecosystems and beaches in the entire region. Some scientists even speculated that a 1994 cyclone in Bangladesh, which killed 100,000 people was precipitated due to climatic changes from the Kuwait oil fires.

## Environmental Damage

The Persian Gulf has a high diversity of ecosystems, including coral reefs, mangroves, and sea grass communities. There are 450 animal species associated with coral reefs alone. Besides 180 species of molluscs, 106 species of fish, 5 species of dolphins, 113 species of overwintering birds,

---

Saudi Arabia (KSA) during 1991 and 1992. It has been reported that approximately 1,080 to 1,370 excess deaths from the increased air pollution exposures provides a strong indication that the population of KSA suffered a substantial adverse health impact from the environmental degradation associated with this conflict. White, Ronald H. and Carl H. Stineman, Premature Mortality in the Kingdom of Saudi Arabia Associated with Particulate Matter Air Pollution from the 1991 Gulf War, Vol. 14, No. 4, *Human and Ecological Risk Assessment*, 2008, p. 645-664.

72  Roberts Adam, Environmental Destruction in the 1991 Gulf War, No. 291, *International Review of the Red Cross*, November-December 1992, p. 542.

3 species of whales and numerous sea turtles, dugongs and sea snakes have been reported in the Gulf. The effect of the oil spill was the most devastating on birds. The feeding grounds of over one hundred thousand wading and migratory birds were destroyed and some populations have been slow to recover. Oil can coat a bird's feathers, hindering flight and causing loss of the feather's insulating properties. Birds can also ingest oil from contaminated food or while cleaning their feathers. This oil is then delivered to the eggs and greatly increases hatching morality. Mistaking the oil slicks to be water bodies, the birds landed on them. They got coated with oil, lost their capability to fly and perished by sinking or due to hunger. Seabirds were the first victims of the environmental damages caused by the Gulf armed conflict.[73] The oil-soaked cormorant became symbolic of the ecological damage caused by the spill. Before the war, there were various seabirds living in the Gulf region and the number of these birds was about 260,000,000. After the war, this number was reduced to 100,000,000 birds. Around 100,000,000 to 150,000,000 seabirds were found dead on the Saudi Arabia coastlines.[74]

The oil spill resulted in immediate threat to human lives through loss of drinking water and affected harvesting of marine food. Important shrimp fisheries declined immediately after the war to around one percent of their pre-war level. The marine environment was exposed to large quantities of petroleum hydrocarbons, the volume of the spills being estimated at between 1 and 1.7 million tons. The spill was broken up into several smaller spills which contaminated most of the Saudi Arabian coastline About 700 km of Saudi Arabian shoreline consisting of sand, gravel, wetlands, lagoons, and muddy tidal flats, covered by vegetation was contaminated. Some oil ended up on the beaches of Kuwait, Iran, Bahrain and Qatar but

---

73 The effects of oil spills on aquatic birds are devastating. An oiled bird is subject to extremes of heat or cold, poisoning from ingested oil and predator attacks. A bird's feathers are its natural protection against the elements. The feathers of aquatic birds are made up of microscopic barbs and barbules that hook together like Velcro to form a watertight seal. This seal is what keeps the bird buoyant and insulates it from heat and cold. As long as a bird's feathers are properly aligned, the feathers overlap each other, keeping the seal intact. Oil disrupts this natural alignment, leaving the bird vulnerable to hypothermia from cold water or overheating from hot temperatures or the heat of the sun. Birds keep their feathers aligned by preening. When a bird is covered with oil, it engages in almost non-stop preening in an attempt to realign its feathers, restore its natural buoyancy and protect itself from heat and cold. During preening the bird ingests oil, which is highly toxic.

74 Philip Elmer, Environmental Damage, A Man-Made Hell on Earth, *TIMES*, 18 March 1991, p. 36;

generally these countries were less affected. Most of the mangroves and marshes along the affected coast was destroyed and 50 to 90 per cent of the fauna, mainly crabs, amphipoda and molluscs, were also killed by the oil. Approximately 50 dugongs and several times as many dolphins were found dead on the beaches of Saudi Arabia after the spill.

The desert bordering Kuwait has a unique ecosystem that was home to snakes, camels, gazelles, spiders, scorpions and sheep. It is protected by an upper layer of sand, pebbles and microorganisms which has been referred to as desert shield. Pebbles ranging from about 0.5 cm to 2 cm in diameter form the natural upper layer of the ecosystem and are large enough to resist movement during most wind storms, thus holding in place the smaller grains below. In addition, a network of microorganisms including bacteria, form an interlocking mesh among the smaller upper sand grains and provide resistance against wind disturbances.[75] Military fortifications and massive-scale vehicle movements destroyed this natural desert-shield in Kuwait, which may take decades to recover.[76] Hydrocarbon depositions from oil well smoke and deliberate spilling of oil in trenches and irrigation channels contaminated groundwater resources and the mines left buried throughout the desert will pose a hazard to travellers for years to come.

Besides the damage to this ecosystem from oil fires and the spill, animals were frequently killed in indirect attacks. Prior to the war, Kuwait had a camel population of 10,000 that was reduced to an estimated 2,000 after the war. Desert warfare at night was often most treacherous for the camel. By night, the troops saw only blips on a radar screen. Assuming these to be caused by approaching Iraqi troops, the tank troops fired at and destroyed whatever caused the blips. Only the following morning, when the desert would be strewn with dead camels, would the troops realize that the blips had not been the enemy. Iraqi troops also destroyed the Kuwait City Zoo,

---

75 Daehler, Curtis C. and Majumdar Shyamal K. 1992. 'Environmental Impacts of the Persian Gulf War' in Majumdar SK, Forbes GS, Miller EW and Schmalz (ed.), *Natural and Technological Disasters: Causes, Effects and Preventive Measures*, The Pennsylvania Academy of Science, p. 329-336.

76 Not only were the Iraqi's guilty of the oil spills, the bomb raids of the Coalition air forces also caused the release of oil into the Persian Gulf as well. The desert surface was disturbed not only during the onset of the ground war, but also due to the movement of thousands of military vehicles and the dropping of high explosives. The digging of trenches and foxholes and the building of berms and walls of sand resulted in the exposure of vast amounts of soils to fluvial and aeolian erosion, providing source material for dust particles and dune sands. Sandstorms caused further spread of soot and oil throughout the region.

killing and maiming the animals. Out of a collection of over 400 animals prior to the war, only twenty-four could be found after the Iraqis left.[77]

Several persistent chemicals were used during the war and much of these were released as pollutants. It is, however, extremely difficult to collect information from the military on additives and chemicals that are used. Halones, a group of carboflouro-brome-compounds, were used to reduce the risk of explosion of the fuel tanks of aircraft.[78]

## Depleted Uranium (DU) Ammunition

The 1991 Gulf War is reportedly the first conflict in which depleted uranium (DU) ammunition was used on a military scale.[79] The Pengaton has admitted that the Coalition Forces dropped at least 320 tonnes of munitions and weapons containing DU over Iraq during the war, although some independent environmental groups believe that the amount dropped was much higher.[80] Overall, 50 tonnes of DU was fired during tank battles and 250 tonnes used in air to ground attacks. The United Kingdom Ministry of Defence (UK MoD) has indicated that less than one tonne of DU ammunition was used during the war, though it has not disclosed

---

77  Lanier-Graham Susan D. 1993. *The Ecology of War: Environmental Impacts of Weaponry and Warfare*, New York: Walker and Company, p. 48-49.

78  It is impossible to estimate the total amount of halones used in the war, as this kind of information is classified. However, a hypothetical calculation shows the following: The Allied aircrafts did approximately 110,000 missions. If each mission consumes 25 kg of halones, the total amount of these substances used during the 43 days of air raids was almost 3,000 tonnes or nearly 10 per cent of the total annual global discharge of halones. Freon is a related group of persistent compounds, which also is a well known greenhouse gas. Freon was used as an additive to the fuel used by the Stealth-bomber, primarily to reduce particulate emissions so that the plane should not be undetectable by radar. The amount of freones used in the aircrafts is also classified but 44 F-117 Stealth-bombers were used in the Gulf War. Sadiq M. and McCain J. 1993. *The Gulf War Aftermath: An Environmental Tragedy*, Kluwer Academic Publishers.

79  DU, a by-product from the process that enriches natural uranium ore for use as fuel in nuclear reactors and nuclear weapons, has both defensive and offensive military applications. Its high density makes it suitable as a component of armour plating (e.g. for part of the turrets of battle tanks), as well as for piercing armour plating. DU munitions are currently manufactured for use by aircraft (including helicopters) and tanks. For more details on DU weapons; see Jha U C. 2013. *Weapons of War: Environmental Impact*, New Delhi: KW Publishers, p. 219 -247.

80  During the Gulf War, American and British forces used more than 290,000 kilograms of depleted uranium contaminated equipment and the soil on the battlefields of north-eastern Saudi Arabia, Kuwait, and southern Iraq. Fahey Dan, Depleted Uranium Weapons: Lessons from the 1991 Gulf War, available at: http://www.wise-uranium. org/dhap992.html12, accessed 12 November 2013.

where the ammunition was used. The US government has to date not released information on DU target coordinates for the 1991 war. DU was reportedly used extensively in the vicinity of Basra and Kuwait. The Iraqi military did not possess or use DU weapon during the conflict.[81]

## Explosive Remnants of War

Kuwait inherited extensive explosive remnants of war (ERW)[82] contamination in the wake of the 1991 Gulf War. Areas of Kuwait are still contaminated with ERW of different types, including rocket-propelled grenades and mortars, as well as significant quantities of anti-personnel and anti-vehicle mines. Ten different types of Allied cluster sub-munitions were amongst the unexploded munitions discovered following the liberation of Kuwait in February 1991 by the Coalition Forces. The accumulation of thousands of US non-landmine sub-munition duds on the battlefield created de facto minefields. There is evidence that 'the dumping of old, unreliable stock on Kuwait and the neighbouring countries increased the probability of a large residual problem caused by munitions failing to explode as intended.'[83]

The widespread ERW contamination affected civilians and military personnel alike, hindering reconstruction and land use in the coasts, deserts, agricultural, residential and recreational areas. The presence of ERW prevents the use and rehabilitation of community infrastructure and resources. These include housing, water and irrigation systems, villages, schools, clinics and markets, and the paths or roads between them. Clearance activities are often needed before they can be used or new construction can go ahead. ERW presence also dissuades the inhabitants of affected communities from certain types of land use, or makes exploitation of local resources less efficient. Ultimately, land denial not only affects economic productivity; it can also produce wholesale change in traditional social and economic practices. At its most extreme, whole communities

---

81 During the 1991 war, the US army recovered and disposed of its own vehicles contaminated by DU during fires and friendly fire incidents. McDonald Avril, Jann K. Kleffner and Brigit Toebes (eds). 2008. *Depleted Uranium Weapons and International Law: A Precautionary Approach*, T.M.C. Asser Press, p. 14-15.

82 An explosive remnant of war is defined as unexploded ordnance of all types except antipersonnel and anti-vehicle mines. It also includes abandoned stockpiles of munitions.

83 *Explosive Remnants of War: A Global Survey*. 2003. Landmine Action, London, UK, p.62-63.

may be abandoned. ERW and other military debris have value as an economic resource in many poor communities. For those on the very margins of society, ERW can be the mainstay of economic survival. This leads people to undertake high-risk activities to locate explosives and scrap that are a major cause of accidents in many countries.

Between February 1991 and June 1997, more than 111,000 tonnes of ordnance was cleared and during 2000-02, nearly 27,000 items of explosive remnants of war were disposed of. Despite a massive and expensive clean-up operation, hampered by environmental conditions such as high temperatures, sand storms and flash floods; cluster sub-munitions, as well as other unexploded ordnance, continue to be encountered in Kuwait.[84] Table 2 provides a summary of extent of damage in Kuwait from oil spillage during the Gulf War.

| S. No. | Type of damage | Extent of damage |
|---|---|---|
| 1. | Damaged oil wells | 720 |
| 2. | Oil seepage into land | 60 million barrel |
| 3. | Oil in lakes | 24 million barrel |
| 4. | Oil lakes | 570 |
| 5. | Area covered by oil lakes | 49 sq km |
| 6. | Total oil-contaminated areas | 960 sq km |
| 7. | Heavily contaminated soil | 40 million tons |
| 8. | Oil lost due to fires and oil flow | 1.8 to 2 billion barrels |
| 9. | Depth of oil in trenches | 60-120 cm |

*Table 2: The Consequences of deliberate oil spillage in Kuwait*[85]

---

84 *Explosive Remnants of War: A Global Survey*. 2003. Landmine Action, London, UK, p. 68.

85 Oil lakes affect soil adversely. Toxic substances resulting from the oil lakes may accumulate in plant tissue, constituting a carcinogen which causes death to any animal eating such plants. Areas within the boundaries of the oil lakes were considered biologically dead. After the oil lake dried, oil tar or sludge remained, causing severe disturbances in the physical, chemical, and biological properties of the soil environment. Dark coloration of the soil surface leads to greater heat absorption, increased soil temperature, and consequently increased water loss by evaporation. A study acknowledged that damages to natural vegetation were caused by the increased temperature of atmosphere and soil, the decrease of photosynthetic activity from the burning of many oil lakes. Polluted soil can be classified in three groups depending on how much pollution presents in the soil: (i) Severely-polluted soil which caused death to all its biological capabilities; (ii) Mid-polluted soils that affected about 25-100 per

## B. Environmental Damage in Iraq

Although the war lasted less than six weeks, the air campaign targeted all types of infrastructure, military and civil, including sewage and water supply plants, power stations, bridges, oil refineries, manufacturing and petrochemical industries as well as nuclear, biological and chemical weapons facilities in Iraq. The environmental fallout of such a massive bombing campaign was potentially significant although it was never scientifically assessed. Immediately after the war, Iraq was placed under strict UN sanctions and made to pay compensation for war damages, including environmental ones.[86] At the same time it was denied the right to restore key social services and infrastructure, including the importation of spare parts to rehabilitate wastewater treatment plants such as that of Al-Rustamiyah, in Baghdad, which was releasing 300,000 m³/day of untreated sewage into the Tigris River with grave humanitarian and environmental consequences.

The Coalition Forces bombed all known chemical factories and chemical weapon storage depots. Hazardous chemicals were released into the surrounding areas and posed a threat to the inhabitants. Clean up attempt of these contaminated sites was never a priority issue. In addition, an Iraqi nuclear reactor was bombed, and it is possible that radioactivity has been released, which may cause further casualties in the years to come.[87]

The impact of Gulf War was unprecedented environmental ruin ever executed by any military force. The war was a laboratory for military scientists and weapon makers. It demonstrated for all to see that recent advances in military technology have given the armed forces extraordinary

---

cent of the soil's biota; and (iii) Slight-polluted soil covered by soot which had fallen from oil smoke caused by oil-well fires. Finally, oil lakes affected the ground water aquifer. Sea water used to extinguish the oil-well fires also contributed to the loss of soil productivity. As for the effect on public health, some studies show that asthma and respiratory system problems increased after the pollution occurred. These studies concluded that children were more vulnerable to these types of disease than adults. For more details see: Eifan, Meshari K., Head of State Criminal Responsibility for Environmental War Crimes: Case Study: The Arabian Gulf Armed Conflict 1990-1991, SJD dissertation, Pace University School of Law, Fall 2007, p. 15-16.

86  For more details on UN Compensation Commission (UNCC), see p. 287.

87  Daehler, Curtis C. and Majumdar SK. 1992. 'Environmental Impacts of the Persian Gulf War' in Majumdar SK, Forbes GS, Miller EW and Schmalz (ed.), *Natural and Technological Disasters: Causes, Effects and Preventive Measures*, The Pennsylvania Academy of Science, p. 334.

new destructive powers.[88] After the war many veterans suffered from a condition now known as the Gulf War syndrome. The causes of the illness are subject to widespread speculation. Possible causes are exposure to depleted uranium (DU), chemical weapons (nerve gas and mustard gas), an anthrax vaccine given to 41 per cent of US soldiers and 60-75 per cent of UK soldiers, smoke from burning oil wells and parasites. The symptoms included chronic fatigue, muscle problems, diarrhoea, migraine, memory loss, skin problems and shortness of breath. Many veterans have died of illnesses such as brain cancer, now acknowledged as potentially connected to service during the war.

## VIII. The Second Gulf War

The Second Gulf War, referred to as 'Operation Iraqi Freedom', started in March 2003. The primary goal of this war was to seek and destroy weapons of mass destruction that the US thought Iraq possessed. Also, it was widely suspected that Iraq was harbouring and supporting Al-Qaeda. The invasion eventually led to the capture of President Saddam Hussein and the military takeover of the country. Many of the tactics used in the first war were also used in this war. With the country hardly having recovered from the first war, the environmental implications were vast when the second war was embarked upon.

Although the bombardment was significantly greater than that in the 1991 Gulf War, it was mainly targeted at military facilities, and civil infrastructure was largely spared. In fact, the principal cause of environmental damage emanated from extensive looting and sabotage of military and industrial facilities as well as oil installations and pipelines. Of the five sites identified by the United Nations Environment Programme (UNEP) as priority contaminated "hotspots", four were looted and one was a military scrap yard.

The Al-Doura refinery warehouses, near Abu Gharaib, 35 km west of Baghdad, were among the largest stores of chemicals in the country. The looting and ransacking of the refinery warehouses after the 2003 conflict has caused a major environmental disaster: over 5,000 tonnes of chemicals, including highly hazardous materials, particularly tetra ethylene lead (TEL) and furfural, were spilled, burnt or stolen. The burning of the chemicals reportedly generated white toxic fumes affecting villages within

---

88 Barnaby, Frank, The Environmental Impact of the Gulf War, *The Ecologist*, Vol. 21(4), 1991, p. 166-172.

a radius of 2–3 km around the storage facility. The area is assumed to be heavily contaminated with a variety of hazardous chemicals and the risk of groundwater pollution is high, given the permeable nature of the sandy soils.[89]

## Depleted Uranium (DU)

The total amount of DU used in the 2003 war is unknown, but speculative figures from various studies put them in the range of 170 to 1,700 tonnes. The US, while admitting to using DU, has not disclosed how much and where it was used, while the United Kingdom has reported firing 1.9 tons.[90] People who may come into direct contact with DU munitions and DU-contaminated equipment, particularly those working in scraping operations are at the greatest risk of radioactive exposure.[91] It is therefore important that DU contaminated areas be identified and assessed and a monitoring programme for potentially affected populations established.[92]

Contamination from DU and other military-related pollution is strongly suspected of causing a sharp rise in congenital birth defects and cancer cases in Iraq, as well as in other nations that have been invaded by NATO

---

89 *Environment in Iraq: UNEP Progress Report*, 2003, United Nations Environment Programme, Nairobi, p. 9.

90 On 24 June 2003, the British Ministry of Defence provided UNEP with a list of fifty-one DU target coordinates for the 2003 Iraq conflict, as well as a map identifying Challenger II tank target points. In addition, the UK disclosed that it had fired a total amount of approximately 1.9 tonnes of DU ammunition during the conflict. *Technical Report on Capacity-building for the Assessment of Depleted Uranium in Iraq*, 2007, United Nations Environment Programme, Geneva, p. 4, 10.

91  This may involve any or all of the following potential risks to the environment and human health: (i) Inhalation of DU dust by anyone in the immediate vicinity who survived the initial blast and subsequent fire is a potentially serious health risk; (ii) Widespread, low-level contamination of the ground surface; (iii) Presence of intact DU penetrators buried in soft ground (which might be dug up and handled by unprotected individuals, leading to a low-level but unnecessary radiation dose to the skin); (iv) Presence of DU penetrator fragments on the ground surface (which might be picked up and handled by unprotected individuals, including 'souvenir' hunters, leading to a low-level but unnecessary radiation dose); and (v) Possible migration of DU into ground water (and from there into drinking water supplies), through corrosion and dissolution of penetrators and penetrator fragments. *Desk Study on Environment in Iraq*, 2003, United Nations Environment Programme (UNEP), p. 80-82.

92 Kammas M. 1999. *Environmental and Health Consequences of the Use of Radiological Weapons (Depleted Uranium) on Iraq in UM-Al-Ma'arek 1991-1999*, Committee for Pollution Impact by Aggressive Bombing (CPIAB).

and the US military forces over the past two decades.[93] Some scientists assert that DU dust can move across hundreds of kilometers through the air. When DU particles, as well as intact ammunition and other weapons materials enter water sources, they may contaminate food chains. When a human inhales, ingests or is contaminated by dust particles from DU weapons, radioactive DU atoms can settle in the lungs, spleen, kidney, and other vital organs. Many prominent doctors and scientists contend that DU contamination is also connected to the recent emergence of diseases that were not previously seen in Iraq, such as illnesses of the kidney, lungs, and liver, as well as a total collapse of the immune system. DU contamination may also be connected to the steep rise in leukaemia and anaemia cases, especially among children, that is being reported in many Iraqi governorates. Additionally, there is a startling jump in miscarriages and premature births among Iraqi women.[94]

## Cluster Munitions

The US and the United Kingdom used 1206 air-dropped cluster munitions containing more than 200,000 explosive sub-munitions from 20 March to 9 April, more than what they used in Afghanistan in six months. Coalition use of ground-launched cluster munitions exceeded even the number of air-dropped types, with 10,782 containing approximately 2 million sub-munitions. The Iraqi forces engaged in a host of practices in breach of international humanitarian law i.e. the use of human shields, the abuse of the Red Cross and Red Crescent emblems and the location of military

---

93  August, Oliver, America Leaves Iraq a Toxic Legacy of Dumped Hazardous Materials, *The Times,* London, 14 June 2010.

94  Due to its radioactivity, DU dust particles primarily produce alpha particles, as well as beta particles and gamma rays. When an alpha particle, the largest and heaviest kind of radiation, enters the body into the blood-stream, some of it will be excreted in urine. Other particles may lodge in different parts of the body for extended periods of time and damage DNA configuration in cells. This can lead to altered gene expression, genetic mutations, and carcinogenesis (the transformation of normal cells into cancer cells). Theoretically, exposure to a single alpha particle from DU can cause devastating diseases. A higher dosage of exposure might greatly increase the risks of developing DU related illnesses, due to greater and more extensive cell damage. Furthermore, beta particles from DU are particularly hazardous to the skin and eyes. DNA mutations caused by DU may be passed from parent to child. Therefore, DU contamination from the First and Second Gulf Wars may continue to cause a persistent national health crisis for the future generations of Iraq. The remaining traces of DU in Iraq represent a formidable long-term environmental hazard, as they will remain radioactive for more than 4.5 billion years. McDonald, Avril. 2008. *Depleted Uranium Weapons and international law: A precautionary approach,* Asser Press.

objectives in civilian residential areas. In retaliation, Coalition ground forces deployed cluster munitions extensively in or near populated areas, causing hundreds of civilian casualties in major Iraqi cities, including al-Hilla, al-Najaf, Karbala, Baghdad and Basra.[95]

Cluster munitions have the potential to miss their targets, thus harming civilians and their properties. They are also infamous for their high dud rates. Many explosive sub-munitions when dispersed, fail to detonate as designed, becoming *de facto* landmines that kill and maim indiscriminately long after the conflict has ended. Terrain can also increase dud rates, for example, soft surfaces like desert sand and jungle marshes may not provide the resistance needed to detonate the bombs. Unexploded sub-munitions are more harmful than other unexploded bombs. A report by the Human Rights Watch suggest that by February 2003, 1,600 civilians had been killed and 2,500 injured in Kuwait and Iraq (60 per cent of victims under 15-years age), because of ground and air based cluster munitions.[96]

## Explosive Remnants of War

Iraq has a long legacy of explosive remnants of war (ERW) and mines dating back to the Second World War. The Iran-Iraq War and the Gulf Wars have compounded the problem as has the military repression by Baghdad of various minority communities of the Southern Marshes. ERW and mine contamination is particularly prevalent along the Iraq-Iran border and the south and central parts of the country (Northern Iraq under Kurdish control is dealt with in a separate section of this study.) ERW is not confined to rural areas. ERW casualties have been reported from urban areas as well.

The multiple military conflicts involving Iraq have resulted in large and widespread quantities of military debris;[97] including unexploded ordnance,

---

95  *Off Target: The Conduct of the War and Civilian Casualties in Iraq*, Human Rights Watch, December 2003, p. 56-60, 80-92. Available at: http://hrw.org/reports/2003/usa1203/usa1203.pdf, accessed 20 January 2010.

96  S. Goose, "Cluster Munitions: Towards a Global Solution," in *Human Rights Watch World Report*, New York: Human Rights Watch, 2004, p. 254.

97  The newly developed Awarisch landfill in south-western Baghdad holds over 10,000 damaged/destroyed military vehicles (tanks, armoured personnel carriers, trucks, Scud launchers) and includes a small recycling facility. The landfill may not be secure, with children recycling aluminium and other valuable metals from the tanks. *Environment in Iraq: UNEP Progress Report*, 2003, United Nations Environment Programme, Geneva, p. 16.

spent cartridges, shells, penetrators, military vehicles;[98] contaminated soils and demolition waste (e.g. containing chemicals or asbestos), and packaging from military and humanitarian supplies. The environmental risks of this toxic waste could be long-lasting and serious.[99]

War, internal policies and external sanctions have combined to confront Iraq with a high risk of desertification. This has been exacerbated by drought and the destruction of the Mesopotamian marshes. The degradation of rangelands has had particularly adverse effects on nomadic pastoralists.[100] Desert ecosystems are particularly vulnerable to physical damage from the movement of heavy military vehicles, which result in the loss of plant cover and disaggregation of soil particles.[101] In recent years, Iraqi health officials have called for in-depth research on war-related environmental pollution as a potential contributor to the country's poor health conditions and high rates of infections and diseases.

---

98  Unexploded ordnance (UXO): It can be expected that significant quantities of UXO are present, especially in and around heavily targeted areas such as Baghdad and Basra and pose risks to the environment and human health. US military officials estimate that 3-5 per cent of bombs, rockets and shells fail to explode, although soft sand may have increased this rate to 15 per cent in some cases. The total number of unexploded ordnance may range from 10,000 to 40,000 individual pieces. *Desk Study on Environment in Iraq*, 2003, United Nations Environment Programme (UNEP), p. 68, 83.

99  *Desk Study on Environment in Iraq*, 2003, United Nations Environment Programme (UNEP), p. 37.

100  Desertification is the process of land degradation in arid, semi-arid and dry sub-humid areas. It is caused primarily by human activities and climatic impacts. Desertification occurs because dry land ecosystems are extremely vulnerable to over-exploitation and inappropriate land use. Poverty, political instability, deforestation, overgrazing and poor irrigation practices can all undermine land quality and productivity. See: http://lnweb18.worldbank.org/ESSD/essdext.nsf/41ByDocName/MiddleEastandNorthAfricaEnvironmentStrategy306KBPDF/$FILE/MNAEnvStrategy2001.pdf, accessed 19 June 2014.

101  The desert crust is a layer of algae, mosses, lichens, fungi, bacteria and cyanobacteria that occupies the top one millimetre of the desert soil. These organisms are dormant when dry, but become active when wetted. The crust has major ecological value in the desert ecosystem as a protector of the thin desert soil against wind erosion, as an absorber of water (from fog and dew as well as rain), as a suitable bed for seed germination, and as a photosynthetic layer that adds a significant amount of organic carbon and organic nitrogen into the desert ecosystem, thus increasing its productivity. The crust is known to be fragile and easily damaged by vehicles and seems to be very slow to repair itself, with scientists estimating recovery over decades rather than months or years. One study of tank tracks in the Arizona desert suggested full recovery only after 1,000 years. *Desk Study on Environment in Iraq*, 2003, United Nations Environment Programme (UNEP), p. 45, 69.

# IX. Azerbaijan

Armenia's aggression against Azerbaijan, during 1988-1994 resulted in serious environmental damage in Azerbaijan. The occupied regions of Azerbaijan (about 20 percent of the territory) was almost totally destroyed and looted. The aggressors pursued the policy of 'burned-land and ethnic cleansing'. As a result, more than 150,000 dwellings were destroyed and robbed and 1 million people were forced to leave their homes and become refugees.

In the occupied zones, about 6,000 manufacturing, agricultural and other kinds of factories and plants were fully plundered and destroyed. More than 1 million hectares of agricultural land, including 127,700 hectares of irrigated land and 34,600 hectares of vineyards and orchards, was damaged; and 1,200 sq km of the irrigation system was totally destroyed. By an estimate, the damage only to Azerbaijani agricultural lands inflicted by the Armenian aggression amounted to US$ 472 million. In addition, flock of about 244,000 sheep and 69,000 cattle were driven from the occupied territories out of Azerbaijan.[102]

There was a considerable damage to the Azerbaijani cultural legacy as well. In all, 22 museums, 4 picture galleries and 9 historical palaces were burned and devastated by the Armenian aggressors. Some 40 thousand museum pieces and exhibits of great historical significance, gold and silver, rare and precious germ stones, carpets and other handmade goods were robbed and 44 temples and 9 mosques were desecrated. Some 4.6 million books and manuscripts were burned and 927 libraries looted.

The combat activities and the following occupation caused serious damage to 280,000 hectares of forest (or 25 percent of the country's forests), 6 major national parks, and more than 200 paleontological and geological sites. In 1993 alone, 206,600 m³ of valuable timber was taken to Armenia.[103] The

---

102 Security Council document A/58/594–S/2003/1090, dated 13 November 2003. Also see: http://www.azerbembassy.org.cn/eng/back_ecdam.html, accessed 13 June 2014.

103 Upon the occupation of the Azerbaijani territories by Armenia, walnut, oak and other tree species were cut down and sold to foreign countries, and forests for cattle grazing were massively destroyed in some of the occupied regions. Some tree and shrub species, which were protected for many years such as yew-tree, Araz oak, Eastern plane, pomegranate, forest grapes, Buasye pear, box(-tree), Eldar pinewood, persimmon (date-palm), willow leafed pear, etc. are now on the edge of vanishing. *Dash-bashi* and *Leshkar* forests were also exposed to fire in 1996. In autumn of the same year, the trees available-for-use in *Leshkar* forest area were completely cut down and taken away. Moreover, Armenians cut down the walnut trees planted

overall damage inflicted was estimated at over US$ 22 billion.

## X. Former Yugoslavia

The Socialist Federal Republic of Yugoslavia (SFRY), which consisted of six republics— Croatia, Bosnia and Herzegovina, Montenegro, Serbia, Macedonia, and Slovenia—broke apart in 1991 and 1992. Four wars were fought thereafter to determine the countries that would succeed the SFRY. The first war occurred in Slovenia and lasted for ten days in June and July 1991, producing few casualties. The second war was fought in Croatia, from July to December 1991 and in the summer of 1995. The third war took place in Bosnia and Herzegovina from 1992 to 1995. The second and third wars resulted in hundreds of thousands of mostly civilian casualties, massive damage to property, and more than 2.5 million refugees. The fourth war, known as the Kosovo war, lasted from March to June 1999. It was an air war conducted by the North Atlantic Treaty Organization (NATO) against the Federal Republic of Yugoslavia, a rump of Yugoslavia, consisting of Serbia and Montenegro.

### Bosnia

Bosnia became independent of Yugoslavia in 1992 and immediately afterwards entered into a war as a consequence of the instability in the wider region of the former Yugoslavia. Approximately 250,000 civilians were killed and there was an outflow of about 800,000 refugees. Numerous landmines, originating mostly from the former Yugoslavian People's Army, were deployed to secure borders and to restrict enemy movement. Some areas were mined even after the war; mostly to prevent the return of refugees. Minefields can still be found across most parts of the country, since they were laid along conflict lines that often changed. The war ended in the winter of 1995 with the Dayton Peace Agreement. From then on, the country has been divided into two entities: the Federation of Bosnia-Herzegovina (FBIH) and Republica Serbska (RS), with their own constitutions and governments.

The environmental damage from the Bosnian War consists mostly of the presence of landmines and unexploded munitions. Bosnia remains the

---

in 1957-1958 and covering 55 ha of *Leshkar* forest area. While paving new roads in *Top* and *Shukurataz* forest areas in 1996-1997, about 350-400 years old oak trees were also cut down and taken by Armenians. See: http://old.azembassy.rs/articles/view/25.

most landmine contaminated country in Europe and among the worst impacted countries in the world. An area with a size of 1820 km², around 3.6 per cent of the total territory, is filled with mines. It is estimated that there were between 3 and 6 million landmines in more than 16,000 minefields in Bosnia and Herzegovina. The clearing of mines is an ongoing challenge to the country, as over 5,000 people have been killed or injured by landmines, including 1520 since the end of the war.[104]

The most prominent environmental impact of landmines is the denial of access to vital resource. The main resources to which access is denied in Bosnia Herzegovina are the forests, agricultural land and potential tourist zones. The poor commonly rely on forests for collecting wood, hunting, gathering food and medicinal plants and for charcoal. It is estimated that about 10,000 hectares of agricultural land cannot be used. Landmines have also threatened biodiversity. There are no exact numerical data on the animals that have been killed or injured by landmines, but it is thought that there are species that are endangered.[105]

## The Kosovo War

Following the failure of the Rambouillet talks, NATO initiated an air campaign, 'Operation Allied Force' on 24 March 1999 against Serbian targets. The campaign was suspended on 10 June 1999. Although the conflict was relatively short, severe damage was inflicted to strategic infrastructure and industrial sites.[106] The Kosovo Conflict also had wider regional impacts: Albania and Macedonia had to receive huge numbers of refugees from Kosovo and they were completely unprepared for the large-scale influx. Other neighbouring countries, especially Bulgaria and Romania, downstream along the Danube, feared the effects of trans-boundary pollution from targeted industrial facilities. The fires in the oil refineries and oil storage depots sometimes lasted for many days and created clouds of pollution over wide areas. Out of 50 bombed industrial sites, four could

---

104 Landmines destroy some vegetation when they explode, but the major damage to vegetation is caused by mine clearance. The machines used to search the ground for landmines and unexploded ordnance (UXO) plough the ground and destroy all vegetation. When a landmine explodes non-biodegradable and toxic waste (lead, cadmium, chromium, TNT, RDX, Tetryl, Depleted Uranium) comes free and can leach into soil and underground water.

105 Edeko, SE, Environmental Impact of the war for the Balkanization of the Balkans, Vol. 1 (2), *Sacha Journal of Policy and Strategic Studies*, 2011, pp. 29-45.

106 UN Human Settlements Programme & UN Environment Programme; *The Kosovo conflict, consequences for the environment*, 1999, UN Habitat & UNEP, Geneva.

be classified as environmental hotspots (sites of special environmental concern)[107], as the toxic chemicals released presented serious risks to human health and required urgent clean-up on humanitarian grounds.

## Pancevo

Pancevo, a town of about 80,000 inhabitants, is located on the eastern bank of the Danube, approximately 20 km north-east of Belgrade. A major industrial complex, including a petrochemical plant, a fertilizer plant, and an oil refinery, lies on the southern edge of the town.[108] An artificial canal, 1.8 km in length, carries wastewater and storm water runoff from the complex directly into the Danube. The industrial zone was heavily targeted during the conflict, with two air strikes on the petrochemical complex (HIP Petrohemija Pancevo) and the fertiliser plant (HIP Azotara), and seven attacks on the oil refinery. Various hazardous substances were released into the environment, either directly from damaged storage facilities, or as a result of fires, with the most obvious impact being the dense clouds of black smoke which poured from burning installations.

According to NATO, the Pancevo petrochemical and fertilizer factory complex and neighbouring Lola-Utva airplane factory produced military chemicals and parts as well as civilian ones. Considerable environmental damage resulted from the destruction of the chemical factory complex at Pancevo, which was hit with at least 56 missiles, resulting in the release of 80,000 tonnes of burning oil into the environment. Among the destroyed targets were the complex's storage tanks, containing thousands of tons of toxic chemicals. Three days earlier, 1,400 tons of ethylene dichloride had poured directly into the Danube, while on another occasion workers

---

107 In terms of natural diversity, the Federal Republic of Yugoslavia (FRY) has been one of the most important geographical regions in Europe. It is home to a wealth of species (plants, fish, birds, mammals) that is matched by few other European nations. The total areas of protected and particularly valuable natural areas cover more than 400,000 hectares of the FRY's territory. Bionet, Federal Ministry for Development, 1997, *Biological Diversity of FR Yugoslavia, Assessments Threats and Polices,* Science and Environment.

108 The fertilizer plant does not have any industrial wastewater or storm-water treatment facilities. Effluent from the plant is discharged directly into a collection channel and subsequently to the open canal. Effluent from the petrochemical plant and the oil refinery initially flows into a sewer channel and undergoes treatment in a wastewater facility before discharge into the canal. United Nations Environment Programme (UNEP), and United Nations Centre for Human Settlements (UNCHS). 1999. *The Kosovo Conflict: Consequences for the Environment and Human Settlements.* Geneva, Switzerland: UNEP and UNCHS.

dumped 9,500 tons of ammonia into the river to reduce the danger from a NATO strike on the ammonia storage tanks. There were reports that mercury also seeped into the groundwater surrounding the complex.[109]

The effects of these attacks were disastrous. Black rain reportedly fell onto neighbouring towns and villages. In addition, a toxic cocktail of compounds and substances leaked into the air, soil and water around Pancevo, including 2,100 tonnes of ethylene dichloride (a substance causing kidney, liver and adrenal damage), eight tonnes of metallic mercury (known to cause severe birth defects and brain damage), 460 tonnes of vinyl chloride monomer (a known human carcinogen and a source of dioxins when burned), and 250 tonnes of liquid ammonia (which can cause blindness, lung disease and death). The city's air was filled with fumes for several days. Local residents experienced respiratory and stomach ailments, as well as burning of eyes. Leaves turned yellow or black. Government officials warned against eating vegetables from the Pancevo area, and temporarily banned fishing in the Danube downstream from Pancevo. Doctors in Pancevo advised pregnant women to have abortions.

## Kragujevac

Kragujevac, a central Serbian industrial town of 150,000 inhabitants, has a car factory, formerly one of the biggest industrial facilities in the entire Balkan region. The factory is located on the banks of the Lepenica River, a small tributary of the Velika Morava, which flows into the Danube some 60 km downstream of Belgrade. The Zdralica river is also close to the factory. The car factory was targeted twice during the conflict. Heavy damage was inflicted to the power station, car assembly line, paint shop, computer centre and truck plant. Some parts of the factory were completely destroyed, and production was halted.[110]

The air strikes reportedly caused extensive environmental pollution, with damage to soil, water and air. The main problems reported were the leaking of several tones of polychlorinated biphenyls (PCBs) contained

---

109 Schwabach, Aaron, Environmental Damage Resulting From the NATO Military Action Against Yugoslavia, Vol. 25, *Columbia Journal of Environmental Law*, (2000), p. 117-130.

110 United Nations Environment Programme (UNEP), and United Nations Centre for Human Settlements (UNCHS). 1999. *The Kosovo Conflict: Consequences for the Environment and Human Settlements*. Geneva, Switzerland: UNEP and UNCHS, p. 38-39.

in transformer oil[111] into the Morava River, and contamination of groundwater by PCBs and heavy metals. It was reported that up to 2,500 kg of oil containing PCBs was released into the environment as a direct result of the air strikes, and underground water tanks below the factory were polluted with transformer oil containing PCBs. The fate of the industrial town of Kragujevac, was similar to that of Pancevo. Unexploded munitions posed a long-term health hazard. Particular concern was expressed over the use of depleted uranium weapons.

## Novi Sad

Novi Sad is the second largest city in the Federal Republic of Yugoslavia. It is located on the banks of Danube, approximately 70 km north-west of Belgrade, in the district of Vojvodina. Novi Sad was heavily targeted during the conflict, with rail and road bridges across the Danube destroyed (together with water pipelines carried by the bridges), and industrial and military facilities damaged or destroyed. One of the principal targets was the Novi Sad oil refinery.[112] More than two-thirds of the 150 storage tanks

---

111 Polychlorinated biphenyls (PCBs) are organochlorines (substances based on carbon and chlorine) that were manufactured until the mid-1980s after which they were banned due to their toxicity and persistence. PCBs were widely used in electrical equipment and are still found in old electrical equipment and releases into the environment continue from waste dump leakages. PCBs are very persistent in the environment taking years to degrade. In rivers they become bound to sediments. They are fat-soluble and accumulate in the tissues of animals. Predators at the top of food chains, such as fish-eating birds, toothed whales and humans have the highest levels in their bodies. Due to long distance transport on air currents towards the Polar Regions and in water, PCBs have become world-wide pollutants. For example, levels in some polar species such as the polar bear are high. The greatest intake of PCBs for the general population is from fatty food, such as meat, fish and dairy products. In mammals, PCBs are passed via the placenta to developing young in the womb and via breast milk to newborn babies. A wide range of adverse effects have been associated with exposure to PCBs in wildlife, including mass die-offs of seals and dolphins, large population declines of European otters, and adverse effects on reproduction and development of young in many species. PCBs cause toxic effects on the nervous system, immune system, reproductive system, and development of experimental animals. PCBs are classified as probable human carcinogens.

112 The refinery is located on the left bank of the river, 3 km to the north of the city centre and just 2 km upstream of bank filtration wells used for the city's water supply. A shipping canal, with loading and unloading facilities for barges, runs along the southern edge of the refinery directly into the Danube. A system of artificial collecting channels within the refinery compound takes surface runoff to the Danube, via a wastewater treatment plant equipped with oil separators. United Nations Environment Programme (UNEP), and United Nations Centre for Human Settlements (UNCHS). 1999. *The Kosovo Conflict: Consequences for the Environment and Human Settlements*. Geneva, Switzerland: UNEP and UNCHS, p. 44.

for crude oil were directly hit or seriously damaged by debris during at least twelve NATO air strikes, and many consequently caught fire or leaked oil and oil products. About 73,000 tonnes of crude oil and oil products are reported to have burnt or leaked into the wastewater collection canals or into the ground.

It was very difficult to estimate the actual amount of oil and oil products discharged into the Danube, however, about 130 tonnes of oil was recovered from the cooling water pumping station at the outflow of the wastewater channel. As a result of fires following the air strikes, parts of Novi Sad and the surrounding districts experienced concentrations of both sulphur dioxide and airborne particles of several hundred $\mu g/m^3$ during the fires. During the conflict period, the health authorities advised the people of Novi Sad to wash food thoroughly, and not to eat food carrying soot deposits. Fishing was banned in the whole Vojvodina district during the time of the conflict. [113]

## Bor

The copper mine and smelting plant outside Bor, a town of 40,000 inhabitants in eastern Serbia, and the neighbouring Jugopetrol oil depot were targeted during the NATO air strikes. The oil depot, which mainly served the Bor copper industry, was completely destroyed and the transformer at the copper mine site was damaged. The air strikes on the power plant, and the consequent disruption of the electricity supply, interrupted the production of sulphuric acid, a by-product of the copper industry. This resulted in the chronic release of sulphur dioxide gas, normally recovered during the manufacture of sulphuric acid. Experts were of the view that the chronic emission of sulphur dioxide would have a serious environmental impact. As Bor is close to the border with Bulgaria, these emissions also had transboundary effects, depending on wind direction.

## Environmental impact of the conflict on the Danube River

During and immediately after the Kosovo conflict, one of the principal environmental concerns was the possible damage to the Danube.[114] Since

113 United Nations Environment Programme (UNEP), and United Nations Centre for Human Settlements (UNCHS). 1999. *The Kosovo Conflict: Consequences for the Environment and Human Settlements*. Geneva, Switzerland: UNEP and UNCHS, p. 47.

114 The Danube Basin covers 817,000 km² of 17 Central European countries, and the river therefore, receives chronic and acute inputs of nutrients and pollutants from an enormous number of industrial, agricultural and municipal sources. The potential

most of the key industrial facilities targeted during the air strikes are located either along the Danube (e.g. Novi Sad, Pancevo), or its tributaries (e.g. Kragujevac), there were fears that large quantities of hazardous substances could have entered the Danube system, posing risks for people in Yugoslavia and, downstream in Bulgaria and Romania, through drinking contaminated water or eating contaminated fish. The Danube is one of Europe's most important corridors of biodiversity. Though there is no evidence of an ecological catastrophe for the Danube, some serious hot spots of contamination by hazardous substances were identified.

During the campaign, it was reported that up to 100 bombs had been jettisoned into the Adriatic Sea by NATO aircraft returning to bases in Italy. This led to pollution fears amongst countries bordering the Adriatic. However, it was later reported that 93 bombs had been located and detonated by NATO, with a small number remaining in deep water (below 250 m).

## Use of Depleted Uranium

Approximately 31,000 rounds of Depleted Uranium (DU) ammunition were used during the Kosovo war. The United Nations Environment Programme (UNEP) report on Kosovo mentioned: (i) DU contamination of drinking water; (ii) the presence of DU in air at two sites; (iii) high surface soil contamination of heavy metals at three ammunition destruction sites; and (iv) workers, civilians and military and mine clearance personnel with access to sites where DU presence was confirmed were unaware of or misunderstood the risks and issues surrounding DU ammunition.[115]

In 2000, the Italian government opened an inquiry into the possible link between DU and 30 cases of serious illness among troops, who served in the Balkans. During this period 12 soldiers developed cancer and five of these

---

environmental contamination and risks to human health were clearly very serious. Neighbouring countries – namely Bulgaria and Romania – expressed their deep concern about trans-boundary air pollution and the possible toxic sludge in the Danube River. While NATO argued that the environmental damage was minimized by the use of sophisticated weapons and selective targeting, the intensity of the air strikes, the targeting of industrial facilities, and the dramatic media coverage combined to raise fears that an environmental catastrophe had resulted from massive pollution of air, land and water in those countries.

115 *Depleted Uranium in Bosnia and Herzegovina: Post-Conflict Environmental Assessment*, United Nations Environment Programme (2003).

died of leukaemia.[116] According to the World Health Organization, the effect of DU on the environment could in some instances increase the levels of contamination in food and ground water after some years.[117] Exposure to DU may have radiological (i.e. due to radiation) and biochemical effects in the human body. The health consequences of such exposure, depending upon the dose or intake, include cancer and malfunction of organs, particularly the kidneys.[118]

The NATO military action against Yugoslavia did not target the environment as the Persian Gulf and Vietnam Wars did. Nonetheless, the aerial bombing campaign to inflicted measurable environmental damage within the territory of the Federal Republic of Yugoslavia, as reported by UNEP team.[119]

# XI. Afghanistan

Afghanistan, a beautiful land inhabited by an ethnically diverse population, has both a rich cultural heritage and a long history of foreign incursions. It is the original home of many agricultural products (varieties of cereal, breeds of sheep and goats, and forest products), and was rich in minerals (gold, copper and semi-precious stones), and other natural resources. Since ancient times Afghanistan's natural resources have serviced many great and small empires.

Until the middle of the 20th century Afghanistan had extensive forest and plant cover. This included high-alpine flora, coniferous and mixed forests, open woodlands with juniper, pistachio and almond trees, semi-desert scrub and marshlands. Apart from the country's most arid deserts and frozen mountains, virtually the entire land surface has been used for

---

116 Capella P. and Bowcott O., NATO urged to clean up its uranium debris in Kosovo, *The Guardian*, 5 January 2001.

117 World Health Organization 'Depleted Uranium: sources, exposures and health effects' available at: http://www.who.int/environmental_information/radiation/depluraniumexecsume.htm , accessed 20 June 2014.

118 Rao S.S. and Balakrishna Bhat T, Depleted Uranium Penetrators - Hazards & Safety, Vol.47 (1), *Defence Science Journal*, (1997), p. 97-105. Also see: Depleted Uranium in Bosnia and Herzegovina: Post-Conflict Environmental Assessment, United Nations Environment Programme, 2003, p. 18.

119 *Depleted Uranium in Bosnia and Herzegovina: Post-Conflict Environmental Assessment*, United Nations Environment Programme, 2003.

centuries, whether for agricultural farming or for livestock grazing, fuel-wood collection and hunting. Managing livelihoods in the mountainous dry lands of Afghanistan has never been easy. The influence of more than three decades of conflict, compounded by years of drought and mismanagement of important resources, has made it that much harder, and has caused widespread human suffering as well as the devastation of almost all natural resources across the country.[120]

## Armed Conflict

The Soviet occupation of Afghanistan started in 1979, when the Soviet Union sent armed forces to assist the then government. An increasing level of conflict ensued between the government and various organized armed groups operating in a loose coalition. The armed groups received substantial assistance from the West in the form of weapons. After a prolonged and devastating war, the occupation ended and the Soviet forces left Afghanistan in February 1989.[121] In 1992, the government fell to the force of the loose coalition known as the Mujahedeen. In the environment of instability, fighting and chaos, certain section of the population welcomed the arrival of the Taliban, which gradually increased its control over the territory and took over Kabul in 1996. The Taliban was recognized as the Government of Afghanistan by only Pakistan, Saudi Arabia and the UAE. It has been reported that Pakistan's military ruler President Musharraf encouraged Pakistanis to go to Afghanistan to fight along with the

---

120 This conflict has killed an estimated 1.7 million, permanently disabled 2 million and caused at least one third of the Afghan population to leave their homes. According to UNHCR estimates, from 1985 – 1990, 6.2 million Afghans –including children born in exile- were living in Pakistan and Iran alone: this was nearly half of the worlds refugee population. Girardet E, and Walter J. 1998. *Essential Field Guides to Humanitarian and Conflict Zones: Afghanistan*, Crosslines Communications Limited, Geneva.

121 Decades of Afghan wars brought about marked demographic changes in Afghanistan. Violating the Geneva Conventions, the Soviets used various nerve gases, and chemical/biological weapons in several provinces. More than half of Afghanistan's 36,000 villages and helmets were turned into ghost towns, millions of anti-personnel mines, especially the 'butterfly mines' were fixed by the Soviets, maiming millions in the countryside. About 6.2 million Afghans, constituting 32 per cent of the projected population, became refugee in Pakistan, Iran and elsewhere, and more than 1.5 million were killed, bringing the total to 7.7 millions, over 40 per cent of the total projected population in 1990. The level of Afghan refugees was such that Pakistan had to close its borders with Afghanistan in 1994. Khan Imtiyaz Gul, Afghanistan: Human Cost of Armed Conflict since Soviet Invasion, Vol. XVII, No. 4, *Perceptions*, Winter 2012, p. 209-224.

Taliban.[122] In October 2001, the US, assisted by many European countries, attacked Afghanistan in its war on terrorism, named 'Operation Enduring Freedom'. The ultimate goal was to replace the Taliban government, and to find the 9/11 mastermind and Al-Qaeda leader Osama Bin Laden.

Nearly 35 years of the combined pressure of armed conflict, civil disorder, lack of governance and drought has taken a major toll on Afghanistan's natural and human resources. The over-exploitation of the country's natural resources has led to grave environmental threats. These include surface and groundwater scarcity and contamination, massive and ongoing deforestation, desertification of important wetlands, soil erosion, air pollution, and depleted wildlife populations. Trees have been cut not only for fuel but also to make it harder for competing armies and rebel bands to hide and ambush one another.[123] A powerful 'timber mafia' has also taken over much of the valuable forest – in 30 years, 60 percent of the deciduous trees have been cut down.

Prolonged lack of water and the rapid disappearance of the country's forests and woodlands have turned thousands of people into environmental refugees. Deforestation has accelerated soil erosion and land degradation, creating ideal conditions for landslides, flash floods and extreme flooding events. This has led to increased population pressure on over-burdened urban areas and could generate new small-scale conflicts over access to scarce resources. The capacity to address these problems is severely limited as a result of the collapse of local and national governance.

## Depleted Uranium Weapons and Cluster Bombs

The US has used depleted uranium (DU) shells on targets inside Afghanistan, most notably against the Taliban frontlines in the northern region of

---

122 Hampson, Francoise J., 'Afghanistan 2001-2010', in Elizabeth Wilmshurst (ed.), *International Law and the Classification of Conflicts*, Oxford: Oxford University Press, 2012, p. 243.

123 When UNEP team visited Afghanistan in 2002 to conduct a post-conflict environmental assessment, it was overwhelmed by the level of deforestation it found. Not a single tree was left standing in many areas of the Badghis and Takhar provinces which boasted complete forest cover, only three decades before. At the majority of sites visited, UNEP observed vast expanses of bare or eroding soil where local livelihoods were devastated, and both the frequency and intensity of floods were reported to have increased threefold. Local rivers have consequently suffered heavy erosion and expansion. The width of the Cheshmanduzuk River near Qala-i-Nau, for instance, has increased from 50 meters to more than 250 meters, wiping out fertile farmland and villages in the process.

the country.[124] Many medical studies have linked DU's radioactivity to increased instances of leukaemia, lung cancer and birth defects.[125] Cluster bombs have also caused a large number of casualties amongst protected persons in Afghanistan.[126] Old Russian-made bomblets still inflict casualties and accidental detonations have killed or maimed hundreds of civilians. A NATO policy banning the use of cluster munitions in Afghanistan has been in place since 2007. Human Rights Watch estimates that hundreds of civilian casualties in the early stages of the Afghanistan War in 2001 were caused by cluster bombs dropped by the US Air Force.[127] The Afghanistan President has condemned the coalition forces for the environmental consequences the war has had on his country. He also accused coalition forces of polluting Afghanistan with nuclear components, an apparent

---

124 The use of DU weapons by the US or allied forces since 2001 in Afghanistan remained uncertain, as claims about the use of DU weapons have neither been confirmed by the US military nor verified by credible investigations. However, most likely the US forces have used some DU weapons and Taliban and/or Al-Qaeda may have possessed DU rounds. McDonald, Avril. 2008. *Depleted Uranium Weapons and international law: A precautionary approach*, TMC Asser Press, p. 19.

125 The urine of eight civilians, 8 drinking water samples and 18 soil samples were tested for the contents and isotopic composition of uranium. The uranium concentrations in urine were in the range of 89 - 478 ng/L, with an average of 275 ng/L. The concentrations in drinking water were in the range of 2.2 - 56.4 μg/L, with an average of 23.8 μg/L. The isotopic composition of all samples was that of natural uranium. Durakovic, Asaf, The quantitative analysis of uranium isotopes in the urine of the civilian population of eastern Afghanistan after operation Enduring Freedom, Vol. 170, No. 4, *Military Medicine*, (2005), p. 277-284. Available at http://www.wise-uranium.org/dissaf.html, accessed 21 January 2014.

126 The 2008 Convention on Cluster Munitions (CCM) prohibits use, production, transfer and stockpiling of cluster munitions. In addition, it establishes a framework for cooperation and assistance to ensure adequate care and rehabilitation to survivors and their communities, clearance of contaminated areas, risk reduction education and destruction of stockpiles. Despite heavy pressure from the US, Afghanistan has signed the treaty on 3 December 2008 and ratified on 8 September 2011..

127 For over a decade, Human Rights Watch documented the devastating effects of cluster bomb used in Afghanistan. Soviet forces used cluster munitions during their invasion and occupation of Afghanistan from 1979 to 1989, and a non-state armed group used cluster munitions during the conflict in the 1990s. Between October 2001 and early 2002, the US aircraft dropped 1,228 cluster bombs containing 248,056 bomblets in 232 strikes on locations throughout the country. According to Cluster Munition Monitor, at least 771 casualties from cluster munitions were recorded in Afghanistan. Available at: http://www.hrw.org/news/2011/09/13/afghanistan-ratifies-global-ban-cluster-bombs, accessed 21 January 2014; Also see: *Fatally Flawed: Cluster Bombs and Their Use by the United States in Afghanistan*, Human Rights Watch, December 2002, p. 15-31. Available at: http://hrw.org/reports/2002/us-afghanistan/Afghan1202.pdf, accessed 23 March 2014.

reference to depleted plutonium used in munitions and armour.[128]

## Landmines

Landmines, although never produced within Afghanistan, have been laid in all phases of armed conflict in Afghanistan,[129] and the country, is thought to be one of the most heavily mined countries in the world, with an estimated 10 to 15 million landmines still on the ground.[130] These mines have been scattered randomly, placed in concentrated clusters, and laid singly as traps.

The Soviet PFM-1 'butterfly' mines, used widely in Afghanistan, were designed to maim. Their small size, light weight and bright colouring makes them particularly attractive to children. Two other Soviet mines found in Afghanistan are the trip-wire activated fragmentation mine, that shoots hundreds of metal fragments when detonated and the large blast mines designed to be virtually impossible to neutralize.[131] These landmines have not only harmed humans and wildlife, but have destroyed large section of irrigation system. Landmines not only accelerate environmental damage through their explosions, but also driving the civilian population from

---

128 The 2003 UNEP's report found that the long-term consequences of nearly 25 years of war and overexploitation of Afghanistan's once rich natural resources created grave environmental threats. These included surface and groundwater scarcity and contamination, massive and ongoing deforestation, desertification of important wetlands, soil erosion, air pollution, and depleted wildlife populations. In addition, the prolonged lack of water and the rapid disappearance of half of the country's forest and woodland cover turned thousands of people into environmental refugees. This has led to increased population pressure on over-burdened urban areas and could generate new small-scale conflicts over access to scarce resources. *Afghanistan: Post-conflict environment assessment.* Nairobi: United Nations Environment Programme, 2003.

129 The bulk of mines found in Afghanistan are Russian made but mines manufactured by Italy, China, US, Pakistan, Egypt, Britain and former Czechoslovakia have been found. Afghanistan has been described as the 'most dangerous museum of unexploded ordinances in the world.' Fifty-two different landmines have been identified, designed either to attack single individuals or threaten anyone within 30 metres or both. Landmine Monitor: Landmine Monitor Report 2000.

130 The use of landmines in Afghanistan has been indiscriminate. Minefields were unmarked and few military mine maps exist. Mines were also laid from the air and were impossible to mark by their nature, sheer numbers and mobility. As a result, mines can be found in even the remotest mountain passes of the country. More strategic placement resulted in contamination of water sources, agricultural land and shelter. *Exposing the Source, US Companies and the Production of Antipersonnel Mines*, Human Rights Watch, 1997.

131 Godrej D, The War Surgeon, Landmines – Trail of Terror, *New Internationalist*, (1997), Issue 294. Available at: http://www.oneworld/ni/issue294/first.htm.

areas thought to be mined to more marginal and fragile environments and thus speeding the depletion of resources and destruction of biodiversity.

In addition to the physical burden on the population, Afghanistan as a country faces the significant socioeconomic repercussions of landmine pollution. Transportation infrastructure has been disrupted reducing exports and imports and environmental damage further delays the rehabilitation of the agricultural based economy. Cleared land suffers accelerated degradation due to desperate attempts to increase yields from smaller areas of available land.

Since 1991, more than 400,000 people in Afghanistan have been killed or maimed by landmines, the majority of victims being civilians, injured well after conflict has resolved. From 1990 to 2000, 205,842 antipersonnel mines, 9,199 antitank mines and 1,054,738 unexploded ordinances were removed from Afghan soil. The absolute number of landmines is of little consequence, because, just one mine, even the fear of a mine's presence can paralyze individuals and communities and prevent resettlement of refugees and Internally Displaced Persons. It seems unlikely that Afghanistan will ever be completely cleared of mines, a total of 717 square km of land remains contaminated and new minefields continue to be uncovered.[132]

In 2002 the UNEP team had first-hand experience of how flooding and landmines can combine to deadly effect. Near the village of Farkhar in Takhar province, a swollen river burst its banks and washed across an active mine field. It swept thousands of landmines downstream, creating untold dangers for unsuspecting villagers and laying a swathe of mines across local roads and fields.

The technology used for clearing mines is primitive and inadequately designed for 'humanitarian mine clearance' where an entire area is completely demined in order to rehabilitate it. Clearing may miss predominantly plastic mines entirely and mechanical mine clearing equipment destroys valuable topsoil compounding the environmental devastation. The demining process in Afghanistan has been equated to the work of archaeologists since collapsed mud walls of compounds can bury the mines metres deep. Predictably the accident rate amongst Afghan

---

132 A major socioeconomic impact study conducted by the Mine Clearance Planning Agency (MCPA) published in December 1999 revealed that this affected land consisted of 61 per cent grazing, 26 per cent agricultural land, 7 per cent roads, 4 per cent residential and 1per cent irrigation. *Landmine Monitor Report: 2000*, Landmine Monitor.

deminers is the highest in the world. Demining is especially dangerous in Afghanistan due to the rugged terrain, hardness of the soil and density and variety of the mines present, especially within urban areas.[133]

## Refugees

Perhaps the greatest environmental impact of the military actions has been the displacement of people and the large number of refugees (at one time, there were close to five million Afghan refugees). Although the existence of these refugees and the need for humanitarian aid is known, the impact these refugees have had on the environment is very rarely discussed.[134] The concentration of large numbers of refugees into areas that were previously sparsely populated or uninhabited has created intense pressure on the environment. Deforestation, soil erosion from overgrazing and from the impact of the large number of people, and water contamination impact the wildlife and the health of the refugees. A secondary effect on wildlife is the migration of mobile species from suitable habitat into less habitable areas.

With most of the borders of being officially closed by neighbouring countries, refugees were forced to use less travelled roads in more mountainous territory where security is weak or nonexistent. Thus there was a sudden and massive influx of people into regions that otherwise had low human presence and pressure, regions which are now the only remaining

---

133 Land mines and unexploded ordnance (UXO) still litter vast areas of the country, making some agricultural land unsafe for public use. Landmines kill or maim an estimated 10 to 12 people every day in Afghanistan. At one point the area contaminated by landmines in Afghanistan covered almost 780 square kilometres (making Afghanistan one of the most heavily mined countries in the world). So far more than 400,000 landmines have been destroyed, but a significant portion of the contaminated land has yet to be cleared (on average, 15–30 sq km of land is cleared annually). *Afghanistan's Environment 2008*, UNEP, p.19.

134 During the fighting and period of severe drought (1990s–2005) some five million Afghans left the country because of insecurity and constrained livelihoods. Another five million were internally displaced. Most of the refugees were forced to live in Pakistan (3.5 million) or Iran (1.5 million). After the Interim Government was established, introducing relative stability, these refugees began to return home. More than three million Afghans have now returned, but a significant number are still in host countries – Pakistan and Iran. Allan (1987) has examined the environmental impact of 3,500,000 Afghan refugees who fled from their homeland into Pakistan. According to Allan; Apart from social, political, and humanitarian concerns, this largest of recent migrations has caused extensive environmental damage, much of it probably irreversible. It appears that Pakistan nationals have taken advantage of the ensuing confusion to indulge in illegal logging." Allan, Nigel J. R., Impact of Afghan Refugees on the Vegetation Resources of Pakistanis Hindukush-Himalaya, Vol. 7, *Mountain Research and Development*, (1987), p. 200-204.

habitat of wild goat, sheep, and snow leopards. Refugees also congregated around the few water sources in this arid land, essentially sealing them off from wildlife that may have historically depended on these waterholes for survival. Refugees, in their quest for food and fuel, cut down trees in these forest patches, which are vitally important wildlife habitat and help control erosion on steep mountain slopes. The loss of these forests and grasslands can have a cascading effect through the ecosystem, as many other plants and animals depend upon them for food, shelter, and breeding[135].

## Environmental damage

The three decades of armed conflict has destroyed or severely damaged the once thriving urban and rural areas, cultural sites and the natural environment.[136] A combination of factors, such as war, internal armed conflict and lack of governance coupled with a series of natural disasters, population growth and increasing demand for natural resources has led to significant depletion of resources, leaving them fragmented and reducing productivity. The vast areas of the country contaminated with landmines and depleted forests, especially in the north and east, are the direct results of the war and conflict-related damage to the environment. The number of livestock, in particular sheep and camels, has substantially decreased.[137]

A few centuries ago, deciduous and evergreen forests covered five per cent of Afghanistan's current land area, including one million hectares of oak and two million hectares of pine and cedar, mostly in the eastern part of the country. Open woodland dominated by pistachios, almonds and junipers occupied a third of the land area. Today most of the original forests have

---

135 Salman Annel, The Afghanistan conflict and its effects on the environment, available at: http://www.tigweb.org/youth-media/panorama/article.html?ContentID =786&start=13363, accessed 22 December 2013.

136 Rangelands, forests and biodiversity products are nature's key constituents as well as important sources of food, shelter, energy, income and cultural heritage for the vast majority of the country's population. These natural resources were considered "the wealth of the poor" in Afghanistan because rural people living close to them depend on natural and agricultural ecosystems to provide tangible goods and services: crops, fruit, grazing, timber, hunting, medicine and also erosion control, pollination and water drainage stability. Alpine pastures, cedar forests, unspoilt wilderness and rare animals have huge tourist potential once Afghanistan becomes politically stable and peaceful.

137 Over the last 30 years livestock populations in Afghanistan have fluctuated from between about four million cattle and more than 30 million sheep and goats to the lowest levels recorded in the country's recent history with 3.7 million cattle and approximately 16 million sheep and goats. *Afghanistan's Environment 2008*, UNEP, p.15.

gone. Forests now occupy less than 2 per cent of county's total area.[138]

Several factors are responsible for the rapid decline and degradation of forests.[139] One of them is the demand for timber in Afghanistan and abroad, especially neighbouring Pakistan. During 1992–2002, massive logging and smuggling significantly contributed to forest reduction (50–200 timber truckloads a day or 150,000–500,000 cubic metres of wood annually) in the eastern provinces. Local communities have lost control over the forests on which they depend for their survival, and forest resources are now largely used for immediate profit by organized crime syndicates and traders.

Armed conflict has also inflicted damage on forest ecosystems. During the 1980s pistachio trees were uprooted by Soviet military forces, and intense fighting led to an increase in the risk of forest fires. Other causes include non-sustainable practices such as tree felling for energy and construction (including increasing urbanization needs); poor forest management; feeble incentives for reforestation; lack of community involvement and awareness; and agricultural and urban encroachments.

The loss of forest cover does not only have environmental impacts, but also

---

138 In 2002, when a UNEP team visited Afghanistan to conduct a post-conflict environmental assessment, it was overwhelmed by the level of deforestation it found. Not a single tree was left standing in many areas of the Badghis and Takhar provinces, which boasted complete forest cover only three decades before. Armed conflicts have also taken their toll on the country's forests. Trees have been cut not only for fuel but also to make it harder for competing armies and rebel bands to hide and ambush one another. The rapid loss of forest and plant cover over the past three decades has accelerated soil erosion and land degradation in the country, making it susceptible to landslides, flash floods, and extreme flooding events. Furthermore, the impacts of climate change are likely to add to water shortages, desertification, and future environmental degradation. *Afghanistan: Post-Conflict Environmental Assessment*, United Nations Environment Programme (UNEP), 2003. Also see: *Afghanistan's Environment 2008*, UNEP, p.16.

139 After years of armed conflict and political chaos Afghanistan faces a severe environmental crisis. During Afghanistan-Russia war, the cutting of vegetation alongside the streets and highways in Kabul province and the adjacent Parwan Province was a perfect example of deliberate environment destruction—a tactics that was also used in the Indochina war. As the Afghan-Soviet war began, the existing surveillance eroded and the need for fuel substantially increased. Wood from the valuable Pistacho forests even appeared in fuel market in Kabul during the war. Numerous air bombing during the war caused major and long-lasting wildfires in the forests of Paktia and Kunar. Trees cut in Afghanistan were sold extensively for fuel or lumber in the neighbouring country Pakistan. The damage to forests may be greatest environmental disaster that occurred in the Afghanistan during the war, when the forest area declined from 3.4 per cent to 2.6 per cent of land area in less than 10 years. Formoli, T.A., The Impact of the Afghanistan-Soviet War on Afghanistan's Environment, Vol. 22, *Environmental Conservation*, (1995), p. 66-69.

leads to economic losses. In the 1970s, the Badghis and Takhar provinces of northern Afghanistan were covered with productive pistachio forests, which earned substantial revenue from their nuts. These forests have almost totally disappeared in just three decades.  It is difficult to calculate the indirect economic losses from the reduction in key forest functions – such as erosion and flood control, soil fertility and biodiversity benefits – but clearly these costs are high. Finally, since the productivity of the country's rangelands and forests is declining, people have been forced to move from rural to urban areas in search of alternative livelihoods, increasing the growth of urbanization. However, with increased international military presence and government control, as well as local infrastructural development and tighter control over timber-smuggling, the rate of deforestation seems to have declined in recent years.

## Biodiversity

Afghanistan has a wide range of ecosystems,[140] including glaciers and high-alpine vegetation, coniferous and mixed forest, open dry woodland with juniper, pistachio or almond, semi-desert scrub, sand and stony deserts, rivers, lakes and marshland. The more closed types of mixed and coniferous forests occur mainly in the east, along the border with Pakistan, where precipitation tends to be more regular and abundant. Areas of open woodland remain mainly on the northern slopes of the Hindu Kush. [141] The

---

140 Afghanistan is comprised of eight bio-geographical provinces; seven belong to the Palearctic Realm, while one small area in the lower Kabul River Valley has Indo-Malayan affinity. A recent classification breaks Afghanistan down into 15 smaller eco-regions of which four are considered as critical/endangered, eight as vulnerable, and only two as relatively stable and intact. Afghanistan has many indigenous species, including 118-147 species of mammals, 472-510 species of birds, 92-112 species of reptiles, 6-8 species of amphibians, 101-139 species of fish, 245 species of butterflies, and 3500-4000 species of vascular plants. Much of the information on Afghanistan's biodiversity is old and no longer reliable. Little significant information has been added since the onset of war in 1978. The few recent investigations that have been made suggest that Afghanistan's biodiversity has suffered enormously during the course of the last three decades. *Implementation of the Convention on Biological Diversity: A retrospective analysis in the Hindu Kush-Himalayan countries*, International Centre for Integrated Mountain Development, Kathmandu, Nepal, June 2011, p. 10.

141 Vegetation cover in Afghanistan has been modified significantly through millennia of human occupation. Most of the country appears to be subject to some degree of land degradation. Much of the land surface is used as rangeland for grazing livestock. Tree cover was formerly more extensive than at present. The potential for re-growth is likely to be seriously affected by heavy fuelwood collection or timber harvesting that far outstrips woodland regeneration, and by browsing and grazing domestic livestock. Soil erosion is also a serious problem due to the loss of protective vegetation cover.

diversity of habitats has given rise to a wide variety of fauna. The natural wildlife heritage of the country too is under threat. Many of the larger mammals in Afghanistan are categorized by the World Conservation Union (IUCN) as globally threatened.[142] Flamingos (*Phoenicopterus ruber*) have not bred successfully in Afghanistan for almost a decade, and the last Siberian crane was seen in 1986. While the Wakhan Corridor contains healthy populations of endangered snow leopards and other mammals including Marco Polo sheep, several mammalian species – such as the Caspian tiger (*Panthera tigris virgata*) is on the verge of global extinction and have not been seen in Afghanistan for decades. Others – such as markhor (*Capra falconeri*) – are considered endemic and live only in Afghanistan and adjacent territories. The salamander (*Batrachuperus mustersi*), which, occurs only in mountain streams in the central Hindu Kush of Afghanistan is also believed to be at risk from habitat modification and armed conflict.

## After Effects of Conflict

Almost 80 per cent of the country's population[143] lives in rural areas and relies heavily on natural resources, which makes it extremely vulnerable to the impacts of local and global phenomena (such as droughts, natural disasters, climate change and desertification) and the degradation of natural resources through erosion and pollution of soil and water. The

*Afghanistan: Post-Conflict Environmental Assessment*, United Nations Environment Programme, 2003.

142 These include snow leopard (*Uncia uncia*), wild goat (*Capra aegagrus*), markhor (*Capra falconeri*), Marco Polo sheep (*Ovis ammon polii*), urial (*Ovis orientalis*), and Asiatic black bear (*Ursus thibetanus*). Other mammals of interest include ibex (*Capra ibex*), wolf (*Canis lupus*), red fox (*Vulpes vulpes*), jackal (*Canis aureus*), caracal (*Caracalcaracal*), manul or Pallas's cat (*Otocolobus manul*), striped hyena (*Hyena hyena*), rhesus macaque (*Macaca mulatta*), and brown bear (*Ursus arctos*). The country has one endemic bird species, Meinertzhagen's snow finch *(Montifringila theresae)*, and major breeding populations of six other restricted regional species: yellow-eyed pigeon *(Columba eversmanni)*, plain willow warbler *(Phylloscopus neglectus)*, Brooks's willow warbler *(P. subviridis)*, variable wheatear *(Oenanthe picata)* and Dead Sea sparrow *(Passer moabiticus)*. The population of yellow-eyed pigeon is particularly important because the species is rare and declining throughout its Central Asian range. Afghanistan also has significant numbers of breeding lammergeier (*Gypaetus barbatus*), black vulture (*Aegypius monachus*) and other birds of prey. Among reptiles, four species are believed to be restricted to Afghanistan: the geckos *Asiocolotes levitoni* and *Cyrtopodion voraginosus*, and the lacertid lizards *Eremias afghanistanica* and *E. aria. Afghanistan: Post-Conflict Environmental Assessment*, United Nations Environment Programme, 2003.

143 The population of Afghanistan is around 31 million, which includes nearly 3 million refugees that are residing in Pakistan, Iran and other countries.

influx of returning refugees, population growth, and the creation of new environmental refugees and internally displaced persons – as a result of droughts, natural disasters, climate change and desertification – could exert additional stress on natural resources.

Afghanistan's fast-growing urban centres consume increasing amounts of agricultural goods and energy. Due to over-population in many urban areas and the high concentration of pollution sources such as cars and industries, the residents suffer from severe air pollution, poorly organized collection and disposal of waste, and lack of sanitation and access to safe drinking water are additional health hazards. There is also a shortage of green, open spaces. Putting the country back on a path towards sustainable development will nevertheless be an enormous challenge. Traditional systems for managing natural resources and existing strategies for adaptation and mitigation have been damaged by past and ongoing conflict, population pressure, the collapse of the rural economy, self-centred control by local groups, and the breakdown of law and order. To establish a sustainable development agenda, a community-based approach to natural resources is needed. Otherwise the current trend of environmental degradation may lead the country deeper into poverty and dependence on international aid, pushing the people of Afghanistan further into the abyss of human insecurity, social conflict and misery. While the Americans may complete their withdrawal by 2016, the toxic chemicals they leave behind will continue to pollute [144]

---

144 The US military presence in Afghanistan consists of fleets of aircraft, helicopters, armoured vehicles, weapons, equipment, troops and facilities. Since 2001, they have generated millions of kilograms of hazardous, toxic and radioactive wastes and virtually all of it has been buried, burned or secretly disposed of into the air, soil or groundwater of Afghanistan. In addition, the water supply has been contaminated by oil from military vehicles and DU from ammunition. Also see: Afghanistan's Environment 2008, UNEP, p. 7.

## XII. Georgia

The Russian military aggression in August 2008[145] caused widespread damage to the natural ecosystems of the Caucasus and Black Sea regions.[146] Although far from conflict zones, three Protected Areas of Georgia were affected by the Russian military operations. These are: the mountain forests of the Borjomi-Kharagauli National Park (IUCN category 2); the terrestrial and marine parts of the Kolkheti National Park (IUCN category 2) on the Black Sea; and the riparian forests of Liakhvi Nature Reserve (IUCN category 1). The damage to the forests of the Borjomi-Kharagauli National Park and the adjacent areas was particularly high.

**Forest fires**

In August 2008, fire in the forests of the Borjomi gorge[147] started after Russian military helicopters flew over the forested areas and dropped flammable bombs. When the fire was put out after about 21 days, the area of burned forests amounted to over 950 hectares, with 250 hectare totally destroyed. The remaining vegetation cover lost its ecological function and material value. In the Ateni Gorge (The Shida Kartli Region) about 20 seats

---

145 During the armed conflict, Russia used cluster munitions of its own production, air-dropped RBK series bombs, containing either 60 or 108 antipersonnel and anti-materiel sub-munitions each, ground-launched Uragan rockets, each containing 30 submunitions with self-destruct mechanisms, as well as at least one ground-fired Iskander missile, carrying 20 sub-munitions each. Georgia, on its part used the Gradlar Multiple Launch Rocket System where each rocket contains 104 submunitions. Altogether, it was confirmed that Russian cluster munitions killed 12 civilians and injured 46, and Georgian cluster munitions killed four civilians and injured eight more. *A Dying Practice: Use of Cluster Munitions by Russia and Georgia in August 2008*, Human Rights Watch, April 2009, p. 24-68.

146 The Caucasus Eco-region is among the Planet's 34 biodiversity hotspots and one of few hotspots that lay in the areas with non-tropical climate. One of the most important reasons of this is a high proportion of endemic and relict species of plants and animals. 20 to 30 per cent of flowering plants, mammals, amphibians, reptiles, fish, and a high proportion of invertebrates living in the Caucasus are not found outside the conventional borders of the region. The Trialeti Priority Conservation Area includes pristine forests, sub-alpine meadows and represents habitat for many endemic, rare and relict species; therefore, Borjomi-Kharagauli NP can be definitely considered as model Park for the Caucasus Ecoregion.

147 The Borjomi area is known for high diversity of plant, insects, amphibians, reptiles and small mammals endemic species that is caused by location of the area on a biological crossroads of different bio-geographic regions (Colchic, Minor Asian, South Caucasian-Iranian, and Caucasian itself/East Caucasian). The area holds populations of the species that, according to the recent genetic studies, are Tertiary relicts that have been maintained here for ten or more millions of years. Accordingly, this area represents the main backbone in establishing of protected areas network in the Caucasus.

of fire were recorded, and by the time the main fire seat was managed, about 50 hectares of forests had been burned down. Fire were also set in the forests of the Kaspi region (the Shida Kartli region), and Kharagauli (the Imereti region) and Kojori (the Kvemo Kartli region) forests.

The fires have completely destroyed the forest massifs, under-wood vegetation and top soil. The fertile humus layer has been completely burned. The physical-mechanical and chemical-biological characteristics of soil as well as soil-forming main rocks have been changed. Micro-biological processes required for maintaining soil functions have been disturbed. Meadow fertile soils have been transformed into an exhausted and scorched mass. The prospects of development of plants in these areas are grim and rehabilitation will be an arduous task. Restoration of destroyed forest cover may take tens or hundreds of years.

Smoke, high temperature and flame generated by fire, as well as noise during the process of fire fighting disturbed the habitats and lifestyle of animals. Forest destruction disturbed the regime of groundwater recovery, with a serious impact on water resources of the Borjomi region. It was estimated that greenhouse gases equivalent to 407,000 tons of carbon dioxide was released into the atmosphere as a result of the forest fires in the Borjomi region. Considering the average market price (15 euros) for the removal of 1 ton carbon dioxide equivalent the loss could be estimated at 6,105,000 euros. Along with the environmental damage, the Russian attack also caused a severe negative impact on tourism.

## Oil spills

The Russian army occupied the Poti (The Samegrelo-Zemo Svaneti Region) coastal base in August 2008 and blasted and sank 12 Georgian vessels. As a result, about 50 tons of oil, including engine and hydraulic oils spilled into the Black Sea. In addition, the bombs in these vessels blew up. The contents of bombs, the chemical composition of which is not known, also spilled into the sea.

Spilled oil and oil products heavily polluted the coastal zone of the Black Sea and threatened the marine part of the Kolkheti National Park and its ichthyofauna (e.g., sturgeon, grey mullet and herring). Oils are lightweight liquids and form a thin film on the water surface, hampering the penetration of oxygen into the water. This causes not only destruction of sea animals but also extinction of water vegetation. The Black Sea current moved the spilled oil to the north of the city of Poti to the direction of the Kolkheti

National Park and its protected sea zone. The Kolkheti National Park located 5 km north from the oil spill site is distinguished for its unique biodiversity and is a part of internationally recognized Ramsar protected sites. Oils spilled in these areas may cause the destruction of many rare and threatened (included in the Red List of Georgia) species of plants and animals. Moreover pollution of soil and water will affect the internationally important peat lands of the Kolkheti lowland.

On August 24, 2008 a train loaded with raw oil was blown up at the Gori-Khashuri section (Shida Kartli region) of the Georgian railway. The explosion was caused by a fragment of a missile shot at a military base of the Georgian Army. In total, 12 tanks (60 tons of oil in each) of oil were burned down. An area of about 4,000 sqm was polluted and about 650 tons of oil was burned.

## XIII. Chechnya

The contamination of the environment of Chechnya[148] by the Second Chechen war came close to a catastrophe. Experts are of the opinion that as a result of the war, over 30 per cent of Chechnya's land has been contaminated and does not meet the accepted environmental conditions for life. Some of the gravest risks the Chechens faced were radiation and petroleum oil leak into the ground and the resulting pollution of soil and water.

The Russian republic of Chechnya, devastated by war, now faces an ecological disaster. A former aide to Boris Yeltsin believes that Russian bombing has rendered Chechnya an environmental wasteland. There is special concern over widespread oil spills from Russian bombardment of plants and refineries. Since 1994, 20,000 tons of oil pollutants have leaked into Chechnya's ground. As a result, 40 per cent of agricultural land has become polluted to the extent that it is no longer arable. In addition, 1.5 to

---

148 The Second Chechen War (War in the North Caucasus), was launched by the Russian Federation on 26 August 1999, in response to the Invasion of Dagestan by the Islamic International Peacekeeping Brigade (IIPB). On 1 October 1999 the Russian troops entered Chechnya. The campaign ended the de facto independence of Chechen and restored Russian federal control over the territory. Although it is regarded by many as an internal conflict within the Russian Federation, the war attracted a large number of foreign fighters. On 16 April 2009, the counter-terrorism operation in Chechnya was officially ended. The exact death toll from this conflict is unknown. Unofficial estimates range from 25,000 to 50,000 dead or missing, mostly civilians in Chechnya. Russian official figures are over 5,200.

2 million tons of these pollutants have leaked into the groundwater, which mainly flows into the two major rivers, Sunzha and Terek, which flow into the Caspian Sea. It has been estimated that about 300,000 tons of toxic waste flowed into the Caspian Sea from Chechnya during the period.[149]

Russian forces also destroyed facilities with 'sources of ionizing irradiation', which have made Chechnya a 'restricted radioactive area'. It was reported that radiation levels in areas such as Chiri-Yurt, Vedeno, Gudermes, Argun and Grozny were ten times above the normal level. Chechnya's wildlife too sustained heavy damage during the hostilities, as animals that had once populated the forests migrated to safer havens.[150] In 2004, the Russian government designated one-third of Chechnya as a 'zone of ecological disaster' and another 40 per cent as 'a zone of extreme environmental distresses'.

The most heavily mined areas[151] are those in which separatists continue to put up a resistance, namely the southern regions, as well as the borders of the republic. No humanitarian mine clearance has taken place since December 1999. In June 2002, UN officials estimated that there were 500,000 landmines in the region. UNICEF has recorded 2,340 civilian landmine and unexploded ordnance casualties in Chechnya between 1999 and the end of 2003.

## XIV. Lebanon

In July 2006, a 34-day war broke out between Israeli Defence Forces (IDF) and Lebanon causing wide-ranging damage to the civil infrastructure and environment of the later.[152] Even though the period of conflict was relatively short, the impact on Lebanon's civilian population was significant.

---

149 The environmental problem was compounded by corruption through approximately 15,000 makeshift refineries, most of which are based on illegal trafficking in oil. There were numerous reports about involvement of the Russian military in this trafficking. In 2002, there were reports of 500-600 million tons of oil illegally refined in make shift refineries, compared to 700 million tons of legally refined oil that year. Batal al-Shishani Murad, Environmental Ramifications of the Russian War on Chechnya, *Central Asia- Caucasus Analyst*, 3 May 2006, p.10-11.

150 Military Operations greatly alter Chechen Mountain life, *Prague Watchdog*, 4 May 2003.

151 Chechnya: Landmines seen as Continuing Scourge: RFE/RL, 19 October 2004. Also see: Batal al-Shishani Murad, Environmental Ramifications of the Russian War on Chechnya, *Central Asia- Caucasus Analyst*, 3 May 2006, p.10-11.

152 Hostilities ended with a ceasefire under UN Security Council Resolution 1701.

An estimated 1,191 civilians were killed and 4,405 injured.[153] In addition almost one million people were displaced, creating four times the number of refugees that the NATO bombardments in Kosovo did. Severe damages were caused to infrastructure, with 130,000 dwelling units destroyed; 900 factories and commercial buildings shattered; 107 bridges and overpasses, approximately 445,000 m² of road network and 27 fuel stations bombed. The hostilities generated a very high level of demolition waste, leading to a new environmental threat. The UNDP classified this type of damage as "severe" and estimated its outcome to have a medium to long-term duration, between 1 and 50 years.[154] The total volume of the generated rubble has been estimated to be up to 3.5 million m³, almost the volume of the biggest pyramid in the world, the Chulula Pyramid.

## Damage to the Energy Sector

Some key infrastructures damaged by IDF include the Jiyeh power plant,[155] the Beirut Rafic Hariri International Airport, and various petrol stations. Two fuel storage tanks containing 15,000 tons of fuel each were hit during the attack resulting in a fire that lasted for 12 days. The fuel also spilled to the sea, causing one of the major environmental disasters experienced by Lebanon. The oil contaminated at least twenty-two areas over a stretch of 150 km out of Lebanon's 225 km coastline. The spill also reached areas on the Syrian coastline and Turkish and Cypriot waters. Fuel storage tanks at the airport were also damaged by a direct Israeli air strike resulting in the burning and release of about 5,000 m³ of kerosene.

The environmental damages caused by these two events were of three main

---

153 *Lebanon: Post-Conflict Environmental Assessment.2007.* United Nations Environment Programme, p. 10.

154 *Lebanon Rapid Environmental Assessment for Greening Recovery, Reconstruction and Reform 2006*, UNDP, 2007.

155 The Jiyeh thermal power plant site, whose total area comprises some 40,000 m², is located directly on the coast, approximately 30 km south of Beirut. The total amount of oil burned and spilled as a result of the air raids has not been ascertained, but up to 75,000 m³ of oil, which was identified as heavy IFP – number 6 fuel, could have been burned, spilled into the sea and leaked into the ground. The military strike on the fuel tanks resulted in massive oil fires and generated a plume of smoke stretching for several kilometres. The fire burned continuously for up to 27 days and the smoke contained a potentially toxic cocktail of pollutants – including soot, particulate matter, carbon monoxide, methane and a range of hydrocarbons – the combination of which could be expected to cause a significant degree of environmental pollution and respiratory problems for local residents. *Lebanon: Post-Conflict Environmental Assessment.2007.* United Nations Environment Programme, Nairobi, Kenya, p. 46.

types. First, the atmospheric pollution deriving from the potentially toxic cocktail of pollutants contained in the smoke released by the burning fuel. This included soot, particulate matter, carbon monoxide, methane and a range of hydrocarbons, the combination of which can be expected to remain in the air for a long time causing respiratory problems for local residents or falling to the ground in the form of acid rain or snow. The second concerns mostly the area surrounding the airport and included contamination of groundwater with a large amount of benzene, toluene, ethylbenzene and xylenes, compounds which are highly toxic and highly mobile. The third environmental loss occurred in terms of damages to the marine and coastal ecosystems caused by the huge amount of heavy oil that spilled in the sea.[156]

A range of ammunition was launched from aircrafts, tanks and stationary positions by the IDF. An average of 200-300 aerial-delivered missiles were fired daily on adjacent areas of Lebanon, Mount Lebanon, North Lebanon and the Bekaa Valley. For the initial weeks of the conflict, the Israeli ground forces maintained a constant delivery of approximately 2,000 rounds per day fired from artillery, which increased to approximately 6,000 rounds per day in the last weeks preceding the ceasefire. IDF fired a total of 1,800 rockets containing cluster bombs, each containing 644 bomb-lets making a total of 1,159,200 bomb-lets that were dispersed over southern Lebanon.[157] The naval artillery also fired approximately 100-200 rounds per day on areas throughout South Lebanon. This ordnance consisted of: 76mm High Explosive rounds and Harpoon-type missiles. An average of 10 per cent of such ordnance fails to function as designed and remains in the ground as a significant explosive hazard. UNEP found evidence of the use of white phosphorus (WP)-containing munitions and their use was confirmed by

---

156 Additionally, the spill had a substantial impact on the fishing and tourism sectors. Contamination of beach resorts and coastal towns led to a reduction in visitors. During the war, Lebanon's 8,500 fishermen were prevented from venturing out to sea due to the Israeli naval blockade, at a time that represents the peak of the fishing season and typically generates more than one third of their annual income. Additionally, some fishing ports such as the Dhalia harbour in the Raouche area of Beirut were hit directly by the spill, as a thick of layer of oil gathered on the sea surface coating the boats and equipment. To make things worse, the consumer market for fish in Lebanon virtually collapsed in the aftermath of the war, as demand for fish has fallen due to health fears.

157 The UN estimates that around 100,000 unexploded bomb-lets now litter 590 sites in south Lebanon posing a serious hazard to civilians who returned to the area after the war and are now trying to rebuild their lives. At least 21 people have been killed by cluster bombs since the ceasefire and more than 100 have been injured. Available at: http://www.mineaction.org/overview.asp?o=540, accessed 22 January 2014.

the IDF. However, the environmental impact of the WP in Lebanon was limited to the burning of olive trees and houses.[158]

## Damage to Agricultural Sector

The agricultural sector was hard hit by the IDF attacks. Many agricultural fields and pastures were rendered useless due the presence of unexploded (UXOs) sub-munitions. Many UXOs were located very close to water sources, making such sources inaccessible for the community. The result was the adoption of unsustainable practices such as the drainage of wetlands for more aggressive irrigation or extensive use of pesticides with associated harmful impacts on water resources and birdlife. The presence of UXOs also posed a major hindrance to reforestation plans. In addition thousands of hectares of scrubland were lost to fires, posing danger to large mammals. Soil compaction due to the movement of military vehicles in the highly affected areas may lead to loss of soil fertility and increased soil erosion.[159]

---

158 White phosphorus is a common form of the chemical element phosphorus. It has extensive military application as an incendiary agent, smokescreen to conceal troop movements and as an antipersonnel flame compound capable of causing serious burns. White phosphorus is a colourless, white or yellow waxy substance with a garlic-like odour. It reacts rapidly with oxygen and catches fire easily. It is used in bombs, artillery and mortar shells, which burst into burning flakes of phosphorus upon impact, and has a long history of military use for offensive and target-marking purposes. Burning WP produces a hot, dense, white smoke, which is usually not hazardous in the concentrations produced by a battlefield smoke shell, although breathing WP for short periods may cause coughing and irritation of the throat and lungs. Breathing WP for long periods causes a condition known as 'phossy jaw', which results in poor wound healing of the mouth and breakdown of the jawbone. In deep soil or sediment with very low oxygen concentration, however, WP may remain unchanged for many years. *Lebanon: Post-Conflict Environmental Assessment, 2007.* United Nations Environment Programme, p. 165.

159 Dutch Values: The standards according to which soil and water samples are evaluated are a matter of international debate between experts and authorities. There are several lists worldwide for Verification Values, Precaution Values, Action Values and Intervention Values. For its environmental assessment in Lebanon, UNEP used the Dutch Intervention Values and Environmental Screening or Target Values, for the following reasons: (i) they have been used around the world for more than two decades, so there is substantial knowledge of their application within the international scientific community;(ii) they are comprehensive in terms of the number and range of parameters for which standards have been set; and (iii) Whenever soil or groundwater assessments lead to a need for intervention, Dutch Values can provide target values for clean-up activities. The Dutch Values can be accessed at: http://lebanonreport.unep.ch.

The quality of air in Lebanon has been compromised by burning of fuel and forest fire. The main pollutants of concern include SO2, NOx, Carbon Monoxide (CO), particulate matter, polycyclic aromatic hydrocarbons (PAHs), and dioxins and furans. Indirect impacts on the air quality are due to reconstruction efforts.

The impacts on fresh water resources were due to damaged to surface water streams from destroyed bridges and infrastructures, decomposition of carcasses and groundwater pollution from polychlorinated biphenyls (PCBs) leakage or leakage of gasoline and diesel from damaged petrol stations.

## Biodiversity Loss

Biodiversity was affected both directly and indirectly. Protected areas and fragile ecosystems, wetlands and a biosphere reserve were damaged during the conflict, leading to the destruction of wildlife and habitat. Use of heavy machinery by the Israeli army (tanks and bulldozers) to clear roads during the invasion resulted in the disturbance and fragmentation of ecosystems and floral and faunal populations as well as eradication of marginal habitats by the sides of roads. The Mediterranean basin suffered significantly during the war. The damage suffered by the Lebanese marine and coastal ecosystems can be imputed to the physical advance of Israeli warships, the direct bombing, and the massive oil spill which occurred as a consequence of the air strikes. UNDP classified the impact on marine biodiversity from the oil spill from the Jiyeh power plant as long-term (10-50 years) and severe damage (the highest grade of the scale). Protected areas and fragile ecosystems, such as the Palm Islands Nature Reserve, were directly harmed by the fuel released. The direct effects are degradation of ecosystems, deterioration of vegetation, disturbance of wildlife, and destruction of delicate habitats.

Several industrial facilities were also severely damaged during the war. In total, 31 industrial facilities in South Lebanon, Beqaa and Beirut suburbs were reported to have been completely or partially destroyed. The environmental concerns relate mainly to soil and groundwater contamination.[160]

---

160 Tranquillo Nicoletta. 2007. *Green Casualties of War: The need for international protection of the environment during armed conflicts and the case of the war between Israel and Lebanon in 2006,* Department of Economic History, Lund University, Sweden.

## XV. The Israel-Palestine Conflict

The conflict between Israel and the Palestinians (27 December 2008 to 18 January 2009) had a profound and lasting effect on the environment in the Gaza Strip. The Israeli Defence Forces (IDF) conducted a major military operation comprising bombardment by land, sea and air, and incursions into the Gaza Strip[161] by troops. Before and during that period, Hamas and other Palestinian militant groups fired rockets from Gaza into Israel and engaged Israeli troops during the ground invasion.[162]

A UNEP report has highlighted the catastrophic environmental consequences of the armed conflict.[163] According to the report, the fighting resulted in extensive casualties and the destruction of homes, livelihoods and infrastructure. Homes and public infrastructure throughout the Gaza Strip sustained extensive damage, with Gaza City being the worst hit.

The environmental situation in the Gaza Strip was already serious prior to the conflict, mainly due to underinvestment in environmental systems. The hostilities caused additional damage and increased the pressure on environmental facilities and institutions. The conflict generated a significant volume of demolition debris and caused serious damage to the sewage system.[164] In addition, there was widespread destruction

---

161 The Gaza Strip is a narrow strip of land on the Mediterranean coast. It borders Israel to the east and north and Egypt to the south. It is approximately 41 kilometres long, and between 6 and 12 kilometres wide, with a total area of 378 square kilometres. In 1948, the Gaza Strip had a population of less than 100,000 people. The current population is estimated to be in excess of 1.5 million, distributed across five Governorates. Gaza City, which is the biggest governorate, has about 400,000 inhabitants. The two other main governorates are Khan Younis (population 200,000) in central Gaza, and Rafah (population 150,000) to the south. The majority of people live in refugee camps. There are no permanent water bodies in the Gaza Strip, though large-scale sewage ponds and sewage flowing through Wadi Gaza has become de facto hydraulic features.

162 *Environmental Assessment of the Gaza Strip following the escalation of hostilities in December 2008 – January 2009,* UNEP, 2009, p. 6.

163 This report and its findings are based on field work by a team of international experts deployed by UNEP following its Governing Council's Decision 25/12 in February 2009, requesting UNEP to assess the environmental damage and carry out an economic evaluation of the rehabilitation and restoration of the environment in the Gaza Strip following the escalation of hostilities in December 2008 and late January 2009. *Environmental Assessment of the Gaza Strip following the escalation of hostilities in December 2008 – January 2009,* United Nations Environment Programme, 2009.

164 According to a UN damage assessment carried out using satellite imagery, 2,660 buildings and 186 greenhouses were destroyed or severely damaged during the hostilities and 167 kilometres of road were damaged. The assessment revealed 220 impact craters on roads and bridges and 711 craters on open or agricultural land. It is

of agricultural areas.[165] Extensive areas of orchards and farmland were seriously physically degraded by the movement of ground forces.[166] According to the Palestinian National Early Recovery and Reconstruction Plan for Gaza 2009-2010, over 35,750 cattle, sheep and goats and more than one million birds and chickens were killed during the armed conflict.[167] The damage to smaller industrial enterprises was significant and there was an increase in pollution discharged into the Mediterranean and seeping into groundwater. The escalation of violence caused pockets of contamination, such as hydrocarbon contamination at industrial sites, sewage contamination around broken storage tanks, continuing sewage contamination around sewage treatment plants, storm water infiltration areas, and contaminated sewage drains and coastline.

A number of environmental and health impacts may ensue from these damages: (i) lack of good quality water may lead to an increase in disease; (ii) drinking water contamination by sewage may exacerbate health problems; (iii) sewage from damaged treatment plants may be released onto agricultural and other land; and (iv) untreated or undertreated sewage may be drained out to sea, causing problems to the marine environment.[168]

---

estimated that air strikes have generated 600,000 tonnes of demolition debris. Pollution levels are such that infants in the Gaza Strip are at risk from nitrate poisoning. It is likely that some of the spillage of sewage from treatment plants, the result of power cuts, has filtered through the porous soil into the underground aquifer. The very nature of the soils in the Gaza Strip means that sewage from overwhelmed and unsealed landfills can easily percolate down into the aquifer. *Environmental Assessment of the Gaza Strip following the escalation of hostilities in December 2008 – January 2009*, UNEP, 2009, pp. 16, 27-31.

165 An estimated 17 per cent of cultivated land, including orchards and greenhouses, has been severely affected, with adverse consequences for farmers' livelihoods and those of the population at large. Destruction of vegetation cover and compacting of soil by strikes and tank movements has degraded the land and made it vulnerable to desertification.

166 *Environmental Assessment of the Gaza Strip following the escalation of hostilities in December 2008 – January 2009*, UNEP, 2009, p. 26.

167 Available at: http://www.reliefweb.int/rw/RWFiles2009.nsf/FilesByRWDoc Unid Filename/PSLG-7QHJQZ-full_report.pdf/$File/full_report.pdf, accessed 12 March 2013.

168 *Environmental Assessment of the Gaza Strip following the escalation of hostilities in December 2008 – January 2009*, UNEP, 2009, p.78.

# CHAPTER 3

# Environmental Damage in Non-International Armed Conflict

Since 1945, non-international armed conflicts (NIAC) have been much more common than international armed conflict. In the 16-years period of 1990-2005, only four of the 57 active armed conflicts were international, while that remaining 53 were non-international.[1] In 2011, 36 of the 37 active armed conflicts were fought within states. Of these, nine were internationalized, meaning that there was international involvement by way of troop support to one or both of the warring parties.[2] The majority of NIAC do not, in fact, remain confined within the borders of a single country, and eventually affect the neighbouring countries in some way.[3] During and following armed conflicts, armed and lawless societies can have both a direct and an indirect impact on the environment. These impacts occur for reasons related to subsistence, or for strategic or commercial reasons, and their root causes are often political, social and economic. NIAC have contributed to severe famine and the wholesale distribution

---

1  *Stockholm International Peace Research Institute (SIPRI) Yearbook 2006*, Oxford: Oxford University Press, p.109. In the post-World War II era conflicts within the states (i.e, non-international armed conflict or NIAC) have been far more common than conflicts between states, although the line is often very difficult to draw Charles. Lysaght, The Scope of Protocol II and Its Relation to Common Article 3 of the Geneva Conventions of 1949 and Other Human Rights Instruments, Vol. 33, *American University Law Review*, (1983), p. 9-12.

2  These conflicts included Afghanistan, Algeria, Iraq, Mauretania, Rwanda, Somalia, Uganda, USA and Yemen. Themner Lotta & Peter Wallensteen, Armed Conflicts: 1946-2011, Vol. 49 (4), *Journal of Peace Research*, (2012), p. 566.

3  *Stockholm International Peace Research Institute (SIPRI) Yearbook 2012*, Oxford: Oxford University Press. Also see: UNEP World Conservation Monitoring Centre, October 2003, p. 5-6. Available at: http://www.cms.int/bodies/ScC/12th_scientific_council/pdf/English/Doc_05_Attach4_MountainGorilla_E.pdf, accessed 16 May 2014.

of antipersonnel landmines and ERWs has been seen to render the land unusable. During an NIAC in a territory where the nation-state is weak, non-state actors remain the major culprits as far as the destruction of the environment and exhaustion of natural resources is concerned.[4]

Armed conflict between competing entities within a state has significant impacts on both the parties involved and the environment. Unfortunately, armed conflict is particularly prevalent in areas known for their biodiversity. Over 80 per cent of the major armed conflicts in the second half of the 20th century took place in the biodiversity hotspots, i.e., areas that contain the entire populations of more than half of all the species of plants and more than 42 per cent of all vertebrates. Armed conflict took place in two-thirds of the world's 34 hotspots during that period.[5] Hotspots are also under particular threat because they are found mostly in the poor countries, and poverty puts great pressure on natural resources. Armed conflict in the hotspots makes conservation even more challenging, as displaced persons and refugees often turn to the forests for food and building materials, putting additional pressure on biodiversity.[6]

Armed conflicts have affected wildlife habitats in numerous countries since 1990. The list includes Afghanistan, Angola, the Democratic Republic of Congo, Cambodia, Central African Republic, Colombia, India, Indonesia, Liberia, Mexico, Myanmar, Nepal, Pakistan, the Philippines, Sierra Leone, Sri Lanka, Sudan and South Sudan. Often armed conflict in some of these countries has taken the form of low-level guerrilla warfare that has continued for years, with the same territory changing hands several times. In addition to the tragic toll they have taken on civilian populations, such conflicts have had considerable environmental impacts. For example, opposing armies engage in deforestation and defoliation, hunt wildlife for food, lay thousands of antipersonnel landmines, and clash over valuable natural resources (such as timber and diamonds) to finance their arms purchases.

---

4    Bailes, Alyson J.K., Global Security Governance: A World of Change and Challenge, *Stockholm International Peace Research Institute (SIPRI) Yearbook 2005*, Oxford: Oxford University Press, p.1-27.

5    Hanson, T., T.M. Brooks, G.A.B. da Fonseca, M. Hoffmann, J.F. Lamoreux, G. Machlis, C.G. Mittermeier, R.A. Mittermeier and J.D. Pilgrim, Warfare in Biodiversity Hotspots, Vol. 23, *Conservation Biology*, (2009), p. 578–587.

6    McNeely Jeffery A. and Susan A. Mainka. 2009. Conservation for a New Era: Conservation and Armed Conflict, International Union for Conservation of Nature (IUCN), Switzerland. Available at: http://data.iucn.org/dbtw-wpd/html/2009-026/section11.html, accessed 13 May 2014.

During NIAC, ecological assaults in combat zones are often kept secret or widely ignored, with the result that the harm to humans and the environmental harm is more devastating still. Nature may also be used as a weapon of conflict and its destruction may affect innocent individuals who depend on their environment. It may also force them to leave the areas that have nourished their communities. Such environmental damage could be expensive, traumatic and sometimes, irreversible.

Scientific literature on the effects of NIAC on environment is extremely scattered and requires a great deal of time to gather. It is generally limited to the sub-Saharan African continent,[7] where most of the information pertains to the effects of conflict on large mammals such as primates, elephants and rhinoceroses, and to the effects on national parks. The environmental effects of armed conflict in Afghanistan are well documented, but hardly any research has been undertaken for other countries such as India, Nepal and Sri Lanka. Most of the literature consists of newspaper reports or single articles rather than any scientific studies on the subject. Due to these limitations, the matter in this chapter is confined to three regions, covering 16 situations in the world.[8]

## I. Angola

Angola's civil war[9] began three months after the country won independence from Portuguese rule in 1975, and lasted until the death of rebel leader Jonas Savimbi in 2002. During the 27 years of civil war, an estimated 500,000 people died and 426,000 Angolans fled their country, while nearly 70,000 Angolans became amputees as a result of landmines, giving the country the dubious distinction of having the most landmine-related amputees

---

7  Africa is the oldest continent on Earth. The array of ecosystems and organisms contained within its forests, rivers, deserts, wetlands, mountains, and savannas, is unequalled in the world. The human species evolved at the margins of the equatorial forests of Africa, and people have substantially influenced African ecosystems for hundreds of thousands of years. The civil wars and internal strife's have been responsible for more African forest destruction in the past 60 years than in the preceding 10,000.

8  The destruction of natural environment of Afghanistan has been extensive during the international and the non-international armed conflict. It started after the Soviet occupation of Afghanistan in 1979 and continues even today. The situation has been covered in the previous chapter.

9  Main parties in contention for power at the time of independence included the National Liberation Front of Angola (FNLA), the Popular Movement for the Liberation of Angola (MPLA) and the National Union for the Total Independence of Angola (UNITA).

per capita in the world.[10]   Angola's vast oil[11] and diamond resources were part of a major bone of contention. Civil conflicts have consistently been exacerbated by the business rivalries between foreign countries vying for African oil and mining resources.[12] In general, Angola suffered from an unstable social, political and economic environment due to: (i) a high number of landmines--over 15 million were planted; (ii) an absence of respect for human rights, including domestic legislation that favoured FDI over the citizens' welfare; and (iii) a high number of refugees and internally displaced persons (IDPs).[13]

The landmines have robbed Angola of its rich biodiversity, as thousands of animals, including antelopes and elephant, fell prey to them. In some cases, landmines were used by poachers to obtain ivory illegally, as a field of mines can kill or wound an entire herd of elephants. Several reports during the late 1980s indicated that National Union for the Total Independence of Angola (UNITA) rebels used landmines to kill elephants so as to use their tusks to buy weapons. In south-eastern Angola, more than 100,000 elephants and 1000 rhinoceroses perished at the hands of rebels and South African soldiers during the years of internecine warfare.[14] Elephant populations in Angola have not recovered from this ordeal. In addition, many subsistence farmers lost their cattle due to landmines and were forced to kill wildlife in order to avoid starvation.

---

10 'Angola's Landmines', The Trade and Environment Database Projects, (1996), The American University, Washington DC. Available at: http://gurukul.ucc.american.edu/ted/LANDMINE.HTM, accessed 10 May 2014. Also see: Pajibo E, *Southern Africa Today*, News Letter dated 7 March 2002. Available at: http://www.afsc.org/intl/africa/saftod07.htm, accessed 10 May 2014.

11 Human Rights Watch (HRW) reported: "The Angolan Government has used oil revenues to finance covert arms purchases that undermined the spirit of the Lusaka Peace Accords. The arms are being used to continue a vicious civil war in which hundreds of thousands of civilians have lost their lives over the last decade and nearly 10 per cent of the population was displaced by the renewed conflict. *The IMF and Angola: Oil and Human Rights*, A Human Rights Watch Backgrounder, Human Rights Watch, London, June 2000.

12 The social life of war, Track Tow: Constructive Approaches to Community and Political Conflict, Vo.8, No.1, July 1999, p.17.

13 Conflict Risk Assessment Report: Angola and Diamond Works, June 2005, available at: http://www4.carleton.ca/cifp/app/serve.php/1055.pdf, accessed 16 August 2013.

14 Breytenbach, J. 2001. *The Plunderers*, Johannesburg: Covos Day Books. Also see: *From Conflict to Peace building: The Role of Natural Resources and the Environment*, The United Nations Environment Programme (UNEP), 2009.

Further, the landmines in Angola set in motion a series of events that led to environmental degradation in the form of soil degradation, deforestation, pollution of water resources with heavy metals and alteration of food chains. Landmines also restricted the movement of people, as refugees are often unable to return to their homes and farm their land. Many people have lost their lives in attempts to rebuild their farming activities around the landmines.[15] It is likely that the effects of the scars left by the civil conflict on the people and environment of Angola will continue for decades to come. Clearing Angola of landmines will prove to be a very challenging task, which will, in fact require a considerable amount of international financial aid and expertise.

## II. Central African Republic

The Central African Republic (CAR) has an area of 623,000 sq km and a population of approximately 3.5 million. The country's population is concentrated largely in the west and around the capital city of Bangui. The CAR is located in the heart of Africa, and the country's rich biodiversity reflects influences from both the east and west of the continent. The topography of the country is largely defined by low-lying and undulating hills and for this reason, most of the habitat differentiation is caused by the climate, mainly variations in rainfall. The CAR has four main climatic zones, extending from north to south.[16] The country's vegetation zones correspond to these climatic zones and include Sahelian savanna, or open savannas; Sudanian savanna, comprising vast grasslands with small groups of trees; Congolian forest-savanna mosaic, which includes wooded savanna and dry, deciduous forests; and Congolian dense forests, ranging

---

15  Nachon, C.T., Environmental Aspects of Landmines, (1999), International Campaign to Ban Landmines. Available at: http://www.icbl.org/, accessed 10 May 2014.

16  The Sahelien Zone is characterized by a longer dry season than rainy season, with annual rainfall totaling less than 1,200 mm. This zone is situated in the extreme north of the CAR, and covers about 10 per cent of the country. The Sudano-Guinean Zone, which comprises the largest part of the country, is characterized by three to six months of dry season with annual rainfall of around 1,400 mm. The Sudano-Oubangian Zone, which covers most of the southern third of the country, is characterized by a three month dry season, high humidity throughout the year, and annual rainfall greater than 1,500 mm. The Guinean-Congolese Zone, which is located in the extreme south (around Bangassou and south of Bayanga) is characterized by the absence of a true dry season, with annual rainfall exceeding 1,500 mm. Allard Blom and Jean Yamindou. 2001. *A Brief History of Armed Conflict and its Impact on Biodiversity in the Central African Republic*, Washington: Biodiversity Support Programme, p.9.

from deciduous to semi-evergreen and evergreen forests.[17]

The CAR's biodiversity is one of the least studied in Africa. The country has approximately 700 species of birds and the region of Dzanga-Sangha is one of its most biologically diverse areas.[18] However, due to the lack of financial resources, the CAR's forest reserves are not well protected. Poaching poses the single largest threat to the conservation of biodiversity and law enforcement to control the rampant poaching in all protected areas is clearly inadequate.

## Armed conflict

During most of the four decades after independence, the CAR remained calm despite being in a region rife with civil unrest and armed conflict. In 1993, after demonstrations and rioting, the then President, Andre-Dieudonne Kolingba, was forced to call elections in which he was defeated. These elections, the first open and free multi-party elections in the CAR, seemed to have been fair, with little or no violence. Following the elections, a new era was ushered in under President Patasse. However, the lack of economic improvement under the new President ultimately triggered a series of events leading to mass-scale violence.

In 1996, members of the CAR army mutinied thrice, demanding payment of pending wages and improved benefits and working conditions. The army took to the streets, firing in the air and looting Bangui's main commercial district.[19] The third mutiny had the most serious consequences

---

17  Blom, A., and J. Yamindou, 'Status of the protected areas and gazetted forests of the Central African Republic', in *Ecological and Economic Impacts of Gorilla-based Tourism in Dzanga-Sangha, Central African Republic*, doctoral thesis, by A. Blom, 2001. Department of Environmental Sciences, Tropical Nature Conservation and Vertebrate Ecology Group, Wageningen University, the Netherlands.

18  Harris, D. 1994. *Interim check-list to the vascular plants of the Dzanga-Sangha Project Area Central African Republic*, Unpublished report, University of Oxford, p. 31. Also see: Fay, J.M., C.A. Spinage, B. Chardonnet, and A.A. Green, 'Central African Republic', in East, R. (ed.). 1990. *Antelopes Global Survey and Action Plans*, Gland: IUCN, p. 99-109.

19  Even though the first mutiny was resolved through negotiations, it created a climate of mutual mistrust. Shortly thereafter, the soldiers took to the streets once again. The second mutiny quickly deteriorated into a vicious cycle of violence. The ranks of the army became divided into those supporting the President and those demanding not only payment of wages, but also political change. Pitched battles ensued in the streets of Bangui, and looters took advantage of the total breakdown of law and order and started looting shops, businesses, and homes. France and other foreign governments tried to mediate and the French army intervened and ended the uprising. A brief period

on the economy, civil society, and the environment. People were forced to evacuate their homes and relocate to areas under the control of their own ethnic affiliation. In April 1998, the United Nations peacekeeping force (MINURCA) was established to bring peace in the country.[20] Negotiations between the warring factions finally resulted in a permanent settlement later that year. Life in the CAR gradually returned to normal pace after more than two years of bloodshed and violence in which at least several hundred people, mostly civilians, were killed. This unrest was devastating for the economy, and had a tremendous impact on the environment.

During the period of unrest, the CAR's central government experienced a slow breakdown of control over its northern provinces. The north has long been an area of unrest, dating back to the slave trade period, when raiding parties from Sudan and Chad came looking for slaves and ivory. Ivory has been a valued commodity for centuries, and in the late 1970s the market saw a new upsurge. This was in part due to the civil wars in Sudan and Chad, which led to an increasing influx of automatic weapons, such as the AK-47, which quickly became weapons of choice for elephant poachers, replacing the traditional spear. The civil wars also fuelled the demand for fast money, and ivory, with its rapidly increasing value, satisfied this demand.

## Socioeconomic Impact

The mutinies in the CAR resulted in 70,000 internally displaced persons (IDPs), 130 destroyed industries and businesses, and loss of job for thousands. These conflicts increased inflation by 3 per cent, decreased exports by 16 per cent, decreased imports by 23 per cent, and decreased state revenues by 33.6 per cent. These changes caused a dramatic increase in external debt, a decrease in overall security in the country. In a country that already had extremely limited medical services, at least three health

---

of calm followed, but underlying tensions remained, with the capital divided into two clear factions, now based mainly on ethnic lineage. Violence eventually erupted again, and heavy fighting ensued. Again, several nations tried to mediate and placed troops between the fighting factions. A cease-fire agreement was reached on January 24, 1997. French troops were quickly supplemented by troops from six African nations, and this mostly African peacekeeping force eventually restored order by the end of 1997. It was replaced by the United Nations peacekeeping force in April 1998. Allard Blom and Jean Yamindou. 2001. *A Brief History of Armed Conflict and its Impact on Biodiversity in the Central African Republic*, Washington: Biodiversity Support Programme, p. 11-12.

20  The World Fact book, 1999 – Central African Republic, CIA 1999. Available at: http://www.odci.gov/cia/publications/factbook/ct.html, accessed 03 December 2013.

centres were destroyed. Funeral services were limited during this time, and people were buried in backyards, causing serious health hazards. Embassies and international organizations closed their offices leading to the suspension or permanent closure of projects. The offices of at least 12 donor-financed projects were ransacked or completely destroyed.

## Environmental Impact

The mutinies increased overall insecurity and resulted in a large migration of people away from Bangui. The movement of displaces persons was relatively short-lived, lasting perhaps for a maximum of four years, however, it led to a rapid increase in deforestation associated with slash-and-burn agriculture as well as firewood collection. Many people turned to hunting and poaching to survive this difficult period. The massive pullout of foreign assistance and funding also had a negative effect on biodiversity conservation. Very few international conservation NGOs were present in the CAR before the mutinies, and most of these left the country during the conflicts. Only two international conservation organizations remain active in the CAR: Wildlife Conservation Society (WCS) and the World Wildlife Fund (WWF). Although some national conservation organizations continued work, they were relatively small-scale and had a limited scope. Most international organizations, such as UNDP, FAO, and the World Bank, pulled out their expatriate staff and had their offices looted and/or vehicles stolen during the mutinies.[21]

Because of its extended duration, the conflict in the north has had a much greater impact on biodiversity than did the short-lived mutinies in the capital. Elephant numbers dropped dramatically as a direct result of the insecurity in the north. The conflict in the north has also led to the disappearance of the rhinoceros from the CAR, which had a rhinoceros population possibly as high as 10,000 some 30 years ago. With the increasing pressure from the north and the subsequent disappearance of elephants, poachers began moving south and this had a severe impact on the elephant populations in the southern forests.[22]

---

21 Allard Blom and Jean Yamindou. 2001. *A Brief History of Armed Conflict and its Impact on Biodiversity in the Central African Republic*, Washington: Biodiversity Support Programme, p. 16-19.

22 Allard Blom and Jean Yamindou. 2001. *A Brief History of Armed Conflict and its Impact on Biodiversity in the Central African Republic*, Washington: Biodiversity Support Programme, p.14-16.

## III. Democratic Republic of Congo

The Democratic Republic of Congo (DRC), formerly Zaire, is a vast country with a land area of 2,267,000 sq km. It has a population of some 58 million, with a high population growth of 3.2 per cent. Over 30 per cent of the population lives in urban areas (25 per cent only in Kinshasa), while 70 per cent resides in rural areas. The urban annual growth rate is 3.8 per cent. 360 ethnic groups speaking 219 languages reside in the country. The DRC holds the world's largest deposits of cobalt and tantalum, as well as significant reserves of copper, gold, diamonds, and other minerals (zinc, iron, uranium, etc).

The DRC possesses more species of birds and mammals than any other African country and is one of the most flora-rich countries on the continent.[23] It has a great diversity of ecosystem. It has the largest number of fauna and the second largest number of flora (after South Africa) on the African continent, and the second largest tropical forest in the world after the Amazon. Its forests are known as the "world's second lung." In addition to logging, they provide many livelihood opportunities, including ecotourism, conservation, agriculture and non-timber forest products such as foodstuffs, medicine or cosmetics. Despite its abundance of natural resources, it is one of the poorest countries in the world. An estimated 16 million people are suffering from hunger and 150,000 people continue to die every year from hunger, disease, and other causes of instability.[24] The DRC has experienced a trade-off between natural resources of known commercial value and biodiversity of undetermined value during its two civil wars.[25]

---

23  Sayer, J. A., C. Harcourt, and N. M. Collins. 1992. *The conservation atlas of tropical forests in Africa,* UK: Macmillan Publishers Ltd, p. 288.

24  According to WHO estimates, there are more than 150,000 annual deaths in DRC due to: diarrhoea caused by polluted water/bad hygiene (67 per cent), indoor air pollution (31 per cent) and outdoor air pollution (2 per cent). Available at: http://www.who.int/ quantifying_ehimpacts/countryprofilesebd.xls, accessed 22 March 2014.

25  First Congo War (1996–1997), which led to the overthrow of Mobutu by Laurent Kabila and his rebels, and Second Congo War (1998–2003), involved nine nations and led to ongoing low-level warfare despite an official peace and the first democratic elections in 2006. The armed conflict is, however, continuing in the country and has claimed an estimated three million lives, either as a direct result of fighting or because of disease and malnutrition. It has been called possibly the worst emergency to unfold in Africa in recent decades. The armed conflict had an economic as well as a political side. Fighting was fuelled by the country's vast mineral wealth, with all sides taking advantage of the anarchy to plunder natural resources.

The DRC stretches from the volcanoes and the Rwenzori Mountains of the Virungas National Park (VNP) in the east to the Atlantic Ocean and the Mangrove Nature Reserve in the west.[26] There are the northern savannas of the Garamba National Park (GNP), the central waterways and dense forests of the Salonga National Park (SNP), and the southern wooded savannas of the Upemba National Park (UNP). Some of Africa's spectacular mammals can only be found in the DRC. These include the okapi (*Okapia johnstoni*), found in the Okapi Faunal Reserve (OFR) and Maiko National Park (MNP); the northern white rhino (*Ceratotherium simum cottoni*), found in the Garamba National Park (GNP); the eastern lowland gorilla (*Gorilla beringei graueri*), found in the Kahuzi-Biega National Park (KBNP) and MNP; and the Bonobo chimpanzee (*Pan paniscus*), found in the Salonga National Park (SNP).[27]

## Armed Conflict in Neighbouring States

Many countries bordering the African Great Lakes have been involved in the armed conflict. Though DRC, Rwanda, Burundi, and Uganda have suffered the most, other countries are also implicated, notably Sudan, Zimbabwe, Tanzania, Angola, and Namibia. Preceding the Rwandan genocide, troops primarily from the Rwandan refugee population in Uganda (largely Tutsi), started a movement in 1990 to regain power in Kigali, the capital of Rwanda. They had Ugandan support as they had assisted Ugandan President Museveni to power in Kampala in 1986. The assassination of Rwandan President Juvenal Habyarimana set off a cycle of violence that resulted in the death of 500,000 to 1 million Rwandans (mainly Tutsi and moderate Hutu). Following a military operation carried out by the French between June and August 1994, about 2 million Rwandan refugees crossed into DRC.

While the Rwandans were trying to reassemble their country following the trauma of genocide, Zaire (as the DRC was known then), in its far western capital, was in the fourth year of its long 'democratic transition'. The transfer of the Rwandan populations into the eastern province of Kivu also marked

---

26 The Congo basin has eighteen protected areas, including seven national parks, of which five have been classified as part of the 'common heritage of mankind'. Many of these species are also protected by existing conventions including the Biodiversity and CITES Conventions.

27 Terese Hart and Robert Mwinyihali. 2001. *Armed Conflict and Biodiversity in Sub-Saharan Africa: The Case of the Democratic Republic of Congo (DRC)*, Washington DC: Biodiversity Support Programme. Available at: http://www.worldwildlife.org/bsp/publications/africa/143/titlepage.htm, accessed 17 May 2013.

the transfer of the Rwandan war into Zaire, which was already nearing complete economic collapse. Zaire's economy had taken an extreme slide in the mid-1970s. Soaring fuel costs and a collapse in the price of copper compounded the negative blow from nationalization of foreign investment. A high level of corruption and an obsession with personal gain choked the nation by the mid-1990s. Infrastructures crumbled, inflation figure reached four digits, and the incipient industry was paralysed.

The Rwandan peasants, ex-Rwandan military persons, and anti-Tutsi guerrillas who poured across the Rwanda/Zaire border, established refugee camps in North and South Kivu. Tension between the Hutus, Tutsis, local populations and Mobutu's forces led to clashes in the Kivu countryside. In 1996, the ethnic violence drove close to 1 million Hutu refugees to Rwanda, and tens of thousands of other refugees into the vast Congolese forests. Less than a year later, with support from Rwanda, Uganda, and Angola, the disparate rebels formed the new Alliance of Democratic Forces for the Liberation of Congo-Zaire (ADFL) and had marched across the country to overthrow Mobutu and established a new regime.

## Refugees and internally displaced persons (IDPs)

Congo has long been a destination for refugees. During the colonial era, its borders were open to peasants fleeing from famine and from ethnic conflicts in Rwanda, Burundi, Sudan and Angola. Refugees were encouraged by the Belgian government, which was in need of labour for its plantations of coffee, tea, quinine, and for mines and road projects. Since independence, the central reason for mass movements into Congo has been armed conflict resulting from ethnic tensions (as in Rwanda and Burundi), religion (Sudan), and politics (Angola and Uganda). Along with this, the DRC has also experienced waves of movement of internally displaced persons (IDPs).[28]

---

28  At the time of independence, there was a massive migration of Luba people out of the city of Kananga in Kasai Occidental, following an abortive secessionist movement. There were numerous groups of displaced people from the muleliste movement, a rebellion started by one of Patrice Lumumba's ministers following Lumumba's assassination. By 1964, the mulelistes controlled the eastern part of the current DRC, an area similar in extent to the current rebel-held territory. During the rebellion of the mulelistes or simbas, IDPs fled the northwestern rim of Lake Tanganyika toward Maniema and south Kivu. Legum, C. 1961. *Congo Disasters*, UK: Penguin Books, p.174.

The impact of the mainly Rwandan refugees on the environment in east DRC has been devastating. When accompanied by armed men, the roaming refugees forced villagers to feed them or raided their fields, while unarmed, refugees were voluntarily helped by the local people. Whatever, the circumstances, the refugees substantially increased the pressure on the available resources. In some instances this resulted in the local population itself being forced to move mainly towards small towns, or to increase its reliance on fish and wildlife.[29] Even before the armed conflict many local people in the DRC were dependent on natural resources for their survival. The collapse of the transport system increased the reliance on bushmeat to about 80 per cent of protein consumed.[30] People learned to adapt to the disturbance caused by refugees or soldiers. In the first instance they will work on their fields at night to avoid being harassed. When this became impossible, or when the pressure from refugees or soldiers was too high, they fled into the forest, where they tried to make a living from fishing and hunting; mainly using snares and traps, but sometimes using traditional methods such as bows and poisoned arrows.[31]

Nearly 115 sq km of the forest of the Virunga National Park (VNP) was cut by refugees.[32] Many camps housed armed and frustrated people, which made protection of the parks almost impossible. The amount of poaching increased substantially. For example, the number of snares and machetes confiscated in VNP tripled in 1994 and 1995. Park guards and gorillas were killed in both VNP and Kahuzi-Biega National Park.[33] Bamboo was

29  Biswas, A. and Tortajada-Quiroz, C., Environmental impacts of the Rwandan refugees on Zaire, Vol. 26, *Ambio*, 1996, p. 403-408.

30  Wilkie, D., Curran, B., Tshombe, R. and Morelli, G., Managing bushmeat hunting in the Okapi Wildlife Reserve, Democratic Republic of Congo, Vol. 32, *Oryx*, (1998), p. 131–144.

31  Draulans Dirk and Ellen Van Krunkelsven, The impact of war on forest areas in the Democratic Republic of Congo, Vol. 36 (1), *Oryx*, January 2002, p. 35-40.

32  In the mid-1990s, the most visibly striking environmental consequence of the refugee camps was deforestation. More than 1 million refugees needed wood for cooking fires. Around Goma, this deforestation happened in the Virungas National Park (VNP). The continuous collection of firewood over two years caused serious ecological transformation over vast areas of the reserve forests and national parks. The deforestation elicited response from the international community. The refugee camps which were sponsored by international humanitarian organizations were seen as directly responsible. Terese Hart and Robert Mwinyihali. 2001. *Armed Conflict and Biodiversity in Sub-Saharan Africa: The Case of the Democratic Republic of Congo (DRC)*, Washington DC: Biodiversity Support Programme.

33  Draulans Dirk and Ellen Van Krunkelsven, The impact of war on forest areas in the Democratic Republic of Congo, Vol. 36 (1), *Oryx*, January 2002, p. 35-40.

harvested in higher elevations primarily by refugees from Kibumba camp. The equivalent of about half of some 19.2 sq km of bamboo was cut.[34]

## Impact on Parks

Although the environmental consequences of the conflict have been unevenly distributed, nearly all the parks and reserves of eastern DRC have been affected. The Garamba National Park (4,900 sq km), located in northern DRC along its border with Sudan, was one of the first protected areas affected by armed conflict. Starting 1991, some 800,000 refugees fleeing the civil war in Sudan were set up in camps on the park's borders. Arms and ammunition were abundant and military units (Sudanese People's Liberation Army, SPLA) were stationed adjacent to the park. As a result, meat poaching escalated, first in the northern sector of the park, but eventually moving toward the southern part of the park, which is the habitat of the only remaining wild population of northern white rhinoceros.[35] During the first of DRC's wars of liberation (1996–97) the park and its headquarters were occupied by mercenaries working for Mobutu until they were ousted by the ADFL. All of the park's logistical equipment was looted, including fuel, radios, and vehicles. The guards were disarmed, and the park's law enforcement capacity was severely crippled. Elephant hunting increased rapidly after 1996, when the DRC conflict began. SPLA rebels, militias hired by Mobutu, and later also the Congolese army (FARDC), were involved in poaching at different times.[36] It has been reported that GNP's elephant population was halved  (from more than 11,000 to less than 5,500) and its buffalo population fell by two-third. (from more than 25,000 to less than 8,000).[37]

The Okapi Faunal Reserve (ORF) with an area of 13,400 sq km, is not on an international border, so it was among the most recently affected protected areas. Poaching of elephants, which was rampant from the late 1970's to

---

34  Brauer Jurgen. 2011. *War and Nature: The Environmental Consequences of War in a Globalized World*, London: AltaMira Press, p.132.

35  Hillman Smith, K, The current status of the Northern white rhino in Garamba, Vol. 25, *Pachyderm*, (1998), p. 104-105.

36  Hart T, and Mwinyihali R. *Armed Conflict and Biodiversity in Sub-Saharan Africa: The Case of the Democratic Republic of Congo (DRC)*, Washington, DC: Biodiversity Support Programme (2001). Available at: http://www.worldwildlife.org/bsp/publications/africa/143/titlepage.htm, accessed 16 Nov 2013.

37  Brauer Jurgen. 2011. *War and Nature: The Environmental Consequences of War in a Globalized World*, London: AltaMira Press, p.136.

the early 1980's stopped almost completely in the OFR after the CITES ban on ivory trade in 1989.[38] However, in 1996, military and rebel factions moved into the area and looted the park headquarters, disarmed guards, brought in hunters, and opened markets around the reserve for bushmeat and ivory. These militias were replaced by Uganda-backed rebels in 1999. The killing of elephants was widespread in 2000, and military deserters set up large poaching camps to the southeast, southwest and west of the reserve, as well as inside the northeastern part.[39] Elephants in the region were killed not just for ivory but also to feed the armed forces. The worst of the killing of elephants happened between 2002 and 2004, when rebel militias clashed in areas of high elephant density. There were reports of elephant poaching during 2007 through 2009.[40]

Elephant meat was sold in the village of the park administrative centre, and the park guards were mocked by an imperious order from the passing military to 'guard' the ivory they had poached and were carrying with them. Four years after the first war, there was a significant increase in the number of illegal 'coltan' and gold mines, which reached the vicinity of the Reserve. The mining camps were the foci for poaching as well as deforestation and serious disturbance to watercourses.

The Kahuzi-Biega National Park (KBNP), with an area of 6,000 sq km, is located on the DRC's eastern border and has suffered consistently since the period of Rwandan refugee camps. The root cause for much of the damage in KBNP was social problems arising from the Rwandan war. A high

---

38  Alers MPT, Blom A, Sikubwabo Kiyengo C, Masunda T, Barnes RFW, Preliminary assessment of the status of the forest elephant in Zaire, Vol. 30, *African Journal of Ecology*, (1992), p. 279–291.

39  During a five month anti-poaching operation, through a collaborative effort of ICCN staff, military, paramilitary and NGO's, 117 kg of ivory, and 215 kg of elephant meat was recovered, and 20 poachers were apprehended. Mubalama L, Mapilanga JJ, Less elephant slaughter in the Okapi Faunal Reserve, Democratic Republic of Congo, with Operation Tango, Vol. 31, *Pachyderm*, (2001), p. 36–41.

40  In the OFR, direct and indirect impacting factors combined to wreak havoc on the elephant population. Despite the protected status of the reserve, up to 50 per cent of the population, or perhaps as many as 3300 animals, have been lost. It was estimated that at least 23 tons of ivory was taken out of the reserve and its surroundings. Assuming an average 6.9 kg of ivory per elephant, this corresponds to 3434 dead elephants. Hunter N, Martin EB, Milliken T , Determining the number of elephants to supply the current unregulated ivory markets in Africa and Asia, Vol. 36, *Pachyderm*, (2004), p. 116–128. For more details see: Beyers RL, Hart JA, Sinclair ARE, Grossmann F, Klinkenberg B, et al., *Resource Wars and Conflict Ivory: The Impact of Civil Conflict on Elephants in the Democratic Republic of Congo - The Case of the Okapi Reserve*, 2011.

population density stressed resources within the Park. In certain sections of the park, internal displacements had made the population density rise to 300 persons per sq km. The people along with the militia were involved in mining gold, castorite, and coltan. These ores, along with ivory, were exported from airstrips, five of which are located outside the borders of the low-altitude sector of the park. The gorilla population suffered heavily during the armed conflict. It was thought that about 8,000 Grauer' gorilla lived in the park during 1994-1995. Apparently due to poaching, this population was reduced to 126 in August 2000.[41] Redmond (2001) has listed the environmental damages caused in the KBNP in Congo and Rwanda due to armed conflict and coltan mining.[42]

- Forest clearance and use of timber to build camps to accommodate workers

- Forest clearance to expose substrate for mining

- Pollution of streams by silt from washing process

- Erosion of unprotected earth during rains leading to land-slips

- Cutting of firewood for heating and cooking

- Hunting for animals for bushmeat to feed miners and camp followers.

- Animals maimed or killed by snares

- Debarking of trees to make panning trays for washing coltan

- Cutting of lianas to make carrying baskets for coltan

- Disturbance of animals by people residing in and moving through forests

- Silting of streams likely to kill invertebrates and reduce photosynthesis

- Reduced productivity of fish stocks in lakes and rivers affected by silt pollution

---

41  Brauer Jurgen. 2011. *War and Nature: The Environmental Consequences of War in a Globalized World*, London: AltaMira Press, p.13-138.

42  Redmond, I., Coltan Boom, Gorilla Bust: The Impact of Coltan Mining on Gorillas and other Wildlife in 2001, p. 9-10. Eastern Congo, A Report from the Dian Fossey Gorilla Fund Europe and the Born Free Foundation, 2001. Available at: http://www.bornfree.org.uk/coltan/coltan.pdf, accessed 1 June 2014.

- Ecological changes due to loss of key species such as elephants and apes

- Loss of biodiversity: only a small population of elephants, gorillas, okapis, and other endangered species remain

- Long-term changes in watershed due to rapid run-off in deforested areas

The Virunga Volcanoes are a mountain chain straddling the borders of Uganda, Rwanda, and the DRC. Three national parks, one in each country, are situated here. Settlement within the park was a major problem for Virungas National Park (VNP). Until the massacre of mid-1994, these protected areas were not severely affected. Once people started fleeing through the Virungas to the Congo and settled in and near the Park in that country, ecological problems emerged on a large scale. Within a matter of days, some two million people flooded across the border and about 720,000 of whom eventually settled near Goma. They remained in five camps for about two years and moved out when the eastern Congo itself became embroiled in armed conflict. The decision of the then-Zairian government to site refugee camps in the aftermath of the 1994 Rwanda genocide on the edge of the VNP led to the deforestation of 113 sq km of the park with all the attendant consequences in biodiversity terms.[43] Displaced people caused significant habitat loss in VNP.[44] The Mount Goma was completely denuded in three days and not a single tree was left standing.[45]

The Salonga National Park (SNP), with an area of 36,560 sq km, is the largest of all DRC's Parks. Its navigable rivers, has been a poacher's paradise for more than two decades. Poachers, who invaded the park soon after its creation in 1970, included heavily armed deserters from Mobutu's army. Poaching in the Maiko National Park also affected the elephant population in the country. As was the case with Kahuzi-Biega lowland forest, there was virtually no protection in this place during this period.

---

43 Central African Region Programme for the Environment (CARPE 1), 'Conservation in a Region of Civil Instability: The Need to Be Present and Assist', available at: http://carpe.umd.edu/products/carpe-cd-02/CARPE-Briefs/Congo-22.html, accessed 1 June 2014.

44 McNeely JA, 'Addressing extreme conflicts through peace parks', in Palo M, and De Jong W, *Extreme Conflict and Tropical Forests*, Netherlands: Springer, 2007, p. 159-172.

45 Biswas A.K. and C. Tortajada-Quiroz, Environmental Impacts of the Rwandan Refugees on Ziare, Vol. 25 (6), *Ambio*, 1996, p. 403-408.

DRC's armed conflict led to widespread lawlessness in protected parks. Government institutions were disrupted or taken apart, or oriented to facilitate illegal extraction and taxation (such as the national police and military). Institutions such as the national parks service, whose mandate is the protection and control of natural resources, were the focus of attack and harassment. Thus, the collapse of wildlife conservation and enforcement during the conflict was profound. Staff ceased normal operations or moved out of protected areas, and many were killed. Hunting increased and was partly linked to the proliferation of small arms. Militias and military occupied protected areas. The exploitation of elephants for ivory and meat was used to provision insurgents or the military, and to generate revenue to fund further expansion of resource takeovers.[46] The populations of elephants were severely reduced by armed militias who also competed to secure control of easily extractable natural resources, such as gold, diamonds, and mineral ores, that could be extracted by low-input artisanal methods. Saw-wood, charcoal and fisheries were also targets of control and conflict. Key resources included ivory and bushmeat, and African elephants were the most important of these targeted species.

Outside the protected areas, along the eastern border with Uganda, there was an uncontrolled incremental increase in logging. There was a constant movement of logging trucks carrying the wood toward the Kasindi border crossing. The logging facilitated settlement and bushmeat hunting.

## IV. Ethiopia

Ethiopia, located in the horn of Africa, has long been recognized for its wealth of natural resources, endemic species, and high biodiversity. These natural assets remained largely unprotected until the mid-1960s, when the government instituted a conservation- and protected-area programme. The primary aim of this programme was to establish by laws and areas for the conservation and protection of a range of species and habitats. The government ensured the establishment of numerous protected areas and the conservation of diverse native species within these areas. These initiatives were undertaken for the sake of education, research, and recreation, and to conserve essential resources such as fuel wood, building materials, forage, traditional medicines, and food.

---

46  Hart T, Mwinyihali R. 2001. *Armed Conflict and Biodiversity in Sub-Saharan Africa: The Case of the Democratic Republic of Congo (DRC)*, Washington DC: Biodiversity Support Programme.

Ethiopia achieved success in conserving the largest area of afro-alpine habitat on the continent (Bale Mountains National Park) and ensured the survival of several endangered species and endemics. These include the Ethiopian wolf (*Canis simensis*), African wild dog (*Lycaon pictus*), mountain nyala (*Tragelaphus buxtoni*), Walia ibex (*Capra walie*), African elephant (*Loxodonta africana*), African wildass (*Equus africanus*), Soemmerring's gazelle (*Gazella soemmerringii*), Swayne's hartebeest (*Alcelaphus buselaphus swaynei*), and the genetic material of many other species.

Ethiopia's conservation and protected area programme also provided varying levels of protection to certain watersheds and many essential natural processes and cycles (e.g., pollination, seed dispersal, soil hydrology). It generated income both nationally and locally through tourism, hunting, and the sale of wildlife (e.g., primate exports) and wildlife products, i.e. crocodile (*Crocodylus niloticus*) skins, ostrich (*Struthio camelus*) skins, and civet (*Viverra civetta*) musk.

## The Conflicts

The Ethiopian-Eritrean civil war and the Ethiopian revolution took place for very different reasons. The civil war had its roots in World War II, when the administration of the region then known as Eritrea was temporarily entrusted to British military rule, until its fate could be decided by the UN General Assembly. The UN elected to adopt a compromise resolution, stating that Eritrea was to establish its own form and organization of internal self-government while existing as a federated state of Ethiopia. Ethiopia was to be responsible for matters pertaining to foreign affairs, defence, foreign and interstate commerce, transportation, and finance.[47] Neither Ethiopia nor Eritrea was particularly pleased with this manner of alliance.

The Ethiopia-Eritrea conflict, known as one of the longest-running civil wars in African history lasted 30 years, primarily because both countries were struggling with a range of internal problems and civil discord.[48] In

---

47 UN General Assembly Resolution, 15 September 1952.

48 Eritrea's problems were ideological and religious in nature and caused a battle among its leading insurgent groups in 1974, at the end of which the Marxist-oriented Eritrean People's Liberation Front (EPLF) emerged as the victor. Ethiopia's problems, on the other hand, were related to the emperor's failure to effect any significant social, economic, or political reform, including transforming Ethiopia from a subsistence-based economy to an agro-industrial based economy. The emperor's problems also stemmed from failure to combat famine and a growing trade deficit. These issues became the

the mid-1980s Ethiopia experienced a series of devastating droughts and insect plagues that led to widespread crop failures and livestock losses. The government forcibly uprooted hundreds of people from the north and resettled them in structured villages. The restriction on peoples' movements and transport associated with their move, however, left people in many areas desperate for food and other commodities. Further, many of the promised services never materialized because natural catastrophes and conflict with Eritrea had left the nation's economy in a state of collapse. These factors, in conjunction with famine, resulted in the displacement and death of hundreds of thousands of people within Ethiopia during the mid-1980s, forced over 100,000 refugees into Somalia, and led many Ethiopians to join forces with Eritrea.

## Conservation and Exclusionary Protected-Area Policy

The Ethiopian Wildlife Conservation Organization (EWCO) was established in 1965 to manage conservation and protected area. This institution was formally recognized as an autonomous body in 1970. The EWCO's responsibilities during that period included establishing nine national parks, four wildlife sanctuaries, seven wildlife reserves, and 18 controlled-hunting areas between 1965 and 1980. It was also responsible for adopting and implementing a range of hunting and conservation policies, including the adoption of IUCN protected-area descriptions and guidelines. Under these policies, all national parks were declared as 'Strict Conservation Areas'. This was termed an exclusionary protected-area policy, as this placed a limitation on all kinds of human use of that area like settlement, exploitation of natural resources, grazing of livestock, mining, etc., except as required for the management of the wildlife and conservation. The imperial government's policy proved most controversial, as it imposed restrictions on the taking of previously unregulated species and natural resources and required the involuntary resettlement of indigenous peoples. Matters did not improve when the Provisional Military Government of Socialist Ethiopia (PMGSE) took over as the new government continued empowerment of the EWCO and public endorsement of the EWCO's conservation and protected-area efforts.

---

incentive for an armed forces-led rebellion that ended with the emperor's deposition on 12 September 1974, and the establishment of the Provisional Military Government of Socialist Ethiopia (PMGSE) as the nation's ruling body. Major Mengistu Haile Mariam eventually emerged as the leader of the PMGSE after three years of power struggles among the revolution's leaders.

The forceful adherence to the exclusionary protected-area policy, in conjunction with a nationwide lack of basic development and a diversion of finances toward conflict contributed to the conservation programme's lack of success. Policies related to resettlement, villagization, movement, and commerce were also were responsible for considerable damages to and losses of protected natural resources.

## Deforestation and soil erosion

Little economic growth and development, and the diversion of finances towards conflict, led to a decline in the availability of food and other commodities, a scarcity of petroleum products, high inflation, and rising unemployment. These, perpetuated a reliance on the land and its resources. The most significant consequence of this reliance was further deforested for agriculture, livestock production, timber and fuel wood. Deforestation on lands adjacent to, and within, certain protected areas resulted in the loss of critical habitat, species isolation, and local species extinction. Farming on steep slopes increased, as land became increasingly scarce. This led to increased rate of soil erosion and gullying and decreased crop yields, forcing people to cultivate newer slopes, and exacerbating the deforestation problem. Excessive soil erosion resulting from deforestation interfered with the operation of several of Ethiopia's hydro-power schemes and was the reason for repeated nationwide power outages during the rainy season. The decline in water quality throughout Ethiopia has been attributed to unregulated deforestation and soil erosion, as has been the decline in rainfall production and stream flow. These impacts had an effect on Ethiopia's wetlands, fisheries, and overall natural biodiversity.

## Impoverishment of conservation programme

The diversion of finances and development energy toward conflict meant that conservation efforts received insufficient funding and lacked in infrastructure and equipment. This contributed to the loss of conservation-related income, because the general lack of facilities limited recreational and educational opportunities. Insufficient funding also prevented in-depth research, effective management, and maintenance, and was a contributing factor to the decline in the morale of EWCO personnel, who were unable to enforce the conservation bylaws and the government's exclusionary protected-area policy. These dilemmas were dealt with by periodically calling in the military to assist in the removal of those deemed encroachers. Use of the military to remove people angered and alienated the once-legitimate residents to an even greater extent, particularly when they felt that their very survival was at stake.

The restriction on people's movement led to the overgrazing of rangelands and exacerbated deforestation and soil-erosion. Many significant and widespread environmental changes took place due to overgrazing, including shrub-land expansion, an increase in undesirable woody species, soil erosion and a decline in forage quality and quantity. These changes also gave rise to settlement-encroachment problems and habitat alterations within the protected areas. In the Awash National Park, encroachment and settlement led to the illegal harvest of fuel wood and shelter wood, increased competition between wildlife and livestock, and forced many species to forage elsewhere. There was an increase in illegal hunting and disease transmission as well, which contributed to the decline of wildlife.

During the period of conflict, modern weaponry (primarily machine guns) was readily available in the black market. Unfortunately, easy access to machine guns increased the frequency and intensity of conflict between ethnic groups. Death and injuries increased as a consequence, as did the displacement of entire ethnic groups from disputed lands. The displaced, sometimes tried to occupy protected areas. The Nechisar National Park was occupied on several occasions. Easy access to arms increased hunting for food, leather, medicinal products and ivory. Species most vulnerable to hunting during the period of conflict included the lesser and greater kudu (*Tragelaphus strepsiceros*), common eland (*Tragelaphus oryx*), buffalo (*Synercus caffer*), beisa oryx (*Oryx gazella*), soemmerring's gazelle, swayne's hartebeest, grevy's zebra, mountain nyala, elephant, giraffe (*Giraffa camelopardalis*), hippopotamus (*Hippopotamus amphibius*), cheetah (*Acinonyx jubatus*), lion (*Panthera leo*), spotted hyena (*Crocuta crocuta*), and jackals (Canis sp.).

## The military's utilization of wildlife

The diversion of finances toward areas of conflict occasionally resulted in a lack of military provisions elsewhere. This forced the Ethiopian military to hunt for food whenever there was a shortage. Reports from several of Ethiopia's protected areas revealed that hunting of this nature occurred particularly when the protected area was located near a training camp. Details of damage to National Parks and Wildlife Sanctuaries in Ethiopia are shown in Table 3.

| S. No. | Protected Area | Damage |
|---|---|---|
| 1. | Abijatta-Shala National Park, established to protects aquatic birds; two rift valley lakes | Infrastructure looted and destroyed, government vehicles burned |
| 2. | Babille Elephant Sanctuary, established to protect endemic sub-species of elephant | No infrastructure or staff; incursions of large numbers of refugees from Somalia |
| 3. | Bale Mountains National Park, established to protect endemic mountain nyala, Ethiopian wolf, and giant mole rat; also protects a rare Afro-alpine habitat and moist highland forest | Livestock control fences cut, all outposts destroyed, mountain nyalas and wolves shot |
| 4. | Gambella National Park, established to protect Nile Lechwe, white-eared kob, and whale-headed stork in extensive swamp habitat | Infrastructure and vehicles destroyed |
| 5. | Kuni-Muktar Mountain Nyala Sanctuary, established to protect mountain nyala and remaining highland forest | Mountain nyalas shot, forestlands cleared; no infrastructure existed |
| 6. | Mago National Park, established for the protection of buffalo, giraffe and elephant | Abandoned by staff; store and houses looted |
| 7. | Nechisar National Park, established to protects Swayne's hartebeest and Burchell's zebra; portions of two rift valley lakes protect crocodile and hippopotamus | Outposts located far from the headquarters damaged and looted; incursions into the main grassland plain by the Gugi agro-pastoralists |
| 8. | Omo National Park, established to protect an extensive grassland wilderness and numerous large mammal species, such as the common eland, buffalo, and elephant | Increased poaching instances |

| S. No. | Protected Area | Damage |
|---|---|---|
| 9. | Senkele Swayne's Hartebeest Sanctuary, established to protects Swayne's hartebeest; most viable population in Ethiopia | All infrastructures destroyed and herd widely dispersed |
| 10. | Simien Mountain National Park, established to protect the Walia ibex and Ethiopian wolf | Inaccessible between 1984 and 1991; all park infrastructure destroyed |
| 11. | Yabello Sanctuary, established to protect of Swayne's hartebeest, Stresemann's bushcrow, and white-tailed swallow | Not developed; no infrastructure |
| 12. | Yangudi Rassa National Park, established to protect the wild ass | Not developed; no infrastructure |

*Table 3: Damage to protected areas in Ethiopia*

Today, several of Ethiopia's protected areas exist on paper only, while others have declined in size or quality. The country has lost the black rhinoceros (*Diceros bicornis*), and several other species now face the threat of extinction. Some of these setbacks are the result of the earliest conflicts for the expansion of empires and wealth, and to control trade throughout the Horn of Africa, and ethno-religious differences. The majority of conservation problems, however, can be attributed to Ethiopia's adoption and implementation of an exclusionary protected-area policy and to the causes and consequences of its prolonged engagement in conflicts.

## V. Liberia

Liberia has been affected by armed conflict for almost 14 years. The conflict has had grave social, economic and environmental consequences. In 1990, one million people – almost a third of the entire population fled the country.[49] By the end of 2003, about a third of these people were still living as refugees in neighbouring countries. Since 1989, about half a million people have been killed in war-related circumstances and of these,

---

49 *Africa Environment Outlook (AEO-2): Our Environment, Our Wealth*, United Nations Environment Programme, Nairobi, 2006, p. 399.

50 per cent were civilians. [50] The conflict also involved large numbers of child soldiers, often supplied with narcotics by militia commanders, and involved in traumatizing attacks on civilians and other atrocities.

One side effect of the conflict has been the increasing pressure that has been put on forests. This was particularly the case after sanctions were imposed on the trade in diamonds, which was linked to the arms trade and enduring violence in Liberia and the sub-region. With diamonds becoming harder to sell, increased emphasis was placed on the production of timber. In 2002, timber exports accounted for more than half of the foreign exchange coming into the country, and more than a quarter of the total GDP.[51] Since then, an embargo has been imposed on the export of timber from Liberia.[52]

An increased dependence on charcoal for fuel has also resulted in deforestation. The infrastructural breakdown caused by the armed conflict, reduced the availability of mains electricity to just 1 per cent of what it was prior to the war. Supplies of kerosene and cooking gas were also disrupted by the war.[53] Between 1990 and 2000, forest cover was reduced by 2 per cent per year, which amounts to 76,000 ha per year. The Forestry Development Authority, which is meant to regulate the industry, has been unable to fulfill its mandate due to the lack of capacity.

Unregulated mining has also created problems. Thousands of Liberians rely upon mining for their livelihoods and prospecting, mining, and hunting became widespread in some protected areas, for example, the Sapo National Park (SNP). Since 2003, intensive mining occurred in the

---

50  The armed conflict devastated the economy, which was struggling even before violence broke out, halving gross domestic product (GDP) and completely halting production in key sectors of the economy such as the export trade in iron ore. Since the end of hostilities, the economy has begun to recover, growing at around 15 per cent in 2004, primarily as a result of donor support. *Desk Study on the Environment in Liberia*, United Nations Environment Programme (UNEP), 2004, Nairobi.

51  *Desk Study on the Environment in Liberia*, United Nations Environment Programme (UNEP), 2004.

52  The UN Security Council Resolution 1521 of 2003.

53  Charcoal was the only option for 99 per cent of the population. As a proportion of the GDP, charcoal production increased from 2 to 9 per cent in 1999. However, during the most violent and unstable periods of conflict (between 1994 and 1996) commercial production of charcoal actually decreased, because of the dangers and difficulties of transporting the commodity in the war zone. Satia, J. 2000. *Woodfuel Review and Assessment in Liberia*, European Commission and Food and Agriculture Organization of the United Nations, Rome.

park and two major mining settlements – called Iraq and Baghdad – were established with a population of between 3,500-5,000 people. Research, in the region of Iraq, showed that gold mining and trading has been the main economic activity, generating for some miners about 198.45 gram of gold a week.[54] There are various negative environmental impacts of the alluvial mining techniques used. Mining results in the discharge of large amounts of suspended solids into watercourses, and the release of large amounts of poisonous chemicals into the environment. For example, it is thought that for every gram of gold extracted, two grams of mercury is released into the environment.

Bushmeat trade is causing widespread local extinction of wild animal species. Bushmeat trade – which includes endangered species, such as chimpanzee (*Pan troglodytes*) – has become so lucrative that many farmers have abandoned agriculture and are dependent on hunting as their main livelihood strategy. Giant pangolin (*Manis gigantea*) are sold for about US$15-20 each while a medium-sized black duiker (*Cephalophus niger*) for about $5-10 and red colobus monkey (*Colobus cercopithecidae*) is sold for about $20. The expansion of commercial logging with an infrastructure of roads and trucks that links forests and hunters to cities and consumers is deepening the problem. The value of the bushmeat trade serving Monrovia alone has been estimated as US$8 million for 10 months of 2003-04.[55]

It is not just terrestrial animals that suffered; all six Atlantic species of sea turtles have fallen prey to poachers.[56] Years of political instability and civil wars have hampered conservation activities and sea turtle conservation initiatives in Liberia may be negated by difficulties in establishing safe,

---

54  At a minimum price of U$ 9 per gram in Monrovia, this amounts to an income of U$1,786 a week. Even though the actual income that accrues to the miners themselves may not be this high, it certainly points to the fact that the mining is actually paying off for the various actors in this economy. Liberia: Under Mining the Forest – Presenting ongoing illegal activities in forest sector – Occasional Briefing Paper – Vol. 1, No. 001/05, Sustainable Development Institute (SDI). Available at:http://www.sdiliberia. org/sdidoc/Liberia%20Under%20Mining%20The%20Forest.pdf, accessed 20 June 2014.

55  See:www.jhr.ca/blog/2013/04/bushmeat-trade-thrives-on-endangered-species-but-creates-livelihood/, accessed 11 July 2014.

56  Green turtle (*Chelonia mydas*), leatherback (*Dermochelys coriacea*), hawksbill (*Eretmochelys imbricate*), olive ridley (*Lepidochelys olivacea*), loggerhead (*Caretta caretta*) and Kemp's ridley (*Lepidochelys kempii*). Formia, A, Tiwari, M, Fretey, J. and Billes, A. 2003. Sea Turtle Conservation along the Atlantic Coast of Africa, Marine Turtle Newsletter 100, 2003, p. 33-37. Available at: http://www.seaturtle.org/mtn/archives/mtn100/mtn100p33.shtml, accessed 20 June 2014.

long-term field projects and enforcing national legislation, or by shifting pressure on natural resources.[57] Marine ecosystems have also been affected by pollution from the many ships that have been damaged and sunk in the harbour. Furthermore, many ships are believed to fly under a Liberian "flag of convenience" (i.e., they are registered in Liberia for financial reasons). Some of these ships do not comply with international standards on the discharge of waste products, and have been associated with serious environmental pollution in the past.

Another problem is the extent of landmines and unexploded ordinance (UXO) littering parts of the country. In 1995, it was estimated that there were seven minefields in the country, containing a total of some 18,250 mines.[58] Many of these have since been removed, although information is lacking on the exact number of landmines removed and the location of de-mining operations. Also, there is no systematic collection of data on landmine casualties. Human casualties continue to be a problem. There is no mine/UXO risk awareness education being conducted. There is only one prosthetic workshop in the country, the other one having been destroyed in fighting in 2003, and access to healthcare for those injured by UXO is extremely limited. Only one-tenth Liberians have access to any formal health care.[59]

## VI. Mozambique

Mozambique, with a land area of 799,000 sq km and a population of 16.1 million, has experienced a turbulent history. It has faced several centuries of Portuguese administration, a long war of independence, an abrupt transition to independence in 1975 followed by a short period of post-independence stability till 1980. An armed conflict between the Mozambique Liberation Front (FRELIMO) and the National Resistance Movement (RENAMO) from 1980 to 1992, affected most of the country.

---

57 Formia, A., Tiwari, M., Fretey, J. and Billes, A., Sea Turtle Conservation along the Atlantic Coast of Africa, *Marine Turtle Newsletter 100*, 2003, p. 33-37.

58 *Human Rights Watch World Report 2004: Human Rights and Armed Conflict*. Human Rights Watch (HRW), New York. Available at: http://www.hrw.org/wr2k4/download/wr2k4.pdf, accessed 12 June 2014.

59 In 2003, two children were killed and another three injured when an anti-vehicle mine found in a swamp exploded after they tried to open it. In 2004, UXO that detonated in an agricultural field killed one person; a boy was injured in the capital city while playing with a hand grenade, and six people were injured in a UXO explosion in Monrovia. *Human Rights Watch World Report 2004: Human Rights and Armed Conflict*. Human Rights Watch (HRW), New York.

It resulted on the displacement of 50 per cent of the rural population, development stalled, and a breakdown of natural resource management occurred in much of the country. The two opposing forces, FRELIMO and RENAMO finally signed a peace accord in Rome in October 1992. The large-scale intervention by the United Nations peace-keeping force in Mozambique (UNOMOZ) contributed to the maintenance of peace and the holding of Mozambique's first democratic elections in October 1994. A critical feature of the UN intervention was the successful demobilization of the armed forces of both parties.

## Environmental Damage

The 12-year armed conflict between FRELIMO and RENAMO impacted the lives of all Mozambicans in one way or another. It is estimated that at least 50 per cent of the rural population was displaced during the war (either internally or as refugees in neighboring countries), economic development was stalled and Mozambique was registered as one of the poorest nations of the developing world. The natural resource base of the country was severely affected during the armed conflict. The wildlife resources, especially large mammal species, were decimated in many areas inside and outside protected areas. Hunting for meat and trophies was particularly severe in areas where troops were stationed for long periods of time e.g., the Northern Sofala Province including the Gorongosa National Park and the Zambezi Delta.

South African and Zimbabwean troops (supporting RENAMO and FRELIMO respectively) contributed to the decline in large mammal species. They hunted for, and exported, wildlife trophies including ivory and rhinoceros horn. Infrastructure within the protected areas was largely destroyed. The natural resource base in peri-urban areas and areas adjacent to guarded transport corridors also came under heavy pressure due to the large influx of displaced persons. This resulted in a dramatic impact on the local natural resource base through hunting, and cutting of woody vegetation for firewood and shelter. The immediate post-war period was followed by largely uncontrolled and illegal harvesting of wildlife and forestry resources that accompanied the de-mining process and the rehabilitation of roads and bridges in the absence of adequate enforcement.

Following independence, most trained Portuguese nationals left Mozambique and capacity across all sectors, including the forestry and wildlife was critically weak. During the ensuing armed conflict, management of natural resources broke down in many areas inside and outside the protected areas, where local communities were forced to flee, protected areas were abandoned, and government controls ceased. Wildlife populations in most protected areas were drastically reduced during the armed conflict.

## VII. Rwanda

Rwanda is one of the smallest countries in Africa.[60] Its high soil fertility, due to rich volcanic soils, has lead to the highest population density on the African continent, with up to 500–700 people per square kilometer.[61] Over 90 per cent of the population, out of an estimated 10.2 million, relies on subsistence agriculture, which puts great pressure on the country's natural ecosystems, whether forested, savanna, or wetland.

By the mid-1950s, Rwanda had established two national parks and several forest reserves for either complete protection or sustainable management. A large portion of these areas was converted to agricultural land over time, but more than 10 per cent of the country was under some form of protection. During the mid-1970s, gorilla research and gorilla tourism started to bring Rwanda into the international spotlight and, by the end of the 1980s, gorilla tourism was a major source of foreign currency for the government, second only to coffee and tea exports. [62] During this time, Rwanda was a major recipient of foreign aid and was considered to be one of the model countries by the development community. However, a growing political divide between factions representing the northwest and the rest of the country soon led to destabilization. During the late 1980s and early 1990s, external aid began to dwindle with donors demanding

60 Rwanda is a small country having an area of 26,338 sq km, with a relatively large population (10.2 million) and high rate of population growth. A central plateau at elevation between 1,400 and 2,200 meters dominates the country. It rises to the west, towards Congo, to heights of over 3,500 meters, and falls in elevation towards Tanzania in the east. The north-western part, between the towns of Gisenyi and Ruhengeri, is the most famous for its five volcanoes. Brauer Jurgen. 2011. *War and Nature: The Environmental Consequences of War in a Globalized World*, London: AltaMira Press, p. 122-123.

61 Olson, J.M., et. al., 1995. Exploring methods for integrating data on socioeconomic and environmental processes that influence land use change: A pilot project, Report to Biodiversity Support Program, Michigan: Michigan State University.

62 Vedder, A., and A.W. Weber. 1990. The mountain gorilla project. In A. Kiss (ed.), *Living with Wildlife: Wildlife Resource Management with Local Participation*, World Bank Technical Publication 130:83–90, Washington, D.C.

economic reforms and a transition to greater democracy. This reduction in aid probably helped to increase the instability in the country. In October 1990, a civil war began that eventually led to genocide in 1994.[63]

Hundreds of thousands of people were killed in the civil war. Two million people were uprooted within Rwanda and another two million fled south to Burundi, Tanzania and Zaire.[64] Most of these refugees settled in and around protected areas of great conservation value. The Volcanoes National Park in the west and the Akagera National Park in the east; the Nyungwe Forest Reserve, and the Gishwati and Mukura Forest Reserves suffered severely as a result.

The Volcanoes National Park encompasses about 425 square kilometers of forest and shares borders with Uganda and the DRC. Rwanda and the DRC are separated by Lake Kivu. The Karisoke Research Station was established in this Park with support from the African Wildlife Foundation (AWF), Fauna and Flora International (FFI) and the World Wildlife Fund (WWF) for the study of mountain gorillas (*Gorilla gorilla beringei*).

When the armed conflict started, the entire Virunga area was deemed unsafe. Both the Rwandan Patriotic Force (RPF) and the Rwandan Armed Forces (RAF) had laid anti-personnel landmines inside and along the perimeter of the Rwandan portion of the Park. However, the park staff continued to patrol in the western section of the park. In 1991, the RAF cut a swathe of vegetation about ten meters wide through the forest to allow them to patrol and prevent any RPF soldiers from moving into the western half of the park.[65] Occasionally, the RAF fired mortars into the forest at the RPF.

---

63   Andrew J. Plumptre, Michel Masozera, and Amy Vedder. 2001. *The Impact of Civil War on the Conservation of Protected Areas in Rwanda*, Washington, D.C.: Biodiversity Support Program. Available at: http://www.worldwildlife.org/bsp/publications/africa/145/pdf/Rwanda.pdf, accessed 14 May 2014.

64   Berry, JA, and CP Berry. 1999. *Genocide in Rwanda: A Collective Memory*, Washington, D.C.: Harvard University Press.

65   Habitat destruction and the accompanying loss of wildlife are among the most common and far-reaching impacts of conflict on the environment, and occur for subsistence, strategic, or commercial reasons. Habitats are sometimes directly affected during armed conflict. For example, vegetation may be cut, burned, or defoliated to improve mobility or visibility for troops. In Rwanda in 1991, the Rwandan army cut a swath 50 to 100 meters wide through the bamboo forest connecting the Virunga Volcanoes in order to reduce the possibility of ambush along a key trail. Kalpers, J. 2001b. Overview of Armed Conflict and Biodiversity in Sub-Saharan Africa: Impacts,Mechanisms, and Responses. Washington, DC, USA: Biodiversity Support Program.

The international and national researchers working in the forest were evacuated several times during 1990-1994, when the security situation deteriorated. At the start of the mass killings in 1994, the director was evacuated to DRC. Most of the park infrastructure was destroyed and buildings were looted. Many refugees from Rwanda were settled close to the Congolese portion of the Virunga Park, leading to the clearing of a large area of forest for firewood.[66] The refugees harvested firewood and poached animals for bushmeat. After the conflict, the Interahamwe,[67] attacked the returning park staff killing several of them.[68] Elephants were reported to have moved from the Rwandan to the Congolose part of the Virunga. It is believed fifteen gorillas were killed as direct consequence of the armed conflict.[69]

The Akagera National Park in the east of Rwanda lies adjacent to the Tanzanian border. It comprised 2,500 square kilometers of savanna woodland, grassland, and wetlands and was extremely rich in large

---

66 Refugee settlements in forests areas can dramatically lead to accelerated conversion of forest to agricultural land, collection of firewood, extraction of surface and ground waters, fishing and hunting. At the same time, the assimilative capacity of environments can be stretched by the additional wastes produced, and this can exacerbate threats to human health. There is evidence that rapid increase in refugee population, places additional stresses on local resources. For example, it is rare for refugees to be provided with construction materials or fuel for cooking, and these resources will often by necessity be collected from local environments. Martin Adrian, Environmental Conflict between Refugee and Host Communities, Vol. 42, No. 3, *Journal of Peace Research*, May 2005, p. 329-346; Also see: Biswas, A.K., and H.C. Tortajada-Quiroz, Environmental impacts of the Rwandan refugees on Zaire, Vol. 25, *Ambio*, (1996), p. 403–408.

67 Organization that was engaged to overthrow the government dominated by Tutsi (Syn: Army for the Liberation of Rwanda).

68 At least 80 of Virunga's park staff have been killed by insurgents. McNeely, J. A. 2002. Overview: Biodiversity, Conflict and Tropical Forests, in Matthew, R., Halle, M., and Switzer, J.(eds.), *Conserving the Peace: Resources, Livelihoods, and Security*, International Institute for Sustainable Development / IUCN – The World Conservation Union, p. 31-55. Available at: http://www.iisd.org/pdf/2002/envsec_conserving_peace. pdf, accessed 20 June 2014.

69 Brauer Jurgen. 2011. War and Nature: The Environmental Consequences of War in a Globalized World, London: AltaMira Press, p. 126. In the Virunga and Volcano National Parks of DRC and Rwanda, infant gorillas were captured for sale, and adult males killed so that their skulls can be sold as souvenirs to tourists. Adults may also be killed in order to gain access to the infants. An infant reportedly fetched as much as £86,000 on the black market. In addition, there were reports that few gorillas were killed and partly eaten by Rwandan militia in the Rwandan side of the Virungas (Volcans National Park). *Report on the status and conservation of the Mountain Gorilla (Gorilla gorilla beringei)*, UNEP World Conservation Monitoring Centre, October 2003, p. 5-6.

mammals, and important for the conservation of the Sitatunga (*Tragelaphus spekei*) and Roan (*Hippotragus equinus*) antelope. In addition, it was home to an extraordinary variety of birds. During the initial invasion in early 1990, this park was invaded by the RPF, but they were driven back to Uganda by the army with support from the Congolese (then-Zairean) army. However, between 1990-1993, military personnel actively hunted and killed animals in the park for survival.[70]

Following the genocide in 1994 and the change of government, official policy allowed many of the returning Tutsis to occupy a major sector of the park. They cleared a large forested area for cattle grazing and in 1998, the park's boundaries were redrawn to less than one-third of its original size. The heavy hunting during the war and the loss of critical habitat resulted in a large reduction in number of large mammals (buffalo, impala, topi, warthog, reedbuck, oribi, and zebra).[71] It is estimated that the reduction in size of the Park led to a loss of 15 per cent of tree and shrub species, 20 per cent of herbaceous species, and about 13 per cent of bird species from the park. [72]

The Nyungwe Forest Reserve, in southwest Rwanda, is spread over 970 sq km of mountainous terrain. It protects one of the largest remaining afromontane forests[73] in Africa. It was administered in four management zones, in accordance with the financial support from external agencies: French, Swiss, European Development Fund, and World Bank.   The Nyungwe forest conservation project, supported by the Wildlife Conservation Society (WCS), was established in 1987 to start a tourism, research, and monitoring program in the nature reserve. The reserve contained many endemic bird species and two regional endemic primates.

---

70  Kanyamibwa, S, Impact of war on conservation: Rwandan environment and wildlife in agony, Vol. 7, *Biodiversity and Conservation*, (1998), p. 1399–1406.

71  Andrew J. Plumptre, Michel Masozera, and Amy Vedder. 2001. *The Impact of Civil War on the Conservation of Protected Areas in Rwanda*, Washington DC: Biodiversity Support Programme, p. 17.

72  Nyilimanzi, V., et. al., 'Clarification of the resumption of support to Akagera National Park', Mission Report to GTZ, 1997, Kigali, Rwanda.

73  Afromontane is a term used to describe the Afrotropic sub-region and its plant and animal species common to the mountains of Africa and the southern Arabian Peninsula. The Afromontane regions of Africa are discontinuous, separated from each other by lowlands, and are sometimes referred to as the Afromontane archipelago, as their distribution is analogous to a series of Sky Island. Although some Afromontane enclaves are widely separated, they share a similar mix of plant species which are often distinct from the surrounding lowland regions.

This forest was less affected by the war, because there was no instability in this region. During the most intense period of the conflict in 1994, this forest was held by the French and witnessed less fighting and destruction. However, the senior staff left Rwanda, leaving the junior staff to manage the project. The chief warden was later murdered and for five months the junior staff carried on working despite receiving no salary. The internationally funded projects in the four management zones were terminated and never resumed after the genocide.

In 1995 and 1996, the Rwandan Patriotic Army (PRA) prevented the local population from entering the forest, as there were suspected pockets of resistance hiding therein, particularly near the Burundi border. Senior staff was appointed and was able to continue operating with security provided by the RPA. By 1998, calm had been restored and the RPA presence was reduced. However, the calm brought increased pressures on natural resources from local communities and the threats to the reserve increased while the government was being rebuilt and there was little law enforcement capability on the ground. This resulted in a very high level of poaching and unregulated agricultural encroachment. A large numbers of traps were set regularly, and the number of ungulates (e.g., duikers), porcupines (*Atherurus africanus*) and Gambian rats (*Cricetomys gambianus*) were reduced drastically. It is believed that the last elephant in Nyungwe was killed by poachers in 1999 for ivory.[74]

The Gishwati Forest Reserve initially spreadover approximately 280 square kilometers and contained populations of chimpanzees (*Pan troglodytes*) and golden monkeys (*Cercopithecus mitis kandti*). It was heavily affected by cattle grazing and other human activities even before the civil war. The World Bank supported an integrated forestry and livestock project that converted 100 square kilometers to pasture and another 100 square kilometers to pine plantations in the early 1980s. A 30-square kilometer area was designated as a military zone in the north of the forest, leaving only 50 square kilometers of natural forest. During and following the war, the northern part of Gishwati was used for camps for displaced persons, which grew rapidly. People settled and farmed within the reserve, and during 1997 and 1998, the forest was also used as a hideout by many of the

---

74 Though the likely effect of the absence of large mammals on the forest is unknown, recent experiments in Kenya have shown that exclusion of large herbivores can induce changes in vegetation and in insect-plant mutualism. Brauer Jurgen. 2011. *War and Nature: The Environmental Consequences of War in a Globalized World*, London: AltaMira Press, p. 124.

Interahamwe, and numerous military operations took place in the forest in an attempt to remove them. As a result of the heightened military presence in the region, the local people often fled their homes and shifted to more stable areas, thus creating further pressures on land and forest degradation. The Mukura Reserve comprised only about 20 square kilometers of forest. This too was severely degraded, and now only eight sq km of the reserve contains a few trees.

## VII. Sierra Leone

Sierra Leone,[75] a former British protectorate and colony, became an independent nation in 1961. Since then it has experienced five coups, decades of single-party rule and a ten-year civil war until 2002. Inequitable benefits-sharing of natural resource wealth was one of the drivers of the civil war that ravaged the country from 1991 to 2002.[76] The conflict

---

75 Located on the western coast of Africa, Sierra Leone covers a land area of 71,325 sq km, of which approximately 120 sq km is water, is one of the smallest countries in coastal West Africa. It is bordered to the southwest by the Atlantic Ocean, with Liberia situated to the southeast and Guinea to the north and northeast. It is divided into four provinces: Northern, Southern, Eastern and West (Western Area Peninsula), and 14 administrative districts. The country is also disaggregated into 149 traditional local chiefdoms, each presided over by a paramount chief. The capital is Freetown, which is located adjacent to the one of the largest natural harbours in the world. Other large cities include Makeni, Kenema, Koidu and Bo, which are all inland. Sierra Leone's relatively small area is endowed, however, with natural riches that include mineral resources and biodiversity. The natural vegetation includes lowland moist and semi-deciduous forests, which constitute the westernmost extent of West Africa's Upper Guinea ecosystem, as well as inland valley swamps, bolilands and wooded savannah. Ten major rivers form the drainage systems, flowing southwest and roughly parallel, from the northern uplands to the extensive mangrove swamps along the coast. The wildlife is typical of the Upper Guinea ecosystem with a few locally endemic species, but with numerous species that find their westernmost range in Sierra Leone. Chris B. Squire. 2001. *Sierra Leone's Biodiversity and the Civil War*; A Case Study Prepared for the Biodiversity Support Programme, Washington DC: Biodiversity Support Programme, p. 9.

76 Britain carved out the country that became Sierra Leone (Declaration of the Protectorate, 1896) during the former's empire building era. Pre- and post-independence policies in areas such as education, economics, culture, politics and religion were characterized by inequity and maximization of profits from exploitation. Throughout Sierra Leone's history, the inequities on which the country was founded have never been acceptable to the silent majority, feeding societal tensions and setting the stage for eventual armed conflict. Independent Sierra Leone's first military coup took place in 1967, followed by a countercoup a few days later. A third coup took place in 1968. The country was declared a republic in 1971 and a one-party state in 1978. Chris B. Squire. 2001. *Sierra Leone's Biodiversity and the Civil War*; A Case Study Prepared for the Biodiversity Support Program. Washington, D.C.: Biodiversity Support Programme, p.17.

which outlived five governments, caused the internal displacement of huge sections of the population, paralyzed the economy, and rendered the country ungovernable, with a consequent breakdown in law and order. The state of destabilization has taken its toll on conservation efforts and on biodiversity. The official cessation of conflict in 2002 brought to a close a period of intense damage to the environment, however, restoration, if at all possible will be an arduous task.

At the start of the conflict, the Revolutionary United Front (RUF)[77] behaved like insurgents, moving weapons along roads and seeking to hold terrain and towns. They were easily driven back into the forest, first by the National Provisional Ruling Council (NPRC) in 1993, and subsequently by the Civil Defence Forces (CDF) from 1995. According to the movement's own account, the leadership was sequestered behind the Gola North Forest Reserve in Nomo Chiefdom, on the border with Liberia, contemplating withdrawal into Liberia.[78] Isolated, the RUF then adopted a new military strategy;[79] which meant living permanently living in the forest reserves. The armed conflict caused both, the direct and indirect impact on the environment in Sierra Leone.[80]

---

77  Abdullah, I., and P. K. Muana, 'The Revolutionary United Front of Sierra Leone (RUF/ SL)'; in C. Clapham (ed.), *African Guerrillas*, 1998, Oxford: James Curry.

78  Davies, A.G. 1987. *The Gola Forest Reserves, Sierra Leone: Wildlife Conservation and Forest Management*, Gland, Switzerland: IUCN.

79  The RUF abandoned the heavy weapons and vehicles, and built camps in the thick forest. Then they embarked on infiltration and pinprick attacks mounted via the numerous forest trails that crisscross the country. Along these trails, small bands of RUF were safe from a motorized enemy at most times without maps. A wedge was driven between civilians and the NPRC government and the army through trickery, such as RUF cadres carrying out attacks dressed in military fatigues, or scattering army identity cards/passes to give the impression that the destruction was the work of government troops. The RUF had 14 bases within natural reserves. As an extension of their forest war strategy, the RUF started abducting large numbers of civilians. The total number of persons living with the RUF in the various forest camps was more than 50,000 at the peak of the campaign. Abdullah, I., and P. K. Muana, 'The Revolutionary United Front of Sierra Leone (RUF/SL)'; In C. Clapham (ed.), *African Guerrillas*, 1998, Oxford: James Curry.

80  The environmental impacts of the conflict are of three main types: direct, indirect and institutional. Direct impacts are those with highly visible environmental consequences, such as the destruction of ecosystems or water supplies as a result of fighting. Indirect impacts, such as those caused by coping and survival strategies, often occur over a longer period, with the effects manifesting more severely over time. And third, institutional impacts, which are comprised of the governance and management changes that occur during the time of conflict, make dealing with direct and indirect impacts much more difficult in both the short and long run. *Sierra Leone: Environment, Conflict*

The RUF repeatedly targeted water stoarge tanks, wells and other water-related infrastructure, which led to further deterioration of an already poor water access situation. The acute water shortages, particularly in the dry season, inhibited activities during the recovery process. A lack of waste management capacity caused surface water degradation and damage to coastal areas. Subsistence agriculture has been the most prominent livelihood in Sierra Leone. The conflict impacted agriculture directly as well as indirectly. Direct damage was caused by rebel fighters as they sacked towns and villages, and by the fact that most displaced owners abandoned their plots for several seasons or years. Forests were damaged by the activities of the RUF, the Sierra Leone Army and government-affiliated militias and mercenaries. The rebels often destroyed crops and vegetation in a senseless manner.[81]

During the conflict, the RUF and other combatants increased the intensity of illicit artisanal diamond mining to support their operations. An estimated annual amount of between US$ 25 million and US$ 125 million in diamonds left the country each year during the war.[82] The mining sites that were expanded were not rehabilitated in any way, leaving effluent, degraded sites and lost arable land. The mining also caused a great damage to the agricultural sector, in terms of reduced flows of natural capital and a heavily degraded environment. The use of diamond revenues[83] to fuel

---

and Peace-building Assessment, Technical Report, United Nations Environment Programme, 2010, p. 44.

81 In Sierra Leone, forests were also a refuge. During the armed conflict, entire communities escaped to the forests, sometimes living there for years. Today, many of these same communities have become dependent on forest resources to survive, including protected forests where people plant, poach, dig rock quarries and cut down timber. As population pressures mount, the lure of protected areas will only grow, putting a range of ecosystem services in jeopardy. Sierra Leone: Environment, Conflict and Peace-building Assessment, Technical Report, United Nations Environment Programme, 2010, p.62.

82 OT Africa Line (2009), Freetown port information report – Port infrastructure. Available at: http://www.otal.com/sierra/#infra, accessed 12 January 2014; Also see: Fithen, C. 1999. Diamonds and war in Sierra Leone: Cultural strategies for commercial adaptation, Unpublished Ph D dissertation, Department of Anthropology, University College, London.

83 Hollywood film Blood Diamond has dramatized the role diamonds played during the civil war that raged in the country from 1991 to 2002 (diamonds both financed and fuelled the conflict). In some ways, the attention drawn to the issue of conflict diamonds by the movie has been beneficial, especially in that it has raised public awareness of the accomplishments of and gaps in the Kimberley Process, which seeks to reduce the number of conflict diamonds in the world market. The Kimberley Process began in May 2000 when the government of South Africa brought together industry,

civil war has ceased, but the environmental and socioeconomic effects of 75 years of artisanal diamond mining remain. Vast expanses of land have been stripped of topsoil, churned up, and abandoned, leaving the land barren and useless. This unproductive land represents a significant loss of potentially valuable agricultural production and livelihoods.

The indirect impacts of armed conflict on the environment and natural resource base are frequently more significant and longer lasting than acute direct impacts. In Sierra Leone, the most visible indirect impact has been the environmental consequences of large-scale displacement during the conflict. More than half the population was forced to move,[84] both internally within Sierra Leone and across its borders, into Guinea and Liberia. Internal migration sped up the process of urbanization, particularly in Freetown, as the people who came in search of a stable situation during the 1990s subsequently decided to settle. The lack of alternative employment opportunity forced both rural and urban populations to over-exploit forest resources, farm land and the small rivers and bays, particularly in the coastal areas.

Neither the local communities nor the government fully realized the true value of natural resource products. For example, extremely valuable hardwood trees were illegally felled and discarded or burned for fuel in Kenema District in order to make room for small-scale subsistence agriculture.[85] The armed conflict also affected the tourism sector. The loss of the tourist trade due to instability incentivized the quick liquidation

NGOs, and governments to discuss the problem of conflict diamonds. The outcome was the Kimberley Process Certification Scheme, which officially went into effect in January 2003. Despite shortcomings in the area of enforcement mechanisms and independent monitoring, the Kimberley Process has been credited with bringing the number of conflict diamonds in the world market down from a high of 15 per cent to the current level of less than 1 per cent. The Foundation for Environmental Security and Sustainability (FESS), USAID, June 2007.

84 During the period of September to November 1999 high internal displacement took place with total numbers reaching 459,430, 605,851, and 592,523 respectively for these three months. In camps, IDPs were normally supplied with rations of rice/bulgur, fish, and oil. Other cooking materials had to be provided by the IDPs. In particular, fuel wood for cooking was harvested from nearby vegetation. Such harvesting was in addition to the demands of the original residents of such towns. It would therefore be reasonable to assume that the consumption of tree species normally used for firewood in these localities would have increased manifolds. Chris B. Squire. 2001. *Sierra Leone's Biodiversity and the Civil War*: A Case Study Prepared for the Biodiversity Support Programme, Washington DC: Biodiversity Support Programme, p. 19-22.

85 *Sierra Leone: Environment, Conflict and Peace-building Assessment*, Technical Report, United Nations Environment Programme, 2010, p. 47.

of natural capital for small gains, such as beach sand mining for urban buildings, or cutting down forests and mangroves near the water. While these activities generated short-term benefits, long-term opportunities for profitable and sustainable tourism were severely affected.

Before the civil war, a number of NGOs were actively involved in environmental education, restoration of degraded lands, biodiversity monitoring, environmental sanitation, and natural resource management. During the war these organizations suffered many setbacks, including the destruction of project infrastructures, carting away of working implements, and the occupation of project sites by combatants. As a result, most of the projects undertaken by these institutions collapsed. The projects located away from combat areas and IDPs did survive. However, even these projects encountered problems like indiscriminate cutting of trees for fuelwood, construction, and medicinal herb collection. The civil war occasioned accelerated breakdown in law and order in the large sections of the country that were under RUF control.[86] Forest reserves that should have been protected were indiscriminately exploited, sometimes with connivance from the people whose duty it was to protect them.

A large number of combatants and of abducted and fleeing civilians had to live off the forest for prolonged periods throughout the conflict period. Combatants as well as civilians indulged in wide-scale mining, often inside reserves, with potentially disastrous consequences for biodiversity. Both the government army and civil defence forces spent prolonged periods in forest reserves and resorted to bush hunting for subsistence.

Negative impacts on biodiversity[87] resulted from various degrees of breakdown in law and order in Sierra Leone predate the civil war. Two consequences of this breakdown have significant negative impacts:

---

86  Chris B. Squire. 2001. *Sierra Leone's Biodiversity and the Civil War*: A Case Study Prepared for the Biodiversity Support Programme, Washington: Biodiversity Support Programme, p. 29.

87  The loss of biodiversity in Sierra Leone has been a major concern since the early 1960s. The threat is manifested by various negative impacts: (i) Loss of unique habitats for wildlife within ecosystems. The loss of biodiversity in a country runs parallel with the loss of such "specialized" habitats, which are destroyed as the vegetation is removed; (ii) Loss of genetic resources and wild types for improving biotechnology; tissue culture, crossbreeding, genetic engineering, and pest control; and (iii) Loss of plant resources with medicinal potential to combat diseases and improve human livelihoods. Chris B. Squire. 2001. *Sierra Leone's Biodiversity and the Civil War*: A Case Study Prepared for the Biodiversity Support Programme, Washington DC: Biodiversity Support Programme, p. 9.

increased illicit diamond mining activities[88] and encroachment on forest reserves. Illegal logging and other activities in forest reserves, occasioned by a breakdown in law and order, have been another source of serious potential negative impact on biodiversity. The breakdown in law and order during the war years led to serious encroachments on the Western Area Peninsula Forest (WAPF) reserve.[89] A stone mining company was also responsible for massive deforestation of reserve. Indiscriminate logging at the No. 2 River reserve has threatened a native bird, white-necked Picathartes or Rockfowl (*Picathartes geymnocephalus*), in the reserve. Instances of illegal logging was during the armed conflict was reported throughout the country. The officers, whose duty was to protect the reserve, also connived at times with loggers and local community residents in illegal encroachment on the reserves.

## IX. Sudan

The long civil war in Sudan (1962-1972; 1983-2002) has directly affected over 60 per cent of the country and greatly influenced its development. The war was a highly complex conflicts, the main one being the long-standing war in South Sudan that encompassed the Nuba Mountains, southern Blue Nile, eastern Sudan and Darfur over time.[90] Although the government

---

88 Diamonds were first found in Sierra Leone in the 1930s with the main deposits in the high forest zones and alluvium and river terraces in the south and the east. The Siaka Stevens All Peoples Congress (APC) regime (1968 to 1985) built its power through taking control of small-scale diamond mining operations in Kono. As part of his plan to control Kono diamonds, Stevens uprooted the old colonial government railway line through the south and the east (the axis on which many of the main provincial secondary schools lay and also the axis of power for the rival Sierra Leone People's Party, (SLPP)) and replaced it with a main road leading directly to Kono through the Northern provincial centers of Makeni and Magburaka. This helped to secure more control of the Kono alluvials for the northern dominated APC elites. Reno, W. 1995. *Warlord Politics and African States*, Boulder, Co.

89 The Western Area Peninsula Forest (WAPF) is located on the hills of the Freetown Peninsula. The total reserve is 17,688 hectares consisting of a narrow chain of hills about 37 km long and 14 km wide; the highest peak rises about 900 meters. The hills are covered with moist forest and they form the westernmost closed canopy forest remaining in Sierra Leone. Teleki, G. 1980. Hunting and trapping wildlife in Sierra Leone: aspects of exploitation and exportation, Special Report to the Ministry of Agriculture and Forestry, Freetown, Sierra Leone. Also see: McNeely Jeffery A. 2000. 'War and Biodiversity: An Assessment of Impacts, In Austin, Jay E., and Bruch, Carl E., (ed.), *The Environmental Consequences of War: Legal, Economic and Scientific Perspectives*, Cambridge: Cambridge University Press, p. 355.

90 The armed conflict in Sudan could be divided into small-scale and large-scale. Tribal and small-scale conflicts fought only with small arms have occurred continuously

forces' weaponry included tanks and heavy artillery, most military confrontations were fought mainly with light weapons such as AK47 assault rifles. The opposition forces generally used light weaponry, with a small number of tanks and other heavy weapons. Only the government forces had airpower. Landmines were used widely in most major conflicts. Minefields were abandoned without marking or extraction and are mostly unmapped. As a result, Sudan now suffers from a severe landmine legacy which continues to cause civilian casualties.

Fighting in Darfur was characterized by a 'scorched earth' campaign carried out by militias over large areas, resulting in a significant number of civilian deaths, the widespread destruction of villages and forests, and the displacement of victims into camps for protection, food and water. Over two million people were displaced, and the casualties are estimated by a range of sources to be between 200,000 and 500,000. There were reports that drinking water wells had been poisoned in Darfur.

In 2007, the UNEP produced its first comprehensive analysis of the potential link between conflict and the environment, focusing on Sudan. According to this report:

The linkage between conflict and environment in Sudan are twofold. On the one hand, the country's long history has had a significant impact on its environment....On the other hand, environmental issues have been and continue to be contributing causes of conflict. Competition over oil and gas reserves, Nile water and timber, as well as land use issues related to agricultural land, are important causative factors in the instigation and perpetuation of conflict in Sudan. Confrontations over rangeland and rain-fed agricultural land in the drier parts of the country are a particularly striking manifestation of the connection between natural resource scarcity and violent conflict. In all cases, however, environmental factors are intertwined with a range of other social, political and economic issues.[91]

The prolonged civil war caused significant indirect impacts on the

---

throughout the history of Sudan. No part of the country has been exempt from such clashes, but they have been concentrated in the south, west and east of the country for the last thirty years. Their causes include disputes over cattle theft, access to water and grazing, and local politics. Most of the large-scale conflicts in Sudan have a connection to tribal friction. *Sudan: Post-Conflict Environmental Assessment*, 2007, United Nations Environment Programme (UNEP), p.73. The US-backed accords brought a halt to half a century of intermittent civil war between north and south Sudan. South Sudan formally declared its independence on 9 July 2011.

91 *Sudan: Post-Conflict Environment Assessment*, UNEP, 2007, p. 8.

environment. The most severe environmental consequences have been caused by the displacement of an estimated five million people. Darfur, with some 2.4 million displaced, may be the most environmentally significant displacement case in the world today due to its fragile dryland conditions. Looting of natural resources in conflict zones by all sides was widespread, the most significant being the extraction of high-value timber in the south and fuel-wood for charcoal in the Nuba Mountains. Ivory poaching decimated elephant and rhinoceros populations in southern Sudan were depleted due to hunting by the warring parties. Environmental governance collapsed not only in active conflict zones but nationwide and both the military as well as civilians took advantage of the opportunity to act with environmental impunity. The conflict also meant that most of the country was inaccessible for scientific data collection, further limiting rational decision-making for resource management and conservation. Finally, the war economy created a funding crisis as provisions for sustainable environmental management practically did not figure in the government's fiscal budget.

Four categories of natural resources were particularly linked to the conflict: (i) oil and gas reserves; (ii) Nile waters; (iii) hardwood timber; and (iv) rangeland, rain-fed agricultural land and associated water points. The revenue from hardwood timber sales helped sustain the north-south civil war. The direct impacts of the conflict include: (i) landmines and explosive remnants of war (ERW); (ii) defensive works; and (iii) targeted natural resource destruction. The indirect and secondary impacts of the conflict include: (i) environmental impacts related to population displacement; (ii) natural resource looting and war economy resource extraction; (iii) environmental governance and information vacuum; and (iv) funding crises, arrested development and conservation programmes.

Landmines and other explosive remnants of war are a major problem in Sudan. Thirty-two per cent of the country is estimated to be affected, with the greatest concentration in Southern Sudan.[92] As many as twenty-one of the country's twenty-five states may be impacted, although the true extent of Sudan's landmine problem remains unknown, as a comprehensive

---

92 The potential impacts of landmines and ERW can be divided into chemical and physical categories. Conventional explosives, such as TNT and RDX, found in artillery shells and mines are highly toxic and slow to degrade. While they present an acute toxic hazard if ingested, the toxic risk is considered insignificant compared to the risk of injury from explosion. *Sudan: Post-Conflict Environment Assessment*, UNEP, 2007, p. 89.

survey of the issue has not been undertaken to date. Though no systematic data collection and verification mechanism exists, the reported and registered number of landmine casualties from the year 2000 to 2005 totals 2,200. There is also no data on animal casualties from mines, but these are expected to be much higher than the human casualty rate.[93] Apart from human casualties, another major impact of landmines is impeded access to large areas for people and their livestock. In Sudan, access to some areas has been reduced for decades, as they have remained mined or suspected as such since the beginning of the conflict.

After civilian deaths and injuries, the most significant effect of the conflict on the population of Sudan has been displacement. An estimated five million people (7 to 12 per cent of the estimated total population of Sudan) were displaced. The great majority of the displaced came from rural areas and migrated to camps on the outskirts of towns and cities. Over two million have relocated to the capital city, Khartoum. The severe and complex environmental consequences of displacement include: (i) deforestation and de-vegetation; (ii) unsustainable groundwater extraction; (iii) water pollution; (iv) uncontrolled urban slum growth; (v) the development of a 'relief economy' which can locally exacerbate demand for natural resources; (vi) invasive weed expansion; and (vii) return- and recovery-related deforestation. However, not all displacement in Sudan is due to armed conflict. Displacement-related environmental issues are widespread and often highly visible in major camps, settlements, urban slums and return areas. Land degradation in camp areas was caused by overharvesting of seasonal fodder and shrubs by camp residents and their livestock (commonly goats).[94]

The countries neighbouring Sudan hosted some 700,000 Sudanese refugees. In addition to a range of chronic environmental problems, these countries suffer from the impact of numerous large camps. Refugees from Darfur in north-eastern Chad, for example, remained a considerable burden to their host communities due to their sheer number (400,000 people). Since their arrival in 2003, pressure was mounted significantly on scarce natural resources such as water, fuel-wood and fodder for livestock, access to which has often been a source of conflict in the region.[95]

---

93  *Sudan: Post-Conflict Environment Assessment*, UNEP, 2007.

94  Ibid, p. 105.

95  For example, Uduk refugees from the Upper Nile province now living in Gambella refugee camp in western Ethiopia have, in the thirteen years since the camp was

There is a large volume of literature on the wildlife of Sudan as recorded by casual observers who travelled through or lived in Sudan during the 19th and first half of the 20th centuries. A 1940s account, for instance, describes large populations of elephant, giraffe, giant eland, and both white and black rhino across a wide belt of Southern Sudan. As late as 1970, Sudan boasted some of the most unspoilt and isolated wilderness in east Africa, and its wildlife populations were world-renowned. The past few decades have witnessed a major assault on both wildlife and their habitats. In the north, the greatest damage has been inflicted by habitat degradation, while in the south, it is uncontrolled hunting that has decimated wildlife populations. Because of the civil war, however, few scientific studies of Sudan's wildlife have been conducted, and coverage of the south has always been very limited. Sudan harbours a number of globally important and endangered species of mammals, birds, reptiles and plants, as well as endemic species. In addition, there are a number of species listed as vulnerable by IUCN, including 16 species of mammals, birds and reptiles. The list includes: hippopotamus (*Hippopotamus amphibius*); cheetah (*Acinonyx jubatus*); African lion (*Panthera leo*); Barbary sheep (*Ammotragus lervia*); Dorcas gazelle (*Gazella dorcas*); red-fronted gazelle (*Gazella rufifrons*); Soemmerring's gazelle (*Gazella soemmerringei*); African elephant (*Loxodonta africana*); Trevor's free-tailed bat (*Mops trevori*); horn-skinned bat (*Eptesicus floweri*); greater spotted eagle (*Aquila clanga*); imperial eagle (*Aquila heliaca*); houbara bustard (*Chlamydotis undulata*); lesser kestrel (*Falco naumanni*); lappet-faced vulture (*Torgos tracheliotos*); and African spurred tortoise (*Geochelone sulcata*).[96]

The ready availability of firearms has been the most significant factor in the reduction of wildlife, and has also compounded the problems of habitat destruction in northern and central Sudan. Uncontrolled hunting has devastated wildlife populations and caused the local eradication of many of the larger species including chimpanzees,[97] elephant, rhino, buffalo, giraffe,

---

established, seriously degraded an area of almost 400 sq km by clearing it for agriculture. Rehabilitating this area will require considerable time and resources. Ibid, p.115.

96 *Sudan: Post-Conflict Environmental Assessment*, UNEP, 2007, p. 252-258.

97 The chimpanzee (*Pan troglodytes*) is found in relatively undisturbed tropical forest regions in central and western Africa; the forests of the far southern edge of Sudan represent the eastern limit of its habitat. Like all of the great apes, the chimpanzee is in danger of extinction. Throughout its range, the species is subject to a variety of threats, including habitat loss and fragmentation, the bush-meat industry, and live capture. While all of these issues are important in Sudan, the predominant problem is

eland and zebra. There has been significant looting of natural resources like timber (lumber and charcoal), ivory and bush-meat by both the sides, with the result that the larger edible mammals such as buffalo, giraffe, zebra and eland are locally extinct.[98]

In northern and central Sudan, the greatest damage has been inflicted by habitat destruction and fragmentation from farming and deforestation. Larger wildlife have essentially disappeared and are now mostly confined to core protected areas and remote desert regions. In the south, uncontrolled and unsustainable hunting has decimated wildlife populations and caused the local eradication of many of the larger species, such as elephant, rhino, buffalo, giraffe, eland and zebra. In Darfur, there have been consistent reports of militias using scorched earth tactics, destroying trees, crops and pastures. Deliberate deforestation and vegetation clearance could have important impacts on the land, water and biotic regimes.[99]

## X. South Sudan

After two decades of armed conflict, South Sudan gained independence in July 2011.[100] Before its division, Sudan had been the largest country in Africa. Most of the people have spent the great part of their lives in the midst of civil war and crisis. The country is faced with a number of environmental problems, including the unregulated exploitation of natural resources; climate change; and large numbers of returnees. The majority of the people in South Sudan use wood charcoal for cooking and heating. Fuel-wood and timber are being collected faster than the time taken for the re-growth of trees to control soil erosion. All these factors have played a part in destroying the natural resource base of the country and compromising the livelihoods of the communities that depend largely on the land and

---

the bush-meat trade and the resulting live capture of animals. Typically, a mother and other family members are shot for meat, and the juveniles are captured alive for later sale as pets. Ibid, p. 271.

98 *Sudan: Post-Conflict Environmental Assessment*, UNEP, 2007.

99 Bashir, M. et. al., Sudan Country Study on Biodiversity. Khartoum: Ministry of Environment and Tourism (2001). Also see: Blower, J.R., Wildlife Conservation and management in the Southern Sudan, UNDP/ FAO Sudan Project Findings and Recommendations, 1997.

100 The Republic of South Sudan became Africa's 54th nation on 9 July 2011, as it officially became independent following a historic referendum on self-determination held on 9 January 2011.

its resources for a living.[101] After a period of over fifty years dominated by wars, and the independence process which created the country, an institutional and regulatory framework to govern environmental issues is now being developed. UNEP has been active since 2009, and is engaged in creating and developing environmental awareness on a national scale to support the government and the population of the country.

A recent study noted the impact of climate change and environmental degradation on water, soil, forests, biodiversity, agriculture and fisheries. Permanent rivers have become seasonal, water tables have been lowered and the rainy season has been shortened. Soil degradation has increased due to water erosion, wind erosion and fire. Deforestation has been accelerated due to firewood collection, charcoal production,[102] livestock grazing,[103] agriculture, and collection of construction materials. In the north and south-east, there is a serious competition for drinking water

---

101 The South Sudan government has drafted an environmental policy to mitigate some of the above threats including charcoal production, poaching and logging, all of which constitute potential triggers for renewed conflict within South Sudan. Jacob K. Lupai, Environmental Sustainability for Development in South Sudan, available at: http://www.southsudannewsagency.com/opinion/articles/environmental-sustainability-for-development, accessed 2 February 2014.

102 The main fuel used in urban centres is charcoal. Many returnees burn wood to make charcoal to generate income because no license is needed and simple tools are required. Moreover, the forest belongs 'to nobody'. The production of charcoal requires large quantities of wood and likely contributes significantly to deforestation. Large quantities of charcoal are also exported. Based on monthly figures on charcoal exportation from the Renk County in Upper Nile State to Sudan, it is estimated that now annually in the order of 60,000 bags of charcoal are exported from Renk County, representing 2,700 hectares of deforested land. This estimate is based on an extrapolation of the annual fluctuations in charcoal production due to seasonality. Since more charcoal may have been exported unregistered or illegally, the real figure is expected to be much higher. Environment Impacts Risk and Opportunities Assessment: Natural Resources Management and Climate Change in South Sudan, Ministry of Environment, Government of the Republic of South Sudan and the United Nations Development Programme, January 2012, p. 37-38.

103 The impact of livestock grazing is less visible and more difficult to quantify than that of clearing for agriculture and cutting for charcoal, fuel wood or construction. The most important contribution of livestock to deforestation is the removal of seedlings, which eliminates the capacity of the forest to regenerate. Heavily grazed forest therefore often shows a very open structure on the ground. Fire is very much associated with livestock keeping, as pastoralists burn grass to promote the re-growth of perennial grasses in the dry season. Again, fire kills seedlings and hence reduces re-growth of trees. Environment Impacts Risk and Opportunities Assessment: Natural Resources Management and Climate Change in South Sudan, Ministry of Environment, Government of the Republic of South Sudan and the United Nations Development Programme, January 2012, p. 40

between people, livestock and wildlife due to desertification. Soil, air and water pollution is increasing due to unregulated industrial and agricultural practices. There has been a loss of fish species and reduction of fish size as a result of rivers becoming increasingly seasonal.

Landmines are another major problem in the country. Of the 137,944,810 square metres estimated to be landmine contaminated area, a total of 6,897,094 square metres of residential and agricultural land has been cleared of mines (till 15 June 2013). This represents 5 per cent of the total known contaminated area.[104]

## XI. Turkey

Since the early 1980s there has been an armed struggle in large areas of eastern Turkey, between the Turkish security forces and the Kurdistan Workers Party (Partiya Karkeren Kurdistan or PKK). In order to establish itself in the countryside, the PKK applied the principles of prolonged guerrilla warfare from 1984, concentrating in southeastern Turkey (Turkish Kurdistan). Guerrilla cells launched incessant and widespread small-scale attacks on the Turkish Armed Forces. The army also attacked to destroy the guerrillas, but these proved ineffective. As the troops got into position, the guerrillas merely slipped away, only to return later unnoticed when the army sweep had ended and the soldiers had returned to their barracks. The conflict caused as many as 35,000 deaths.

In 1993, in response to the tactics adopted by PKK, the security forces started village evacuations and the burning of buildings, crops, and forests.[105] It has been reported that during the period 1991 to 2001, as many as 3200 villages were burnt.[106] The local population was forbidden to go

104 The United Nations Mine Action Service and its partners surveyed 404 kilometres of roads, including the main road between Bor and Malakal. The Mine Action Service is collaborating with the UN police and other partners in training national police explosive ordnance disposal teams. The UN Security Council, Report of the Secretary General on South-Sudan, S/2013/366 dated 20 June 2013, para 63.

105 An eye witness, Twenty-four-year-old person informed Human Rights Watch that, during the spring of 1994, helicopters were frequently used to burn down the forests surrounding Yazioren, a small village of thirty homes. He informed that the security forces poured gasoline or some kind of flammable liquid over the tree and then set the trees afire; and the Jandarma [Gendarmerie] ordered villagers not to enter into the forests, which were declared free-fire zones. *Weapons Transfer and Violations of the Laws of War in Turkey*, Washington: Human Rights Watch, 1995.

106 Jongerden, J., 2007. *The Settlement Issue in Turkey and the Kurds: An Analysis of Spatial Politics, Modernity and War*, Brill Academic Publishers, Leiden and Boston.

into the burned and burning areas because of the continuing operations. On the other hand, security forces permitted illegal tree cutting in forests. An estimated three million people were displaced as Turkish security forces systematically evacuated or destroyed villages.[107]

Military, paramilitary and insurgent forces intentionally destroyed forests, crops, livestock, foodstuffs, seeds, buildings, and other assets of economic, cultural, and biological value. Jongerden (2006),[108] using remote sensing data, reported that in Eastern Turkey, the Turkish Armed Forces have systematically used forest burning as a part of a counterinsurgency (COIN) campaign directed against the PKK. They burnt about 11,000 hectares (110 sq km) or 7.5 per cent of forests. Even larger non-forest areas amounting to 52,000 hectares (520 sq km) were burned.

## XII. Iraq-Marsh Arabs

In 1991, after the First Gulf War, the Marsh Arabs of southern Iraq rose up against Saddam Hussain. In retaliation, the Iraqi government embarked on a massive water diversion project to drain the wetlands where the Marsh Arabs had been settled for generations and adapted to the marsh environment. The plight of the Marsh Arabs has received very little attention from legal scholars, possibly due to a lack of information about the region or to the obscurity of international law concerning domestic environmental damage.[109]

The Mesopotamian marshlands constitute the largest wetland ecosystem in the Middle East. They are a crucial part of intercontinental flyways for migratory birds, support endangered species, and sustain freshwater fisheries, as well as those of the Persian Gulf. In addition to their ecological importance and outstanding natural resources, these marshlands are unique from the global perspective of human heritage. They have been

---

107 Etten, Jacob van, Joost Jongerden, Hugo J. de Vos, Annemarie Klaasse, and Esther C.E. van Hoeve, Environmental destruction as a counterinsurgency strategy in the Kurdistan region of Turkey, *Geoforum*, 2008.

108 Jongerden, Joost, et.al., Forest burning as a counter-Insurgency strategy, 2006, available at: http://www.joostjongerden.info/ForestBurning_website.pdf, accessed 25 June 2014. Also see: Biswas, A.K., 'Scientific assessment of the long-term environmental consequences of war', in J.E. Austin and C.E. Bruc. 2000. *The Environmental Consequences of War: Legal, Economic, and Scientific Perspectives*, Cambridge University Press, p. 303-315.

109 Michael Posner and Fiona McKay, The Iraqi Justice System: Challenges in Responding to Iraq's Past Abuses of Human Rights, Vol. 42, *JUDGES' J.*, (2003), p. 14-15.

home to indigenous communities for millennia and are regarded as the site of the legendary 'Garden of Eden'. In the early 1970s, the marshlands, consisting of interconnected lakes, mudflats and wetlands, extended over 20,000 sq km of Iraq and Iran.[110]

In 1991,[111] the Saddam Hussein government seeking to punish the Marsh Arabs launched a massive engineering campaign to drain the wetland system. Huge canals and earthworks were constructed to divert the waters of the Tigris and Euphrates away from the marshes and into the Gulf.[112] This substantially reduced the water supply and effectively eliminated the flood pulses that sustained the wetland ecosystems in the lower basin. In addition, it led to a marked degradation of water quality in the mainstreams of the Tigris and Euphrates, due to saline return drainage from irrigation schemes and dam retention of sediment and nutrients. The futility of the marshland and the ecosystem processes were also affected by contaminants, such as industrial and agricultural chemicals and urban effluent.[113]

The destruction of the Mesopotamian marshlands has been documented by the UNEP. The study reveals that in their lower courses, the Tigris and Euphrates created a vast network of wetlands, comprising a complex of tall reeds, seasonal marshes dominated by desert shrub and grasses, shallow

110 *Environment in Iraq: UNEP Progress Report*, 2003, United Nations Environment Programme, p. 22-24.

111 Before the first Gulf War, Southern Mesopotamia held South-western Asia's most extensive wetlands, at the confluence of the Tigris and the Euphrates. For thousands of years these wetlands had been occupied by the ancestors of the people known today as the Marsh Arabs The culture of the Marsh Arabs, existing in harmony with the marsh environment, was completely dependent on marsh resources: the plants, animals and water of the marshes. The duration of the culture testifies to the sustainability of its uses of those resources. The reeds that grew in the marshes were the primary building material for houses and boats; the fish and waterfowl of the marshes were a primary source of food. The marshes themselves were known to outsiders for their spectacular displays of spring wildflowers.

112 Massive drainage works in southern Iraq in the late 1980s and early 1990s, together with the effects of major upstream damming devastated the wetlands (overall loss of 90%), such that only minor and fragmented parcels remain today. Massive loss and degradation had taken place by 2000, with the greatest change occurring between 1991 and 1995. The central and Al Hammar marshlands had been almost completely destroyed, with 97% and 94% of their respective cover transformed into bare land and salt crusts. The water-filtering role of the marshland had ceased and the remaining drainage canals carried polluted irrigation wastewater directly toward the Gulf, with potentially harmful impacts on local fish resources. The Marsh Arabs of Iraq: Do They Want to Go Back in Time? *ECONOMIST*, 5 June 2002.

113 Partow, H. 2001. *The Mesopotamian Marshlands: Demise of an Ecosystem: Early Warning and Assessment Technical Report*, UNEP.

and deep-water lakes, slightly brackish seasonal lagoons, and regularly inundated mudflats. The wetlands extended from Basra in the south to within 150 km of Baghdad, but the core of the system was located around the confluence of the Tigris and Euphrates.[114] The Marsh Arabs who had lived in the wetlands for five thousand years were forced to flee and many died.[115] While the exact number of deaths and of persons displaced as a result will probably never be known, most sources give numbers of displaced persons between 200,000 and 400,000.[116]

The drainage of the wetlands was a deliberate and calculated act of genocide and ecocide.[117] Over 90 per cent of the marshlands have dried out and largely transformed into a barren landscape of desert and salt flats. A further 30 per cent of the remaining 1,084 square kilometers of the marshland, the trans-boundary marsh straddling the Iran-Iraq border, dried out between 2000 and early 2003, leaving just 7 per cent of the original area. This has had a catastrophic impact on biodiversity and wildlife which go beyond Iraq's borders and are of regional and international importance. Prominent losses include the possible extinction of the endemic smooth-coated otter *Lutra perspicillata maxwellii*, bandicoot rat *Nesokia bunnii*, long-fingered bat *Myotis capaccinii* and an endemic species of barbel fish *Barbus sharpeyi*. Several aquatic birds are critically threatened, including the African darter *Anhinga rufa* and sacred ibis *Threskiornis aethiopica*, which may now be extinct in the Middle East. A further 66 bird species are considered to be at risk. A wide range of migratory aquatic species have been affected – including penaied shrimp, and Hilsa shad *Tenualosailisha* (a fish), which migrate between the Gulf and nursery grounds in the marshlands – with serious economic consequences for coastal fisheries. Increasing salinity in the Shatt al-Arab estuary (due to upstream hydrotechnical works) has also damaged the breeding grounds of another important fish species, silver pomfret *Pampus argenteus*.[118]

---

114 For more details see: Partow, H. 2001. *The Mesopotamian Marshlands: Demise of an Ecosystem: Early Warning and Assessment* Technical Report, UNEP.

115 The Marsh Arabs of Iraq: Do They Want to Go Back in Time? *ECONOMIST*, June 5, 2002.

116 Emma Nicholson and Peter Clark (eds.). 2002. *The Iraqi Marshlands: A Human and Environmental Study*, London: Politico's Publishing.

117 Schwabach Aaron, Ecocide and Genocide in Iraq: International Law, the Marsh Arabs and Environmental Damage in Non-international Conflicts, 2003, Paper 35, The Berkeley Electronic Press. Available at: http://law.bepress.com/expresso/eps/35, accessed 31 March 2014.

118 *Desk Study on Environment in Iraq*, United Nations Environment Programme (UNEP),

Several mammals that were previously abundant are now under enormous pressure or locally extinct. These are the grey wolf, honey badger, striped hyena, jungle cat, goitered gazelle and Indian crested porcupine. Previously, the most common mammal in the marshes was the wild boar, which posed a major threat to the Marsh dwellers' crops and was their main enemy. Their numbers have also been in drastic decline. Other frequently-sighted mammals which are also threatened include the small Indian mongoose, the Asiatic jackal and the red fox. The desert monitor, previously common in desert regions bordering the marshes, is now rare.[119] The destruction of the wetlands was disproportional to the goal of eliminating a handful of impoverished and already defeated rebels. The military goal of capturing the last few rebels could have been achieved with considerably less destruction. The vast majority of the Marsh Arabs who were uninvolved in the rebellion were made to suffer and no apparent attempt was made to distinguish between civilians and rebels. Besides, the Genocide Convention clearly prohibits acts such as those committed by the Iraqi government against the Marsh Arabs.[120]

## XIII. India

North-east India, comprising the seven States of Assam, Arunachal Pradesh, Nagaland, Meghalaya, Manipur, Mizoram and Tripura, has earned the dubious distinction of persistent underdevelopment and growing insurgency. The fire of insurgency has been engulfing the region in such a way that in many areas there seems to be a parallel authority of the insurgents who indulge in unrestricted acts of abduction, extortion, killing and environmental damage.

The environment has been a major victim of the insurgency. Both the insurgents and the personnel involved in anti-insurgency operations have caused denudation of forests. Not only are conservation activities and other forestry operations hampered, resulting in the loss of valuable natural resources, but also there is a grave threat to the fragile ecology of

---

2003, p. 39-44.

119 Partow, H. 2001. *The Mesopotamian Marshlands: Demise of an Ecosystem: Early Warning and Assessment Technical Report*, UNEP, p. 34.

120 Schwabach Aaron, Ecocide and Genocide in Iraq: International Law, the Marsh Arabs and Environmental Damage in Non-international Conflicts, 2003, Paper 35, The Berkeley Electronic Press. Available at: http://law.bepress.com/expresso/eps/35, accessed 31 March 2014.

the region.[121]

The Manas Wildlife Sanctuary (Assam) was included in the World Heritage List in 1985. The IUCN 1985 evaluation report specifically noted that: "Manas provides critical and viable habitat for more rare and endangered species than any of the Indian sub-continents protected areas." However, the long-running conflict has had such a detrimental impact on the forests and wildlife populations of the park (particularly rhinoceros, tiger and swamp deer) that it was included in the List of World Heritage in Danger in 1992.[122]

Insurgency has also been on the rise in other parts of India, where disaffected tribes have turned against the government and have been supporting groups such as the Maoist guerrillas. The Maoists control vast areas of forested land in central and eastern India – areas that serve as prime tiger habitat. While they may not be targeting tigers intentionally, they are preventing conservation activities in the regions they control, which may be as much as 30 per cent of India's tiger range.

Left-wing extremist and insurgency are being cited as the major reason for the rising number of tiger deaths reported across various forests reserves in India. It has been estimated that there are barely 1,411 tigers left in the country. An assessment made by the National Tiger Conservation Authority (NTCA), a nodal body set up by the Ministry of Environment and Forests (MoEF), revealed that tiger density has decreased in as many as six reserves. [123] According to the NTCA report, tiger density has fallen in reserves such as Palamu (Jharkhand),[124] Valmiki (Bihar), Simplipal

---

121 P.R. Bhattacharjee P R and and P. Nayak, Vicious Circle of Insurgency and Under Development in North-east India, available at: http://www1.freewebs.com/nehu_economics-a/vcircle_ner.pdf, accessed 13 May 2014.

122 Report on the UNESCO-IUCN Mission to the Manas World Heritage Site India, Draft of 20/22 April, 2005. Manas Wildlife sanctuary was taken over by guerrillas from the Bodo tribe, who burned down the park, buildings, looted most park facilities, killed guards, destroyed bridges, poached rhinos, elephants, tigers and other wildlife, cleared forests, and depleted fish stock in the Manas river. Himraj Dang. 1991. *Human Conflict in Conservation: Protected Areas, the Indian Experience*, New Delhi: Har-Anand and Vikas Publications House.

123 Insurgents don't spare endangered tigers too, *Times of India*, New Delhi, 1 January 2010.

124 The Palamu National Tiger Reserve which is situated in backward district of Jharkhand was established in 1973 and spread across 1,014 sqkm. The reserve had 22 tigers. In spite of a nationwide drive to conserve tigers, the big cat's population in this district has been dwindling. The 2007 census put the Palamu tiger population at 17, which was

(Orissa), Nagarjunsagar (Andhra Pradesh), Indravati (Chattisgarh) and Nampdapha (Arunachal Pradesh). Tigers are killed as insurgents come in close contact with them deep inside the forests. And even if they are not targeted, the excessive harvesting of tiger prey such as deer and wild pigs, is forcing tigers to prey on domestic animals (or even people) and come into conflict with rural communities.

The Government of India has recently moved the Indian Army into the conflict theater of Bastar (Chattisgarh), close to the strongest military base of the Maoists. An area of about 100 sqkm at the foothills of Abujhmad, a thickly forested plateau, has been earmarked for training of the army, which maintains that its plans are limited to training and there will be no active troop deployment. Another view is that the training range will bring the army tantalizingly close to the Maoists, and hence could be a part of future strategic positioning.[125] Whatever may be the aim of this movement, the ultimate sufferer would be the environment. [126]

Internal conflict has plagued Kashmir since 1950.[127] The 'paradise on

---

further reduced to 13. However, the actual figure are not known as the district is has been affected by the activities of the Maoist, and their presence has impeded survey. Increased naxal activities are also affecting routine forest management. More than 70 per cent of the reserve remains unprotected as the officials and staffs have come under attacks from Maoists. In May 1999 a ranger was abducted and robbed, in August 2003, a forest tracker was killed and in September 2004, a forester and driver were killed in a landmine blast. In 2009, the rebels robbed and killed a ranger. Scarcity of water is also affecting the reserve. It is one of the poorest districts in India and classified by the state government as "food insecure". Naxal threat affects tigers too, *The Hindu*, 20 December 2010.

125 Finally, Army moves into Maoist territory, *The Times of India*, New Delhi, 14 December 2010.

126 There were few allegations of poaching of chinkaras (Indian Gazelle), a protected species, in the Thar deserts by few military personnel in November 2011. *The Hindu*, 20 December and 22 December 2011. As reported a junior commissioned officer (Subedar) and four other ranks under him allegedly killed three chinkaras which were later found in the military premises by the officials of the Forest Department. While the Forest Department was pressing for the trial of military personnel in a civil (criminal) court, the army authorities were insisting on trial by a military court. The Indian Criminal Court and Court Martial (Adjustment of Jurisdiction) Rules, 1978 provides that in case of any disputes as to the forum of trial, the Central Government is the final authority. In case the Central Government decides that the proceedings against such person(s) should be instituted before a Magistrate, the commanding officer of such person is to deliver him to the Magistrate for a trial (Rule 9 as amended by SO 4010 of November 24, 1986; and the Regulations for the Indian Army, Paragraph 418).

127 Asthana Vandana and Shukla A C, Environmental Consequences of Armed Conflict in South Asia, *South Asian Journal*, October-December 2008, p. 83.

earth', and home of many rare and endangered species, has faced habitat destruction, loss of wildlife, over-exploitation and degradation of natural resources.[128] The wildlife population throughout the valley is rapidly declining due to extensive deforestation and poaching. The massive presence of Indian and Pakistani armies on the borders of Kashmir, resulted in large scale poaching as the troops living in the border areas indulged in killing rare species like the ibex, blue sheep, urian, the big horned sheep, antelope and snow leopard.[129] There are reports that the snow leopard hunted for its precious skin and teeth, is now almost extinct. [130] The Hygam Weyland, 50 km north of Kashmir, once home for many migratory birds, has shrunk to only 4.5 sq km, the rest having been transformed into grazing ground for cattle.

## XIV. Nepal

The 'people's war', an armed uprising by the Maoist extremists in Nepal began in February 1996. It grew over the years and gradually engulfed almost the entire country. The conflict came to an end when the Maoists joined the political mainstream in 2006. The conflict had several direct and

---

128 The militancy and continued presence of military in the valley has also taken a heavy toll on Kashmir's ecosystem. Thousands of trees have been felled to facilitate military manoeuvres against militants and to build access routes to uninhabitable terrains near the line of control. Timber smuggling has become a major business, with nearly 500 hectares of forests disappearing every year. Militants have killed over 100 forest department officers to deter them from patrolling the forests, thereby indirectly ceding the timber smugglers an open space to operate in. Soil erosion due to deforestation has lead to frequent flash floods in the state. Bhatt Semu, Kashmir: A choice between History and Future, available at: http://www.amankiasha.com/detail_news.asp?id=311&page=65, accessed on 30 November 13.

129 The consequence has been that some of the rare species of animal like the Snow Leopard, Flying Squirrel and Long Tailed Himalayan Marmot have been pushed to being on the verge of extinction. Barking Deer, Cheetal, Nilgai, Musk Deer, Himalayan Black Bear, Shapu, Ibex, Blue Sheep, Marmot and Lynz may soon become extinct if their unrestricted slaughter is not checked. Over 300 species of birds which included Pheasants, Quills, Partridges, Vultures, Kites, Eagles and a large number of colorful birds, all of which use to reside in the lush forests of Kashmir have virtually disappeared. Today those forests stand naked and void of any visible sign of bird life. Crook, J, War in Kashmir and its Effect on the Environment, Conflict and the Environment in Kashmir, ICE Case Studies, (1998), Case Number: 76. Available at: http://www1.american.edu/ted/ice/kashmiri.htm, accessed 14 May 2014.

130 Ejaz Ur-Rehman, Impact of Armed Conflict on Environment in the State of Jammu and Kashmir: An Overview, 2010. Available at: http://ejaz.blog.com/2010/05/09/impact-of-armed-conflict-on-environment-in-the-state-of-jammu-and-kashmir-an-overview/, accessed 14 May 2014.

indirect impacts on the environment.[131] First, it resulted in the destruction of forests and other natural resources; second, the conflicting groups exploited natural resources to raise funds; third, the conflict situation was exploited by vested groups for smuggling and illicit trade in wildlife and natural resources; and the fourth, the displacement and resettlement of people placed grater stress on natural resources.

Nearly 18.33 per cent of the total land area of Nepal is protected forest area.[132] The Royal Nepalese Army was positioned in these areas to prevent poaching and illicit trade of wildlife species. These areas became regular targets of the Maoists who destroyed the infrastructure in the protected areas.   After November 2001 the army was withdrawn from these protected areas. The heavy presence of Maoists resulted in the departure of personnel associated with conservation and protection, leaving no staff to monitor or oversee wildlife and habitat preservation.[133] This disturbed forest management. There was over exploitation of some high-value medicinal plants by the rebels for the economic benefits and to raise funds. Smugglers also had the opportunity to indulge in poaching, illegal logging and smuggling of forest produce.[134] There was large-scale poaching of endangered animals such as the one horned rhinoceros, musk deer, snow leopard and tiger in the Royal Bardia National Park and Royal Chitwan National Park and other places.[135]

Even before the insurgency, Nepal served as a conduit for illegal trafficking in wildlife products, such as shatoosh (a fine wool made from the throat hairs of the endangered Tibetan antelope, or chiru) brought from Tibet

---

131 Nepal has been an agrarian economy with over 80 per cent of the people dependent on agriculture. Land distribution has been inequitable and poor people live on lands that measure less than one hectare which can hardly support a family's needs. There is intense and widespread competition for the available natural resources, which are fast depleting. These together with rapidly increasing population, faulty land distribution system and insecure tenancy rights have caused problems particularly for the tenant farmers and agricultural laborers.

132 Ministry of Forests and Soil Conservation, Nepal Biodiversity Strategy, Government of Nepal, 2002.

133 Stubblefield Cynthis H. and Mahendra Shrestha, Status of Asiatic black bears in protected areas of Nepal and the effects of political turmoil, Vol. 18 (1), *Ursus*, 2007, p. 101–108.

134 Upreti B.C. 2011. 'Conflict in Nepal: Impact on Nepal and its Cross-border Consequences', in Raghavan V.R. (ed.), *Internal Conflict in Nepal: Transnational Consequences*, New Delhi: Vij Books India Pvt. Ltd., p. 100-118.

135 The Impact of Nepal's Armed Conflict on Conservation Efforts, available at: http://nepal.usembassy.gov/env_page5.html, accessed 20 June 2014.

to Nepal and then to India. Similarly, tiger bones and skins from India transit through Nepal on the way to Tibet, China, and Southeast Asia. Wildlife watchers believe that the level of trafficking has now reached alarming proportions and that banned items are freely sold in the markets of Kathmandu.[136]

When the government mobilized the armed forces to control the Maoist rebels in rural areas, many posts were established in remote forested areas. In order to ensure the safety of the personnel, the forests surrounding the military camps were cleared. It was also reported that the army was involved in logging high-value trees without notifying the forest committee, collaborating with timber smugglers and hunting.[137] The bodies of people killed in attacks were thrown into rivers or left to decompose in the forests, causing pollution. Landmines laid by the Maoists and fires set by the security forces also destroyed forests.[138]

A six-month long extensive research was undertaken to assess the impact of the conflict on protected areas. The study, which covered 16 parks and reserves, highlighted the damage to infrastructure, deforestation and illegal hunting of endangered species, and declining security measures within the protected areas.[139] Some protected forests like the Makalu – Barun National Park and Dhorpatan Hunting Reserve, suffered extensive damage due to the establishment of training camps by the Maoists.[140] The Nepal Department of Forests reported that the insurgents destroyed 40 out of 92 area forest offices; and 190 out of the 696 range posts.[141] Wildlife smuggling

---

136 The Impact of Nepal's Armed Conflict on Conservation Efforts, available at: http://nepal.usembassy.gov/env_page5.html, accessed 20 June 2014.

137 Roka Krishna B., Armed Conflict and its Impact on Community Forestry in Nepal, Vol. 26, *Tropical Resources Bulletin*, Spring 2007, Yale Tropical Resource Institute, Yale School of Forestry and Environmental Studies, p. 55-62.

138 Upreti Bishnu Raj. 2004. *The Price of Neglect: From Resource Conflict to Maoist Insurgency in the Himalayan Kingdom*, Kathmandu, Nepal: Bhrikuti Academic Publications.

139 The study highlighted the wild life trade in Chitwan, Kathmandu and Rasuwa; increased threat to endangered one-horned rhino; the presence of strong poacher network in Chitwan; increased illegal trade of wildlife parts in Kathmandu and increased evidence of Rasuwa district being used for transporting such illegal goods. Wildlife Watch Group (WWG), Annual Report 2007, Kathmandu, Nepal.

140 Upreti B.C., 'Conflict in Nepal: Impact on Nepal and its Cross-border Consequences', in Raghavan V.R. (ed.), *Internal Conflict in Nepal: Transnational Consequences*, New Delhi: Vij Books India Pvt. Ltd. 2011, p. 100-118.

141 The Impact of Nepal's Armed Conflict on Conservation Efforts, available at: http://

increased tremendously during 1998 to 2005.[142]

Community forestry has been a highly successful strategy for the regeneration of forests in Nepal. It involves handing over user rights and management of the forests to local people who have been using the forests traditionally to ensure a proper balance between resource utilization and management.[143] The armed conflict and the fear of Maoists was a serious setback for community forestry. In some areas, the Maoists forced the NGOs working for community forestry to register with the people's government so that they could keep track of the flow of funds to these organizations and levy taxes on them.

## XV. Sri Lanka

The Democratic Socialist Republic of Sri Lanka is an ethnically, linguistically and religiously diverse country of 21 million people. It has remained in the global map of conflict for more than two decades. What began as a conflict between the Sinhala and the Tamil communities gradually grew into a demand for the creation of separate homeland for the Tamils. After almost three decades of brutal armed conflict, on 19 May 2009, the Government of Sri Lanka declared its victory over the Liberation Tigers of Tamil Eelam (LTTE). The final stages of the conflict saw numerous allegations of violations of IHL and international human rights law.[144]

---

nepal.usembassy.gov/env_page5.html, accessed 24 June 2011.

142 Ek Raj Sigdel, Poaching- How to Fight It, The Kathmandu Post, 6 March 2003; K.C. Shandip , Nepal Still a Hotspot for Illegal Wildlife Traders, *The Kathmandu Post* , 7 April 2002.

143 Nepal has more than 11,500 forest user groups in nearly all of its 75 districts, with participation by about 1.2 million households, and has been lauded internationally for its exemplary success in reclaiming denuded hillsides through community forestry efforts. Years of painstaking effort by local communities in partnership with the Nepalese government and donors such as USAID and the Danish and British development agencies had resulted almost 9,000 square kilometers of forests being turned over to community management forests. The Impact of Nepal's Armed Conflict on Conservation Efforts, available at: http://nepal.usembassy.gov/env_page5.html, accessed 20 June 2014.

144 In the wake of discriminatory State policies and anti-Tamil violence in the 1950s, the Tamil struggle for rights, which began as non-violent protests, increasingly gave rise to Tamil militancy and armed revolt, with a central demand for a separate State. A number of Tamil politico-militant groups, including LTTE, emerged in the 1970s, as the discourse shifted from accommodation to separatism. Violent repression of Tamils by Sinhala nationalists increased in intensity, alongside increasing attacks by Tamil armed groups against the security forces. Elements in the Governments encouraged anti-Tamil violence which culminated in an extensive 1983 anti-Tamil attacks. It

The conflict had detrimental impacts on the environment. As early as in 1986, the Wilpattu National Park was attacked by Tamil rebels, who killed twenty-one members of the staff and destroyed facilities. This caused a withdrawal of conservation staff and an increase in military activity in the area.[145] The biodiversity, natural resource base and wealth of the nation have been significantly harmed by bombings, planting of landmines and aerial attacks. Elephants and their terrain, one of the most fiercely guarded wildlife reserves of Sri Lanka, have been adversely affected. Human habitation has also been through dreadful ruin and degradation and has been a cause of serious concern to the government and people.

Landmines set with the intent to maim rather than kill in order to use up more resources in the care of the injured, are an issue for both human and elephant populations that draw severely on the already depleted resources. Both the government forces and the LTTE used mines during the conflict and it is estimated that approximately 482 sq km is contaminated by mines and UXO in the North.[146] Vast areas were mined by the LTTE without any documentation.[147] Severe flooding in 2011 uncovered landmines from the country's decades-long civil war. These unexploded mines are just another problem in a long list of difficulties for some of the poorest people in a country that is still recovering from the civil war.

The mines and ERWs are wreaking renewed havoc on herds of elephants returning to the lands they inhabited before they were forced to relocate

---

resulted in thousands of deaths, large-scale displacement, and destruction of Tamil property and migration of abroad. The 1983 is commonly regarded as the start of armed conflict between the Government and LTTE. Report of the Secretary-General's Panel of Experts on Accountability in Sri Lanka, 31 March 2011, p. 8. Available at: http://www. un.org/News/dh/infocus/Sri_Lanka/POE_Report_Full.pdf, accessed 14 May 2014.

145 McNeely Jeffery A. 2000. 'War and Biodiversity: An Assessment of Impacts, In Austin, Jay E., and Bruch, Carl E., (ed.), *The Environmental Consequences of War: Legal, Economic and Scientific Perspectives*, Cambridge: Cambridge University Press, p. 364.

146 Landmine and Cluster Munition Monitor (LCMM), a programme providing research and monitoring for the International Campaign to Ban Landmines (ICBL) and the Cluster Munition Coalition (CMC), has reported a total of 21,993 landmine-related casualties in Sri Lanka since the 1980s, including 1,419 civilian returnees. From 1999 to the end of 2009 the casualty figure was 1,310, including 123 killed, 453 injured and 734 unknown. Abhayagunawardena, Vidya, Vicious killer, Vol. 28, Issue 18, *Frontline*, 27 August- 9 September 2011.

147 Fonseka Bhawani, Landmines and Land Rights in Sri Lanka, August 2010, available at: http://www.gichd.org/fileadmin/pdf/ma_development/wk-landrights-oct2010/ LMAD-wk-Sri-Lanka-case-study-Nov2010.pdf, accessed 20 May 2014.

away from violent clashes. In many cases, elephants working for humans are injured in remote areas and cannot be helped for many days.[148] The injured elephants are put down as a result of the inherent difficulty in finding veterinary help and keeping the wounds and amputations clean. The resettlement of human populations may result in further developments of land for housing and agriculture, resulting in the displacement of many elephant populations. This increases both the chance of human-elephant clashes and the chance that elephants will be forced to scavenge for food in areas that have not been cleared of landmines because they do not have the same value to human populations as other areas.[149]

The ERW problem in Sri Lanka is not just about unexploded ordnance (UXO)[150]; there is also large contamination from abandoned ordnance as frontlines have shifted and army camps have been deserted. These unexploded munitions in rural and urban areas are causing humanitarian problems. They are impeding efforts at resettlement, rehabilitation and reconstruction. ERW accidents generally result in the death and/or injury of one or more people. Common injuries include amputation, loss of sight, abdominal injuries, burns and lacerations from fragmentation. Most victims are from low-income households and children, particularly boys are most at risk. Most incidents occur when people interact with ERW, either

---

148 Electronic Mine Information Network, 2011, Portfolio of Mine Action Projects: Sri Lanka, (2011), available at: http://www.mineaction.org/projects.asp?c=24, accessed 12 May 2014.

149 On April 4, 2011--International Mine Awareness Day-- while many advocates for mine removal were celebrating the inclusion of 10 more states to the Mine Ban Treaty, two elephants were killed in Sri Lanka by landmines. This came after a decision made by the Sri Lankan government to relocate the Sri Lankan Nature Conservatory to a former war zone containing as many as 1.5 million active landmines; proving even more that elephant safety depends on the actions taken and decisions made by humans in affected regions. As many as seven organizations are currently working in Sri Lanka to clear mines and promote mine education, but the demining process is not the only factor in helping elephants. Windy Borman, 2 Elephants Step on Landmines in Sri Lanka on International Mine Awareness Day, 4 April 2011, The Eyes of Thailand, Available at: http://www.eyesofthailand.com/2011/04/04/2-elephants-step-onlandmines-in-sri-lanka-on-intl-landmine-awareness-day/, accessed 12 May 2014.

150 Unexploded ordnance (UXO) refers to a wide range of explosive weapons in many different conditions: artillery shells, grenades, mortars, rockets and airdropped bombs as well as explosive sub-munitions (or bomblets) that form the contents of cluster munitions, either air-dropped or delivered from land-based systems. According to International Mine Action Standards (IMAS), UXO is 'explosive ordnance that has been primed, fuzed, armed or otherwise prepared for use or used. It may have been fired, dropped, launched or projected yet remains unexploded either through malfunction or design or for any other reason'.

out of curiosity or deliberately due to economic need or social conscience. They also occur during the clearing of land, the gathering of firewood or water, and the tending of animals. ERW pose a greater risk to children than landmines. ERW prevent people from using their land, although not to the same extent as landmines do. Once discovered, people are reluctant to use their land for agriculture and are afraid to let their children play freely. Nevertheless, sometimes economic needs outweigh the risk of contact. Although most explosives are not harmful to the environment, detonated explosives are toxic. White phosphorous is extremely toxic when released and can contaminate soil and water through secondary exposure. There is also a significant accumulation of heavy metal contamination in areas that have been subjected to prolonged exchange of fire.[151]

## Vegetation

The armed conflict led to the felling of over 5 million trees, including 2.5 million palmyrah palm (*Borassus flabellifer*).[152] Palmyrah palm help to retain water in the soil, and being the tallest trees in the region, they act as wind breaks and prevent wind erosion. Between 1956 and 1985, natural high forests decreased from 44 per cent to 27 per cent of the total land area. Most of the deforested area has been now converted into low productivity grasslands. In the early years of the militancy, a number of camps were established by the militants in the forested area of Vanni. The militants, who had no knowledge or understanding of the natural environment, brought urban utilitarian practices. There was the incursion of domesticated species of plants, particularly food plants and in many areas militant groups were also engaged in illegal logging and marketing of timber as a source of revenue.[153]

During the subsequent period of the conflict, both sides fortified themselves

---

151 Cave, Rosy, *Explosive Remnants of War in Sri Lanka*, London: Landmine Action, 2003, available at: http://www.landmineaction.org/resources/ERW_Sri_Lanka.pdf, accessed 24 June 2014.

152 In the early 1980's there were an estimated 5 million palms in the Jaffna peninsula. T. Saverimuttu, T., N Sriskandarajah, and VIS Jayapalan, Ecological Consequences of the War in the Tamil Homeland in Sri Lanka, Proceedings of International Conference On Tamil Nationhood & Search for Peace in Sri Lanka, Ottawa, Canada 1999. Available at: http://www.tamilcanadian.com/page.php?cat=22&id=18, accessed 5 June 2014.

153 T. Saverimuttu, T., N Sriskandarajah, and VIS Jayapalan, Ecological Consequences of the War in the Tamil Homeland in Sri Lanka, Proceedings of International Conference On Tamil Nationhood & Search for Peace in Sri Lanka, Ottawa, Canada 1999. Available at: http://www.tamilcanadian.com/page.php?cat=22&id=18, accessed 5 June 2014.

by building bunkers, defence lines and camps for soldiers. Trees were cut to build thousands of bunkers and for firewood. Government troops moved along the Colombo-Jaffna highway, pushing the Tamils back. Bulldozers followed the infantry and artillery units, clearing 500 metres on both sides of the road. All houses and trees were flattened so that the soldiers deployed in the area could have a clear view. The use of artillery, aerial bombing and the naval cannons by the Sri Lankan armed forces had a major impact on natural vegetation, agricultural land, and wild animals and birds. There have also been a number of reports of incendiary devices being used to burn forests, leading to the destruction of flora and fauna, and the disruption of the ecological balance.

## Wildlife

Both government troops and the guerrillas have hunted wildlife for food. Their impact was the most severe on large mammals with slow reproductive rates. Subsistence hunting was also engaged in by the poor people living along the edges of the conservation areas,[154] especially where refugees had resettled. In Vanni, where hunting has always been a part of the local culture, villagers hunted animals such as the jungle fowl (*Gallus lafayetti*), land monitor lizard (*Varanus bengalensis*), black naped hare (*Lepus nigricollis*), spotted deer (*Axis axis*), sambar (*Cervus unicolor*), barking deer (*Muntiacus muntjak*), mouse deer (*Tragulus meminna*) and wild boar (*Sus scrofa*).[155]

The free availability of guns during the war and the use of wire snares appear to have had a serious impact on wildlife. The spotted deer (*Axis axis*) used to be the most common and numerically abundant large herbivore in the Wilpattu National Park. But today, its numbers have declined significantly. Other protected areas (like the Yala East (Kumana) National Park and Flood Plains National Park) were also affected by illegal timber extraction and poaching. Uncontrolled hunting of wildlife not only reduces the population of the target species, but it caused serious changes in flora and fauna.

---

154 Unless regulated, even subsistence hunting for bushmeat can become a conservation problem, especially if the number of people who practice it increases. Hardin, G., *Science*, 1968, p. 1243–1248.

155 Data on the impact of war on wildlife were difficult to obtain while the armed conflict was going on. The information was gathered from visits made to the Vanni region in the northwest of the island. Santiapillai Charles and S. Wijeyamohan, The impact of civil war on wildlife in Sri Lanka, Vol. 84, No. 9, *CURRENT SCIENCE*, 10 May 2003, p. 1182-1183.

The Udawalawe National Park in the South Eastern region of Sri Lanka is a major eco-tourism attraction. The park is particularly known for its Sri Lankan Elephants, a sub-species of the endangered Asian Elephant. Other wildlife include the water buffalo, spotted deer, barking deer, sambar deer, striped-neck mongoose, leopard and fishing cats. During the last decade, over 1300 wild elephants have been killed in Sri Lanka due to gunshot wounds, poisoning, electrocution, land mines and collisions with vehicles and trains. Increased agriculture and human settlement is also causing loss and increased fragmentation of elephant habitat. [156]

Population displacements have occurred due to the armed conflict, natural disasters and development projects. The conflict-induced displacement has been the most prominent in the last few decades. Warring factions and displaced civilian populations can take a heavy toll on natural resources. As many as 600,000 Sri Lankans were internally displaced over the two-decade long armed conflict, creating a buffer strip between the Sinhala and Tamil communities. Some villages were abandoned for more than 10 years. During the last phase of the conflict, over 300,000 civilians were displaced from their homes in the Vanni region. Sri Lankan armed conflict has led to the felling of large number of trees, robbing farmers of income as many poor people were critically depended on forests for food and medicines.[157]

Human-elephant conflict is becoming increasingly common throughout Asia as humans and elephants battle for land and resources. Shrinking elephant habitats and expanding human populations mean people and elephants increasingly come into contact. Elephants can be dangerous to humans, and can devastate crops and buildings. The problem is compounded by the elephant's attraction to crops such as sugar cane, bananas and other fruits grown by humans. Elephants are killed due to the conflicts and other threats include land mines and cross fire as a result of war and collisions with vehicles and trains.[158]

---

156 Sri Lankan Elephants (Elephas maximus maxiums) are listed by the IUCN Threatened Species Red List as endangered with between 3000 and 4000 remaining in the wild. Of these only half are found in protected areas. Taronga Conservation Society, Australia; Report on Udawalawe National Park, Sri Lanka. Available at: http://www.taronga. org.au/animals-conservation/animals/asian-elephant/elephant-conservation-projects, accessed 20 May 2014.

157 In Defence of the Environment, Putting Poverty to the Sword, 2007, UNEP. Available at: http://www.unep.org/Documents.multilingual/Default.asp?DocumentID=288&Arti cleID=3810, accessed 17 November 2013.

158 Taronga Conservation Society, Australia; Report on Udawalawe National Park, Sri Lanka. Available at: http://www.taronga.org.au/animals-conservation/animals/asian-

## XVI. Colombia

Colombia is one of the twelve "megadiversity" country on the planet. Nearly all the topographical features in the world are present in Colombia, including dense tropical jungles, extreme alpine regions, lush Andean valleys, bleak savannas, and arid deserts. Ranking second only to Brazil in species diversity, Colombia accounts for about 10 per cent of the world's biological diversity, even though it occupies a mere 0.77 per cent of the earth's surface. It has the third highest number of vertebrate species in the world (about 2,890), including 27 species of neo-tropical primates (over one-third of the world's species), 7 per cent of the world's mammals (358 species), 6 per cent of the world's reptiles, and 10 per cent of the world's amphibians. It is also home to about 20 per cent of the world's birds (1,721 species), which is more than any other country's share, and 1,900 species of fish. It has 970 species of crustaceans, 2,200 types of mollusks, 150 types of coral, and 290 types of starfish (echinoderms).[159]

However, long years of internal conflict, military actions, migrant movements, excessive natural resource exploitation, and deficient management and institutional capacities have seriously damaged the nation's environment.[160] Conservationists and environmentalists all over the world are concerned with the harm being done to Colombia's rich natural habitats and unique flora and fauna. Colombia's lush ecosystem supports millions of people who depend on its water, forests, food sources, and medicinal plants.[161] The southern part of the country, which forms an important part of the Amazon basin, is under immense pressure from

---

elephant/elephant-conservation-projects, accessed 20 May 2014

159 Nagle Luz E., Placing Blame Where Blame is Due: The Culpability of Illegal Armed Groups in Narco-traffickers in Colombia's Environmental and Human Rights Catastrophes, Vol. 29, *William & Marry Environmental Law and Policy Review*, (2004), p. 61.

160 The conflict concerns several actors: left-wing guerrilla groups, right-wing paramilitary combatants, and narco-traffickers, pitted against the Colombian government and foreign military and civilian advisers charged with various tasks and goals. The situation related to complex issues concerning property rights, social inequity, economic disparity, institutional corruption, narco-trafficking, terrorism, significant capital flight, and a debilitating brain drain. Nagle Luz E., Placing Blame Where Blame is Due: The Culpability of Illegal Armed Groups in Narco-traffickers in Colombia's Environmental and Human Rights Catastrophes, Vol. 29, *William & Marry Environmental Law and Policy Review*, (2004), p. 5-6.

161 Carlos Alberto Chica, Colombia: Environmentalists Declare "All-Out" War, *Inter Press Service*, 4 June 1984.

logging and accidental fires. It has been estimated that more than 16 per cent of the Amazon's original rainforest cover is gone and the percentage increases at an alarming rate during times of drought.[162] The internal conflict has also forced a large section of the rural poor away from their sources of livelihood, placing tremendous pressure on biodiversity and the ecosystem.[163]

Colombian rebels have been detonating petroleum pipelines, spilling millions of barrels of crude oil into rivers, contaminating drinking and irrigation water, killing fish and other wildlife, contributing to forest fires and air pollution, sterilizing soil, and harming riverside communities. The Colombian government's estimated damages include, among others, US$ 26 million in lost crude oil, US$ 1.5 billion in lost oil revenues, and US$ 26 million in environmental clean-up costs. The aquatic impacts have extended beyond the national borders to Venezuela, where the government is trying to determine how to remedy the impact on its rivers.[164]

Despite the obvious threat posed by NIAC, none of the rules of international humanitarian law applicable to such situations provide specifically for the protection of the environment. There is no provision in either the Hague or Geneva laws or elsewhere to deal specifically with environmental protection during NIACs. The Common Article 3 of the Geneva Conventions of 1949 and Additional Protocol II of 1977 (AP II), which deals with NIAC does not even mention the subject. A proposal submitted to the Diplomatic Conference to introduce into AP II, a proposal analogous to Article 35, paragraph 3, and Article 55 of Additional Protocol I (AP I) was explicitly

---

162 The Amazon often is referred to as the 'Earth's Lungs' because of the massive quantities of carbon dioxide the rainforests absorb from the atmosphere. Unfortunately, those vital organs are beginning to resemble the lungs of a lifelong smoker. Stephanie Kriner, Amazon Rainforest Is Fading Faster than Originally Thought, 26 May 1999, available at http://www.disasterrelief.org/Disasters/990414Amazon/, accessed 11 January 2014.

163 More than 250,000 Colombians have been killed in NIAC and approximately 2.3 million people have been displaced during the period of 1996 to 2003. Nagle Luz E., Placing Blame Where Blame is Due: The Culpability of Illegal Armed Groups in Narco-traffickers in Colombia's Environmental and Human Rights Catastrophes, Vol. 29, *William & Marry Environmental Law and Policy Review*, (2004), p.7-8.

164 Colombia Urges UN to Designate Bombing of Pipelines as Environment Treaty Violation, Vol. 21, *International Environmental Reporter*, 1998, p. 175, (referring to Protocol Additional II and UN General Assembly Resolution 48/30 of Dec. 9, 1993); Let's take Out Nature from the War: Ministry of the Environment, available at:,http://www.presidencia.gov.co/noticias/generales97/97072114.htm, accessed 9 September 2013.

rejected.[165] AP II, which prohibits attacks upon installations containing dangerous forces, the prohibition of starvation of civilians, and certain provisions aimed at protecting the civilian population could be indirectly relevant.[166], [167] According to Adam Roberts:

The implementation of rules of restrains is often difficult in civil wars. First, such wars are often conducted by forces with minimum training and weak command structures. Second, the aim of the parties in such wars is often to drive people from their homes and land, and aim which in itself is likely to involve violations of the law of war. Finally, government and their foreign allies may feel free to engage in actions that would be more open to question if carried out beyond their national borders, and in an undeniably international war. Further, the governments may consider their internal adversaries to be criminals, not lawful belligerents.[168]

---

165 Bouvier Antoine, Protection of the natural environment in time of armed conflict, No. 285, *International Review of the Red Cross*, December 1991, p. 576.

166 According to Bouvier (1991), the concept of environmental protection is not totally absent from Additional Protocol II. Article 14 (Protection of objects indispensable to the survival of the civilian population), which prohibits attacks against "foodstuffs, agricultural areas for the production of foodstuffs, crops, livestock, drinking water installations and supplies and irrigation works", and Article 15, which prohibits any attack against "installations containing dangerous forces....if such attack may cause the release of [such] forces", contribute to protecting the environment in time of non-international armed conflict. Bouvier Antoine, Protection of the natural environment in time of armed conflict, No. 285, *International Review of the Red Cross*, December 1991, p. 556-578.

167 For instance, the action of Iraqi government in Mesopotamia violated Article 14 of AP II, which provides: "Starvation of civilians as a method of combat is prohibited. It is therefore prohibited to attack, destroy, remove or render useless, for that purpose, objects indispensable to the survival of the civilian population, such as foodstuffs, agricultural areas for the production of foodstuffs, crops, livestock, drinking water installations and supplies and irrigation works." In addition under Article 17 of AP II, there is a prohibition on the forced movement of civilians. Though, Iraq was not a party to AP II, its action was violative of principles of distinction, proportionality and humanity. Discrimination requires that attackers distinguish military targets from civilian ones. Proportionality requires that the force used be proportional to the desired objective. Humanity requires that military forces avoid inflicting suffering, injury, or destruction beyond that actually necessary for the accomplishment of legitimate military objectives.

168 Roberts Adam, The Law of War and Environmental Damage, in Austin, Jay E., and Bruch, Carl E., (ed.). 2000. *The Environmental Consequences of War: Legal, Economic and Scientific Perspectives*, Cambridge: Cambridge University Press, p. 75.

# CHAPTER 4

# Military Activities and Post Conflict Situations

George Washington, in his first inaugural address, said: "To be prepared for war is one of the most effectual means of preserving peace."[1] Countries spent a large percentage of their GNP on military preparedness[2] and militarism.[3] Today, 165 of 196 sovereign states maintain regular armed forces and about 10 percent of all government expenditure in the world is devoted directly to maintaining these regular armed forces,[4] although many of the states are at peace most of the time, with their armed forces engaged primarily in training, garrison duty, weapon-testing and patrolling within their own borders. The construction of facilities for the militaries such as

---

1   George Washington, first annual address to Congress, January 8, 1790.

2   Military preparedness includes all activities necessary to plan, staff, arm, maintain and deploy national military forces, in the absence of actual armed conflict. Industrial support activities are also related to military preparedness. These are conducted largely by civilians on contract to the military establishments. Such activities include production, testing, storage, and transportation of war material; research and development; and other activities involved in industrial support of the military. Gaines, Arthur G., Comments: The Environmental Threat of Military Operations, in Grunawalt Richard J., King John E. and McClain Ronald S. (eds). 1996. *Protection of the Environment During Armed Conflict*, Newport, Naval War College, International Law Studies, Vol. 69, p. 137.

3   The dictionary meaning of militarism: "the belief or desire of a government or people that a country should maintain and readily draw upon a strong military capability and be prepared to use it aggressively to defend or promote national interest." Pearsall Judy (ed.), *The New Oxford Dictionary of English*, First Edition, 1998, p. 1173. Militarism may best be understood as the conjunction of the state and a society. For details see: Trauschweizer Ingo, On Militarism, Vol. 76, No. 2, *The Journal of Military History*, April 2012, p. 507-556; Also see: Militarism: The Environmental Cost, available at: http://www.indymedia.org.uk/media/2009/08//436986.pdf, accessed 26 August 2013.

4   World military expenditure in 2012 is estimated to have been $1756 billion representing 2.5 per cent of global gross domestic product or $249 for each person. Military Expenditure, *SIPRI Yearbook 2013: Armament, Disarmament and International Security*, p. 125.

ports, fortifications, airfields, barracks, maintenance and repair depots, and fuel storage facilities have a significant environmental consequence. The routine maintenance of ships, aircraft, combat and support vehicles, and the storage and discard of weaponry produce pollutants such as used oil and solvents, polychlorinated biphenyls (PCBs), photographic chemicals, battery and other acids, paint sludge, heavy metals, asbestos, cyanides and plating residues. The training of military troops contributes to land, air and water pollution.

Both during the preparation for and war, the militaries of most nations consume huge amounts of fossil fuels and other non-renewable materials. Energy consumption by military equipment can be substantial. Approximately one quarter (42 million tonnes per year) of the world's jet fuel is used by armed forces.[5] An F-16 fighter jet burns as much fuel in an hour as the average American motorist uses in two-years. An armoured division of 348 battle tanks operating for one day consumes more than 2.2 million litre of fuel, and a carrier battle group operating for one day consumes more than 1.5 million litre of fuel.[6] Bombing exercises destroy ecosystems, kill wildlife and create long-term hazards due to unexploded ordnance. The military bases also produce large amount of ordinary garbage, medical wastes, and sewage; which may be disposed of casually. The use of oil-fuelled weapon systems and transport vehicles, including naval vessels and aircraft leads to significant environmental damage.[7] In sum, military activities contribute to global environmental problems such as climate change,[8] the destruction of the ozone layer and loss of biological

5   It has been estimated that nearly one-quarter of all jet fuel, i.e., 42 million tonnes per year was used for military purpose in the late 1980s. Michael Renner. Environmental and Health Effects of Weapons Production, Testing and Maintenance, in Levy and Sidel (ed.), *War and Public Health*, p. 117-135.

6   In the late 1980s, the United States military consumed 18.6 million tons of fuel (more than 44 percent of the world's total) annually, and emitted 381,000 tons of carbon monoxide, 157,000 tons of oxides of nitrogen, 78,000 tons of hydrocarbons, and 17,900 tons of sulphur-dioxide. Renner M. 2000. 'Environmental and health effects of weapons production, testing, and maintenance', in: Levy B.S., Sidel V.W., (eds), *War and Public Health*, Washington, DC: American Public Health Association, p. 117-136.

7   McNeill J.R., 'The Global Environmental Footprint of the US Military', in Closmann Charles E., (ed.). 2009. *War and the Environment: Military Destruction in the Modern Age*, USA: Texas A&M University Press, p. 22-28.

8   The projected impacts of climate change will be more than threat multipliers; they will serve as catalysts for instability and conflict. In Africa, Asia, and the Middle East, the impacts of extreme weather, such as prolonged drought and flooding—and resulting food shortages, desertification, population dislocation and mass migration, and sea level rise—are posing security challenges to these regions' governments. The

diversity. Greenhouse gases in the atmosphere are at their highest level for 800,000 years and have continued to rise at an average of about 2.7 per cent annually over the past decade.[9]

The armed forces of the world are both 'normal' and 'special' polluters producing toxic and radioactive wastes.[10] They are also 'protected polluters' because there are no environmental legislations to control their activities.[11] The overall and worldwide pollution by the armed forces could be as high as 30 percent.[12] The worldwide military use of aluminium, copper, nickel and platinum is greater than the demand for these materials in the Global South. Almost 30 percent of all the aluminium produced goes to the arms trade. Aluminium smelting is one of the most environmentally destructive processes. The mining of bauxite destroys tropical rainforests and releases chemicals into riverine and groundwater systems in the countries like Jamaica, India, Trinidad and Australia. Military manoeuvres destroy natural vegetation, disturb wildlife habitat, erode and compact soil, silt up streams, and cause flooding. Bombing ranges transform the land into a moon-like wasteland, while shooting ranges for tanks and artillery contaminate soil and groundwater with lead and other toxic residues. The impact of military

---

projected impacts of climate change—heat waves, intense rainfall, floods and droughts, rising sea levels, more acidic oceans, and melting glaciers and arctic sea ice will not only affect local communities but also have international impacts. Climate change may increase the frequency, scale and complexity of future military missions. *National Security and the Accelerating Risks of Climate Change*, CNA Military Advisory Board, USA, Alexandria, VA: CNA Corporation, 2014.

9   *Our Planet: Greening Business*, The Magazine of the United Nations Environment Programme, UNEP, 2014, p. 8.

10  Normal polluter: Military presence and peacetime activities relating to the use of natural resources and energy causing land, waters and air pollution. Special Polluter: the use and maintenance of specialized weapons such as nuclear, chemical, depleted uranium and their routine disposal causing environmental pollution.

11  For example, the Government of India has promulgated a number of acts, rules, and notifications for the protection and preservation of the environment that are addressed at various sectors – agriculture, industry, forestry, energy, mining, tourism, transportation and human settlement. The defence sector has not been explicitly included within their purview, perhaps out of deference to the military mission. The armed forces in India carry out operations across the country and have strong presence in ecologically sensitive areas. Sustainable environmental management of the installations and military sites is, therefore, critical for their continued use and ensuring India's long-term defence preparedness. Rao, N.H., Environmental management: Relevance and implications for management of defence installations for sustainability, Vol. 88, No. 11, *Current Science*, 10 June 2005, p. 1753-1758.

12  Renner M, 'Assessing the Military's War on the Environment', in *State of the World 1991*, New York: Norton.

preparedness on the natural environment is difficult to document as related data and reports are not made public by the governments.

Military operations associated with military preparedness involve (i) activities related to weapon research, development, testing, storage and transportation, and the destruction of old or phased out weapons; and (ii) training, arming, weapon-testing, maintenance, deployment, and activation of armed forces. While the first category of activity may be undertaken in civilian establishments, the second is conducted largely on military bases and military ships and aircraft. The US armed forces generate some 750,000 tons of toxic waste annually—more than that generated by the five largest US chemical companies combined. This pollution occurs globally on US bases in dozens of countries,[13] and some 8,500 military properties on American soil. The military not only emits toxic material directly into the air and water, it is also responsible for poisoning of the land of nearby communities, resulting in increased rates of cancer, kidney disease, increasing birth defects, low birth weight and miscarriage.

Not only is the environment a major victim during the military preparedness and armed conflict, but also during the post-conflict situations. Further, the presence of military in ecologically fragile areas also causes considerable damage to environment.[14] Long after the armed forces are withdrawn from conflict areas, landmines, explosive remnants of war (ERW), pollutants, and leaking chemicals continue to cause havoc.[15]  Landmines not only

---

13  The Pentagon's document of 1999 reported serious pollution at the US bases in Canada, Germany, Great Britain, Greenland, Iceland, Italy, Panama, the Philippines, South Korea, Spain, and Turkey. Since US military bases abroad are treated as US territory, the installations typically remain exempt from the environmental authority of the host country. An analyst comments: "While the US war machine bombards civilians in places like Serbia, Afghanistan, and Iraq, it also makes 'war on the earth', both at home and abroad". Feldman Bob, War on the Earth, available at: http://www.dollarsandsense. org/archives/2003/0303maps.pdf, accessed 26 August 2013.

14  In June 2014, the Government of India has cleared a proposal from the armed forces for setting up a radar station on Narcondam Island in the Bay of Bengal. The tiny Island, part of the Andaman and Nicobar Island group, is the only home of the endemic Narcondam hornbill. The existing police outpost at the island has itself caused some loss of habitat. It is dependent on the single freshwater source available on the island, and any additional human presence and installations will only compound the problems for the island and its unique flora and fauna. In February 2012, the Director, Bombay Natural History Society, made a site visit on behalf of the Standing Committee of the National Board for Wildlife (NBWL), a high-level statutory advisory body of the Government, and strongly recommended rejection of the proposal, as it posed a grave threat to the only population of Narcondam hornbills in the world.

15  Landmines cause dramatic harm to the environment, in terms of the pollution of air and

cause the death and destruction of soldiers and military objects, they also kill civilians, and domestic and wild animals. The presence of minefields can prevent access to safe drinking water. Laying and removing landmines degrades the soil and can cause evaporation of water from sand and soil. Furthermore, animals and plants killed by landmines can pollute the waters around where they are killed.

Finch (1996), has presented a hazard model (Table 4) to the phases of military operations: pre-mobilization, mobilization, military operations, and post-conflict operations.[16]

---

water, loss of agricultural lands and fields, and impairment of economic growth and land use development. For example, sand and soil are damaged when landmines are laid, exploded, and cleared. The nature of the soil can be changed after the explosion of landmines. Explosives commonly used in landmines, such as trinitrotoluene (TNT), seep into the soil. The decomposition of these substances can cause many environmental problems because they are often water soluble, carcinogenic, toxic, and long lasting. This substantially decreases the productivity of agricultural land and increases an area's vulnerability to water and wind erosion, which in turn can add sediment into drainage systems, adversely affecting water habitats. Unexploded ordnance (UXO) detonations have similar results. One study has shown that the detonation of UXO in the Vietnamese province of Quang Tri has drastically reduced soil productivity. According to estimates, rice production per hectare has decreased 50 percent in this area. The slow degradation of landmines and their devastating impact on surrounding land can render resources unusable for many generations. The environmental impact of landmines is particularly pronounced when viewed in conjunction with socioeconomic factors and other consequences of landmine contamination. *Global Landmine Crisis, Environmental Impact, Adopt-A-Minefield, Clear a Path to a Safer World*, available at: http://www.landmines.org/GlobalCrisis/TheProblem/TheProblem-all.htm, accessed 12 December 2013.

16 For instance, in the pre-mobilization phases, explosives must be manufactured and assembled into bombs, mortars, grenades, etc. Manufacturing represents as acute and chronic risk to workers and they are likely to get injured in this process. Also the waste products of these processes represent acute and chronic risk to environment. More military arsenal means larger production capacity and greater potential for contamination. The long-term environmental effects of contamination are very complex and costly to mitigate. In the mobilization phase, population in the vicinity of military camps as well as environment may get affected by accidental releases of explosives or hazardous material. Environmental damage in military operations can occur both as a result of acts of deliberate destruction and malice, and as an unintentional by-product of military activity. Targeting or accidental damage to chemical, petroleum and nuclear facilities could pose serious threat to environment. Further, the effects of explosives are not only immediate, but can last into the post conflict phase. The effects of the uses of Agent Orange during Vietnam War are still visible in Vietnam. Unexploded landmines and ERW are the most chronic problem in the post-conflict phase. The exposure to DU weapons can have long-term health effects on soldiers. For more details see: Finch, Frank R., 'This Land is Our Land: The Environmental Threat of Army Operations', in Grunawalt Richard J., King John E. and McClain Ronald S. (eds). 1996. *Protection of the Environment During Armed Conflict*, Newport, Naval War College, International

| Combat Phase | Source | Hazard classification | Pathway | Receptor |
|---|---|---|---|---|
| **Pre- mobilization** (i) Acute | Manufacturing and Training | Physical damage | Air, Water, Soil | Workers, training land and flora, fauna |
| (ii) Chronic | Spills during exercises, maintenance of garrison | Chemical, physical, biological | Air, Water, Soil | Workers, training lands, humans, flora, fauna |
| **Mobilization** (i) Acute | Industrial production, accidental releases, explosions | Chemical, physical, biological | Air, water, soil | Population in the vicinity, flora, fauna |
| (ii) Chronic | Release of hazardous material used in industries | Chemical, physical, biological | Air, water, soil | Population in the vicinity, flora, fauna |
| **Military Operations** Acute | Explosives | Physical damage | Contact | Soldiers, civilians, flora, fauna, land |
| | Medical wastes | Biological, physical, chemicals | Water, air, soil | Soldiers, civilians, flora, fauna, air, water and land |
| | POL/hazardous waste spills and chemicals | Chemical, physical | Water, air, soil | Soldiers, civilians, flora, fauna |
| | War damage to industrial facilities producing military items | Biological, chemicals, physical | Air, water, soil | Soldiers, civilians, flora, fauna |

| Combat Phase | Source | Hazard classification | Pathway | Receptor |
|---|---|---|---|---|
| Post-Conflict (i) Acute | Landmines, unexploded ordnance | Chemical, physical | Contact | Civilians, land, flora, fauna, soldiers |
| (ii) Chronic | Disposal of contaminants, leaking weapons | Biological, chemicals, physical | Air, water, soil | Soldiers, civilians, flora, fauna, air, water and land |

*Table 4: Hazard Model--Phases of Military Operations*

According to Westings (2001), unintentional environmental degradation during armed conflict begins with the preparation for conflict. It is associated with: (i) establishing military fortifications and other military facilities; (ii) equipping the armed forces with weapons and other military equipments, and disposing of obsolete and unwanted weapons; (iii) training armed forces and testing of the weapons; and (iv) deployment of armed forces in the conflict zone within the national jurisdiction or abroad.[17]

Militaries world-over are the biggest land users. It is estimated that globally, the amount of land used for military purposes ranges between 750,000 and 1500,000 sq km, an area that would be equal to the total surface areas of France and United Kingdom.[18] Among other things, land is used for the testing of aircraft weapons, missiles, bombs, and weapon systems, which lead to the formation of craters, compaction and erosion of soil, and contamination by toxic and hazardous residues. The presence of landmines and other remnants of war render large tracts of land unfit for purposes such as urbanization, agriculture and habitat preservation.

---

17 Westing, Arthur H., Warwick Fox and Michael Renner, Environmental Degradation as both Consequence and Cause of Armed Conflict, Working Paper for Nobel Peace Laureate Forum participants by PREPCOM subcommittee on Environmental Degradation, June 2001. Available at: http://www.timelessfaith.org/BOOKS_pdf/EnviromentaDegradation.pdf, accessed 22 May 2014.

18 In Kazakhstan, for example, more land is currently reserved for the use of military than is made available for wheat production. Biswas Asit K. 2000. 'Scientific Assessment of the Long-term Environmental Consequences of War', In Austin, Jay E., and Bruch, Carl E., (ed.), *The Environmental Consequences of War: Legal, Economic and Scientific Perspectives*, Cambridge: Cambridge University Press, p. 304.

The contribution of military activities to environmental deterioration has not received due attention for two main reasons. First, the military is not seen as an 'industry', though in many ways it behaves like one; and second, states are not willing to subject their armed forces to the levels of transparency and accountability that are required of other governmental or civil society actors.[19] Some of the issues related with the environmental damage caused by military preparedness, the presence of military in an ecologically fragile area, and in post-conflict situations are discussed in this chapter.

## Nuclear Weapon Development and Testing

Nuclear weapons technology continues to dominate concerns regarding potential hazards to the environment. Radioactivity, released into the environment in many phases of production and testing processes, poses a serious threat to the health of biological species, including humans. The assessment of this threat begins with estimating the amount of radiation released, and then evaluating health risks on the basis of what can be found in epidemiological studies of exposed populations and ecosystems over time. These studies are based on relatively small samples and look at areas affected by above-ground tests, areas near nuclear weapons production and storage facilities and areas used for radioactivity tests. They raise concern in terms of human health effects, costs of environmental clean-up and continued environmental contamination. Massive amounts of radioactivity have been released in the last half of the 20th century from the nuclear weapons testing programs of all the major nuclear powers.[20]

---

19 *The Military's Impact on the Environment: A Neglected Aspect of the Sustainable Development Debate*, A Briefing Paper for States and NGOs, International Peace Bureau, August 2002, p. 3. Available at: http://www.ipb.org/i/pdf-files/The_Militarys_Impact_on_the_Environment.pdf, accessed 21 November 2013.

20 The testing phase of nuclear weapons included 423 atmospheric tests (conducted from 1945 to 1957) and about 1400 underground tests (from 1957 to 1989). In the US, radiation releases from the military production of nuclear weapons has been enormous. Production sites that have been investigated, found to have caused significant environmental contamination. Geiger HJ, Rush D. *Dead reckoning: a critical review of the Department of Energy's epidemiologic research*. Washington: Physicians for Social Responsibility; 1992.The US government has recently acknowledged that occupational exposures to nuclear and other toxic materials justifies the awarding of compensation to over 3000 current and retired workers whose health has been adversely affected. *Secretary Richardson announces proposal to compensate thousands of sick workers* [press release]. Washington: US Department of Energy; 12 April 2000, available: www.doe.gov/news/releases00/aprpr/pr00103.htm, accessed 22 March 2014.

The manufacture and testing of weapons involves the leakage of nuclear material.[21] The production of nuclear weapons has polluted vast amounts of soil and water at hundreds of nuclear weapons facilities all over the world. Many of the substances released, including plutonium, uranium, strontium, cesium, benzene, polychlorinated biphenyls (PCBs), mercury and cyanide, are carcinogenic and/or mutagenic and remain hazardous for thousands, some for hundreds of thousands, of years. Contaminants from nuclear weapons production and testing have often travelled far, carried by wind and water. Production facilities for nuclear weapons are heavily polluted, for example in the United States there are over 4500 contaminated Department of Energy sites.[22]

Of all the activities concerning nuclear weapons, testing has been the most destructive of the environment. Even placing tests underground does not avoid atmospheric pollution. Radioactivity released from nuclear testing — including plutonium, strontium, cesium, carbon-14, and radioactive iodine — has been widely dispersed throughout the world. Underground tests have contaminated soil and groundwater.[23] Producing and maintaining

---

21 Nuclear-weapon test explosions have been carried out in all environments, releasing culpable amounts of radiation above ground, underground and underwater. Nuclear tests have occurred on top of towers, aboard barges, suspended from balloons, on the Earth's surface, underwater to depths of 600m, underground to depths of more than 2400m and in horizontal tunnels. Test bombs have been dropped by aircraft and fired by rockets over 320km into the atmosphere. Every nuclear-weapon testing has been responsible for environmental and health problems. Radiation has leaked into the environment from underground nuclear tests, atmospheric and underground nuclear testing has rendered large areas of land uninhabitable, and the health and livelihoods of indigenous people, their children, and their children's children, have been profoundly affected.

22 Arjun Makhijani, Howard Hu, and Kahterine Yih (eds.). 1995. *Nuclear Wastelands: A Global Guide to Nuclear Weapons Production and its Health and Environmental Effects*, Cambridge, Mass: MIT Press. Workers involved in the production of weapons as well as the people in the surrounding communities, have been exposed to radiation. In June 1999, the US government settled legal proceedings filed by the employees of nuclear weapons facilities who alleged that they were exposed to dangerous radiation and were not informed about it for many years. The impact of this radiation has been disproportionately concentrated in the areas where poor people and people of colour were residing. Gini Egan, Social Injustices of Nuclear Weapons Development, Vol. 4 (2), *PSR Health Res. Bull.*, Fall 1997.

23 Underground nuclear explosions give rise to ground disturbance effect. These include slides, subsidence, ground fractures, cliff falls and minor fault displacements which contribute to aftershocks. The aftershocks generally result from small movements along pre-existing fault planes associated with release of tectonic strain. The shock waves radiating from the detonation point of a deep underground explosion, on reaching the surface cause an upward heave of the ground. This may cause surface rock and soil

nuclear arsenals also entails tremendous environmental and human health costs. More than 3,200 US sites were identified as having soil and/or groundwater tainted by radioactive contamination. Similar problems have been found in sites under the former Soviet Union.

It is not only the US and Russia that have caused environmental damage through nuclear technology and nuclear-powered war machinery.[24] All nuclear weapons and nuclear energy producing nations have caused some level of environmental contamination, both in their own countries and abroad. Nuclear testing in the South Pacific, China, India and Pakistan; water and airborne discharges from reprocessing plants in the UK and France; and uranium mining in Namibia, Canada, former East Germany and Australia are a few examples. Moreover, the ongoing production of both nuclear weapons and nuclear power continues to create nuclear waste.[25]

---

to separate from the material below. Depending on soil and rock type there may be a slight mound or depression. Leakage of radioactive material from an underground testing site may occur if there is ground water present at the emplacement depth at the time of explosion, or if fracturing rock subsequently allows ground water access to the cavity. There is a possibility that this ground water is subsequently mixed with drinking water supplies or irrigation and enters into human environment. McEwan A.C. 1988. 'Environmental Effects of Underground Nuclear Explosions', in Goldblat Jozef and David Cox (ed.), *Nuclear Weapon Tests: Prohibition or Limitation*, SIPRI, Oxford: Oxford University Press, p. 75-91.

24   In 1989, a fire occurred in the after-part of the Russian Komsomolets nuclear-powered submarine (NPS). The submarine surfaced only to sink after several hours of futile attempt by the crew to keep it afloat in the Norwegian Sea. Forty-two crew members died. The disabled NPS bottomed at a depth of 1680 meters off Bear Island, 300 nautical miles away from the Norwegian coast. The release of radio-active substance in the near future would contaminate sea bottom and may cause economic loss of up to 2.5 thousand million roubles (in 1991 price). Kolesnikov Sergei and Aleksander Yemelyanenkov, 'Nuclear Pollution in the Former USSR', in Taipale Ilkka, P. Helena Makela and Kati Juva (ed.). 2001. *War or Health? A Reader*, London: Zed Books, p. 420-425.

25   Many square miles in Russia, Belarus and the US have been rendered unusable by contamination of the soil. Also the Irish Sea and the Arctic Ocean have been poisoned. In Russia nuclear submarines, some still armed with nuclear warheads, are rusting away in the fjords of Murmansk. Elsewhere, rivers have been polluted and open reservoirs and lakes have been used to hold large quantities of liquid radioactive materials. In 1957, a waste storage tank at the Chelyabinsk nuclear weapons site in Russia exploded and a radioactive cloud dispersed over more than 200 square kilometres of an agricultural region containing numerous rivers and lakes. Nearly all the trees within the most radioactive zone were damaged or killed. Radioactive waste has been routinely dumped into Lake Karachay, recognized as the world's most radioactive body of water, also at Chelyabinsk.

The clean-up of contaminated sites, the disposal of excess fissile material and dismantling of nuclear weapons also contaminates the environment. The burial of radioactive materials is presently being promoted as the solution to radioactive waste disposal. However, this too may not be free of hazards. One of the most likely mechanisms of pollution in connection with waste disposal underground is the contamination of groundwater through contact with radioactive elements that have leached out from the waste and contaminate the drinking water of both local and distant communities.[26]

The cost of making nuclear weapons and their delivery systems are known,[27] but the cost of the environmental harm caused by these weapons is often neglected. In the 1966 study *Atomic Audit*, it was concluded that the US had spent between $ 270 billion and $ 515 billion in environmental cleanup costs (2006 value) related to its nuclear programme.[28] It has been estimated that the equivalent costs in the Soviet Union could be at least three times higher. A large number of discarded nuclear-powered submarines, belonging to the Russian Navy's Northern Fleet are deteriorating, with the increasing risk of radioactive material leaching out.[29]

## Deployment in sensitive areas

The mere presence of armed forces in ecologically fragile areas can cause considerable damage to the environment. For instance, the Siachen Glacier, [30] the world's highest battlefield in the Himalayan region is facing

---

26 Leaning Jennifer, Environment and Health: Impact of War, Vol. 163 (9), *CMAJ*, 31 October 2000, p. 1157-1161.

27 The US spent approximately $ 7.5 trillion developing, producing, deploying, and maintaining tens of thousands of nuclear weapons from 1940 to 2005. Joseph Cirincione, 'Lessons Lost', *Bulletin of Atomic Scientists*, November 2005, p. 47.

28 Mahkijani Arjun, Stephen I. Schwartz, and William J. Weida, 'Nuclear Waste Management and Environmental Remediation', in Schwartz Stephen I.,1998. *Atomic Audit: The Costs and Consequences of US Nuclear Weapons Since 1940*, Washington DC: Brookings Institution Press, p. 355.

29 *Nuclear Wastes in the Arctic: An Analysis of Arctic and Other Regional Impacts From Soviet Nuclear Contamination (1995)*. Available at: http://www.fas.org/ota/reports/9504.pdf, accessed 26 June 2014.

30 The Himalayas have the largest concentration of glaciers outside the polar region. These glaciers are a freshwater reserve; they provide the headwaters for nine major river systems in Asia – a lifeline for almost one-third of humanity. Himalaya-Karakorum-Hindukush (HKH) together forms the largest mountain chain on earth; they run almost east-west, drawing a border between China and the South Asian nations. They are a blessing for South Asia, not only protecting it from the cold northerly winds, but also

environmental crisis due to the presence of the Indian and Pakistani militaries. The Siachen Glacier lies between the Karakoram and Zaskar ranges, and borders Pakistan, India, and China. It has been described as a 46-mile river of slow-moving ice surrounded by stupendous towers of snow, where human habitation is neither possible nor does it exist.[31]

About 15 thousand soldiers from Indian and Pakistan armies are deployed in a restricted area in and around the glacier. Several camps are located on the glacier itself. Temperatures go down to -50°C which necessitates burning kerosene to keep warm.[32] A forward base on the glacier is supported by air drops.[33] All supplies are brought by helicopter or air-dropped: tents, food, fuel, heaters, cookers, equipment, arms, ammunition, weapons, and rocket launchers. Heavy artillery is taken apart and the pieces flown in to be assembled at high altitude. Thus, Siachen is now polluted by the remains of crashed helicopters, worn out gun barrels, splinters from gun shelling, empty fuel barrels, burnt shelters, telephone wires, skid boards, parachute dropping boards, edible oil containers, canisters, gunny bags, rotten vegetables, expired tinned meat, cartons, wrappers, shoes, clothing,

---

confining the monsoon precipitation to this region. The HKH frozen water reserves are like a rooftop water tank the operation of which is regulated by temperature. Unfortunately its thermostat has been tampered with by global warming and much of its solid mass has been converted into liquid flowing downstream. The accelerated depletion of the solid mass is a threat to future generations which may suffer a paucity of this precious commodity essential for all the living creatures. The conflicting claims to the glacier, and the failure of negotiations to settle the dispute, led to the militarization of Siachen in 1984, when both India and Pakistan stationed their troops in the region. Even after the 2003 cease-fire, the region has remained militarized and the mere presence of the military has had a significant impact on the environment. Kemkar, Neal A., Environmental Peacemaking: Ending Conflict Between India and Pakistan on the Siachen Glacier through Creation of a Transboundry Peace Park, Vol. 25, *Stanford Environmental Law Journal*, No. 1, (2006), p. 1-56.

31 Glaciers in the eastern and central regions of the Himalayas appear to be retreating at alarming rates, while those in the western parts are more stable and could be even growing. A study report from the National Research Council examines how changes to glaciers in the Hindu Kush-Himalayan region, which covers eight countries across Asia, could affect the area's river systems, water supplies, and the South Asian population. The mountains in the region form the headwaters of several major river systems-including the Ganges, Mekong, Yangtze, and Yellow Rivers, which serve as sources of drinking water and irrigation supplies for roughly 1.5 billion people. Himalaya glaciers melting rapidly in some regions, *The Times of India*, New Delhi, 14 September 2012.

32 Nair Pavan, The Siachin War: Twenty-five Years On, *Economic & Political Weekly*, March 14, 2009, Vol XLIV, No. 11, p. 35-40.

33 Verma Kunal and Brig Rajiv Williams. 2010. *The Long Road to Siachen: The Question Why*, New Delhi: Rupa Publications, p. 403-404.

etc.[34] The area has become a massive garbage and sewage dump. The World Conservation Union's World Commission on Protected Areas (WCPA) estimates that on the Indian side alone, over 2000 lb of human waste is dropped daily into crevasses.

There are reports that clothing used by the soldiers are washed in the hot springs near the base camps, and toxic residue flows freely into the river. Siachen lacks natural biodegrading agents, so metals and plastics simply merge with the glacier as permanent pollutants, leaching toxins such as cobalt, cadmium, and chromium into the ice. This waste eventually reaches the Indus River, affecting drinking and irrigation water used by millions of people downstream from the Siachen. The glacier has also experienced large-scale loss of plant and animal diversity as habitats of ibex, brown bears, cranes, snow leopards, and many other species are threatened. The decrease in the number of these species, as well as the constantly eroding glacier line, has led the World Wide Fund for Nature to designate the entire Tibetan Plateau Steppe, which encompasses the Siachen Glacier, as one of 200 areas 'critical' to global conservation.[35]

## Unwarranted Ammunition (UWA)

The armed forces of almost all countries possess large quantities of munitions that are surplus to their requirement or have exceeded their design life. When weapons and ammunitions become obsolete— either because of changed political and military circumstances or due to the passage of time— the surplus stocks need to be decommissioned. Surplus arms were long incinerated, exploded, or simply jettisoned without much thought as to the release of toxic materials. After World War II, 122,000 tonnes of UWA were left in the Netherlands. Most of this was dumped in shallow waters. Due to the degradation of the casings, hazardous materials will eventually leak into the environment. Predictions were made that it would take at least 500 years for all the components to dissolve into the seawater.[36]

The disposal of energetic materials requires great care and involves considerable cost. Chemical residues from ordnance detonations have

---

34 Cariappa N., The Siachen Standoff, *The Hindu*, 11 November 2002.

35 Bhatt Semu, Kashmir: A choice between History and Future. Available at: http://www.amankiasha.com/detail_news.asp?id=311&page=65, accessed 30 November 2013.

36 Environmental Impact of Munition and Propellant Disposal, NATO Research and Technology Organization, Final Technical Report of Task Group TR-AVT-115, 2010.

potential ecological consequences in addition to being threats to human health. Past practices of dumping at sea or into land-fill sites are no longer acceptable and long-term storage is neither safe nor cost effective. Weapons must be dismantled and the energetic material must be destroyed or recycled/reused in a manner that does not harm the environment. Governments have a duty of care to the members of their armed forces, the general public and environment and all reasonable precautions must be exercised to ensure safe disposal of munitions.

UWA are dangerous and economically unprofitable in the context of dismantling for the following reasons: (i) They are unpredictable because irreversible physical and chemical changes can result in the ignition and explosion of the main charge; (ii) They are stored in roofed premises which are close to populated areas and hence raise the probability of human injury; (iii) Their storage in field conditions increases the probability of non-authorized access to ammunition and their use for terrorist purposes; and (iv) Their storage and preservation leads to significant regular financial expenses.[37]

Chemical weapons were not used as instruments of war during WW II, although all the belligerents had stockpiled these weapons. In the aftermath of the Cold War, environmental concerns received far greater attention in disarmament efforts, particularly with regard to chemical weapons disarmament. The Chemical Weapons Convention (CWC),[38] bans chemical weapons and requires their destruction within a specified period of time. The CWC is implemented by the Organization for the Prohibition

---

37 For example, Bulgaria had approximately 76,100 tonnes of UWA as on 1 January 2005. The major part of the UWA contained dangerous substances and components with hazardous properties, such as explosion, fire risk and toxicity and posed a significant environmental risk. The programme for UWA utilization needed urgent financing of approximately € 30 million, which the country could not afford.

38 The Convention on the Prohibition of the Development, Production, Stockpiling and Use of Chemical Weapons and on Their Destruction (CWC), 1997 was opened for signature on 13 January 1993 in Paris, and entered into force on 29 April 1997. To date 188 nations are party to this treaty. Two signatories—Israel and Myanmar—have yet to ratify the convention. CWC bans the stockpiling, transfer, production, development, and use of chemical weapons. While the CWC does not stipulate which technologies governments must use to eliminate their stockpiles, it requires that destruction be "irreversible" and safe for humans and the environment. Therefore, the environmentalists have been apprehensive about the possible dangers associated with eliminating these lethal weapons. The CWC required states-parties to destroy (i) all chemical weapons, and (ii) all chemical weapons production facilities (CWPF) under their jurisdiction or control which were involved in the production of chemical weapons by 29 April 2007.

of Chemical Weapons (OPCW). The CWC requires states-parties to declare in writing to the OPCW their chemical weapons stockpiles, chemical weapons production facilities (CWPFs), relevant chemical industry facilities, and other weapons-related information. The OPCW's main functions are to carry out verification activities and ensure treaty compliance. The State parties were allowed to determine how to destroy their chemical weapons, with the exception of the prohibited measures of sea dumping, land burial and open-pit burning, which were banned for ecological reasons. The selected destruction technology[39] was to minimize the risk of agents released during disposal/destruction, as well as reducing to a minimum the public health and environmental impact from process effluents. In order to ensure the safety of the people and protection of the environment and to verify compliance with environmental standards, effluents and solid wastes were to be monitored, sampled and analyzed before their release. The State parties were to consider the impact of the destruction process across the entire environmental spectrum and subsequently apply the best environmental option.[40] The biggest arsenals of chemical weapons that need to be destroyed are in Russia and the United States.[41] However, most of the information relating to chemical weapons disposal remains hidden from public.

The disposal of unnecessary weapons platforms (tanks, warplanes, or

---

39 Destruction is broadly defined as a process (such as high-temperature incineration or chemical neutralization) that converts chemical warfare agents and munitions irreversibly into a form in which they are no longer usable as weapons. Although the choice of destruction method is left to the discretion of each state party, it must be approved by the treaty organization. Declared chemical weapons stockpiles and former production facilities must be secured and subject to routine inspection until they are completely destroyed, and the destruction process is monitored on a continuous basis by international inspectors. Tucker Jonathan B. (ed.). 2001. *The Chemical Weapons Convention: Implementation Challenges and Solutions*, Washington: Centre for Nonproliferation Studies, Monterey Institute of International Studies, p. 2.

40 Kopte, Susanne, Michael Renner, and Peter Wilke, The Cost of Disarmament: Dismantlement of Weapons and the Disposal of Military Surplus, *The Non-proliferation Review,* Winter 1996, p. 33-45. Also see: Koplow David A. 2001. 'Green Chemistry: Dismantling Chemical Weapons While Protecting the Environment', in Guruswamy Lakshman D (ed.), *Arms Control and the Environment*, New York: Transnational Publishers, Inc, p. 143-157.

41 Destruction of other CWPFs must start within one year after the CWC enters into force for a state-party. States-parties must complete destruction by April 29, 2002. States-parties may request to convert CWPFs to facilities that they can use for non-prohibited purposes. Once their requests are approved, states-parties must complete conversion by 29 April, 2003. Member countries cannot destroy chemical weapons in any way that they like; they have to strictly follow the obligations of the CWC.

intercontinental missiles); munitions, and fuels and propellants damage the natural environment. Whichever technology is chosen, the expectation is that it should meet the following criteria: (i) be easily verifiable; (ii) make renewed military use difficult or impossible; (iii) prevent the theft or diversion of militarily usable materials released in the dismantling process; (iv) meet the deadlines for completing weapons disposal and other stipulations of arms treaties; and (v) comply with local, national, or international safety and environmental standards. All of these criteria have an impact on the cost of dismantlement and disposal, but environmental concern is a particularly potent factor.[42]

## Maintenance of Military Bases

The world's armed forces control large expanses of land. Military training grounds cover extensive areas with various valuable natural habitats. They are usually in remote, sparsely inhabited locations that are off limits to outside visitors. While some of these have thrived as wildlife refuges, land used for weapons testing and military manoeuvres suffer tremendous degradation and pollution. [43] Manoeuvres demolish the natural vegetation and compact and erode soil. Bombing and shooting ranges leave behind a wasteland contaminated and littered with unexploded ammunitions. All these factors exert a strong anthropogenic pressure which may directly or indirectly damage the stability of natural habitats in these territories and to cause the vanishing of rare species of flora and fauna.

During the Soviet period, 10 military bases were established in Lithuania. As a rule, they were situated in remote woodlands of great environmental value. Military sites in that period were considered strictly secret and environmental security was not given any priority. Environmentalists had no information on the radioactive, chemical and explosive materials stored in these military units. Radioactive materials and chemical pollutants

---

42 Kopte, Susanne, Michael Renner, and Peter Wilke, The Cost of Disarmament: Dismantlement of Weapons and the Disposal of Military Surplus, *The Non-proliferation Review,* Winter 1996, p. 33-45.

43 The key environmental problems possible on a typical military camp could be as follows: (i) ruined and damaged layer of soil; (ii) loss of biodiversity; (iii) polluted environment with chemical substances; (iv) damaged trees in the surrounding forests with bullets and splinters; (v) increased hazardous wastes; (vi) improper waste management; (vii) noise pollution; and (viii) problems associated with the specific activity of a military base, like radioactivity, chemical pollutants, etc. Ignatavicius Gytautas and Vytautas Oskinis, Some aspects of interaction between military activities and environmental protection on Lithuanian military grounds, Vol. 53, *Ekologija,* Supplement 2007, p.18.

produced during military activities were most often secretly transported from the territories of the units. The amounts of these materials and the dumps were never recorded. It is possible that until 1988 some radioactive waste was discharged into household waste dumps or buried in the territories of military units and adjacent areas.[44]

In June 1991, when the Soviets left Hungary, there were 171 abandoned garrisons. The environmental damage assessment performed during the withdrawal of troops set the cost of damage in excess of 600 million US dollars; 40 percent of this was damage to the soil and groundwater, 28 percent was damage to fauna, flora and landscape and 18 percent was due to inappropriate waste disposal. Of the greatest concern were the facts that more than 5,000,000 m$^3$ of soil and a huge volume of groundwater had been polluted with hydrocarbons.[45]

In 1992, the US completed its withdrawal from the Philippines, ending a century of US military presence. For almost half a century, the Philippines had played host to two of the most valuable military bases in the world: the Clark Air Force Base and the Subic Naval base, which were crucial to the US defence of the Asian region. However, it was discovered that the US had left behind several contaminated sites due to inadequate hazardous waste management. The US maintains that it is under no obligation to undertake further cleanup at its former installations, as the Philippines has waived its right to demand this under the basing agreement. However, under customary international law, the US is obliged to ensure that activities within its jurisdiction or control do not cause damage to the environment of other states.

In 1989, the US General Accounting Office (GAO) reported that the US

---

44  The key environmental problems possible on the present Lithuanian military territories left by the Russian armed forces could be grouped as follows: (i) the ruined and damaged layer of soil; (ii) techno-genially modified soil; (iii) loss of biodiversity; (iv) presence of chemical pollutants in soil; (v) damage of trees in the surrounding forests with bullets and splinters; (vi) untreated military waste; (vii) management of harmful radioactive substances; (viii) wastewater management. However, it was also found that two bird species, willow grouse (*Lagopus lagopus*) and short-toed eagle (*Circaetus gallicus*), already considered to be extinct in Lithuania, were found in these formerly closed territories. Ignatavicius Gytautas and Vytautas Oskinis, Some aspects of interaction between military activities and environmental protection on Lithuanian military grounds, Vol. 53, *Ekologija*, Supplement, 2007, p.16–21.

45  Magyar Balazs, Janos Stickel and Laszslo Vero, Assessment and Remediation of Environmental Damage: Proceedings of the Rome Symposium, September 1994, IAHS Publ. No. 233 (1995). Available at: http://iahs.info/redbooks/a233/iahs_233_0255.pdf, accessed 23 December 2013.

military is a major generator of hazardous waste in the US, generating more than 400,000 tons each year.[46] Negligent handling of toxic wastes (such as fuels, paints, solvents, propellants, explosives, etc.) during the decades of the Cold War resulted in more than 17,000 contaminated sites on 1,855 US military bases.[47] Hazardous waste management and past disposal practices at US bases have resulted in environmental problems, such as unexploded ordnances, PCB contaminations, soil and ground water contamination, unlined landfills, toxic spills, leaking underground storage tanks and off-base migration of contaminants.

Conventional military activities have many negative environmental consequences. The direct impacts include: (i) formation of craters and compaction, erosion, and contamination of soils by bombs, missiles, and military vehicles and their hazardous and toxic residues,[48] (ii) land pollution from causes ranging from latrines and garbage dumps to landmines, unexploded ordnance, and radioactive dust, (iii) defoliation

---

46  Hazardous waste includes solvents, paints, contaminated sludge, contaminated fuel and oil, phenols (poisonous acidic compounds), munitions, polychlorinated biphenyls (PCBs), metals, cyanides and other poisons which are dangerous to humans and environment. These wastes are generated by motor pools, paint shops, fire department, hospitals, medical clinics, laundries and industrial processed used mainly to repair and maintain weapon systems and equipments. US General Accounting Office, Hazardous Waste management Problems Continue at Overseas Military Bases (1991) GAO/NSIA-91-231.

47  Perhaps the worst case of contaminated site is at US army's Jefferson Proving Ground in Indiana. Jefferson Proving ground has been a munitions' test area since 1941. In the ensuing fifty years, the military test-fired an estimated 23 million rounds of ammunition. Today, it is estimated that 1.5 million of those test rounds remain unexploded, littering the facilities' 55,000 acres. There are reportedly munitions buried 24 feet beneath the earth's surface. Lanier-Graham Susan D. 1993. *The Ecology of War: Environmental Impacts of Weaponry and Warfare*, New York: Walker and Company, p. 87.

48  The US Marine Corps training area of Camp Schwab is close to Kushi Village which is adjacent to on the main island of Okinawa (Japan). Camp Schwab was built in 1960s and is used for the training. It was used for training of the US soldiers before they were sent to Vietnam. It played the similar roles in the Gulf War, Afghan War and the war in Iraq. As a result of the heavy training programs conducted for such roles, serious impacts have been imposed on the environment surrounding village Kushi. In the background of the village lie natural forests and mountains out of which is called 'Kushi-dake', which is about 3 km away from the village. The base of mountain has been used as a shield for live-firing and bombing by the US Marines. Due to 20mm heavy machine gun the firing, the red-soil dust is blown very high and, in the winter time, north wind carries the dust as far as the village. The live-firing causes not only forest deterioration by explosion but also deterioration by forest burning. The mountain is showing a miserable figure and the river and the sea are heavily polluted with red soil. The explosion often shakes the buildings in the neighbourhood and few residents reported cracks in their houses.

and deforestation, (iv) contamination of surface waters and groundwater, (v) atmospheric emissions and resulting air pollution from military equipment and vehicles, (vi) direct and collateral killing of animals and plants and loss of habitat, (vii) degradation and destruction of protected natural areas, and (viii) noise pollution of 140 decibels or more from low-flying aircraft and weapons that can lead to long-term hearing impairment in people and animals.[49] These environmental harms can in turn (i) disrupt or destroy the social and economic infrastructures of human communities, (ii) dislocate human populations, and (iii) create new opportunities for pathogenic microbes and the spread of infectious diseases among human populations.[50]

The construction and upgradation of roads has a serious negative impact on the environment in ecologically fragile areas.[51] It has been estimated that in the Indian Himalayas, for each linear km of mountain road, nearly 10 small to medium landslides occur as a result of slope instability caused by the road. Deforestation caused by road construction has deprived the region of all the tangible and intangible ecosystem services that forests provide in terms of watershed protection and soil conservation, enhancing the susceptibility to landslides. Besides, the illegal smuggling of timber and other kinds of forest produce tends to increase with better road connectivity, threatening the overall biodiversity in the Himalayas. The generation and disposal of road debris is another source of environmental degradation. A kilometre of road requires the removal of nearly 60,000 to 80,000 cubic metres of debris, which causes slope instability prompting landslides. The debris is usually dumped down-slope, causing damage to vegetation, forests, pastures and agricultural lands.[52]

The militaries are major users of ozone depleting substances (ODS).[53]

49  Robyn Eckersley, Ecological Intervention: Prospects and Limits, Vol. 21, No. 3, *Ethics & International Affairs*, Fall 2007, p. 293-316.

50  Biswas, Asit K. 2000. 'Scientific Assessment of the Long-Term Consequences of War', p. 303-315; McNeely, Jeffrey A. 'War and Biodiversity: An Assessment of Impacts', p. 353-378; both in Austin Jay E. and Bruch Carl E. (eds.), *The Environmental Consequences of War: Legal, Economic and Scientific Perspectives*, Cambridge: Cambridge University Press.

51  Nair, Colonel Yoesh, Integrated Road Network, Vol. CXLII, No. 587, *USI Journal*, Jan-Mar 2012, p. 67-74.

52  Sarkar, Rinki, Rural Accessibility and Development: Sustainability Concerns in an Ecologically Fragile Mountain Belt, Vol. XLV, No. 21, *Economic & Political Weekly*, 22 May 2010, p. 63-71.

53  The ozone layer, a thin band in the stratosphere (layer of the upper atmosphere),

In recent years, increasing quantities of CFC have been released into the atmosphere, seriously threatening to deplete the stratospheric ozone layer and foster global climate changes, which may cause the migration of food-growing belts, change in monsoon patterns, sharp rises in ocean levels and flooding of coastal areas due to the melting of polar ice caps, increasing hurricane activity and storms, salt water intrusion into supplies of fresh water, destruction of wildlife habitats, and the impairment of port facilities."[54]

The continued depletion of the ozone layer and the consequent increase in ultraviolet radiation may lead to a growing number of skin cancers and cataracts and reduce the ability of the immune system to respond to infection. Additionally, the growth of the world's oceanic plankton, the base of most marine food chains, would decline. Phytoplanktons are photosynthetic organisms that use up carbon dioxide. So, a decline in plankton populations would lead to increased carbon dioxide levels in the atmosphere and thus to global warming. Recent studies suggest that global warming, in turn, may increase the amount of ozone destroyed. Even if the manufacture of CFCs is immediately banned, the chlorine already released into the atmosphere will continue to destroy the ozone layer for many

---

serves to shield Earth from the Sun's harmful ultraviolet rays. In the 1970s, scientists discovered that chlorofluorocarbons (CFCs)—chemicals used in refrigeration, air-conditioning systems, cleaning solvents, and aerosol sprays—destroy the ozone layer. CFCs release chlorine into the atmosphere; chlorine, in turn, breaks down ozone molecules. Because chlorine is not affected by its interaction with ozone, each chlorine molecule has the ability to destroy a large amount of ozone for an extended period of time. The 1987 Montreal Protocol on Substances that Deplete the Ozone Layer sets firm targets for reducing and eliminating consumption and production of a number of ozone-depleting substances and has the elimination of all ozone-depleting substances as its final objective. Amendments and adjustments adopted in 1990 and 1992 brought the timetables forward and added new controlled substances. As a result, production and consumption of ozone-depleting substances such as chlorofluorocarbons (CFCs) and halons were to be totally phased out by 1 January 1996. Ozone depleting substances are used in the air force for fire-fighting in the crash fire tenders as well as on every aircraft as a fire repressant. In the navy they are used for fire-fighting operations in ships and submarines. In the army, all motorized armoured carriers utilize them for fire-fighting. As refrigerants, the ODS are used in all central air-conditioning plants, mobile communication hubs, missile batteries, armoured carries and cockpits. After the international agreement, the Montreal Protocol on phasing out of ODS came in force, the militaries are facing challenges in selecting and introducing new alternatives. Kumar Manoj, Challenges for the Indian Military: Managing Ozone Depleting Substances, Vol. 5, No. 2, *AIR POWER*, summer 2010, p. 117-132.

54  John S. Hannah, *Chlorofluorocarbons: A Scientific Environmental, and Regulatory Assessment*, Vol. 31, *A.F.L. Rev.*, (1992), p. 92.

decades.

The Montreal Protocol on Substances that Deplete the Ozone Layer (1987) set specific targets for all nations to achieve in order to reduce emissions of chemicals responsible for the destruction of the ozone layer. Many had hoped that this treaty would cause ozone loss to peak and begin to decline by the year 2000. In fact, in the fall of 2000, the hole in the ozone layer over Antarctica was the largest recorded until then. The hole the following year was slightly smaller, leading some to believe that the depletion of ozone had stabilized. However, in 2006 US scientists reported that the ozone loss over Antarctica reached its greatest extent ever. Ozone loss can vary with temperature, and many scientists believe that the 2006 record loss was due to lower-than-normal temperatures. It has been reported that although CFC levels in the atmosphere peaked in 2001, many of these chemicals are long-lasting and the ozone layer over Antarctica may not fully recover until 2065.[55]

## Post-conflict

Recovery from the environmental damage caused by wars has often proven to be very slow, extremely costly, and in some cases impossible. Modern lethal weapons, particularly depleted uranium and chemical weapons containing persistent toxic chemicals, such as dioxins and radio-active substances can have an impact over generations. Another major concern relates to landmines and unexploded ammunition and ordnance, which are "hidden killers." Many of the battlefields of World War I and II and the Vietnam War [56] for instance, are still unfit for cultivation today, and dangerous to people and animals due to unexploded devices and projectiles embedded in the soil.

One study estimated that 70 per cent of the conventional bombs dropped by the US over Iraq in the Gulf War missed their target, and that of the

---

55  EDEKO Sunday E, An Overview of the Environmental Implications of War, Vol. 1, No. 2, *Sacha Journal of Environmental Studies*, 2011, p 50.

56  The US forces used 15 million tons of bombs and ammunition during the Vietnam War and an estimated 800,000 tons of unexploded ordnance still contaminates 20 percent of the country's area. Unexploded ordnance left over from the Vietnam War has killed more than 42,000 people and injured some 62,000 since the end of the war in 1975. These deadly accidents continue daily. It may take more than 100 years to clear the contaminated area. Vietnam War ammo has killed 42k since, *Times of India*, New Delhi, 30 June 2009.

88,500 tons of bombs dropped on Iraq, 17,700 tons never exploded.[57] Some of the ordnance used by the US contained depleted uranium. After the war, many rounds of this ammunition remained in the ground causing radiological contamination. Uranium can become airborne and may be inhaled or ingested. Unexploded ordnance can remain undetected for many years. Mines have been used routinely in wars for nearly two centuries, and today, 80 percent of mine victims are civilians. Discarded materials including radioactive debris, trash and explosives can present environmental hazards long after battles have ceased. The destruction of endangered species, poisoned water supplies, soil pollution, deforestation, and desertification are some other grave environmental problems.

During the 1980-1988 Iraq-Iran War, mines were used extensively on the high sea, involving even non-belligerent ships. Iran dispersed mines in the path of neutral shipping in the Gulf water. Iraq planted more than half a million mines in Kuwait in order to seal off Kuwait's coastline. It also mined the Gulf with thousands of explosive devices that had to be detonated by Allied naval forces in order to permit them to manoeuvre. These mines still pose a threat to the marine ecosystem of all Gulf waters.[58]

War debris and abandoned military equipment pose another serious threat to the environment. In 1991, during Gulf War II, the Allied forces bombarded Iraqi military locations, destroying about 3,000 tanks and about 2,100 artillery pieces. In Kuwait, the "Highway of Death" was covered with thousands of vehicles, cans, tanks, damaged military hardware as well as dead bodies.[59] In addition, sanitary waste, including leftover food for more than half a million troops, littered the Northern Saudi desert. Organic waste of barbed wire and material used to maintain military vehicles were dumped in battlefields. Spent lubricating oil was collected and burned and

57  Cassady B. Craft and Suzette R. Grillot, *Conventional Arms Control and the Environment: Mitigating the Effects of War,* Conventional Arms Control and the Environment: Mitigating the Effects of War," at the Symposium *Arms and the Environment: Preventing the Perils of Disarmament,* Tulsa, Oklahoma, December 1999, The University of Tulsa College of Law, University of Oklahoma.

58  Al-Duaij Nada. 2004. *Environmental Law of Armed Conflict,* New York: Transnational Publishers, p. 48.

59  The Highway of Death refers to a road between Kuwait and Basra on which civilians and minor retreating units of the Iraqi army were brutally attacked and completely destroyed by American aircrafts during the United Nations Coalition offensive in the Gulf War, on the night of 26 February-27 February 1991. It is known officially as Highway 80, and it runs from Kuwait City to the border towns of Abdali (Kuwait) and Safwan (Iraq), and then on to Basra. The road was repaired during the late 1990s, and was used in the initial stages of the 2003 invasion of Iraq by the US and British forces.

its residue was buried, resulting in soil contamination.[60]

Since 2001, the US military has generated millions of kilograms of hazardous, toxic and radioactive wastes in Afghanistan.[61] The US military has not revealed details of its waste disposal systems; and it appears that wastes have been buried, burned or secretly disposed into the air, soil, groundwater and surface waters of Afghanistan. When the US forces withdraw from Afghanistan, the toxic chemicals they leave behind will continue to pollute for centuries. Any abandoned radioactive waste may stain the Afghanistan country side for thousands of years. Afghanistan was described in the past as graveyard of foreign armies. Today it has a different title, "A toxic dumping ground for foreign armies." The American military is using a few burn pits in place of incinerators to destroy hazardous waste. The pollution of water bodies would lead to the extraction of more groundwater in the post-conflict settlement period. This would cause further stress on critical water resources.

In 2006, the UNEP undertook a preliminary assessment of an abandoned military storage site located near Astana, a small village in the Panjshir Valley, Afghanistan. The site is currently used by local inhabitants to graze livestock. The site was used as a helicopter base by the Russian Army during the 1980s, and by the Afghan Northern Alliance as storage ground for stockpiles of military hardware in the 1990s. Hazardous chemicals

---

60 The invasion and occupation of Kuwait by the Iraqi forces and the resulting Gulf War in 1991 led to unprecedented environmental contamination, the effects of which will be felt for years to come. The air was polluted by emissions from hundreds of burning oil wells, the sea fouled by the largest oil spill in history, and the land scarred by massive bombardment and troop movement. For more details see: Sadik M. and McCain J.C. 1993. *The Gulf War Aftermath: An Environmental Tragedy*, Springer.

61 The American military waste in Afghanistan consists of: (i) Fuel leaks and spills; (ii) Paints, asbestos, solvents, grease, cleaning solutions and building material containing formaldehyde, copper, arsenic and hydrogen cyanide; (iii) Hydraulic fluids, antifreeze and used oil; (iv) Pesticide/poison leaks and spills; (v) Lead, nickel, zinc and cadmium battery waste and acids, having toxic and corrosive properties; (vi) Electronic waste, including computers, printers, screen, television, radios, refrigerators, and communication equipments; (vii) Light bulbs having toxic level of mercury; (viii) Plastic; (ix) Medical waste; (x) Ammunition waste; (xi) Radioactive waste, which may contain depleted uranium, radium 226, thorium, cesium 137 and plutonium; and (xii) Grey and black water containing latrine, shower and shave wastes (LSS) and soap residue. The local contractors have dumping these wastes in streams and rivers. While military in the US adheres to strict rules regarding the discharge of such waste, it faces no restrictions in Afghanistan. Nasuti Matthew, The American Military is Creating an Environmental Disaster in Afghanistan, available at: http://www.globalresearch.ca/index.php?context=va&aid=18883, accessed 24 March 2014.

and other miscellaneous materials associated with the fuelling, arming and firing of SCUD missiles remain on site. The hazardous substances stored at Astana include (i) unsymmetrical dimethylhydrazine (UDMH)--a probable human carcinogen, (ii) nitric acid--approximately 10m3, (iii) radioactive materials--radium or tritium, and (iv) unexploded ordnance—about 4,800 kg. The UNEP report concluded that in its current state, the Astana site represents high risks for a number of environmental and human receptors.[62]

## Rebuilding and Resettlement

Deforestation occurs not only during an armed conflict, but also after it, to support rebuilding efforts and occupation forces.  The complete recovery of forest ecosystems may take several centuries. After World War II, about 500 million board feet of lumber and 100 million square feet of plywood were needed for occupation troops and family housing.[63] There was massive deforestation in Europe during and immediately following WW II. Though great efforts have been made to reforest this area, complete recovery may take a couple of centuries.

The return of refugees to their place of origin leads to over-exploitation of resources to meet food and energy needs. The collapse of economic and environmental governance leads to breakdowns in waste collection arrangements, followed by pollution and the risk of infectious diseases. Such situations are regularly accompanied by the appearance of slums and shanty towns, which lead to social vulnerability and insecurity. Communities may come into conflict over access to and control of resources, threatening the delicate balance of the peace settlement.

The shortage of natural resources may lead to fresh conflict in post-conflict settlement zones. For instance in Afghanistan, there were a number of conflicts regarding access to the summer pastures in the central highlands between the local Hazara people and the Kuchis – nomadic Pashtun pastoralists. The conflicts resulted in scores of deaths, large-scale human displacement, ethnic tensions at the local and national level, and

---

62 *Ground Contamination Assessment Report: Military Waste Storage Site, Astana, Afghanistan*, United Nations Environment Programme, Post-Conflict Branch (PCoB), UNEP, 2006, Nairobi, p. 27.

63 Lanier-Graham Susan D. 1993. *The Ecology of War: Environmental Impacts of Weaponry and Warfare*, New York: Walker and Company, p.67.

devastation of livestock and property.[64] When people are driven off their most productive agricultural land they may be forced to depend on a smaller area of land to survive or earn a living. This land may be over-cultivated and depleted of its minerals. Poor soils are fragile, vulnerable to erosion and yield less. Over-cultivation accelerates the process of desertification, which destroys complex ecosystems.

Simon has advanced certain reasons as to why militarism is bad for the environment. [65]

1. **Militaries are notorious polluters:** Anywhere in the world, a military presence is virtually the single most reliable predictor of environmental damage. Military pollution is not limited to bases; it causes significant damage to the environment at large. Together, the world's militaries produce an estimated 6-10 per cent of global air pollution. Since the end of the Cold War, many plans to convert military bases to civilian use have been cancelled because the sites are contaminated beyond any hope of restoration.

2. **Nuclear weapons:** Nuclear weapons pose an environmental threat to humanity unprecedented in human history. Although the world escaped nuclear holocaust during the Cold War, the nuclear arms race has not stopped. The radiation from weapons testing alone may eventually cause about 2.4 million cancer deaths worldwide.

3. **Nuclear wastes:** Even if they are never used, nuclear weapons leave in their wake wastes unlike any other in human history, remaining deadly for hundreds of thousands - sometimes millions of years. There is no completely safe place for these wastes over geological time. The Soviet military is guilty of probably the single most egregious failure to contain nuclear waste; dumping waste directly into Lake Karachay, and creating the most polluted spot on the planet.

4. **Military toxins:** Military bases produce large quantities of hazardous toxics, mostly without informing the neighbourhood population. For more than fifty years, the US Navy has contaminated Vieques, Puerto Rico, leaving residents with cancer

---

64 *The UNEP Programme in Afghanistan: Annual Report 2010*, UNEP (2011), p. 27.

65 Doolittle Simon, There are ten Reasons Why Militarism is Bad for the Environment, available at http://www.envirosagainstwar.org/know/10_reasons_militarism_bad.html, accessed 18 December 2013.

rates 26 per cent higher than the Puerto Rican average. Pollution by Kelly Air Force Base in San Antonio has elevated cancer rates and birth defects in the surrounding Latino neighborhoods.

5. **Militaries are exempt from environmental regulation:** Militaries are routinely exempted from environmental regulations in the name of national security.

6. **Destruction of ecosystems and livelihoods:** In military training routinely leaves ecosystems ravaged and agricultural livelihoods destroyed.

7. **Hazardous effects of weapons on civilians:** In post-conflict situations, abandoned weapons and hazardous wastes keep killing civilians. Vietnamese parents and children today are still being poisoned by the millions of gallons of Agent Orange the US dumped on them during the war. Congenital birth defects more than tripled between 1966 and 1996, while Vietnamese women suffer spontaneous abortion and cervical cancer at rates among the world's worst. The country remains littered with unexploded weaponry. In Iraq, allied forces fired between 320 and 350 tons of DU, and as a result radioactivity has been found in Iraq's groundwater and both plant and animal tissues. DU can cause kidney failure, cancers, reproductive problems, genetic damage, and a weakened immune system. The bombing of Iraq's oil infrastructure released thousands of tons of very toxic hydrocarbons and chemicals. Infant mortality and death of children under five each doubled between 1989 and 1999, while birth defects have also dramatically increased. Since the war, cancer rates have gone up by five times, and cancer victims are getting younger.

Military activities have obvious detrimental impacts on the environment. Weaponry, troop movements, landmines, creation and destruction of buildings, destruction of forests by defoliation or general military usage, target-shooting of animals for practice, consumption of endangered species out of desperation etc., are just some examples of how peacetime military activities harm the environment. In the early 1990s withdrawing Russian troops left behind thousands of square miles of polluted territory in Estonia, where 570 Soviet military facilities occupied almost two percent of the entire country. Experts have now found thousands of unexploded rockets, toxic wastes of nuclear power plants, and oil seepage at twenty feet below the surface. In the mid-1990s, the cost of cleanup was estimated at $6 billion, to which the Russian government refused to contribute.

In recent years, the United Nations Environment Programme (UNEP) has undertaken field research on the impacts of armed conflict.[66] However, detailed examination of the impact of the presence and preparedness of the armed forces on the natural environment is yet to be fully ascertained. Over time, the environmental impact of military preparedness has grown, as technology has boosted the firepower and range of weapons which need to be tested and maintained by the armed forces. Forests, jungles, and wetlands are sometimes used for weapon testing and military operational training. Massive movement of troops and equipment during military tactical exercises in a fragile desert environment can translate into tremendous environmental devastation.

While treaties like 1977 Additional Protocol I and the 1976 ENMOD have tried to limit the environmental consequences of war, they have all made broad exceptions for peacetime activities of the military. Besides, they have weak, even nonexistent, enforcement mechanisms, and the definition of "militarily necessity" has been highly flexible.

---

66  UNEP's Post-Conflict Assessment Unit has undertaken both field research and desk studies concerning Afghanistan, Albania, Bosnia-Herzegovina, Kosovo, Serbia and Montenegro, Macedonia, Iraq, Liberia, and the Occupied Palestinian Territories. These studies demonstrate that the environment can have major implications for human livelihoods and for sustainable economic development in the post-conflict period. As such, environmental issues must be integrated across all sectors in post-conflict situations. Citizens may have fears about environmental threats from air pollution, drinking water contamination, and the presence of hazardous substances, including heavy metals and depleted uranium. There could also be severe contamination of surface water by sewage and other wastes.

# CHAPTER 5

# Legal Protection

At present, there are several bodies of regulations intended to protect the environment in peacetime and during armed conflict. International humanitarian law (IHL) contains isolated provisions to protect the environment during armed conflicts. International environmental law (IEL) provides general protection for the environment and the environment is also protected by international human rights laws (IHRL). The question and, to some extent, the problem is how these different bodies of regulations relate to one another before, during and after armed conflicts. There is an uncertainty about which rules apply during an armed conflict, particularly in situations of non-international conflict (NIAC).

## I. International Humanitarian Law

International humanitarian law (IHL) is a body of law that applies in situations of armed conflict and plays a considerable role in imposing restrictions on combatants. IHL is traditionally classified as The Hague Laws and the Geneva Laws. The Hague laws define the rights and duties of belligerents in the course of military operations and restrict the parties in their choice of the means of injuring the adversary. The body of this law is made up of the conventions adopted at The Hague Peace Conference of 1899 and 1907, excluding the rules which in 1929 and 1949 were taken over into the Geneva Conventions, such as the provisions on prisoners of war and the civilian population of the occupied territories, but including the St. Petersburg Declaration of 1868 and the Geneva Protocol of 1925. The Geneva laws are concerned with the protection of soldiers rendered *hors de combat* and keeping civilians out of hostilities. However, while the Geneva laws are characterized by strict, non-derogable prohibitions, the Hague laws are vaguely worded and permissive, enabling powerful States to use advanced military technology with no regard to humanitarian consequences. Some international law experts use the narrow term Geneva Law as a synonym for IHL rules.[1] IHL has given recognition to environmental concerns and seeks to prevent environmental destruction, directly or indirectly. A number of international conventions also pertain to the proscription of environmental damage during armed conflict as well as peacetime. In addition, a few IHL instruments refer to the protection of private and public property, without addressing environmental protection *per se*, while other instruments address environmental protection broadly.

## A. Treaty Provisions: Direct Protection

### The Hague Conventions of 1899 and 1907

It was in the Hague Peace Conferences in 1899 and 1907 that the first successful efforts were made to codify the existing customary laws of war.[2] Because the Hague Conventions are considered to be customary law today, they are binding on States that were not formal parties to the agreements originally. The 1899 Hague Convention Number I and its annexed regulations addressed the customs and laws of war on land. The Second Hague Peace Conference, convened in 1907, amended and replaced the 1899 Hague Convention Number II with Convention IV. The regulations of the Hague Conventions, reflecting a balance between the principles of

---

1 Roger Normand and Chris Jochnick, The Legitimation of Violence: A Critical History of the Laws of War, Vol. 35, *Harvard International Law Journal*, (1994), p. 387.

2 The first Hague Peace Conference in 1899, which was a step towards international disarmament, resulted in three conventions: for the peaceful adjustment of international differences; regarding the laws and customs of war on land; and for the adaptation of maritime warfare of the 1864 Geneva Convention. There were also three declarations: to prohibit the launching of projectiles and explosives from balloons or by other similar new methods; to prohibit the use of projectiles, the only object of which is the diffusion of the asphyxiating or deleterious gases; and to prohibit the use of bullets which expand or flatten easily in the human body ('dum-dum' bullets). A second Hague Peace Conference was held in 1907. This conference revised the three 1899 conventions and adopted ten new conventions: respecting the limitation of the employment of force for the recovery of contract debts; relative to the opening of hostilities; relative to the status of enemy merchant ships at the outbreak of hostilities; respecting the rights and duties of neutral powers and persons in case of war on land; relative to the conversion of merchant ships into warships; relative to the laying of automatic submarine contact mines; respecting bombardment by naval force in time of war; relative to the creation of an International prize Court; and concerning the rights and duties of neutral powers in naval war. In addition the 1899 declaration prohibiting the discharge of projectiles and explosives from balloons was revised.

proportionality and military necessity, provide limited protection to the environment by protecting property.

Article 22 of the 1907 Hague Regulations sets forth the principle underlying all laws of war. It provides that the right of belligerents to adopt means of injuring the enemy is not unlimited. This concept of 'limits' provides protection to the environment. Article 55 of the regulations provides that "the occupying State shall be regarded only as administrator and usufructuary of public buildings, real estate, forests, and agricultural estates belonging to the hostile State, and situated in the occupied country. It must safeguard the capital of these properties in accordance with the rules of usufruct." Under this principle, the occupying power may not permanently alter or destroy enemy territory and may not act irresponsibly or maliciously in using the natural resources found therein.

The 1907 Hague Convention prohibits environment damage. Article 23 (a) forbids the use of poison and poisoned weapons, while Article 23 (b) prevents the unnecessary suffering of civilians and combatants. Article 23(g) provides another source of limits on environmentally harmful behaviour, although it is directed specifically at property rather than at natural resources: "it is especially forbidden...to destroy or seize the enemy's property, unless such destruction or seizure be imperatively demanded by the necessities of war". Besides, the provision does not offer real protection to the environment because it justifies the wanton destruction of the environment when military necessity arises.[3] However, some scholars are of the view that Article 23 (g) provides adequate protection to the environment since the environmental resources of a country are the property of the State or of its citizens, which the Article seeks to protect.[4]

---

3   For example, in World War II, the German General Lothar Rendulic ordered the evacuation of all the inhabitants in Finmark province, Norway, and destroyed all villages. Although the Nuremberg Military Tribunal later accused General Rendulic of wanton property destruction, the tribunal exculpated him on the basis that military necessity justified his actions at that time. Ensign Florencio J. Yuzon, Deliberate Environmental Modification Through the Use of Chemical and Biological Weapons: "Greening" the International Laws of Armed Conflict to Establish an Environmentally Protective Regime, 11, *Am. U. J. Int'l L. & Pol'y* (1996), p. 793; and *United States v. List*, XI Trials of War Criminals before the Nuremberg Military Tribunals 757, 1295-97 (1946-49).

4   Schwabach Aaron, Environmental Damage Resulting from the NATO Military Action against Yugoslavia, Vol. 25 (1), *Columbia Journal of Environmental Law*, 2000, p. 117-140.

The Annexed Regulations of the 1899 Hague Convention II and the Annexed Regulations of the 1907 Hague Convention IV prohibit actions that cause unnecessary suffering or destroy the enemy's property, towns and cultural artifacts. Under those provisions, it is forbidden to destroy or seize the enemy's property, unless such destruction or seizure be imperatively demanded by the necessity of war. Though these provisions though do not provide protection to the natural environment directly, they can be interpreted to prohibit environmental damage.

## The Fourth Geneva Convention

The four Geneva Conventions of 1949 are mainly concerned with protecting victims of war. However, a few provisions of the Fourth Convention[5] cover aspects of environmental harm. Article 53 of the Convention prohibits the destruction of real or personal property, by articulating that: "Any destruction by the Occupying Power of real or personal property belonging individually or collectively to private persons, or to the State, or to other public authorities, or to social or cooperative organizations, is prohibited, except where such destruction is rendered absolutely necessary by military operations." Article 53 protects only one environmental element, i.e., property in a restricted manner. However, a few legal systems identify all valuable things, including the environment, as the property of the State if they have no owner. Thus, any destruction of such properties would be considered a violation of Article 53. In addition, Article 55 of the Convention ensures the maintenance of food and medical supplies of the population. Though this provision fails to protect the environment directly, it does so indirectly by protecting what is necessary for human survival and well-being. Article 56 provides for the maintenance of medical facilities and services, and indirectly provides protection for the environment through measures to control diseases.

Article 147 defines the "extensive destruction and appropriation of property, not justified by military necessity and carried out unlawfully and wantonly" as one of several "grave breaches" of the Convention. Articles 146 and 148 establish criminal and civil liability for grave breaches of the

---

5    The four conventions are the Geneva Convention I Relevant to the Wounded and Sick in the Field; the Geneva Convention II Relevant to the Wounded, Sick and Shipwrecked at Sea; the Geneva Convention III Relevant to the Prisoners of War; and the Geneva Convention IV Relevant to the Protection of Civilians. Further, the Geneva law includes the 1977 Additional Protocol I Relevant to the Protection of Victims of International Armed Conflicts, and the Additional Protocol II Relevant to the Protection of Victims of Non-International Armed Conflicts.

Convention. Article 146 of the Fourth Geneva Convention imposes the following additional obligation on all nations:

> Search for persons alleged to have committed, or to have ordered to be committed, such grave breaches, and shall bring such persons, regardless of their nationality, before its own courts. It may also, if it prefers, and in accordance with the provisions of its own legislation, hand such persons over for trial to another High Contracting Party concerned, provided such High Contracting Party has made out a prima facie case.

However, destructive conduct may be justified by military necessity and there is rarely a situation where the excuse of necessity may not be used to justify such conduct.[6]

## The Convention on the Prohibition of Hostile Use of Environmental Techniques (ENMOD)

The ENMOD Convention[7] came in response to the environmental modifications made by the US in Vietnam, Laos, and Cambodia in the 1960s and 70s. The US resorted to widespread spraying of chemicals (Agent Orange and other defoliants) to deprive its foes of food supplies and shelter. The ENMOD Convention, which is a short document consisting of a preamble, ten articles, and a set of four understandings in an annex, prohibits the use of environmental modification techniques as a method of warfare. Article I (1) of the treaty states: "Each State Party to this Convention undertakes not to engage in military or any other hostile use of environmental modification techniques having widespread, long-lasting or severe effects as the means of destruction, damage or injury to any other State Party". Also, Parties undertake not to assist, encourage or induce any State, group of States or international organization to engage in such activities. Some environmental manipulation is permitted. For example, armies may use herbicides or other means to denude the perimeter of military bases in order to reduce the chance of sneak attack.

---

6   Huston Meredith DuBarry, Wartime Environmental Damage: Financing the Cleanup, Vol. 23, *U. Pa. J. Int'l Econ. L.*, (2000), p. 903.

7   ENMOD was adopted by the United Nations General Assembly in 1976 and entered into force in October 1978. Today, almost 35 years after ENMOD was negotiated, the treaty is all but forgotten and only 74 countries have ratified it. Parties to ENMOD have met only twice, in 1982 and 1992. Despite the fact that ENMOD was recognized as a flawed treaty, no international civil society group has seriously tried to fix it.

Article I of the Convention provides a definition of environmental modifications the treaty is meant to cover. That definition entails two standards, the first on the magnitude of the modification, and the second on the intent or purpose of the modification. With response to magnitude, Article I sets out that for a technique to fall within the scope of ENMOD, at least one out of three criteria must be met: widespread, long lasting or severe. These criteria are together known as the *troika*, and set the magnitude threshold for violation. If the threshold is met, the exception of military necessity cannot be claimed. The three criteria are defined as follows:

(a) Widespread: encompassing an area on the scale of several hundred square kilometres;

(b) Long-lasting: lasting for a period of months, or approximately a season;

(c) Severe: involving serious or significant disruption or harm to human life, natural and economic resources or other assets.[8]

The second standard relates to the intent of the modification. ENMOD bans environmental modification only for military or hostile purposes. Peaceful modifications of the environment aimed at the potential future developments of technology, are recognized as potentially desirable. "Military" refers to armed conflicts – those between States Parties (i.e. countries which have ratified ENMOD).[9] "Hostile", a much wider concept, includes both armed and unarmed conflicts. The spraying of herbicides by the United Kingdom on opium poppies in Myanmar without permission from the government is a hypothetical example of a non-military hostile conflict.

For an action to be considered a violation of ENMOD, an attempt to manipulate natural processes is required. The treaty does not protect incidental environmental damages resulting from hostile actions. In other words, collateral damage incidental to warfare is not prohibited. Article

---

8    The *travaux* of the United Nations Committee of the Conference on Disarmament (CCD) indicate how to interpret the key terms: 'long-lasting', for instance, signifies 'lasting for a period of months, or approximately a season'. Understanding annexed to the text of ENMOD, contained in the report of the UN Committee of the Conference on Disarmament to the General Assembly, Official Records of the General Assembly, 31st Session, Supplement No. 27 (A/31/27).

9    The phrase "armed conflict" and the word "war" are not to be found in the 1977 ENMOD Convention.

II lists examples of environmental modification techniques and includes among them provocation of earthquakes, tsunamis, hurricanes (typhoons), disruption of ecological balance in climatic elements, causing changes in ocean currents, and in the state of the ozone layer.[10]

Article IV imposes on each party the obligation to take additional measures it considers necessary to prevent any violation of the provisions of the Convention. On the whole, the ENMOD Convention is clearly intended to govern conduct between States.[11] However, it could also be said to apply to NIAC, because it prohibits both military and hostile modifications of the environment.[12]

## Shortcomings of ENMOD

The ENMOD Convention has been the object of much criticism. ENMOD entails at least four specific weaknesses: First, ENMOD does not define the terms widespread, long-lasting, and severe. Second, ENMOD includes thresholds of environmental modifications below which it does not apply. Third, ENMOD refers to "deliberate" acts and what was or not was deliberate may be impossible to establish in international court. And fourth, "the complaint procedure ultimately depends upon the UN Security Council" and is thus subject to veto.[13] In particular Article III, which authorizes the

---

10  An attached understanding to Article II in ENMOD contains a list of events that could be caused by environmental modification techniques. These include: Earthquakes, tsunamis, an upset in the ecological balance of a region, changes in weather patterns (clouds, precipitation, cyclones of various types and tornadic storms), changes in climate patterns, changes in ocean currents, changes in the state of the ozone layer and changes in the state of the ionosphere. According to the US Operational Law Handbook (2007), the application of the ENMOD Convention is limited, as it only bans efforts to manipulate the environment with extremely advanced technology. The simple diversion of a river, destruction of a dam, or even the release of millions of barrels of oil do not constitute "manipulation" as contemplated under the provisions of the ENMOD. Rawcliffe, Maj John (ed.), *Operational Law Handbook-JA 422 (2007)*, International and Operational Law, The Judge Advocate General's Legal Centre and School, US Army, Virginia, p. 232-234.

11  Sharp Walter G., The Effective Deterrence of Environmental Damage During Armed Conflict: A Case Analysis of the Persian Gulf War, Vol. 137, *Military Law Review*, (1992), p.19.

12  In Colombia, the War on Drugs has included the massive spraying of broad spectrum herbicides in ecologically fragile areas. In a single two-week period in 2000, approximately 25,000 hectares were fumigated from the air with a glyphosate-based chemical agent. The plant eradication effort is meant both to squelch narcotics production and to assist in regaining state control over rebel-held land.

13  Westing, Arthur H. 1993. The Environmental Modification Convention, in Arthur

use of environmental modification techniques for peaceful purposes, is considered vague. It leaves open the possibility that prohibited uses of such techniques may be carried out under the cover of peaceful uses.[14] Critics of ENMOD have focused on the *troika* arguing that the threshold that has been set is so difficult to cross that the treaty is practically unusable. Also, the treaty does not prohibit parties from threatening to use environmental modification techniques. Another flaw is that the damage must be proven. Providing proof of damage becomes extremely complicated when the affected ecosystems are complex and poorly understood, as is the case in many areas of the tropics. The relative lack of scientific knowledge of particular ecosystems may hamper accurate assessment of the effects of hostile environmental modification. ENMOD requires assessment after damage is done. However, the true environmental extent of the damage can never be known in ecosystems not fully characterized before the damage is done.

While ENMOD may offer some degree of protection to non-parties, the responsibilities imposed by the Convention are restricted to those who have ratified it. Severe environmental modification techniques have been used in conflicts after ENMOD came into force. Some examples are the use of defoliants in Central America during the 1980s and the severe environmental modifications made during the Gulf War. In the latter, Iraq set fire to over 600 oil wells and sought to damage Kuwait's desalinization plants by polluting the nearby sea.[15]

ENMOD does not outlaw the development and testing of hostile environmental modification techniques, nor does it include verification mechanisms for identifying attempts by Parties to develop such techniques. It does not include a system of compensation for damages resulting from breach of its obligations as it lacks provisions for penalizing State Parties that breach its provisions. A State party can be held responsible, but not liable. Liability and redress, therefore, must be sought through other international legal instruments. In lieu of imposing liability, or as a

---

Burns (ed.), *Encyclopedia of Arms Control and Disarmament*. New York: Scribner's Sons, p. 947-954.

14 Antoine Philippe, International Humanitarian Law and the Protection of the Environment in Time of Armed Conflict, No. 291, *International Review of the Red Cross*, November-December 1992, p.522.

15 The UN Security Council passed a resolution condemning Iraq's invasion of Kuwait and holding it liable for damages. ENMOD, however, was not applied because Iraq is not a Party to the Convention.

mechanism to force acceptance of liability, the Security Council could decide to punish violators through the application of trade or other sanctions. The veto power granted to the Security Council's five permanent members is, without doubt, a major constraint on the effectiveness of ENMOD since it places five States in a permanently privileged position.[16] Although many major powers are Parties to ENMOD, the overall number of ratifications is limited, particularly in the political South. To date, ENMOD has been ratified by only 74 State Parties. The UN General Assembly has called for global ratification on several occasions, but without much success.

## The 1977 Additional Protocol I (AP I)

AP I, which resulted from the worldwide outcry against the US action in Vietnam,[17] represents a considerable development of IHL regarding environmental protection in times of armed conflict.[18] It recognizes that environmental protection is necessary to human health and survival and contains two important provisions (Articles 35 and 55) relating to the protection of environment and limitation on ecological destruction during IAC.

Article 35 forbids the use of weapons and methods of warfare that may

---

16 During the 1984 First Review Conference of the ENMOD Convention, Sweden raised the issue of the role of the Security Council in dealing with the complaints. It was particularly concerned with the fact that members of the Security Council, with the power to decide on the breach of the obligations of the Convention, were not necessarily parties to the Convention (e.g. China and France). Moreover, permanent members of the Security Council could use their veto power to halt a complaint against it. Sweden then proposed a system that would enable State Parties to examine the report of the Committee of Experts prior its submission to the Security Council. East Germany, the United Kingdom, the Soviet Union and the US nevertheless expressed satisfaction with the complaints-procedure; hence no changes were made to it. The First Review Conference ENMOD (1984), available at: http://www.sunshine-project.org/ENMOD Convention/revcon1.html, accessed 22 March 2014.

17 The US' widespread use of heavy munitions; incendiary weapons; herbicides; antipersonnel chemicals; weather manipulation; and bombing raids against dams, dikes, and seawalls, during the Vietnam War had serious environmental effects. The international community objected to these measures, kindling controversy over their employment. The result of the controversy was Protocol I to the 1949 Geneva Conventions of 1949. It advanced additional restraints on the means and methods of waging war and was perhaps the first significant development of IHL since 1907. Diederich Michael, Law of War and Ecology: A Proposal for a Workable Approach to Protecting the Environment through the Law of War, Vol. 136, *Military Law Review*, Spring 1992, p.137-160.

18 The AP I has been ratified by 172 States. The US, China, India and a few other major powers have consistently refused to do so.

cause unnecessary injury to humans or the environment. Article 35 (3), which appears under the heading 'Basic Rules', states, "It is prohibited to employ methods or means of warfare which are intended, or may be expected, to cause widespread, long-term and severe damage to the natural environment."

Article 55, which appears in Part IV on the Protection of the Civilian Population, states:

> 1. Care shall be taken in warfare to protect the natural environment against widespread, long-term and severe damage. This protection includes a prohibition of the use of methods or means of warfare which are intended or may be expected to cause such damage to the natural environment and thereby to prejudice the health or survival of the population.

> 2. Attacks against the natural environment by way of reprisals are prohibited.

The obligation of 'protection' in Article 55(1) suggests that States Parties must take positive steps to guard and defend the environment and keep it safe from damage. The obligation of protection could, therefore, include a wide range of actions; (a) undertaking a rigorous environmental assessment to evaluate potential environmental harm to a particular attack scenario, including a full appraisal of the environmental effects of proposed weapons, as well as risks to particular kinds of environment; (b) the alteration of an attack scenario to avoid potential environmental harm; and (c) calling off a planned attack due to the potential environmental harm.[19]

Article 55 must be interpreted as a 'governing principle' that requires that the effects (or consequences) of permitted actions do not result in escalating damage or cause expressly prohibited widespread, long-term and severe damage to the natural environment. The scope of Article 55 thus extends beyond that of Article 35 in so far as it concerns issues relating to the health or survival of the civilian population. Article 55 could also be interpreted as applicable to instances in which environmental damage is caused by the actions of civilians and refugees, and not just by combatants (directly or as a consequence of their actions).[20]

---

19 Hulme Karen, Taking Care to Protect the Environment against Damage: A Meaningless Obligation, *International Review of the Red Cross*, Vol. 92, No. 879, September 2010, p. 681.

20 Such situations may, for example, arise in an armed conflict where civilians or refugees resort to the destruction of wildlife, as was the case in the Democratic Republic of Congo. Letetia van der Poll and ashraf Booley, In Our Common Interest: Liability and Redress for Damage Caused to the Natural Environment During Armed Conflict, Vol.

In Hulme's opinion (2010: 681), "The real gem hidden behind Article 55 (1), is not the prohibition of means and methods causing widespread, long-term, and severe damage, but the obligation on states parties to take 'care' to protect the environment against such harm."[21] The opening sentence of Article 55(1), i.e., "Care shall be taken in warfare to protect the natural environment against widespread, long-term and severe damage," encapsulates the *raison d'etre* or the 'underlying concept' of the provision.[22] According to Cohan (2003), the 'care clause' suggests a "supervening standard or a general governing principle of due care in military deployments".[23]

A question often raised is why AP I contains two provisions [Articles 35(3) and 55(1)] that appear to cover the same ground. According to Hulme (2010), while there is some overlap in the language of Articles 35(3) and 55(1), the two provisions are different in emphasis. Article 35(3), is a part of the fundamental provisions on means and methods, and its placing pertinent to the absolute limit that it imposes. This section of the Protocol is not limited by the reference in Article 49(3) to warfare having effects on land, and so it appears to apply to the environment, including the marine environment and areas beyond national jurisdiction. The second sentence of Article 55(1) echoes Article 35 (3). However, it has the additional requirement of risk to the human population. The prohibition does mention means and methods causing such harm, but it is indicated as being only an example of the notion of protection elaborated in the first sentence.[24]

Articles 35 and 55 appear to be limited to proscribing systematic environmental warfare through the use of unconventional means, such as herbicides and chemicals. Collateral damage incidental to conventional

---

15, *Law, Democracy and Development*, (2011), p.12.

21  Hulme Karen, Taking Care to Protect the Environment against Damage: A Meaningless Obligation, *International Review of the Red Cross*, Vol. 92, No. 879, September 2010, p. 675-69.

22  Yoram Dinstein. 2001. 'Protection of the environment in international armed conflict', in *Max Planck Yearbook of United Nations Law*, Vol. 5, 2001, p. 531.

23  John A. Cohan, Modes of warfare and evolving standards of environmental protection under the international law of war, Vol. 15, *Florida Journal of International Law*, (2003), p. 504.

24  Hulme Karen, Taking Care to Protect the Environment against Damage: A Meaningless Obligation, *International Review of the Red Cross*, Vol. 92, No. 879, September 2010, p. 677.

warfare is not prohibited, and nor is short-term environmental damage, such as that caused by bombardment. It is doubtful that either Article offers significant protection to the natural environment except in most serious cases.[25] Firstly, the term 'natural environment' has not been defined in AP I, which complicates the pragmatic application of Articles 35(3) and 55. The ICRC commentary on the AP I calls for a broad definition of the term 'natural environment', but the fact that Article 55 is placed under the 'Protection of Civilian Population', suggests that the article's primary concern is for human health and survival. While Article 35 protects the natural environment *per se*, it is doubtful whether the essential obligation created by both the provisions are the same. The reference in Article 55 to 'prejudice the health or survival of the population' indicates that the prohibition encompasses only very serious harm.

Secondly, these provisions are aimed at precluding only very serious significant harm. Compared to ENMOD, Articles 35(3) and 55 set a very high threshold, as the three limiting criteria, 'widespread, long-term and severe', are cumulative rather than alternative. It would appear extremely difficult to develop a *prima facie* case upon the basis of these provisions, even assuming they were applicable. For instance, it is thought that the notion of 'long-term' damage in AP I would need to be measured in years rather than months, and that as such, ordinary battlefield damage of the kind caused to France in World War I or in Vietnam War would not be covered. One significant improvement over ENMOD is that proscribed environmental damage is not limited to injuring another State Party.[26]

Articles 35 and 55 are binding only on States Parties to AP I. AP I does not have universal ratification. Several recent international armed conflicts which have caused massive destruction of the environment have been waged by non-State Parties to AP I, notably the United States and Iraq.

---

25  Tarasofsky Richard D, 1993, 'Legal Protection of the Environment During International Armed Conflict', Vol. XXIV, *Netherlands Yearbook of International Law*, p. 49.

26  The US Army's Operational Law Handbook identifies a key innovative element in AP I. It states: The primary difference between AP I and the protections found within the Hague Regulations or Geneva Conventions is that once the degree of damage to the environment reaches a certain level, AP I does not employ the traditional balancing of military necessity against the quantum of expected destruction. Instead, it establishes this level as an absolute ceiling of permissible destruction. Any act that exceeds that ceiling, despite the importance of the military mission or objective, is a violation of environmental law of war. Rawcliffe, Maj John (ed.), *Operational Law Handbook-JA 422*, International and Operational Law, The Judge Advocate General's Legal Centre and School, US Army, Virginia, 2007, p. 232.

And even those States that have ratified AP I (e.g. the UK), have made declarations and reservations intended to limit their liability. Some States have, for instance, maintained that the rules of set forth in AP I would not apply to nuclear weapons but to conventional weapons only.[27]

The UK maintains that the rules introduced by AP I apply exclusively to conventional weapons. In particular, the rules so introduced do not have any effect on and do not regulate or prohibit the use of nuclear weapons.[28] The British Joint Service Manual of the Law of Armed Conflict states, "There is no specific rule of international law, express or implied, which prohibits the use of nuclear weapons. The legality of their use depends upon the application of the general rules of international law, including those regulating the use of force and the conduct of hostilities".[29] However, the damage to natural environment has been expressly prohibited in a number of State military manuals. These include the manual of Argentina, Australia, Belgium, Benin, Canada, France, Germany, Italy, the Netherlands, New Zealand, Russia, Spain, Sweden, Switzerland, Togo, the US and Yugoslavia.[30]

The liability regime established under AP I also appears inadequate. It offers no guidelines as to how, or even to whom, compensation should be paid. Although Article 91 of AP I holds the State responsible for violations and declares that the State is liable to pay compensation, "if the case demands", for the actions of its armed forces, it cannot be determined from the provisions of AP I alone whether compensation should include

---

27  The Joint Service Manual of the Law of Armed Conflict, JSP 383 (2004), UK: Ministry of Defence.

28  *The Joint Service Manual of the Law of Armed Conflict, JSP 383*, UK: Ministry of Defence, 2004, Para 5.29.3, p. 76.

29  The Manual states: "Whether the use, or threatened use, of nuclear weapons in a particular case is lawful depends on all the circumstances. Nuclear weapons fall to be dealt with by reference to the same general principles as apply to other weapons. The threshold for the legitimate use of nuclear weapons is clearly a high one. The UK would only consider using nuclear weapons in self-defence, including the defence of its NATO allies, and even then only in extreme circumstances. The UK has given a unilateral assurance that it will not use nuclear weapons against non-nuclear weapons states parties to the Treaty on the Non-Proliferation of Nuclear Weapons 1968. The assurance does not apply in the case of an invasion or any other attack on the UK, its Overseas Territories, its armed forces, its allies, or on a state towards which it has a security commitment, carried out by a non-nuclear weapon state in association or alliance with a nuclear weapon state." Ibid, para 6.17, 6.17.1 and 6.17.2.

30  Henckaerts JM and Doswald-Beck L (eds). 2005. *Customary International Humanitarian Law*, Vol. I, p. 152.

restitution or whether compensation should be in the form of a monetary award only.[31]

## AP I and ENMOD

Although Articles 35 (3) and 55 (1) prohibit 'widespread, long-term and severe', harm to the environment, AP I itself does not define these terms.[32] The Vienna Convention provides a general rule that a treaty shall be interpreted in good faith in accordance with the ordinary meaning of the terms contained in it; the terms shall be interpreted in their context and in the light of the object and purpose of the treaty.[33] In the preparatory meeting for AP I, the States made it very clear that the terminology used therein does not have the same meaning as has been attributed to the terminology adopted in ENMOD.[34]

Though the language used to define threshold in AP I is almost identical to that in ENMOD, the States categorically rejected the idea that the terms be interpreted as being the same as those of ENMOD. The scale of environmental damage caused in the Vietnam War was prominent in the minds of the delegates when AP I was being drafted.[35] Therefore, the threshold intended was clearly between that established in ENMOD and 20,000 square km, which was the area damaged in Vietnam. Since the meaning of these terms (widespread, long-term and severe) used in AP I

---

31 Letetia van der Poll and ashraf Booley, In Our Common Interest: Liability and Redress for Damage Caused to the Natural Environment During Armed Conflict, Vol. 15, *Law, Democracy and Development*, (2011), p.14.

32 Hulme Karen. 2004. *War Torn Environment: Interpreting the Legal Threshold*, Leiden: Martinus Nijhoff Publishers, p. 88.

33 The 1969 Vienna Convention on the Laws of Treaties, Article 31 (1). However, the US is of the view that the three terms in AP I are not be understood in layman's term, but in the technical-legal use of those terms within the context of AP I.

34 The differences between the texts of AP I and ENMOD are not an oversight but intentional. The three conditions, or the threshold, of the prohibition in AP I are cumulative (joined by 'and'), while the conditions in ENMOD are alternatives (joined by 'or'). Furthermore, the meaning of the three adjectives limiting the scope of prohibited damage differs (at least according to the negotiating history of the two provisions) depending on whether they are being interpreted in the context of AP I or ENMOD. The competent Conference committee intensively discussed all three in the context of AP I. Federal Republic of Germany, Plenary Meeting, 25 May 1977, O.R. Vol. VI, CDDH/SR, Annex, 113.

35 For example, in South Vietnam over five million acres (approximately 20,200 square kms) was spread with defoliants, representing more than 10 per cent of the country. Westing Arthur H. 1976. *Ecological Consequences of the Second Indochina War*, Stockholm: Almqvist and Wiskell International, p. 28.

is not clear, the most practical working definition would be the minimum area possible. In this way, arbitrariness could be avoided in the attribution of a definition that never existed.[36]

The three thresholds are interconnected, as the intensity of any harm to environment is a composite of the geographical scale, the duration of impact and the severity or seriousness of damage. The International Law Commission (ILC) has suggested that at least two of the three criteria might be connected, in that one is generally present with the other. The ILC adopted the same terminology as that included in Article 35 (3) and 55 for its *Code on Crimes Against the Peace and Security of Mankind*, and remarked that: "The word 'long-term' was necessary because, if the damage was not long-term, it could not be serious; and, for the damage to be serious, it had to be long-term." [37]

Hulme (2004) has suggested that the elements 'widespread' and 'severe' might also be connected. For instance, damage to land on the scale of "X square kilometers" whilst fulfilling the 'widespread' criterion, might also entail a large percentage of a small country or certain environmental components of that country, and hence simultaneously fulfill the criterion 'severe'. If such damage resulted in a change of terrain or ecosystem, the element of 'long-term' harm might also be fulfilled. The threshold of prohibited environmental damage (widespread, long-term and severe) in AP I could therefore be decided as follows:

- The definition of 'widespread' should be considered in terms of a minimum of 'X square kilometers', where X is above several hundred as in ENMOD.

- The definition of 'long-term' should be considered in terms of 20 to 30 years.

- The definition of 'severe' should be considered along the lines of 'significant' damage and should demonstrate a possible threat to the health and survival of the population.

- The threshold should be tested regarding the use of weapons in a separate, distinguishable military operation, as well as the overall effect of a particular weapon on the environment.

---

36  Hulme Karen. 2004. *War Torn Environment: Interpreting the Legal Threshold*, Leiden: Martinus Nijhoff Publishers, p. 93.

37  ILC, Summary Records of 2241st Meeting, 12 July 1991, *YBILC*.

- The minimum threshold of each criterion must be satisfied before it can be termed as either 'widespread', 'long-term', or 'severe'.[38]

Another issue that needs to be considered is whether all the provisions contained in AP I have acquired customary status. According to Cassese, Article 55 'already reflects a general consensus and thus is binding on all members of the world community';[39] while Greenwood has argued that 'the core of the principle [contained in Article 35 (3)] may well reflect an emerging norm of international law'.[40] Dinstein has, however, opined that Articles 35 (3) and 55 do not reflect customary international law.[41] On several occasions, the US has expressed the opinion that AP I is not universally binding.[42]

The provisions of both AP I and the ENMOD place a limit upon the mindless mayhem that normally accompanies war. However, a number of military activities potentially devastating to the environment remain insufficiently regulated. For example, collateral damage from weapons does not appear to be covered under either AP I or the ENMOD. Second, even intentional direct damage to the environment is permissible if it is not covered specifically by the prohibitions. Moreover, the pertinent definitions are unclear and ambiguous. It must also be noted that no clear 'proportionality' equation exists to balance 'military necessity' against harm to the environment.[43]

While AP I has been ratified by 172 countries, a number of important countries like India, Indonesia, Iran, Iraq, Israel, Malaysia, Morocco, the

---

38  Hulme Karen. 2004. *War Torn Environment: Interpreting the Legal Threshold*, Leiden: Martinus Nijhoff Publishers, p. 99-100.

39  Antonio Cassese. 2005. *International Law*, 2nd ed., Oxford: Oxford University Press, p. 419-420.

40  Christopher Greenwood. 1991. 'Customary Law Status of the 1977 Geneva Protocols', in Astrid J.M. Delissen and Gerard J. Tanja (eds.), *Humanitarian Law of Armed Conflict: Challenges Ahead,* Dordrecht: Martinus Nijhoff Publishers, p. 105.

41  Dinstein Yoram. 2004. *The Conduct of Hostilities Under the Law of International Armed Conflict,* Cambridge: Cambridge University Press, p. 185.

42  The US DoD Report, Conduct of the Persian Gulf War, Appendix O, p. 617. Also see: Roscini Marco. 2009. Protection of the Natural Environment in the Time of Armed Conflict, in Bhuiyan Md. J. H., Louise Doswald-Beck, and A.R. Chowdhury (eds.) *International Humanitarian Law – An Anthology*, Nagpur: LexisNexis Butterworths, p. 155-179.

43  Diederich Michael, Law of War and Ecology: A Proposal for a Workable Approach to Protecting the Environment through the Law of War, Vol. 136, *Military Law Review*, Spring 1992, p.104.

Philippines, Thailand, Turkey and the US have not ratified the treaty. A large number of ratifying States have expressed reservations and made an interpretative declaration with regards to the provisions. According to the International Court of Justice (ICJ), for a rule to be a customary rule, it is of primary importance that it should be of a fundamentally norm-creating character, such that it could form the basis of a general rule of law.[44] Therefore, the Articles 35 and 55 of AP I cannot be considered customary in nature.

According to Adede (1994), AP I and the ENMOD Convention no not duplicate each other due to the following reasons. First, AP I is aimed at protecting the natural environment against damages which could be inflicted on it by any weapon, while the ENMOD Convention prevents the use of only one such potential weapon, i.e. environmental modification techniques. Whereas AP I was primarily motivated by the desire to protect human beings from environmental destruction in wartime, the elaboration of the ENMOD Convention was primarily motivated by the desire to contribute to general and complete disarmament and the preservation and improvement of the environment *per se* for the benefit of the present and future generations. Second, AP I applies only to armed conflict, while the ENMOD Convention deals with the prohibition of environmental modification techniques for "military or any other hostile purposes", and thus has wider application (for example, in cases where no other weapon has been used). Third, ENMOD deals with short-term damage to the environment (short-term damage having been interpreted as referring to a period of months). AP I, by contrast, deals with long-term damage (long-term having been interpreted as referring to a period of decades). ENMOD overlaps with other arms control agreements, such as the Convention on Biological and Toxin Weapons (BWTC), particularly in instances in which the tool used to modify the environment is a biological agent, as in the case of modification of the environment by the dissemination of a disease.

AP I and the ENMOD are similar in one important respect---both conventions are aimed at protecting the earth's natural environment, even though both have very high damage thresholds. The ENMOD and the environmental provisions of AP I effectively give nature a 'standing', that is, they do not depend upon direct injury to identifiable human beings. Rather, they focus on the environment itself. In so doing, these conventions have

---

44  North Sea Continental Shelf cases, the International Court of Justice (ICJ) judgment of 20 February 1969, para 72. Available at: http://www.icj-cij.org/docket/index.php?p1=3 &p2=3&k=cc&case=52&code=cs2&p3=4, accessed 10 June 2014.

gone a step further in the field of environmental protection during IAC.

## B. Treaties Protecting the Environment Indirectly

The following international conventions, while not specifically directed towards environmental protection, nonetheless have a general bearing on the environment. There are other treaties that offer limited environmental protection in conflicts. These include: the Treaty Governing the Activities of States in the Exploration and Use of Outer Space, including the Moon and Other Celestial Bodies (Outer Space Treaty) of 1967; the Treaty on the Prohibition of the Emplacement of Nuclear Weapons and Other Weapons of Mass Destruction on the Seabed and the Ocean Floor and the Subsoil Thereof (Seabed Treaty) of 1971; and the Agreement Governing the Activities of States on the Moon and Other Celestial Bodies (Agreement on Celestial Bodies) of 1979.

## The 1925 Gas Protocol

The Protocol for the Prohibition of the Use in War of Asphyxiating, Poisonous or Other Gases, and of Bacteriological Methods of Warfare, 1925, which builds on the generally accepted principles prohibiting the use of particularly inhumane weapons and cruel methods of warfare, was adopted as a collective response to the horrors of the use of chemical weapons during the First World War.[45] In so far as the use of chemical and biological weapons may cause harm to the environment, the Protocol can be seen to provide some level of environmental protection during armed conflict. The Protocol, however, suffers from major limitations: (i) it prohibits only the *use* of chemical and biological means of warfare, and not the research on the development, stockpiling and possession of such weapons, and (ii) it lacks control mechanisms and provisions for establishing responsibility for violations, thereby limiting its ability to serve as a deterrent.

## The 1959 Antarctic Treaty

The Antarctic Treaty was motivated by the desire to preserve the fragile

---

45 The principal purpose behind chemical and biological warfare prohibitions has been to avoid direct human suffering. These restraints, however, also have provided an incidental benefit to the environment. Poison gas or biological weapons sufficient to kill humans certainly are destructive to the non-human portion of the environment. Therefore, the earth's natural resources, including its flora and fauna, are spared to the extent that poison gas or other toxins are not used against combatants.

ecology of the Antarctic region. It prohibits military activities and nuclear test in the region.

> Article I (1). Antarctica shall be used for peaceful purposes only. There shall be prohibited, inter alia, any measures of a military nature, such as the establishment of military bases and fortifications, the carrying out of military maneuvers, as well as the testing of any type of weapons.

> Article V (1). Any nuclear explosions in Antarctica and the disposal there of radioactive waste materials shall be prohibited.

## The Biological Weapons Convention (BWC), 1972

The BWC [46] prohibits, without exception, the development, production, stockpiling or possession of microbial agents, toxins and weapons, as well as equipment or means of delivery designed to use these agents or toxins for hostile purposes or in armed conflict. No later than nine months after its entry into force, all Parties to the BWC undertook to destroy all such agents, weapons and equipment. However, States were only obliged to destroy biological agents above a certain threshold. Stock levels under this threshold were deemed to indicate non-peaceful purposes.

The actual 'use' of biological weapons is not prohibited by the BWC, as the drafters of the agreement considered that this aspect had been regulated by the 1925 Protocol. The BWC does, however, prohibit the transfer of biological agents to other States, groups of States, international organizations or "any recipient whatsoever." The BWC does not create a mechanism of verification, although it does allow complaints to be made to the Security Council.

This weakness was rectified to some extent after the Third Review Conference in 1991, which set up an *ad hoc* body of governmental experts who were requested to examine potential verification measures from a scientific and technical standpoint. The State Parties have agreed to seek solutions through cooperation and negotiations in case any dispute arises regarding the application of the BWC. The BWC also addresses several limitations of the 1925 Protocol and creates a comprehensive regime to deal with biological and chemical weapons. By banning the use of these weapons, the BWC and the Protocol protect the environment---

---

46 Convention on the Prohibition of the Development, Production and Stockpiling of Bacteriological (Biological) and Toxin Weapons and on Their Destruction, 10 April 1972.

particularly fauna and flora---from significant environmental degradation.

## The 1977 Additional Protocol I (AP I)

The 1977 AP I contains certain provisions which indirectly protect the environment in IAC. The 'basic rule' for the protection of civilian objects against the effects of hostilities is contained in Article 48. This provides indirect protection for the environment by stating: "In order to ensure respect for and protection of the civilian population and civilian objects, the Parties to the conflict shall at all times distinguish between the civilian population and combatants and between civilian objects and military objectives and accordingly shall direct their operations only against military objectives."[47]

Article 54(2) of AP I also indirectly protects the environment by prohibiting attacks against "objects indispensable to the survival of the civilian population," meaning objects that are of basic importance to the population's livelihood. Natural resources, such as agricultural land, foodstuffs, crops, cattle, and drinking water could, in many instances, be seen as falling under this category.[48] In addition, Article 54(3)(b) applies even when farmlands and foodstuffs are used in direct support of military action, if such use causes starvation or forced relocation of the civilian population. In effect, this provision also excludes, except in defence of a State's own territory, recourse to scorched-earth strategies that cause severe environmental destruction. The precautionary measures contained in Article 57, recall the proportionality principle and in addition, seek to protect the environment by discouraging acts that cause severe environmental destruction. Finally, Article 56 prohibits attacks against works and installations containing dangerous forces, such as dams, dykes and nuclear electrical generating stations. This prohibition applies even when such a target constitutes a military objective. Paragraph 56 (2) of AP I, however, restricts this protection if (i) such installations are used for something other than its normal function and is in regular, significant and direct support of military operations and if such attack is the only feasible

---

47 This basic rule is an explicit affirmation of the general principle of distinction. This principle is re-emphasized within the rule contained in Article 52 of AP I, which explains what constitutes a military objective as opposed to a civilian object. In case of doubt whether an object which is normally dedicated to civilian purposes, such as a place of worship, a house or other dwelling or a school, is being used to make an effective contribution to military action, it shall be presumed not to be so used.

48 This provision is generally considered to reflect customary international law as its violation would constitute a grave breach of IHL if it amounted to any of the acts enumerated within Article 147 of the Geneva Convention IV.

way to terminate such support; or (ii) other military objectives located at or in the vicinity of these works or installations provide regular, significant and direct support of military operations.

## The 1977 Additional Protocol II (AP II)

AP II specifically addresses non-international armed conflicts (NIAC), but has not gained as much acceptance among States as have the 1949 Geneva Conventions.[49] Though AP II does not mention environmental protection, Article 14 of the Protocol states, "starvation of civilians as a method of combat is prohibited. It is therefore prohibited to attack, destroy, remove or render useless for that purpose, objects indispensable to the survival of the civilian population such as foodstuffs, agricultural areas for the production of foodstuffs, crops, livestock, drinking water installations and supplies and irrigation works". This Article is similar to Article 54 of AP I, which deals with the protection of objects indispensable to the survival of the civilian population, as well as the prohibition of attacks on environment-related targets. Article 15 of AP II extends the protections contained in Article 56 of AP I to NIAC, thereby protecting dams, dykes and nuclear electrical generating stations from being targeted in NIAC. Besides, Article 16 provides considerable protection to monuments, works of art, and places of worship, because they are part of the human environment.

## UN Convention on Conventional Weapons, 1980[50]

The UN Convention on Prohibitions or Restrictions on the Use of Certain Conventional Weapons which May be Deemed to be Excessively Injurious or to Have Indiscriminate Effects (CCW), and its five protocols deal with specific conventional weapons. The Preamble to the CCW reiterates

---

49 AP II has been ratified by 166 States. The prominent non-signatory states are India, Indonesia, Iran, Iraq, Israel, Mexico, Myanmar, Pakistan, Sri Lanka, Thailand, Turkey, the USA, and Vietnam.

50 AP I and II of 1977 prohibit the indiscriminate use of weapons, but not weapons themselves, and do not specify to which weapons the prohibition applies. This problem prompted the ICRC to organize conferences for government experts, in Lucerne in 1974 and in Lugano in 1976. These and subsequent conferences in September 1979 and September 1980 led to the adoption on 10 October 1980 of the Convention on Prohibitions or Restrictions on the Use of Certain Conventional Weapons which May be Deemed to be Excessively Injurious or to Have Indiscriminate Effects, and its three protocols: Protocol I on non-detectable fragments, Protocol II on mines, booby-traps and other devices and Protocol III on incendiary weapons. Antoine Philippe, International Humanitarian Law and the Protection of the Environment in Time of Armed Conflict, No. 291, *International Review of the Red Cross*, November-December 1992, p.528.

Article 35 (3) of AP I: "It is prohibited to employ methods or means of warfare which are intended, or may be expected, to cause widespread, long-term and severe damage to the natural environment." Because it links human injury to environmental injury, the CCW also provides collateral environmental protection while recalling "the general principle of the protection of the civilian population against the effects of hostilities."

The protection provided to civilian populations by Protocol II of the CCW (on Prohibition or Restrictions on the Use of Mines, Booby Traps and Other Devices), is better than that provided by the CCW itself. For instance, Article 3 (2) of the Protocol states: "it is prohibited in all circumstances to direct weapons to which this Article applies, either in offence, defence or by way of reprisals, against the civilian population as such or against individual civilians." This Article not only prohibits such attacks against civilian populations, it also prohibits the indiscriminate use of such devices. Moreover, it requires combatants to avoid foreseeable injury to civilians or civilian objects. Article 2 (5) of the Protocol defines objects, as "all objects which are not military objectives". A military object is defined as "any object which by its nature, location, purpose or use makes an effective contribution to military action and whose total or partial destruction, capture or neutralization, in the circumstances ruling at the time, offers a definite military advantage". Thus, national parks, zoos, reservoirs, rivers, forests and other elements of the environment are, by their nature to be considered civilian objects unless they are misused by military forces.

Protocol II requires the States to take all feasible precautions necessary to ensure the protection of the civilian population from the effects of weapons. Therefore, any severe, widespread, and long-term environmental damage that may reflect on public health and safety should be avoided. The Protocol also prohibits the use of mines, booby traps, and other devices in areas where civilians are concentrated, such as cities, towns, and villages, except for explicit military purposes, since such devices can affect both people and animals that trigger them. Article 6 (2) of the Protocol prohibits causing any superfluous injury or unnecessary suffering. The protection to civilians does not end with the cessation of combat; it continues after combat as well. Protocol II attempts to limit the harmful effects of landmines by requesting States to take protective measures, such as recording the location of targets, so that the unexploded devices can be collected later. To a great extent, this would also facilitate the restoration of the environment to its former condition.

Protocol III of the CCW on Prohibitions or Restrictions on the Use of Incendiary Weapons, which consists of only two articles, [51] stipulates that "it is prohibited in all circumstances to make the civilian population as such, individual civilians or civilian objects the object of attack by incendiary weapons". Article 2(4) of the Protocol directly addresses environmental protection, as it prohibits "making forests or other kinds of plant cover the subject of an attack by incendiary weapons except when such natural elements are used to cover, conceal, or camouflage combatants or other military objectives, or are themselves military objectives".[52] The Protocol thereby affirms the provisions of Articles 51 and 52 of AP I.[53] An amendment to Article 1 of the CCW introduced in 2001 extends the scope of the Convention to situations referred to in the common Article 3 of the 1949 Geneva Conventions relating to NIAC.

Finally, Protocol V to the CCW on Explosive Remnants of War, which was adopted in 2003 and was the first international legal instrument dealing with the problem of unexploded and abandoned ordnance, sets out guidelines for the indirect protection of the environment in post-conflict situations.

The CCW uses the Martens Clause[54] to cover all cases that are not covered

---

51  Article 1 defines certain terms like 'incendiary weapons', 'military objectives, 'civilian objects', and 'feasible precautions.' Article 2 deals with the protection of civilians and civilian objects.

52  Article 2 (4) CCW Protocol III grants the armed forces the right to ignore the protection of natural resources if they are "used to cover, conceal or camouflage combatants or other military objectives, or are themselves military objectives." Al-Duaij Nada. 2004. *Environmental Law of Armed Conflict*, New York: Transnational Publishers, p.294.

53  Antoine Philippe, International Humanitarian Law and the Protection of the Environment in Time of Armed Conflict, No. 291, *International Review of the Red Cross*, November-December 1992, p.529.

54  The Martens Clause is so called after Friedrich von Martens, the Russian delegate who chaired the 11th meeting of the Second Committee of the Second Commission of the First Hague Peace Conference of 1899. In 1980, The Martens Clause was been adopted by the Preambular paragraph five of the Convention on the Prohibition or Restrictions on the Use of Certain Conventional Weapons (CCW). The inclusion of The Marten's Clause in that document affirmed its importance again in protecting civilian populations and combatants as they consider substantial part of the environment. Its wording is reflected in articles and preambles in a number of subsequent treaties, including the four Geneva Conventions of 1949, the 1977 Additional protocols I and II, and the 1980 UN Convention on Certain Conventional Weapons. The Martens Clause is important because it stresses the importance of customary norms in the regulation of armed conflicts. However, today there is no formal agreement amongst lawyers on the interpretation of the Clause, as it is subject to a variety of meanings: both narrow and expansive.

by its provisions, the three Protocols or other international agreements. It provides that "the civilian population and the combatants shall at all times remain under the protection and authority of the principles of international law derived from established custom, from the principles of humanity and from the dictates of public conscience". The Martens Clause does not deal directly with environmental protection. It offers protection only to civilian populations and combatants. Therefore, the environment is not accorded as high a priority in the CCW as injury to persons.

## Chemical Weapons Convention, 1993

The main purpose of the Chemical Weapons Convention (CWC)[55] is to ban the use, development and production of chemical weapons. Chemical substances have both a direct and acute impact on the (natural) environment and, for this reason; the CWC imposes obligations on States Parties not to develop, produce, transfer, stockpile or retains chemical weapons. Article 1 of the Convention specifically prohibits the use of chemical weapons, including assisting, encouraging or inducing anyone to engage in any of the prohibited activities. States Parties are mandated to destroy all chemical weapons owned and abandoned on the territory of another State Party or possessed by them. The CWC requires States to destroy existing chemical weapons and production facilities. In relation to the environment, Articles 4(10), 5(11) and 7(1) of the CWC mandate States Parties to ensure the protection of the environment during the transportation, sampling, storage, and destruction of all chemical weapons. The CWC specifically prohibits the destruction of chemical weapons by "dumping in any body of water, land burial and open-pit burning", thereby ensuring that the human and environmental costs of disposal are minimized.

In particularly serious cases of violation, i.e., in which a State Party's actions threaten the objective and purpose of the CWC,[56] collective measures may be undertaken. In such situations, the matter can also be referred to the

---

55 The Chemical Weapons Convention (CWC) was adopted in January 1993, and it came into force in 1997. It has been ratified by 190 States.

56 The CWC has three principal objectives: (i) It categorically prohibits any use of chemical weapons, whether as "first use" or as a reprisal. State Parties must also refrain from engaging in military preparations for such use, including stockpiling. (ii) The CWC seeks to offer means to verify that State Parties do not initiate or resume chemical weapons production and storage. Situations of non-compliance are to be resolved through peaceful means, including cooperation and negotiations. (iii) The CWC requires that existing chemical weapon stockpiles and production facilities be declared and destroyed.

UN General Assembly or Security Council.[57] The Organization for the Prohibition of Chemical Weapons (OPCW), an independent international body based in The Hague, monitors the implementation of the CWC by the state parties.

As is the case for the Biological Weapons Convention, the CWC has an immediate bearing on the protection of the natural environment during armed conflict, as chemical substances may have direct and severe impacts on the environment. In addition, the CWC has effective mechanisms for monitoring, verification and non-compliance that may serve as a model for other treaties. The CWC appears to cover NIAC as it mandates States Parties to establish both civil and criminal liabilities under international law.

### The Ottawa Treaty, 1997

The Convention on the Prohibition of the Use, Stockpiling, Production and Transfer of Anti-personnel Mines and on their Destruction, commonly referred to as the Ottawa Treaty, completely prohibits the use of anti-personnel landmines. It also forbids their development, production, stockpiling, and transfer. According to the treaty, the States' obligations are to cease the use of anti-personnel mines, to prohibit their development, production, stockpiling and transfer, and to never assist, encourage, or induce anyone to engage in these activities. The use of landmines by a signatory State is considered a breach of its international obligations, since under Article 18 of the Vienna Convention on the Law of Treaties, "a State is obliged to refrain from acts which would defeat the purpose of a treaty when....it has signed the treaty".

Anti-personnel mines harm the environment not only when they are used, but also when they are destroyed as their destruction releases toxic materials which may be released into the soil, water and air. A single mine may cost as little as US$ 3, but expenditure incurred on its removal may be between US$ 200 and US$ 1,000, depending upon where it is placed.[58]

---

57 Article 12 of the CWC provides for measures to redress an existing situation and to ensure compliance, including sanctions. The Conference of the States Parties is empowered to redress and remedy any situation which contravenes the provisions of the CWC. The Conference may restrict or suspend a State Party's rights and privileges under the Convention. It may also recommend collective measures to States Parties where serious damage to the object and purpose of the Convention results from prohibited activities.

58 Swart, M.J.F., *The Effects of Landmines in a Rural Community in Angola: a Case Study*

Some environmental problems associated with landmines include degradation of habitat, reduced access to water points and other vital resources, loss of species, alteration of natural food chains, and additional pressure on biodiversity. When landmines are found in national parks, game reserves and other conservation areas, they undermine the tourist trade. Endangered or vulnerable species[59] can also be directly affected by landmines.

## The Hague Convention on Cultural Property, 1954

The Hague Convention for the Protection of Cultural Property in the Event of Armed Conflict (the Hague Convention on Cultural Property) of 1954 and its Protocols accord enhanced protection to civilian objects during armed conflict.[60] In essence, the Convention seeks to protect and safeguard cultural property and ensure respect for it.[61] Article 28 allows States Parties to "prosecute and impose penal or disciplinary sanctions" on "persons who commit or order" breaches of its provisions. Since the Convention applies expressly to IAC and to cases of occupation of territories, the liability regime relates only to IAC and not NIAC.[62]

---

of *Huambo Province*, 2003, Master's Thesis, University of Johannesburg, available at: http://etd.rau.ac.za/theses/available/etd-05182004-123500/restricted/angolanthesis. pdf, accessed 22 August 2013.

59 In Angola, thousands of animals including antelopes and elephants fell prey to landmines. In some cases, landmines have even been used by poachers, as a field of mines can kill or wound an entire herd of elephants. Nachon, CT, 'The Environmental Impacts of Landmines', in Matthew, R. (ed.). 2004. *Landmines and Human Security: International Politics and War's Hidden Legacy*, New York: State University of New York Press.

60 Article 1(a) defines cultural property as "movable or immovable property of great importance to the cultural heritage of every people, such as monuments of architecture, art or history, whether religious or secular; archaeological sites; groups of buildings which, as a whole, are of historical or artistic interest; works of art; manuscripts, books and other objects of artistic, historical or archaeological interest; as well as scientific collections and important collections of books or archives or of reproductions of the property defined above". Cultural property would also include "buildings whose main and effective purpose is to preserve or exhibit" movable cultural property such as museums, large libraries and depositories of archives, including refuges intended to shelter, in the event of armed conflict, the movable cultural property. Centres "containing a large amount of cultural property" would also be included under this definition. Article 1(b) and (c) of the Hague Convention on Cultural Property, 1954.

61 Articles 2, 3, 4 8, 9, 12, 13, 14, 16 and 17, The Hague Convention on Cultural Property, 1954.

62 Article 18, The Hague Convention on Cultural Property.

The First Hague Protocol (for the Protection of Cultural Property in the Event of Armed Conflict) of 1954, which applies only to IAC, prohibits the export and sale of cultural property from an occupied territory. Yet, unlike the Hague Convention on Cultural Property, the First Hague Protocol fails to provide for any liability in case of a breach of its provisions.

To remedy the deficiencies of both The Hague Convention and its First Protocol, the Second Hague Protocol was adopted in 1999, to establish an enhanced system of protection for specifically designated cultural property. Articles 3 and 22 of the Second Hague Protocol extend the scope of the protection accorded to cultural property to NIAC. Chapter 4 of the Second Protocol introduces a liability regime which covers individual criminal responsibility.[63] It adopts the principle of universality and provides for the extradition of offenders. Articles 15(1) and 21 expressly include offences such as attacks on protected cultural property and the misuse of cultural property, and thus remedy the First Hague Protocol by defining an offence and creating a liability.[64]

On the whole, the Second Hague Protocol provides an improved regime of protection to certain extent. It clarifies the particular precautionary measures to be implemented, and also articulates more clearly the types of conduct that would lead to criminal sanctions and insists that States Parties exercise jurisdiction over such violations. In addition, it extends the protection provided by the Hague Convention on Cultural Property to NIAC. It introduces innovative concepts that could serve to enhance the protection of cultural property and related natural resources in wartime.[65]

---

63 Article 15(2) of the Second Hague Protocol reads: "Each Party shall adopt such measures as may be necessary to establish as criminal offences under its domestic law the offences set forth in this Article and to make such offences punishable by appropriate penalties. When doing so, Parties shall comply with general principles of law and international law, including the rules extending individual criminal responsibility to persons other than those who directly commit the act".

64 Article 15(1) of the Second Hague Protocol reads: "1. Any person commits an offence within the meaning of this Protocol if that person intentionally and in violation of the Convention or this Protocol commits any of the following acts: a. making cultural property under enhanced protection the object of attack; b. using cultural property under enhanced protection or its immediate surroundings in support of military action; c. extensive destruction or appropriation of cultural property protected under the Convention and this Protocol; d. making cultural property protected under the Convention and this Protocol the object of attack; e. theft, pillage or misappropriation of, or acts of vandalism directed against cultural property protected under the Convention".

65 Roberts Adam. 2000. 'The Law of War and Environmental Damage', In Austin, Jay E.,

## C. The Rome Statute of the International Criminal Court

Though not conceptualized with the intention of prosecuting environmental crimes, the Rome Statute of the International Criminal Court (ICC)[66] includes a reference to environmental degradation in its list of justiciable offences. Article 8(2)(b)(iv) of the Rome Statute states, "intentionally launching an attack in the knowledge that such attack will cause.... widespread, long-term and severe damage to the natural environment which would be clearly excessive in relation to the concrete and direct overall military advantage anticipated", would be a war crime. Article 8(2)(b)(iv) is a significant advance for international law. It recognizes for the first time that environmental damage caused by unnecessary military attacks should be prohibited even when that damage does not directly harm human interests and that the only effective sanction for such attacks is individual criminal responsibility. [67]

In addition, other war crimes mentioned in the Rome Statute could incidentally address environmental harm. For example, Article 8(2)(a)(iv) (prohibiting extensive destruction and appropriation of property not justified by military necessity and carried out wantonly and unlawfully), Article 8(2)(b)(xvii) (prohibiting the use of poison and poisoned weapons), and Article 8(2)(b)(xviii) (prohibiting the employment of asphyxiating, poisonous, or other gases) may be used to address issues related to the environment. However, these are not related to environmental crimes in the strict sense.

### Prosecution under the Rome Statute

Prosecution for war crimes under Article 8(2)(b)(iv) of the Rome Statute has been considered a novel provision in international criminal law. In reality, however, there are a number of limitations to the effectiveness of the

---

and Bruch, Carl E., (ed.), *The Environmental Consequences of War: Legal, Economic and Scientific Perspectives*, Cambridge: Cambridge University Press, p. 57.

66 The ICC, governed by the Rome Statute, is the first permanent, treaty based, international criminal court established to help end impunity for the perpetrators of the most serious crimes of concern to the international community. It is an independent international organization, and is not part of the United Nations system. The Rome Statute entered into force on 1 July 2002 after ratification by 60 countries. The ICC is a court of last resort. It will not act if a case is investigated or prosecuted by a national judicial system unless the national proceedings are not genuine.

67 Kevin Jon Heller and Jessica C. Lawrence, The First Ecocentric Environmental War Crime: The Limits of Article 8(2)(b)(iv) of the Rome Statute, Vol. 20 (1), *Georgetown International Environmental Law Review*, Fall 2007, p. 61-96.

provision in holding an individual guilty of environmental harm during armed conflict. To establish a war crime, such harm would have to be:

- among the most serious crimes of concern to the international community as whole;

- committed as part of a plan or policy or as part of a large-scale commission of such crimes;

- the result of intentionally launching an attack in the knowledge that such an attack will cause....widespread, long-term and serious damage to the natural environment which would be clearly excessive in relation to the concrete and direct overall military advantage anticipated.

These provisions set the bar very high for ICC action. First, the three elements—widespread, long-term, and severe—must be proved conjunctively. These terms are not defined in the Rome Statute or in the Elements of the Crimes. In case the ICC decides to charge an individual under article 8(2)(b)(iv), it would have to turn to the ENMOD Convention and AP I. While the interpretation of ENMOD yields fairly accessible definitions of widespread, long-lasting, or severe, it is unclear whether these can facilitate the interpretation of the Rome Statute because ENMOD's requirements are disjunctive. If AP I's definitions were imported into article 8(2)(b)(iv), proving a violation would be virtually impossible.

The stringent *mens rea* requirement is yet another limitation. The harm must be inflicted intentionally and with knowledge that the attack will create such damage. As a result, only the most invidious offender may be held guilty, namely, an individual who *knows* that his behaviour *will cause* widespread, long-term, and severe damage to the environment and, notwithstanding proof of this knowledge, still commits the act with the full *intention* of causing such damage. The *mens rea* is purely subjective and, consequently, there is no room to hold anyone responsible for negligent, willfully blind, or reckless behaviour.

A third limitation is the proportionality requirement. The proportionality between the *actus reus* and the *concrete* and *direct overall* military advantage anticipated seems vague. The impugned conduct has to be *clearly excessive* in relation to the overall *military advantage anticipated*. The use of modifiers such as 'clearly', 'concrete', and 'direct overall' is also vague and conspires to make the successful establishment of the requisite level of proportionality very difficult for the ICC prosecutor. In addition, article 8(2)(b)(iv) does not apply to NIAC. This limitation is particularly problematic because most armed conflicts in the modern age are internal, and no evidence demonstrates that NIAC are *per se* less environmentally destructive than IAC.

The fact that the ICC is unlikely to serve as an enforcement mechanism for wartime environmental damage runs counter to the thinking that IHL may offer the possibility of an effective response to wartime environmental destruction. The effectiveness of the ICC is also hampered by the fact that States such as the US, India, and China are not parties to the Rome Statute. According to Heller and Lawrence, these issues have already "played a critical role in the refusal of the Committee that reviewed NATO's bombing campaign against Yugoslavia to recommend investigating that campaign's environmental damage."[68] Drumble (2000: 630) drew an appropriate conclusion in stating that the international community's decision to criminalize the willful destruction of widespread, long-term and severe damage to the natural environment is cause for limited celebration, considerable disappointment, and concern.[69] There is a little possibility that in the near future, the ICC would rise to the challenges of convicting an individual for environmental damage in an armed conflict.

### D. The ICRC Guidelines

Concern over the extensive damage caused to the environment during the Gulf War, prompted the International Committee of the Red Cross (ICRC) to issue 'Guidelines for military manuals and instructions on the protection of the environment in times of armed conflict' in 1994.[70] The guidelines were drawn from existing international legal obligations and from State practice concerning the protection of the environment against the effects of armed conflict.[71] In the recommending note, the ICRC stated:

---

68 Lawrence C. Jessica & Kevin Jon Heller, The First Eco-centric Environmental War Crime: The Limits of Article 8(2)(b)(iv) of the Rome Statute, Vol. 20 (1), *Georgetown International Environmental Law Review*, Fall 2007, p. 61-96.

69 Drumbl Mark A., 'Waging War Against the World: The Need to Move from War Crimes to Environmental Crimes', in Austin, Jay E., and Bruch, Carl E., (ed.), *The Environmental Consequences of War: Legal, Economic and Scientific Perspectives*, Cambridge: Cambridge University Press, p.620-646.

70 Available at: http://www.icrc.org/eng/resources/documents/misc/57jn38.htm, accessed 02 July 2012.

71 The ICRC study quoted the following sources: General principles of law and customary international law; Hague Convention (IV) and (VIII) of 1907; the fourth Geneva

To the extent that the Guidelines are the expression of international customary law[72] or of treaty law binding a particular State, they must be included in military manuals and instructions on the laws of war. Where they reflect national policy, it is suggested that they be included in such documents.

## Specific rules on the protection of the environment:

1. Destruction of the environment not justified by military necessity violates international humanitarian law. Under certain circumstances, such destruction is punishable as a grave breach of international humanitarian law.

2. The general prohibition on destroying civilian objects, unless such destruction is justified by military necessity, also protects the environment.

3. In particular, States should take all measures required by international law to avoid:

   (a) Making forests or other kinds of plant cover the object of attack by incendiary weapons except when such natural elements are used to cover, conceal or camouflage combatants or other military objectives, or are themselves military objectives;

   (b) Attacks on objects indispensable to the survival of the civilian population, such as foodstuffs, agricultural areas or drinking water installations, if carried out for the purpose of denying such objects to the civilian population;

   (c) Attacks on works or installations containing dangerous forces, namely dams, dykes and nuclear electrical generating stations,

---

Conventions of 1949; Hague Convention for the Protection of Cultural Property of 1954; The ENMOD Convention of 1976; Additional Protocols I and II of 1977 to the Geneva Conventions; UN Convention on Certain Conventional Weapons of 1980 (CCW); CCW Protocol on the Use of Mines, Booby-traps and Other Devices; CCW Protocol on the Use of Incendiary Weapons. The Guidelines have been published as an annex to UN Doc. A/49/323 (1994). GA Resolution 49/50, of 9 December 1994. Available at: http://www.icrc.org/eng/resources/documents/misc/57jn38.htm, visited 14 June 2014.

72 The rules grounded in Articles 35 (3), 55 and 56 of AP I, though included in the ICRC's text cannot be regarded as having customary status. Boothby William H. 2009. *Weapons and the Law of Armed Conflict*, Oxford: Oxford University Press, p. 100.

even where they are military objectives, if such attack may cause the release of dangerous forces and consequent severe losses among the civilian population and as long as such works or installations are entitled to special protection under Protocol I additional to the Geneva Conventions;

(d) Attacks on historic monuments, works of art or places of worship which constitute the cultural or spiritual heritage of peoples.

4. The indiscriminate laying of landmines is prohibited. The location of all pre-planned minefields must be recorded. Any unrecorded laying of remotely delivered non-self-neutralizing landmines is prohibited. Special rules limit the emplacement and use of naval mines.

5. Care shall be taken in warfare to protect and preserve the natural environment. It is prohibited to employ methods or means of warfare which are intended, or may be expected, to cause widespread, long-term and severe damage to the natural environment and thereby prejudice the health or survival of the population.

6. The military or any other hostile use of environmental modification techniques having widespread, long-lasting or severe effects as the means of destruction, damage or injury to any other State party is prohibited. The term "environmental modification techniques" refers to any technique for changing - through the deliberate manipulation of natural processes - the dynamics, composition or structure of the Earth, including its biota, lithosphere, hydrosphere and atmosphere, or of outer space.

7. Attack against the natural environment by way of reprisals are prohibited for States party to Protocol I additional to the Geneva Conventions States are urged to enter into further agreements providing additional protection to the natural environment in times of armed conflict.

8. States are urged to enter into further agreements providing additional protection to the natural environment in times of armed conflict

9. Works or installations containing dangerous forces, and cultural

property shall be clearly marked and identified, in accordance with applicable international rules. Parties to an armed conflict are encouraged to mark and identify also works or installations where hazardous activities are being carried out, as well as sites which are essential to human health or the environment.

10. States shall respect and ensure respect for the obligations under international law applicable in armed conflict, including the rules providing protection for the environment in times of armed conflict

11. States shall disseminate these rules, making them known as widely as possible in their respective countries, and include them in their programmes of military and civil instruction.

12. In the study, development, acquisition or adoption of a new weapon, means or method of warfare, States are under an obligation to determine whether its employment would, in some or all circumstances, be prohibited by applicable rules of international law, including these providing protection to the environment in times of armed conflict.

13. In the event of armed conflict, the parties thereto are encouraged to facilitate and protect the work of impartial organizations contributing to preventing or repairing damage to the environment, pursuant to special agreements between the parties concerned or, as the case may be, the permission granted by one of them. Such work should be performed with due regard to the security interests of the parties concerned.

14. In the event of breaches of rules of international humanitarian law protecting the environment, measures shall be taken to stop any such violation and to prevent further breaches. Military commanders are required to prevent and, where necessary, to suppress and to report to competent authorities breaches of these rules. In serious cases, offenders shall be brought to justice.

The ICRC concluded that existing law, if properly implemented, was capable of providing adequate protection.[73] The guidelines are a summary of the existing applicable IHL rules, which must be respected by the armed

---

73 Gasser Hans-Peter, For Better Protection of the Natural Environment in Armed Conflict: A Proposal for Action, Vol. 89 (3), *American Journal of International Law*, (1995), p. 637-645.

forces during an armed conflict. The UN General Assembly decided in its 49th session not to formally approve the guideline but to invite States to 'give due consideration' to their incorporation into military manuals and instructions.[74] The efforts of the ICRC in issuing model set of guidelines for military manuals[75] have not been very successful, in part because the model incorporates the main elements of AP I, which countries such as the US, China and India have not ratified.[76] In 2010, the ICRC in its presentation on 'Strengthening Legal Protection for Victims of Armed Conflict' drew the conclusion that humanitarian law needs to be reinforced in order to protect the natural environment.[77] It was of the view that the extensive development of international environmental law in recent decades has not been matched by a similar development in IHL.

## E. United Nations General Assembly Resolutions

The UN General Assembly Resolutions have made a significant contribution to the framing of international law on the protection of the environment during armed conflict. In 1969, following reports of the use of chemical agents such as herbicides by the US in the Vietnam War, the UN General Assembly passed a resolution declaring that the 1925 Gas Protocol prohibits the use of following in armed conflicts:

(a) Any chemical agents of warfare i.e., chemical substances, whether gaseous, liquid or solid, which might be employed because of their direct toxic effects on man, animals or plants;

(b) Any biological agents of warfare i.e., living organisms, whatever

---

74 Boothby William H. 2009. *Weapons and the Law of Armed Conflict*, Oxford: Oxford University Press, p. 99.

75 Military manuals are an essential component in the international law-making process, often the litmus test of whether a putative prescriptive exercise has produced effective law. Without adequate dissemination, this putative international law-making is an exercise in the elaboration of myth through *lex simulata* rather than the installation of an effective operational code. Reisman W. Michael and William K. Leitzau, 'Moving International Law from Theory to Practice: The Role of Military Manuals in Effectuating the Law of Armed Conflict', in Horace B. Robertson, Jr, (ed.), *The Law of Naval Operations,* Vol. 64, US Naval War College, International Law Studies, 1991, p. 1-18.

76 Cohan John Alan, Modes of Warfare and Evolving Standards of Environmental Protection under International Law of War, Vol. 15, *Fla. J. Int'l L.* (2002-03), p. 481-539.

77 Available at: http://www.icrc.org/eng/resources/documents/statement/ihl-development -statement-210910.htm, accessed 23 March 2014.

their nature, or infective material derived from them, which are intended to cause disease and death in man, animals or plants, and which depend for their effects on their ability to multiply in the person, animal or plant attacked.[78]

The UN General Assembly, in its Resolution of 9 February 1993, stated that the "destruction of the environment, not justified by military necessity and carried out wantonly is clearly contrary to existing international law". The resolution also expressed concern that the relevant provisions of international law on the matter "may not be widely disseminated and applied". The States were urged "to take all measures to ensure compliance with the existing international law" on this issue, including by "becoming Parties to the relevant international conventions" and "incorporating these provisions of international law into their military manuals". [79] Resolution A/RES/50/7(M) specifically recognizes the importance of considering environmental safeguards in treaties and agreements regarding disarmament, and further highlights the detrimental environmental effects of the use of nuclear weapons, as well as "the positive potential implications for the environment of a future comprehensive nuclear-test-ban treaty".[80]

Guided by the purposes and principles enshrined in the Charter of the United Nations and the rules of IHL, the General Assembly has also addressed the issue of depleted uranium (DU). The Resolutions of 2007 and 2009 could eventually lead to the codification in treaty law of norms protecting human health and the environment from DU armaments.[81]

The UN Security Council has also recognized the role that natural resources can play in armed conflict and post-conflict situations.[82] This

---

78  UN G.A. Res. 2603 A, U.N. GAOR, 24th Sess., U.N. Doc. A/7890 (1969).

79  UNGA Resolution 47/37 (9 February 1993). The resolution did not, however, identify specific gaps in the existing international legal framework, and consequently did not recommend developing or strengthening particular measures.

80  Among the recent objects under consideration by the General Assembly in relation to armed conflict and the environment was Resolution 63/211 (19 December 2008) on the oil slick on Lebanese shores caused by the bombing of the El-Jiyeh power plant during the 2006 war. The resolution emphasizes "the need to protect and preserve the marine environment in accordance with international law."

81  UNGA Resolutions 62/30 of December 2007 and 63/54 of January 2009 request the Secretary-General to produce reports on the issue. The resolution recognizes "the potential harmful effects of the use of armaments and ammunitions containing depleted uranium on human health and the environment".

82  Statement of the UN Security Council President on 25 June 2007, S/PRST/2007/22.

is an important indication of the increasing awareness of the complex and important linkages between the environment and armed conflict at the international policy level. In Resolution 1856 (2008), the Security Council has recognized "the link between the illegal exploitation of natural resources, the illicit trade in such resources and the proliferation and trafficking of arms as one of the major factors fuelling and exacerbating conflicts in the Great Lakes region of Africa, and in particular in the Democratic Republic of Congo". [83] The Security Council consequently decided that the UN Mission to the Democratic Republic of Congo (MONUC) should have the mandate to "use its monitoring and inspection capacities to curtail the provision of support to illegal armed groups derived from illicit trade in natural resources". It also urged States in the region to "establish a plan for an effective and transparent control over the exploitation of natural resources". This resolution appears to open a new avenue for stronger implementation and enforcement of existing law on the protection of the environment and natural resources during armed conflict. By suggesting new means of enforcement, it implicitly recognizes the weakness of the existing enforcement mechanisms and the relevance of mandating peacekeeping missions, whose primarily objective is the preservation of peace and security, to address natural resource issues.

## F. The International Law Commission

The International Law Commission in its 2011 report has argued that the effect of an armed conflict on the environment differs from other consequences in that the former may be long-term and irreparable. It may remain long after the conflict and prevent an effective rebuilding of the society, destroy pristine areas or disrupt important ecosystems. The protection of the environment in armed conflicts has been primarily viewed through the lens of the laws of warfare, including IHL. However, this perspective is too narrow as modern international law recognizes that the international law applicable during an armed conflict may be wider than the laws of warfare. It has been proposed that the ILC should examine the issue in its long-term programme of work. The final outcome could be either a Draft Framework Convention or a Statement of Principles and Rules on the Protection of the Environment in Times of Armed Conflict. [84]

---

83 UNSC Resolution 1856 on the Situation concerning the Democratic Republic of the Congo, 22 December 2008.

84 A few proposal are: (i) to identify the extent of the legal problem, (ii) to identify any new developments in case law or in customary law, (iii) to clarify the applicability of

## G. Principles of IHL

The general principles of IHL are a source of law on their own.[85] They complement and underpin the various IHL instruments and apply to all countries. While customary principles such as distinction, proportionality and humanity, relate to the protection of the environment during warfare, they are treated as subordinate to the principle of military necessity. The principle of distinction is the keystone of the law regulating protection of civilians during hostilities. It stipulates that the parties to a conflict must distinguish at all times between combatants and civilians. Parties may not attack civilians and civilian objects and may direct attacks against only military objectives.[86] Civilians or civilian objects like schools, hospitals, parks, bridges, dams, water bodies should be excluded from military operations.[87] It protects the environment to the extent that the civilian environment is linked to the natural environment, and presumes that a clear distinction can be made between civilian and military environments.

The principle of proportionality states that even if there is a clear military target, it must not be attacked, if the risk of civilians or civilian property being harmed is greater than the expected military advantage.[88] The proportionality principle places limits on belligerents in choosing methods and tactics of warfare.[89] It requires that prior to destroying a natural resource site by military activity, the military authority should weigh the

---

and the relationship between IHL, ICL, IEL and IHRL, and (iv) to develop the work on the effect of armed conflict on treaties, particularly on matters concerning the continued application of treaties relating to the protection of the environment and human rights. Jacobsson Marie G., *Protection of the environment in relation to armed conflicts*, UN: Report of the International Law Commission, Annex E, Sixty-third session, (26 April–3 June and 4 July–12 August 2011); General Assembly Official Records, Sixty-sixth session, Supplement No. 10 (A/66/10), p. 347-364.

85  Statute of the International Court of Justice (ICJ), Article 38.

86  Military objectives are members of the armed forces, other persons taking a direct part in hostilities, and "those objects which by their nature, location, purpose or use make an effective contribution to military action and whose total or partial destruction, capture or neutralization, in the circumstances ruling at the time, offers a definite military advantage." IHL prohibits attacks "of a nature to strike military objectives and civilians or civilian objects without distinction."Additional Protocol I, Articles 51(3), (4) and 52.

87  Tarasofsky Richard D, 1993, 'Legal Protection of the Environment During International Armed Conflict', *Netherlands Yearbook of International Law*, Vol. XXIV, p. 27.

88  The concept of proportionality is described in Article 22 of 1907 Hague Regulations IV.

89  The proportionality principle is contained in Articles 35 (2), 51(5)(b), and 57(2)(a) and (b) of the Additional Protocol I of Geneva Conventions.

expected environmental harm against the military benefits expected to be gained. If the environmental damage outweighs the military advantage, the military operation should be avoided.[90]

The principle of humanity prohibits inflicting unnecessary suffering and destruction.[91] Therefore, in an armed conflict, a Party cannot use starvation as a method of warfare; or attack, destroy, remove or render useless such objects as are indispensable to the survival of the civilian population. All forms of deliberate ecological disruption would appear to fall within the ambit of this overall prohibition.[92]

Military necessity justifies the infliction of suffering upon an enemy combatant, but only that much suffering is justified as is necessary to bring about the submission of the enemy. To be lawful, weapons and tactics involving the use of force must be reasonably necessary to the attainment of their military objective. No superfluous or excessive application of force is lawful, even if the damage done is confined to the environment, thereby sparing people and property.[93] This principle ensures the minimization of human and environmental loss, especially in an armed conflict between the armed forces of a developed State and a developing one.[94]In addition, the

---

90  Michael D. Diederich, Law of War and Ecology, A Proposal for a Workable Approach to Protecting the Environment through the Law of War, Vol. 136, *Mil Law Rev*, (1992), p.137.

91  1907 Hague Regulations, Article 23 (e).

92  The British Manual of Military Law (2004) defines military necessity as: "The principle whereby a belligerent has the right to apply any measures which are required to bring about the successful conclusion of a military operation and which are not forbidden by the laws of war". The Manual further provides that the humanity forbids the infliction of suffering, injury, or destruction not actually necessary for the accomplishment of legitimate military purposes. The principle of humanity is based on the notion that once a military purpose has been achieved, the further infliction of suffering is unnecessary. The principle confirms the basic immunity of civilian populations and civilian objects from attack because civilians and civilian objects make no contribution to military action.

93  Richard Falk, 1992. 'The Environmental Law of War: An Introduction', in Glen Plant (ed.), *Environmental Protection and the Law of War: A 'Fifth Geneva' Convention on the Protection of the Environment in Time of Armed Conflict*, John Wiley & Sons, p. 84.

94  The Committee Established to Review the NATO Bombing Campaign Against the Federal Republic of Yugoslavia was of the view that the environmental impact of that bombing campaign was "best considered from the underlying principles of the law of armed conflicts such as necessity and proportionality". Committee Established to Review the NATO Bombing Campaign Against the Federal Republic of Yugoslavia, Final Report. Available at: http://www.icty.org/x/file/Press/nato061300.pdf, accessed

principle limits environmental damage to within the battlefield and seeks to ensure that damage does not spill over to the neighbouring environment. However, any rule in relation to a neutral environment cannot be absolute, since neighbouring environments will always be affected by warfare. A further limitation of this principle is that it applies only to States and does not cover global commons, which belligerents are otherwise free to abuse.[95]

The Martens Clause[96] has formed a part of modern IHL instruments, and deals with the protection to civilians and belligerents during armed conflict. It has imported into humanitarian law a dynamic dimension that is not limited by time, bringing in fundamental principles beyond those contained in written conventions. It permits the constant and spontaneous development of norms as needed due to scientific, technological, military, social and historical evolution in the common interest of humanity. It is based on the fundamental purpose of humanitarian law: the preservation of humanity. It originally appeared in the Preamble to the 1989 Hague Convention II Respecting the Laws and Customs of War on Land, as:

> Until a more complete code of the laws of war has been issued, the High Contracting Parties deem it expedient to declare that, in cases not included in the Regulations adopted by them, the inhabitants

---

12 September 2012.

95  For example, the rules of maritime neutrality operate only to limit the exercise of belligerency within the territorial waters of neutral States, while the high seas can be treated by belligerents as a 'region of war'; Hague Convention XIII of 1907, Concerning the Rights and Duties of Neutral Powers in Naval War.

96  The Martens Clause is so called after Friedrich von Martens, the Russian delegate who chaired the 11th meeting of the Second Committee of the Second Commission of the First Hague Peace Conference of 1899. In 1980, The Martens Clause was been adopted by the Preambular paragraph five of the Convention on the Prohibition or Restrictions on the Use of Certain Conventional Weapons. The paragraph declares that "the civilian population and the combatants shall at all times remain under the protection and authority of the principles of international law derived from established custom, from the principles of humanity and from the dictates of public conscience." The inclusion of The Marten's Clause in that document affirmed its importance again in protecting civilian populations and combatants as they consider substantial part of the environment. Its wording is reflected in articles and preambles in a number of subsequent treaties, including the four Geneva Conventions of 1949, the 1977 Additional protocols I and II, and the 1980 UN Convention on Certain Conventional Weapons. The relevance of this clause to environmental protection has been widely accepted. Roberts Adam. 2000. 'The Law of War and Environmental Damage', In Austin, Jay E., and Bruch, Carl E., (ed.), *The Environmental Consequences of War: Legal, Economic and Scientific Perspectives*, Cambridge: Cambridge University Press, p. 52.

and the belligerents remain under the protection and the rule of the principles of the law of nations, as they result from the usages established among civilized peoples, from the laws of humanity, and the dictates of the public conscience.

The Martens Clause broadens the range of applicable norms governing conduct during armed conflict beyond those that are laid out in the treaty instruments. The Clause is generally considered to constitute a foundational principle of IHL protecting the environment in the absence of other provisions in treaty or customary law. However, specialists in IHL are not in agreement over the interpretation of the Martens Clause.[97]

## H. Customary IHL

Customary international law (CIL) fills certain gaps in the protection provided to victims of armed conflict by treaty law. These gaps result either from the lack of ratification of the relevant treaties or from the lack of detailed rules on NIAC in treaty law. The rules of customary law are not restricted in their field of application, and many apply to all forms of conflict, whether international or non-international. These rules bind all belligerents on both sides of a conflict, and fill the gaps in the treaty rules applicable to NIAC, including targeting, proportionality, precautions in attack and the protection of civilians and civilian property. Although most of IHL has now been codified in treaties, important aspects of belligerent activity, especially in naval warfare, continue to be regulated by customary law.

The ICRC study on customary law (2005) [98] contains four rules relating to the protection of the natural environment. There are: (i) No part of the natural environment may be attacked unless it is a military objective; Destruction of any part of the natural environment is prohibited, unless required by imperative military necessity; and Launching an attack against

---

97  *Protecting the Environment during Armed Conflict: An Inventory and Analysis of International Law*, November 2009, UNEP, p.12.

98  In the ICRC study, 161 rules have been catalogued in six parts: (i) Principle of distinction, (ii) specifically protected persons and objects, (iii) specific methods of warfare, (iv) weapons, (v) treatment of civilians and persons *hors de combat*, and (vi) implementation. Of the 161 rules identified, 159 apply in IAC and 149 in NIAC. Although key States such as Israel, India, and the US are not party to AP I, they recognize many of the Protocol's provisions as reflective of the customary law of armed conflict. Henckaerts Jean-Marie, Study on Customary International Humanitarian Law: A contribution to the understanding and respect for the rule of law in armed conflict, *International Review of the Red Cross*, Vol. 87, No. 857, March 2005, p. 175-212.

a military objective which may be expected to cause incidental damage to the environment which would be excessive in relation to the concrete and direct military advantage anticipated is prohibited;[99] (ii) The means and methods of warfare must be employed with due regard to the protection and preservation of the natural environment. In the conduct of military operations, all feasible precautions must be taken to avoid, and in any event to minimize, incidental damage to the environment. Lack of scientific certainty as to the effects on the environment of certain military operations does not absolve a party to the conflict from taking such precautions;[100] (iii) The use of methods or means of warfare that are intended, or may be expected, to cause widespread, long-term and severe damage to the natural environment is prohibited. Destruction of the natural environment may not be used as a weapon;[101] and (iv) The use of herbicides as a method of warfare is prohibited, if they would cause widespread, long-term and severe damage to the natural environment.[102] The ICRC study, however, fails to deliver because some of its rules are *lex ferenda* (what the law should be) with insufficient evidence of State practice or *opinio juris*.[103] The Study, therefore, is not a concrete measure. It merely represents the ICRC's idealistic notion of what States should consider customary IHL.[104]

## I. San Remo Manual on International Law Applicable to Armed Conflict at Sea (1994)

The San Remo Manual, which codifies the law of naval warfare and includes provisions for environmental protection in warfare, constitutes an

---

99 Rule 43, Customary Law, applicable in both IAC and NIAC.

100 Rule 44, Customary Law, applicable in both IAC and NIAC.

101 Rule 45, Customary Law, applicable in both IAC and NIAC.

102 Rule 76, Customary Law, applicable in both IAC and NIAC.

103 For a practice of states to become a rule of customary international law it must appear that the states follow the practice from a sense of legal obligation (*opinio juris sive necessitatis*).

104 Marsh J Jeremy, *LexLata* or *Lex Ferenda*? Rule 45 of the ICRC Study on Customary IHL, Vol. 198, *Military Law Review*, Winter 2008, p. 116-164. According to Dinstein (2006), the Study clearly suffers from an unrealistic desire to show that controversial provisions of [AP I] are declaratory of customary international law (not to mention the occasional attempt to go even beyond [AP I]). By overreaching, the Study has failed in its primary mission. Yoram Dinstein, 'The ICRC Customary International Law Study', in Anthony M. Helm (ed.). 2006. *The Law of War in the 21st Century: Weaponry and the Use of Force*, Naval War College Press.

instrument of soft law in relation to the marine environment.[105] The manual "encourages" conflicting parties "to agree that no hostile actions will be conducted in marine areas containing: (a) rare or fragile ecosystems; or (b) the habitat of depleted, threatened or endangered species or other forms of marine life." Para 44 of the Manual states: "Methods and means of warfare should be employed with due regard for the natural environment taking into account the relevant rules of international law. Paragraph 47(h) of the Manual further provides that vessels designated or adapted exclusively for responding to pollution incidents in the marine environment are exempt from attack.[106]

The San Remo Manual indicates that there should be "due regard for the natural environment" in naval warfare. This includes the prohibition of "damage to or destruction of the natural environment not justified by military necessity and carried out wantonly." Formulated slightly differently from AP I, it focuses on the justifications for and carelessness towards the environment. This approach is also recognized under other formulations of customary international law where "due regard for the natural environment" necessitates that all feasible precautions be taken to avoid incidental environmental damage whether or not there is scientific certainty that it will occur.[107]

---

105 The ICJ in the Nuclear Weapons Advisory Opinion stated (in para 30): "States must take environmental consideration into account when assigning what is necessary and proportionate in the pursuit of legitimate military objectives". This obligation was expressed as due regard in the non-binding 1994 San Remo Manual on International Law Applicable to Armed Conflicts at Sea and drafted by the International Institute of Humanitarian Law.

106 Dietrich Schindler and Jiri Toman (eds.). 2004. San Remo Manual on International Law Applicable to Armed Conflict at Sea, The Laws of Armed Conflict, Leiden and Boston. *San Remo Manual on International Law Applicable to Armed Conflict at Sea*, also available at www.icrc.org/eng/resources/documents/misc/57jmst.htm.

107 San Remo Manual, Paragraph 11 provides: "The Parties to the conflict are encouraged to agree that no hostile actions will be conducted in marine areas containing rare or fragile ecosystems or the habitat of depleted, threatened or endangered species or other forms of marine life." Although this provision is not mandatory, such a preventative measure could clearly be in everyone's best interest, particularly because criminal sanctions for individuals causing excessive environmental damage are now possible under the statute of the International Criminal Court (ICC). It can be argued that this provides leeway for states in that as long as the damage caused has a legitimate military purposes, it may be acceptable. Christopher Waters and Ashley Barnes, The Arctic Environment and the Law of Armed Conflict, Vol. 6, No. 4, *Canadian Naval Review*, Winter 2011, p. 16-21.

## J. The 2009 HPCR Manual on International Law Applicable to Air and Missile Warfare

The HPCR Manual provides the most up-to-date restatement of existing international law applicable to air and missile warfare. As an authoritative restatement, the HPCR Manual contributes to the practical understanding of international legal framework.[108] Rules 88 and 89 of the HPCR manual deal with specific protection of the natural environment and provide: "The destruction of the natural environment carried out wantonly is prohibited"; and "When planning and conducting air or missile operations, due regard ought to be given to the natural environment".

The 'commentary' to the Manual provides that the wanton destruction of the natural environment is clearly prohibited under Rule 88, which is also applicable in NIAC. It means that the natural environment is a civilian object unless and until portions of it constitute a military objective.[109] Similarly, when a military objective is attacked, and expected collateral damage is assessed compared to the anticipated military advantage, the proportionality analysis also needs to take into account the expected collateral damage to the natural environment.

Rule 89, also applicable in NIAC, does not require a prior assessment of all possible environmental impacts of air and missile attacks. Those who plan an attack are obliged to take into account that information on the natural environment that is reasonably available to them at the relevant time of planning. In this context, the pilot is not usually expected to make such decisions on his own. The protection of the natural environment 'must' be taken into account when planning and conducting air or missile attacks. The expected collateral damage to the environment, if excessive, requires that any air or missile attack against lawful targets be aborted.

## Problems in Enforcement of IHL

The provisions of IHL governing the protection of the environmental during

---

108 The HPCR Manual and its Commentary are the results of a six-year-long endeavour led by the Program on Humanitarian Policy and Conflict Research at Harvard University (HPCR), during which it convened an international Group of Experts to reflect on existing rules of international law applicable to air and missile warfare. The Manual on International Law Applicable to Air and Missile Warfare by the Program on Humanitarian Policy and Conflict Research at Harvard University (HPCR), 2009. Available at: http://www.ihlresearch.org/amw/manual/ accessed 08 June 2014.

109 Rule 11 HPCR Manual: Attacks directed against civilians or civilian objects are prohibited.

armed conflicts consists of international treaties, diverse body of general principles, customary law and soft law that have developed over a century in response to a wide range of practical problems. Concern for environmental damage during armed conflicts is relatively a new development and these provisions are inadequate in the context of modern armed conflicts. The rules of IHL adopted by the international community before the 1970s offered no real environmental protection. Even when the international NGOs condemned the use of weapons of mass destruction (biological, chemical and nuclear weapons) they did not envisage environmental protection in times of armed conflict. Even now, most IHL provisions are subject to constraints, such as 'necessity of war' used in Article 23 (1)(g) of the 1907 Hague Convention IV or 'necessary by military operations' used in Article 53 of the Fourth Geneva Convention of 1949. Military necessity is used as a part of the legal justification for attacks on legitimate military targets that may have adverse, even terrible, consequences for civilians and civilian objects. For example, during the Vietnam War, the US considered the use of chemical and environmental modification techniques necessary to counter the guerrilla tactics of North Vietnam.

Theoretically, IHL provisions apply not only to the contracting parties, but also the non-contracting States, because they are broadly accepted as customary law. Nonetheless, a number of violations of these provisions have been reported during recent conflicts. IHL directs the States to fulfill a number of obligations. For example, Article 80 of AP I requires the parties to take all necessary measures for the execution of their obligations. Similarly, Article 82 and 83 requires that legal advisors be available in the armed forces to advise commanders on the application of the Conventions and Protocols in times of peace and armed conflicts. Article 87 instructs the parties "to require military commanders, with respect to members of the armed forces under their control, to prevent and where necessary, to suppress and report to competent authorities breaches of the Convention and AP I". But if the military commanders and the local authorities are ignorant of a breach, these provisions provide little help.

Recent conflicts have demonstrated that IHL rules applicable to the protection of the environment during IAC are largely unenforceable and often disregarded. In cases where IHL might apply to the environmental effects of armed conflict, limitations in application and enforcement mechanisms hinder the effectiveness of its provisions. In addition, a lack of synergy and coherence between the existing provisions of IHL has given rise to several loopholes. The absence of effective punishments for environmentally destructive conduct reinforces the ineffectiveness of the current system in preventing environmental harm due to combat.[110]

NIAC have multiple, long- and short-term impacts on environment, and on development and human well-being. The affects could be felt at various levels, within the immediate area of conflict, and often in neighbouring countries.[111] While most recent and ongoing conflicts are non-international, the body of IHL treaty and customary law governing NIAC is relatively limited. In the absence of explicit and direct provisions, the current legal framework on the preservation and protection of environment during NIAC appears insufficient.[112] There is no treaty norm that explicitly addresses the issue of environmental damage during NIAC, and obligations applicable in this context are generally far less restrictive than for IAC. The principal treaty law regulations for NIAC are contained in Common Article 3 to the four Geneva Conventions and AP II. Common Article 3 merely restates the basic protections for persons *hors de combat*, and is of little direct relevance to environmental protection, while Protocol II does not provide detailed limitations regarding methods and means of warfare.[113] Besides,

---

110 Huston Meredith DuBarry, Wartime Environmental Damage: Financing the Cleanup, Vol. 23, *U. Pa. J. Int'l Econ. L.*, (2000), p. 908.

111 *Overview of African Development 2005: Conflict in Africa and the Role of Disarmament, Demobilization and Reintegration in Post-conflict Reconstruction*, United Nations Office of the Special Adviser on Africa, New York. Available at: http://www.un.org/africa/osaa/reports/Overview%20African%20issues%20FINAL.pdf, accessed 2 February 2014.

112 Express treaty law governing NIAC is limited. It includes Common Article 3 of the 1949 Geneva Conventions for the Protection of War Victims; the 1977 Protocol Additional (II) to the Geneva Conventions of August 12, 1949, and Relating to the Protection of Victims of Non-international Armed Conflict (AP II); the 1980 Convention on Certain Conventional Weapons, as amended, and its Protocols; the 1998 Statute of the International Criminal Court; the 1997 Ottawa Convention banning anti-personnel land mines; the 1993 Chemical Weapons Convention; and the 1954 Hague Convention for the Protection of Cultural Property and its 1999 Second Protocol. Unless it is reflective of customary international law, treaty law binds only States Parties thereto.

113 Armed conflicts in important habitats for wildlife have affected numerous countries since 1990. A partial list includes Angola, Bosnia, the Democratic Republic of Congo, Cambodia, Central African Republic, Colombia, Guatemala, India, Indonesia, Liberia, Mexico, Myanmar, Nepal, Pakistan, Peru, the Philippines, Sierra Leone, Senegal, Sri Lanka, the Solomon Islands, and Sudan – quite a depressing catalogue. These typically non-international armed conflicts are often in areas distant from government control where few public services are available to the hundreds of millions of people who live in these remote areas. McNeely Jeffery A. and Susan A. Mainka, Conservation for a New Era: Conservation and Armed Conflict, International Union for Conservation of Nature (2009), Switzerland: IUCN. Available at: http://data.iucn.org/dbtw-wpd/html/2009-026/section11.html, accessed 2 January 2014.

its ratification status is low. Thus, it could not be applied as a source of treaty law in the NIAC in Afghanistan, Angola, Congo, Haiti, Iraq, Somalia and Sri Lanka. Further, non-state actors involved in NIACs also do not consider themselves bound by provisions relating to any environmental protection, such as prohibitions on pillage, or destruction of resources necessary for the survival of the civilian population. The ability to protect the environment from the conduct of non-state actors in NIAC remains limited.[114]

Unfortunately, the case law of international judicial bodies on IHL is also not comprehensive. Though some claim that the general principles of IHL and customary law may be applicable in NIAC, it is unclear as to which provisions of IHL relating to the environment (directly or indirectly) have entered into customary law and may, therefore, be applicable to such conflicts. Finally, aside from the ICC, and some *ad hoc* criminal tribunals, there are few effective mechanisms for enforcing the provisions of IHL, particularly relating to damage to the environment.

According to Bothe (2010: 569), there are three main shortcomings in the existing body of IHL relating to the protection of the environment during armed conflict: (i) the definition of impermissible environmental damage is both too restrictive and unclear; (ii) there are legal uncertainties regarding the protection of elements of the environment as civilian objects; and (iii) the application of the principle of proportionality where harm to the environment constitutes 'collateral damage' is also problematic. These gaps present specific opportunities for clarifying and developing the existing framework. Some of the inadequacies of IHL could be addressed by application of international environmental law (IEL) to armed conflict.[115]

---

114 Theodor Meron, 'Comment: Protection of the Environment During Non-international Armed Conflicts', in Richard J Grunawalt , John E. King and Ronald S. McClain (ed.), *Protection of the Environment During Armed Conflict*, Volume 69, International Law Studies, 1996, NewPort: Naval War College, p. 353.

115 Bothe Michael, Carl Bruch, Jordan Diamond, and David Jensen., International Law Protecting the Environment during Armed Conflict: Gaps and Opportunities, Vol. 92, No. 879, *International Review of the Red Cross*, September 2010, p. 569-592.

## II. International Environmental Law

International environmental law (IEL) is a new legal regime[116] evolving in response to the rapid growth of industrialization, the expansion of transportation, the population explosion and the use of highly noxious substances, all of which have greatly exacerbated harm to the environment in the post WWW II era.[117] In view of the significant gaps and deficiencies in the IHL framework regarding the protection of the environment during armed conflict;[118] it has been suggested that some provisions of IEL may be applied during an armed conflict.[119] IEL provides a well-established body of multilateral environmental agreements (MEAs), principles, norms, standards and approaches preventing and redressing the damage to the environment during times of peace. It also covers numerous cases of environmental damage that give rise to responsibility and potential liability during times of peace.

The laws and commentaries of IEL may be applicable during armed conflict have been covered under three headings: (i) Multilateral environmental agreements (MEA), (ii) Customary international environmental law, and (iii) The international institutions.

### A. Multilateral Environmental Agreements (MEA)

MEAs are binding international instruments to which more than two States are a Party. The breach of an MEA gives rise to State responsibility. In addition, a growing number of compliance mechanisms provide means

---

116 The prevention of environmental damage is the underlying objective of all environmental law instruments and requires the avoidance, reduction or control of activities that are damaging to the environment. Hulme Karen. 2004. *War Torn Environment: Interpreting the Legal Threshold*, Leiden: Martinus Nijhoff Publishers, p. 52. The term 'international environmental law' (IEL) as used in this work, is the aggregate of all rules and principles aimed at protecting the global environment and controlling activities within national jurisdiction that may affect another State's environment or areas beyond national jurisdiction.

117 Leibler Anthony, Deliberate Wartime Environmental Damage: New Challenges for International Law, *California Western International Law Journal*, Vol. 23, No. 1, 1992-1993, p. 69.

118 Loets Adrian, An Old Debate Revisited: Applicability of Environmental Treaties in Times if International Armed Conflict Pursuant to the International Law Commission's Draft Articles on the Effects of Armed Conflict on Treaties, *RECIEL*, Vol. 21 (2) 2012, p. 129.

119 Bothe Michael, Carl Bruch, Jordan Diamond, and David Jensen., International Law Protecting the Environment during Armed Conflict: Gaps and Opportunities, Vol. 92, No. 879, *International Review of the Red Cross*, September 2010, p. 569-592.

to facilitate States to compliance with MEA provisions.[120]

The UN Convention on the Law of the Sea (UNCLOS) establishes a framework for marine governance designed to foster international peace and security.[121] The convention identifies the principal sources of pollution as land-based sources, vessels, exploitation of sea-bed resources, and other equipment operating in the marine environment.[122] UNCLOS provides for freedom of the high seas, which are explicitly reserved for "peaceful purposes."[123] Article 192 of the Convention declares that the States have the obligation to protect and preserve the marine environment, and Article 194 requires States to take measures to prevent, reduce and control marine pollution. Articles 207, 208 and 212 impose the same requirement with regard to pollution from land-based sources, from seabed activities, and through the atmosphere.

These general provisions are limited by Article 236, which provides: "The provisions of this Convention regarding the protection and preservation of the marine environment do not apply to any warship, naval auxiliary, other vessels or aircraft owned or operated by a State and used, for the time being, only on government non-commercial service." The Article further states that such vessels or aircraft must comply with the protective provisions "as far as is reasonable and practicable".[124] Various provisions of UNCLOS, when taken together, suggest that the environmental protection provisions may not apply during times of armed conflict. In fact, Article 236 exempts warships, and the Preamble implies that application was only contemplated during peacetime.

The International Convention for the Prevention of Pollution of the Sea by Oil (OILPOL), 1954, prohibits ships from discharging oil within 50 miles of the shore. OILPOL directly addresses the question of its applicability during times of armed conflict. Article XIX declares that "In case of war

---

120 *Protecting the Environment During Armed Conflict: An Inventory and Analysis of International Law*, November 2009, UNEP, p. 35.

121 United Nations Convention on the Law of the Sea (UNCLOS) concluded on 10 December 1982 and entered into force in 1994.

122 UNCLOS Article 14, para 3.

123 UNCLOS Article 88.

124 The fleets of modern warships of countries such as Australia, Canada, USA and the UK are now either equipped with systems that minimize environmental impacts or are moving rapidly in that direction. Colin Trinder and Steve Cole, Military activities and high seas biodiversity conservation, available at: http://www.highseasconservation. org/documents/trinder.pdf, accessed 16 June 2014.

or other hostilities, a Contracting Government which considers that it is affected, whether as a belligerent or as a neutral, may suspend the operation of the whole or any part of the present Convention in respect of all or any of its territories."

The International Convention for the Prevention of Pollution from Ships (MARPOL), 1973 expands on the prohibitions contained in OILPOL. It aims to eliminate all intentional pollution and to minimize accidental discharge of harmful substances. However, it exempts State military vessels and aircraft by a sovereign immunity clause. Article 3 (3) of the MARPOL provides: "The provisions of this Convention regarding the protection and preservation of the marine environment do not apply to any warship, naval auxiliary, other vessels or aircraft owned or operated by a State and used, for the time being, only on government non-commercial service." This provision further requires state Parties to make sure that such vessels and aircraft comply with the obligations of the treaty to the extent possible.

The Antarctic Treaty, 1959 protects a specific portion of the earth's environment from nuclear weapons and warfare. Article I and V of the treaty prohibits any aggressive military use and nuclear explosions in Antarctica. The disposal there of radioactive waste material in Antarctica is also prohibited.[125]

The World Heritage Convention, 1972, declares that State Parties should recognize their duty to identify and safeguard for present and future generations certain places that constitute part of the heritage of humankind.[126] The Convention states that "the outbreak or the threat of an armed conflict" is sufficient to place a property on the World Heritage in Danger List.[127] A threatened site can also benefit from a reinforced monitoring mechanism if it is at risk of losing the values for which it was inscribed on the World Heritage List. The inclusion of a provision

---

125 See "Treaties Protecting the Environment Indirectly", at p.203 .

126 However, the Convention for the Protection of Cultural Property in the Event of Armed Conflict, 1954, provides a more appropriate protection in cases where heritage sites are at the same time cultural property. Bothe Michael, Carl Bruch, Jordan Diamond, and David Jensen., International Law Protecting the Environment during Armed Conflict: Gaps and Opportunities, Vol. 92, No. 879, *International Review of the Red Cross*, September 2010, p. 580.

127 The World Heritage List includes 962 properties forming part of the cultural and natural heritage having outstanding universal value. These include 745 cultural, 188 natural and 29 mixed properties in 157 State Parties. As of March 2012, 189 State Parties have ratified Convention. Available at: http://whc.unesco.org/en/list, accessed 20 June 2014.

specifically triggered by armed conflict indicates that the Convention continues to apply during hostilities.[128] Article 6 (3) of the Convention indirectly provides for continuance during hostilities by mandating that each Party "undertakes not to take any deliberate measures which might damage directly or indirectly the cultural and natural heritage" of another Party. Thus any destruction of cultural or natural heritage[129] during armed conflict should be interpreted as a violation of this provision. The protection offered by this provision extends to member States only; the cultural and natural heritage of non-members is not covered by this protection.[130]

Certain multilateral environmental agreements (MEAs) explicitly suspend, derogate, or terminate the agreement between belligerents during armed conflict. For example, the 1993 Convention on Civil Liability for Damage Resulting from Activities Dangerous to the Environment, the

---

128 UNESCO has been running a pilot project in the Democratic Republic of Congo since 2000 to try to use the World Heritage Convention as an instrument to improve the conservation of World Heritage sites in regions affected by armed conflict. *Protecting the Environment During Armed Conflict: An Inventory and Analysis of International Law*, November 2009, UNEP, p. 38.

129 Article 1 of the Convention defines the term cultural heritage. It states: For the purposes of this Convention, the following shall be considered as cultural heritage: (i) Monuments: architectural works, works of monumental sculpture and painting, elements or structures of an archaeological nature, inscriptions, cave dwellings and combinations of features, which are of outstanding universal value from the point of view of history, art or science; (ii) Groups of buildings: groups of separate or connected buildings which, because of their architecture, their homogeneity or their place in the landscape, are of outstanding universal value from the point of view of history, art or science; (iii) Sites: works of man or the combined works of nature and man, and areas including archaeological sites which are of outstanding universal value from the historical, aesthetic, ethnological or anthropological point of view. Similarly Article 2 defines the term natural heritage. It states: For the purposes of this Convention, the following shall be considered as natural heritage: (i) Natural features consisting of physical and biological formations or groups of such formations, which are of outstanding universal value from the aesthetic or scientific point of view; (ii) Geological and physiographical formations and precisely delineated areas which constitute the habitat of threatened species of animals and plants of outstanding universal value from the point of view of science or conservation; and (iii) Natural sites precisely delineated natural areas of outstanding universal value from the point of view of science, conservation or natural beauty.

130 In Gulf War II, Iraq, a signatory to the Convention for the Protection of the World Culture and Natural Heritage, 1972, deliberately destroyed the cultural and natural heritage of the State of Kuwait, such as the Seif Palace and the national and the scientific Museums of Kuwait. However, Kuwait had no protection as it is not a Party to this Convention. Al-Duaij Nada. 2004. *Environmental Law of Armed Conflict*, New York: Transnational Publishers, p.161.

1960 Convention on Third Party Liability in the Field of Nuclear Energy,[131] the 1963 Vienna Convention on Civil Liability for Nuclear Damage, and the 1971 International Convention on Civil Liability for Oil Pollution Damage.[132]

Many MEAs, like the 1973 Convention on International Trade in Endangered Species of Wild Fauna and Flora (CITES); the 1982 United Nations Framework Convention on Climate Change; the 1985 Vienna Convention for the Protection of the Ozone Layer; the 1986 Convention on Early Notification of a Nuclear Accident; the 1987 Montreal Protocol on Substances that Deplete the Ozone Layer; the 1989 Convention on Control of Trans-boundary Movements of Hazardous Wastes and their Disposal (Basel Convention); the 1992 Convention on Biological Diversity;[133] the 1994 Convention to Combat Desertification; and  the 2001 Stockholm Convention on Persistent Organic Pollutants contain no reference to their applicability during armed conflict.

## B. Customary International Environmental Law

In 1941, an arbitration panel settled a dispute between the United States and Canada regarding trans-boundary air pollution. The *Trail Smelter Case* decision was based on a fundamental property right *sic utere tuo ut alienum non laedas* – that one must use one's property in such a way as not to cause harm to that of another. [134] The Trail Smelter principle, though not expressly

---

131 The Convention on Third Party Liability in the Field of Nuclear Energy, 1960 exempts operators for damage directly resulting from armed conflict or similar activities. However, Austria and Germany made reservations to this provision, explicitly declaring their right to hold an operator liable for such damage.

132 The Convention expressly provides that its liability obligations will not apply to an owner that can demonstrate that the violations occurred as a result of war or other armed hostilities. The requirements of the Convention generally do not apply to warships or other government vessels used for non-commercial purposes. Articles III and XI, International Convention on Civil Liability for Oil Pollution Damage, 1971.

133 Article 3 of the Convention on Biological Diversity (CBD) provides: "States have, in accordance with the Charter of the United Nations and the principles of international law, the sovereign right to exploit their own resources pursuant to their own environmental policies, and the responsibility to ensure that activities within their jurisdiction or control do not cause damage to the environment of other States or of areas beyond the limits of national jurisdiction". CBD covers a broad subject matter but does not impose precise obligations. Loets Adrian, An Old Debate Revisited: Applicability of Environmental Treaties in Times if International Armed Conflict Pursuant to the International Law Commission's Draft Articles on the Effects of Armed Conflict on Treaties, *RECIEL*, Vol. 21 (2) 2012, p. 129.

134 Trail Smelter Case (*United States v. Canada*), 16 April 1938 and 11 March 1941,

concerning armed conflict, could be applied in situations of armed conflict. The Trail Smelter arbitral panel held that Canada had a responsibility to prevent harmful trans-boundary air emissions from the smelter, and was liable for the damages that such emissions caused. This principle has been used as a reference and incorporated in numerous judicial opinions and international documents, including binding instruments such as UNCLOS and non-binding agreements such as the Stockholm and Rio Declarations.

In the *Corfu Channel Case*,[135] the ICJ practically extended the Trail Smelter principle to the actions of parties during conflict, although the case did not specifically address trans-boundary pollution. In this case, the ICJ held Albania responsible for damage from mines laid in Albanian waters to British ships travelling through these waters, observing that international law obliges the State "not to allow knowingly its territory to be used for acts contrary to the rights of other states".

The ICJ also recognized the Trail Smelter principle in the *1996 Advisory Opinion on the Legality of the Threat or Use of Nuclear Weapons*. ICJ advisory opinions, although not legally binding, provide persuasive evidence of customary international law and the application and implementation of international law. In this advisory opinion, the Court noted that a State's general obligation "to ensure that activities within their jurisdiction and control respect the environment of other States or of areas beyond national control is now part of the corpus of international law relating to the environment." The same concept of neighbourly protection from harm is seen in the 2010 decision by the ICJ in the *Pulp Mills* case.[136] The Court decided that the construction and operation of Pulp Mills in Uruguay required the country to undertake a trans-boundary environmental impact assessment. It recognized that a State must take specific measures to prevent harm to its neighbours, thus extending the general principle of the Trail Smelter decision.

There are a few soft-law instruments, which explicitly refer to armed conflict. For instance, the Declaration of the United Nations Conference on the Human Environment (Stockholm Declaration) of 1972 articulated an overarching principle that may have a bearing on the applicability of

---

Reports of International Arbitral Awards (RIAA), Vol. III, p. 1905.

135 ICJ, Corfu Channel Case (*United Kingdom v. Albania*), Merits, Judgment of 9 April 1949, ICJ Reports 1949, p. 4.

136 ICJ, Case Concerning Pulp Mills on the River Uruguay (*Argentina v. Uruguay*), Merits, Judgment of 20 April 2010.

IEL during armed conflict. Principle 21 provides that "States have ... the responsibility to ensure that activities within their jurisdiction or control do not cause damage to the environment of other States or of areas beyond the limits of national jurisdiction".

The Resolution of the World Charter for Nature[137] directly addresses the need to prohibit environmental harm resulting from armed conflict. Principle 5 of the Resolution mandates that nature shall be secured against degradation caused by warfare or other hostile activities. Principle 11 states that activities which might have an impact on nature shall be controlled, and the best available technologies that minimize significant risks to nature or other adverse effects shall be used. It also specifies the types of harm and the need to rehabilitate degraded areas. Finally, Principle 20 of the Resolution declares that "military activities damaging to nature shall be avoided".

The Declaration on Environment and Development (Rio Declaration) of 1992 states (Principle 24) that: "Warfare is inherently destructive of sustainable development. States shall therefore respect international law providing protection for the environment in times of armed conflict and cooperate in its further development, as necessary". The Rio Conference in its Programme of Action for Sustainable Development (Agenda 21) in Article 39(6), detailing the means of implementation, states that "measures in accordance with international law should be considered to address, in times of armed conflict, large-scale destruction of the environment that cannot be justified under international law". In 2002, the World Summit on Sustainable Development affirmed the principles of the Rio Declaration and Agenda 21, but did not issue any additional recommendations, resolutions or declarations directly related to environmental protection during armed conflict.

The most encouraging provision in the Rio Declaration is that "national authorities should endeavour to promote the internalization of environmental costs...the polluter should, in principle, bear the cost of pollution".[138] There seems to be no reason why this principle may not be applied to wartime as well as peacetime environmental harm, although this has not been the practice of States.[139]

---

137  World Charter for Nature, UNGA Resolution 37/7, 1982.

138 Principle 16 of the Rio Declaration.

139 The exception is the Security Council's imposition of financial liability on Iraq for harm, some of it environmental, done to Kuwait during the Gulf War. See Security

## C. International Institutions

### The IUCN' World Charter for Nature

The International Union for the Conservation of Nature (IUCN) formulated the World Charter for Nature, which was adopted by the UN General Assembly in 1982. Though the Charter is a soft law and not binding, it reflects a general international law principle and covers military activities in peacetime as well as in times of armed conflict. Principle 5 of the Charter declares that "nature shall be secured against degradation caused by warfare or other hostile activities." It also seeks to protect environmental interests by calling for preparation of environment impact assessment (EIA) prior to any military activity. Principle 11 (a) states that activities which might have an impact on nature shall be controlled and the best available technologies that minimize significant risk to nature or other adverse effects shall be used. In particular: (a) Activities which are likely to cause irreversible damage to nature shall be avoided." Principle 20 of the Charter directs that military activities that cause damage to nature shall be avoided, while Principle 21 (d) and (e) of the Charter reaffirm that countries have a duty not to harm another nation's environment, either by activities within their territories or under their control, which have impact in other countries.

The World Charter for Nature expresses a kind of general principle of law, rather than merely an aspiration. Though a soft law, it was adopted by a vote of 111 in favour to only 1 against, that of the United States. The overwhelming support for the World Charter reflects, to some degree, its more binding nature.

In order to strengthen the international legal protection of important protected areas, the IUCN-Commission on Environmental Law (CEL) and the International Council on Environmental Law (ICEL) initiated development of a draft Convention on the Prohibition of Hostile Military Activities in Protected Areas.[140] Article 1 of the draft Convention defined

---

Council Resolution 687, UN SCOR, U.N. Doc. S/RES/687 (1991); see also Security Council Res. 674, UN SCOR, UN Doc. S/RES/674 (1990); S.C. Res. 686, U.N. SCOR, UN Doc. S/RES/686 (1991).

140 Protected areas serve to preserve ecosystems, landscapes and biological processes. There are domestic as well as international legal instruments for creation, maintenance and safety of protected areas. Apart from directly contributing to emergence, escalation and incidence of conflict, protected areas can also play a strategic role in sustaining ongoing military conflicts. The remote and relatively inaccessible location of some

the term protected areas: "Meaning natural or cultural area of outstanding international significance from the point of view of ecology, history, art, science, ethnology, anthropology, or natural beauty, which may include areas designated under any international agreement. Such areas could be terrestrial or marine". Article 2 created mechanism whereby the Security Council designates protected areas as non-target areas, where all military activities are prohibited. The protection provided by the listing is temporary, lasting only for the duration of the particular armed conflict. This protection is not absolute, as Article 3 provides that the protected status could be lost if the State Party in whose territory the area is located, uses it for military activities during armed conflict.

The basic theme behind the draft Convention was similar to that used by the Security Council during the armed conflict in Bosnia and Herzegovina, where number of 'safe areas' were designated, which were prohibited from attacks.[141] Article 9 of the draft Covenant provides protection to the environment against military activities.[142]

---

protected areas can make them refuges for military groups, as they offer physical protection, food, water, fuel and medicine. During international and non-international armed conflict, these areas remain unprotected and have been harmed through pillage, fire, placing of explosive devices, construction of fortifications, cutting and smuggling trees, etc. The idea of the draft Convention grew out of several meeting of experts, including consultation sponsored by IUCN-CEL and ICEL in 1991 and 1992. The World Conservation Congress endorsed the concept in 1996.

141 Tarasofsky Richard G., 'Protecting Specially Important Areas during International Armed Conflict: A Critique of the IUCN Draft Convention on the Prohibition of Hostile Military Activities in Protected Areas', in Austin, Jay E., and Bruch, Carl E., (ed.). 2000. *The Environmental Consequences of War: Legal, Economic and Scientific Perspectives*, Cambridge: Cambridge University Press, p. 574.

142 Article 9 of the draft Covenant dealing with 'Military and Hostile Activities' provided: 1. States shall not engage in military activities resulting in widespread, long-lasting or severe damage to the environment. 2. States shall not engage in any military or other hostile use of the environment as a direct means of destruction, damage or injury. 3. States shall take special measures to protect resources, sites and installations from acts of terrorism or sabotage which may result in damage to the environment. 4. States whose military activities contravene the provisions of paragraphs 1 and 2 shall be held responsible for the subsequent environmental restoration. 5. States shall avoid or minimize, as far as possible, all military activities harmful to the environment when not engaged in armed conflict. Draft of the Working Group of Legal Experts on Environmental Law convened by the International Council of Environmental Law (ICEL) of the International Union for Conservation of Nature and Natural Resources (IUCN), Bonn, draft of April 29, 1991 submitted to UNCED and circulated as UN Doc. A/CONF.151/AG/WG.III/4.

# IUCN Amman Clause

The IUCN Amman Clause was adopted unanimously by the 72 States in the IUCN World Conservation Congress. [143] The Congress urged all United Nations Member States to endorse the following policy:

> Until a more complete international code of environmental protection has been adopted, in cases not covered by international agreements and regulations, the biosphere and all its constituent elements and processes remain under the protection and authority of the principles of international law derived from established customs, from dictates of the public conscience, and from the principles and fundamental values of humanity acting as steward for present and future generations. [144]

The Amman Clause applies in times of armed conflict as well as peacetime. It was intended to apply "until a more complete international code of environmental protection has been adopted," which reflects the drafters' intention to promote environmental protection, both in peacetime and times of armed conflict. The Amman Clause recognizes that environmental destruction may result from military activities in peacetime, and seeks to guarantee the same environmental standards under all conditions.

Further, the Amman Clause urges the UN Member States to adopt a comprehensive international code of environmental protection. Such a code would address environmental matters not governed by existing international environmental laws, or by laws that do not provide real environmental protection. For example, the ENMOD Convention does not include peacetime environmental modification techniques. The Amman Clause seeks to provide protection in such circumstances, although it does not set forth specific criteria for doing so. In attempting to begin the formulation of a comprehensive code of environmental protection the Amman Clause goes far beyond the Marten's Clause from which it sprang. While the Marten's Clause mentioned environmental concerns only as a small part of its focus on the regulation of war, the Amman Clause focuses directly on the environment. This reflects the increased global awareness of the importance of environmental concerns. Additionally, the

---

143 The IUCN Amman Clause was adopted by The World Conservation Congress at its 2nd Session in Amman, Jordan, 4-11 October 2000, to govern environmental matters.

144 The recommendation was drafted by Commission on Environmental Law (CEL) members Dinah Shelton and Alexandre Kiss; See: Martens Clause for Environmental Protection, Vol. 30, No. 6, *Environmental Policy and Law*, (2000), p. 285-286.

Amman Clause does not consider only the present generation, but future generations as well. It specifically refers to the "...fundamental values of humanity acting as steward for present and future generations."[145]

The Amman Clause could offer great environmental protection by itself and may pave the way for additional environmental protection. Under it, States are required to apply the international minimum standard of environmental protection derived from principles of international law, the laws of humanity, and the dictates of the public conscience in peacetime and during armed conflicts. Like the Martens Clause, the IUCN resolution reflects the need for appropriate measures at the national and international, individual and collective, private and public levels to ensure human survival against the environmental consequences of destructive human activities. However, the clause being a soft law, may not have a strong support base among the community of States.

## UNEP Report of 2009

At the international level, the main response to the environmental consequences of conflict has come from the United Nations Environment Programme (UNEP). It was after the Gulf War of 1991 that the UNEP examined the environmental risks of an international armed conflict for the first time. In 1999, the UNEP published its scientific assessment of the Kosovo conflict, which also included a detailed field-based evaluation of DU contamination. The UNEP established a dedicated Post-Conflict and Disaster Management Branch in 2001 with a global mandate to address the environmental impacts of war.

UNEP's scope of work on the environment and conflict is centered on supporting post-conflict countries in four main areas: (i) scientific assessment of environmental impacts; (ii) remediation of contaminated 'hot spots'; (iii) building and strengthening environmental governance capacity; and (iv) integrating environmental considerations in post conflict reconstruction and development. In early 2008, UNEP launched a new programme on the role of the environment in peace-building which aims to address the environmental causes of conflict. The UNEP has published over 20 environmental assessment reports which include post-conflicts situations in Afghanistan, Iraq, Lebanon, the Occupied Palestinian

---

145 Shelton Dinah and Alexandre Kiss, Martens Clause for Environmental Protection, Vol. 30, No. 6, *Environmental Policy and Law*, (2000), p. 285-286.

Territories, Somalia, Congo and Sudan.[146] These flagship reports have by and large succeeded in raising the environment's profile within high-level political agendas, both nationally and internationally. Strengthening environmental governance has been UNEP's core activity in post-conflict countries. UNEP has designed and delivered environmental clean-up and mitigation measures to reduce direct risks from conflict, such as in Iraq where it collected and secured highly hazardous materials.

The UNEP Report of 2009 [147] identifies gaps and weaknesses in the existing legal framework of the four main bodies of international law that provide protection to the environment during armed conflict: international humanitarian law (IHL), international criminal law (ICL), international environmental law (IEL), and international human rights law (HRL). The main findings of the Report are:

- The general humanitarian principles of distinction, necessity, and proportionality may not be sufficient to limit damage to the environment.

- AP I does not effectively protect the environment during armed conflict due to the stringent and imprecise threshold required to demonstrate damage. The triple cumulative standard is nearly impossible to achieve, particularly given the imprecise definitions for the terms "widespread," "long-term" and "severe."

- Provisions in humanitarian law that regulate the means and methods of warfare or protect civilian property and objects provide only indirect protection of the environment. In addition, these protections have rarely been effectively implemented or enforced.

- The majority of international legal provisions protecting the environment during armed conflict were designed for IAC and do not apply to NIAC. Given that most armed conflicts today are non-international, most of the existing legal framework does not apply. This legal vacuum is a major obstacle for preventing the often

---

146 *Protecting the Environment During Armed Conflict: An Inventory and Analysis of International Law*, November 2009, UNEP.

147 This legal assessment was jointly conducted by experts from UNEP and the Environmental Law Institute (ELI). It is also based on the outcomes of an expert meeting of twenty leading specialists in international law that was held by UNEP and the International Committee of the Red Cross (ICRC) in March 2009. *Protecting the Environment During Armed Conflict: An Inventory and Analysis of International Law*, November 2009, UNEP.

serious environmental damage inflicted during internal conflicts. There are also no institutionalized mechanisms to prevent the looting of natural resources during armed conflict.

- The provisions for protecting the environment during conflict under the four bodies of international law have not yet been seriously applied in international or national jurisdictions. This lack of case law contributes to the sense that there is reluctance or difficulties in enforcing the applicable law.

- There is no permanent international mechanism to monitor legal infringements and address compensation claims for environmental damage sustained during IAC.

- The provisions of multilateral environment agreements (MEAs) should be regarded as continuing to apply during both IAC and NIAC, unless they specifically stipulate otherwise. IEL could be used in the interpretation of incomplete or insufficiently clear norms of international humanitarian law.[148]

In December 2009, the UNEP held an international meeting on environmental norms and military activities in Geneva.[149] It was pointed out that military activities could affect the environment in a number of ways, for example, through the production and testing of weapons, military training and exercises and the establishment, maintenance and abandonment of military bases. The remnants of war, such as unexploded munitions, abandoned weapons and polluted land, were also a serious issue. Environmental problems caused by military activities included soil contamination, water pollution and destruction of the landscape, while military activities also contributed to global environmental problems such as climate change, the destruction of the ozone layer and loss of biological

---

148 The UNEP report is an important document which argues for more consistent enforcement and clarification of the standards for environmental protection during armed conflict. Breau Susan, 'Protection of Environment during Armed Conflict', in Shawkat Alam (ed). 2013. *Routledge Handbook of International Environmental Law*, London: Ruotledge, p. 617-632.

149 The meeting was attended by representatives of the following States: Algeria, Austria, Bangladesh, Belgium, Bhutan, Bolivia, Brazil, Burkina Faso, Chile, Colombia, Cote d'Ivoire, Djibouti, Egypt, Germany, Hungary, Indonesia, Israel, Japan, Jordan, Kenya, Kuwait, Madagascar, Mali, Morocco, Namibia, Pakistan, Panama, Paraguay, Qatar, Republic of Korea, Romania, Russian Federation, Samoa, Sao Tome and Principe, Senegal, Spain, Sri Lanka, Sweden, Turkey, United Republic of Tanzania, United States of America, and Venezuela. UNEP/Env.Law/Mil/IG/1/2, 10 December 2009.

diversity. With the aim of the implementing environmental practices across UN peacekeeping missions, the UNEP's latest report[150] makes suggestions to the peacekeepers to minimize their environmental impact and improve operational performance.

The IUCN has recently proposed a draft International Covenant on Environment and Development.[151] The stated objective of the draft Covenant emphasizes the indivisibility of 'environmental conservation' and 'sustainable development'. Article 36 of the draft covenant provides:

Military and Hostile Activities

1. Parties shall protect the environment during periods of armed conflict. In particular, the Parties shall:

   (a) observe, outside combat zones, all national and international environmental rules by which they are bound in times of peace;

   (b) take all reasonable measures to protect the environment against avoidable harm in areas of armed conflict;

   (c) not employ or threaten to employ methods or means of warfare which are intended or may be expected to cause widespread, long-term, or severe harm to the environment and ensure that such means and methods of warfare are not developed, produced, tested, or transferred;[152] and

---

150 As of 30 April 2014, there were 118,043 peacekeeping personnel employed in 17 missions world over. Their supporting infrastructure places considerable demands on the local environment. The UNEP report suggests 12 good practices, which the peacekeepers must observe. This includes: adopting an environmental policy and training of personnel, the use of alternative construction materials to reduce deforestation pressure, energy efficiency and the use of renewable energy resources, waste management and recycling, wastewater treatment and reuse, supporting local conservation efforts, preventing environmental crimes, and a comprehensive environmental management improvements plan. *Greening the Blue Helmets: Environment, Natural Resources and UN Peacekeeping Operations*, 2012, United Nations Environment Programme (UNEP).

151 Fourth edition of the IUCN Draft International Covenant on Environment and Development, conveyed to the UN Member States on occasion of the High-level Event on Biodiversity on 22 September 2010 during the 65th UN GA, Environmental Policy and Law Paper No. 31 Rev. 3, prepared by IUCN and International Council of Environmental Law (ICEL).

152 Subparagraph (c) contains a threshold of permissible harm that departs from existing precedents, with the particular elements to be understood in accordance with their ordinary meaning. This provision is expressed in the disjunctive ("or") along the lines

    (d) not use the destruction or modification of the environment as a means of warfare or reprisal.

2. Parties shall cooperate to further develop and implement rules and measures to protect the environment during armed conflict; until a more complete code of environmental protection has been adopted, in cases not covered by international agreements and regulations, the biosphere and all its constituent elements and processes remain under the protection and authority of the principle of international law derived from established custom, from dictates of the public conscience, and from the principles and fundamental values of humanity acting as steward for present and future generations.

3. Parties shall take the necessary measures to protect natural and cultural sites of special interest, in particular sites designated for protection under applicable national laws and international treaties, as well as potentially dangerous installations, from being subject to attack as a result of armed conflict, insurgency, terrorism, or sabotage. Military personnel shall be instructed as to the existence and location of such sites and installations.

4. Parties shall take measures to ensure that persons are held responsible for the deliberate and intentional use of means or methods of warfare which cause widespread, long-term, or severe harm to the environment and/or for terrorist acts causing or intended to cause harm to the environment.

5. Parties shall ensure that military personnel, aircraft, vessels and other equipment and installations are not exempted in times of peace from rules, standards, and measures for environmental protection.

Although environmental protection is still not a priority for military, efforts can still be made to raise awareness of and provide alternatives to

---

of ENMOD Convention (1976), as compared with the conjunctive ("and") in Additional Protocol I (1977), although "long-term" (from AP I) is used instead of "long-lasting" (from ENMOD). This provision is intended to reinforce the requirement set forth in subparagraph (b) by regulating the means and methods of warfare. Weapons systems are internationally regulated if they cause indiscriminate effects or excessive injuries. Chemical and nuclear weapons and anti-personnel land mines, in particular, are all governed by international agreements. See: Commentary to IUCN Draft International Covenant on Environment and Development, p.114.

protected area destruction during armed conflicts. Declaring protected areas as 'non-militarized' zones, or heightening security around these areas to prevent incursions area few options for the protection of environment during armed conflict.

## Applicability of Environmental Treaties during Armed Conflict

There is no agreement amongst researchers that peacetime environmental treaties are applicable to belligerent states during an international armed conflict.[153] According to Schmitt (1997),[154] there are two different views on the applicability of MEAs during armed conflict: (i) the application of all such treaties immediately ceases with the outbreak of hostilities, and (ii) such treaties survive to the point of inconsistency with armed conflict. The indicators for survivability of treaty during an armed conflict are: (i) treaties governing purely private interests are more likely to survive, for citizens may continue to reap their benefits even after the outbreak of hostilities without damaging the state's interests; (ii) it is more likely that a bilateral treaty will be abrogated, suspended or terminated than a multilateral treaty; (iii) bilateral treaties between non-belligerents are far less likely to be abrogated, suspended or terminated than a bilateral treaty between belligerents; (iv) the finality of a treaty is a powerful indication that it should remain in effect and only in extraordinary circumstances like fraud or coercion, the treaty would be altered and not the existence of armed conflict; and (v) the extent of the hostilities should be considered, and military operations other than war should not affect a treaty's applicability as much as war itself.[155] According to Sharp (1992), if the treaty is directed at sovereign relations (for example, commercial transactions), then it would be suspended or terminated during armed conflict. Conversely, a bilateral convention that has the protection of the environment as its object and purpose will not terminate a state's obligations during armed conflict.[156]Non-compliance with peacetime environmental standards is justified if it is the only means to secure the safety of the nation, so long as

---

153 Voneky Silja, A New Shield for the Environment: Peacetime Treaties as Legal Restraints of Wartime Damage, Vol. 9, No. 1, *RECIEL*, 2000, p. 20-32.

154 Schmitt Michal N., Green War: An Assessment of the Environmental law of International Armed Conflict, Vol. 22, No.1, *Yale Journal of International Law*, Winter 1997, p. 1-109.

155 Ibid, p. 39-41.

156 Sharp Walter G., The Effective Deterrence of Environmental Damage During Armed Conflict: A Case Analysis of the Persian Gulf War, Vol. 137, *Military Law Review*, (1992), p. 23-25.

no interest of greater importance is violated.[157]

UN General Assembly has urged the States for protecting the environment during armed conflict[158] and has recommended for incorporating international law relating to environmental protection into military manuals.[159] If militaries follow environmental protection in peacetime, they are more likely to adhere to them during armed conflict. Military manuals of a few countries incorporate environmental provisions, yet these tend to focus on the requirements found in IHL. [160]

In 2004, the General Assembly approved the International Law Commission's (ILC) proposal to include work on the 'effects of armed conflict on treaties' in its long-term programme. In 2008, the ILC issued a set of draft articles that attempt to regulate the applicability of treaties during armed conflicts. The draft articles state that the onset of armed conflict 'does not necessarily terminate or suspend the operation of treaties' between belligerents or belligerents and neutral parties. Rather, this is determined by a complex body of different considerations: express provisions and subject matter of the treaty, treaty interpretation according

---

157 Voneky Silja, Peacetime Environmental Law as a Basis of State Responsibility for Environmental Damage Caused by War, in Austin, Jay E., and Bruch, Carl E., (ed.), *The Environmental Consequences of War: Legal, Economic and Scientific Perspectives*, Cambridge: Cambridge University Press, p.221.

158 UN General Assembly resolution 47/37, 9 February 1993, Protection of the Environment in Times of Armed Conflict, UN Doc. A/RES/47/37.

159 Quinn John P., Richard T. Evans and Michael J. Boock. 2000. 'United States Navy Development of Operational Environmental Doctrine', In Austin, Jay E., and Bruch, Carl E., (ed.), *The Environmental Consequences of War: Legal, Economic and Scientific Perspectives*, Cambridge: Cambridge University Press, p. 156-170.

160 The US Army's Operational Law Handbook contains a rule regarding the application of peacetime environmental treaties: Peacetime Environmental Law (PEL). (i) In cases not covered by the specific provisions of the laws of war, civilians and combatants remain under the protection and authority of principles of international law derived from established principles of humanity, and from the dictates of public conscience. This includes protections established by treaties and customary law that protect the environment during periods of peace (if not abrogated by a condition of armed conflict). (ii) In the aftermath of Operation Desert Storm, the international community generally accepted the application of the Martens Clause as a useful contributor to the protection of the environment in times of armed conflict. *The Operational Law Handbook 2007*, Judge Advocate General's Legal Centre and School, US Army, Virginia, p. 233. Available at: http://www.fas.org/irp/doddir/army/law2007.pdf, accessed 16 June 2014. Other military manuals, for example of Germany and Canada base their environmental provisions on the rules of *jus in bello* without taking into account the applicability of peacetime environmental treaties.

to Articles 31 and 32 of the Vienna Convention on the Law of Treaties (VCLT) of 23 May 1969, the nature and extent of the armed conflict, and the effect of the armed conflict on the treaty. In November 2011, the UN General Assembly's Legal Committee has adopted the ILC's "Draft Article on the Effects of Armed Conflict on Treaties".

Rules aimed at protecting the environment in general are only found in supportive non-binding instruments like Stockholm Declaration, the World Charter of Nature, and the Rio Declaration. These treaties only protect particular parts, objects or assets of the environment—like the ozone layer, particular territories, seas or ocean regions, or particular species—or prohibit the use of disposal of particular hazardous or toxic substances. The protective values of these treaties in times of armed conflicts are far from clear and indisputable. For instance, the Law of Sea Convention does not provide any guidelines on how to solve problems arising from the apparent contradiction between, on the one hand, the rights of belligerents to use the oceans for military purposes and, on the other, its rules on the preservation, reduction, and control of marine pollution.[161]

MEAs, rules of customary environmental law, and soft-law provisions of IEL afford numerous examples of rules and decisions that establish norms (including on responsibility and liability) relating to environmental damage. There is no uniform agreement that these provisions continue to apply during armed conflict.[162] Though environmental treaties can be applied to situations of armed conflict, their provisions are often too flexible and ambiguous to provide any real guidance to military commanders on the battlefield or to be enforced after the event.[163] Further, soft-law instruments

---

161 UNCLOS, Articles 88 and 141.

162 Falk, Richard. 2000. 'The Inadequacy of the Existing Legal Approach to Environmental Protection in Wartime', In Austin, Jay E., and Bruch, Carl E., (ed.), *The Environmental Consequences of War: Legal, Economic and Scientific Perspectives*, Cambridge: Cambridge University Press, p. 137-155; Low Luan and David Hodgkinson, Compensation for Wartime Environmental Damage: Challenges to International Law After the Gulf War, Vol. 35, No. 2, *Virginia Journal of International Law*, p. 405-483. International Environmental agreements and relevant rules of customary law may continue to be applicable in times of armed conflict to the extent they are not inconsistent with the applicable law of armed conflict. Henckaerts Jean-Marie, Towards Better Protection for the Environment in Armed Conflict: Recent Developments in International Humanitarian Law, *RECIEL*, Vol. 9 (1), 2000, p.18.

163 Alice Louise Bunker, 'Protection of the environment during armed conflict: one gulf, two wars', Vol. 13, No. 2, *Review of European Community & International Environmental Law*, 2004, p. 211. However, environmental protection is now an

are not legally binding unless they rise to the level of customary IEL.

There is also a doubt whether IEL continues to apply during NIAC. The principles established in the Stockholm Declaration, Rio Declaration, World Charter for Nature, and the UN GA resolutions, for example are not binding. So far as the Rome Statute is concerned, Article 8(2)(b)(iv) prohibits an attack causing "widespread, long-term, and severe damage to the environment that would be clearly excessive to….the military advantage anticipated". However, this provision is very controversial and does not provide for environmental protection in NIAC mainly due to its inapplicability in NIAC. Bothe (2010) concludes that the question, as to how various provisions of IEL apply during armed conflict, requires additional research.[164]

### III. International Human Rights Laws

International human rights law (IHRL) is composed of international[165] and regional instruments in the form of declarations, treaties, protocols and principles. These provide a legal framework for the worldwide protection and promotion of human rights. In addition, specific standards have

---

established element of public international law; more than 20 cases have reached international courts since 2000, courts no longer shy away from arguments based on environmental protection, and there is no doubt that extensive protection for the environment exists in international law, albeit in an uncoordinated collection of legal instruments. MacKenzie Catherine P., Barking Up the Wrong Tree: Current Challenges in International Environmental Law, Vol. 58, *Virginia Lawyer*, February 2010, p. 44-49.

164 Bothe Michael, Carl Bruch, Jordan Diamond, and David Jensen., International Law Protecting the Environment during Armed Conflict: Gaps and Opportunities, Vol. 92, No. 879, *International Review of the Red Cross*, September 2010, p. 592.

165 The foremost among these are the 1948 Universal Declaration of Human Rights (UDHR), the 1966 International Covenant on Civil and Political Rights (ICCPR) and the International Covenant on Economic, Social and Cultural Rights (ICESCR). These three instruments are together known as the International Bill of Human Rights. Other conventions relating to human rights are: the International Convention on the Elimination of All Forms of Racial Discrimination (ICERD), the Convention on the Elimination of All Forms of Discrimination against Women (CEDAW), the Convention against Torture and Other Cruel, Inhuman or Degrading Treatment or Punishment (CAT), the Convention on the Rights of the Child (CRC) and its Protocol, the International Convention for the Protection of All Persons from Enforced Disappearance, and the Convention on the Rights of Persons with Disabilities (CRPD). While IHL and IHRL have developed separately, recent treaties include provisions from both the bodies of law. Some examples are the CRC and its Optional Protocol on the Participation of Children in Armed Conflict, the Convention for the Protection of All Persons from Enforced Disappearance and the Rome Statute of the International Criminal Court.

been developed by the United Nations in various fields. Some of these standards are intended to protect all people from human rights abuses such as discrimination, genocide, torture and slavery, while others are meant to safeguard members of specific groups whose human rights are often violated, e.g., stateless persons, refugees, prisoners, workers, children and women. IHRL may provide additional guidance about State conduct affecting the environment and natural resources during armed conflict. However, difficulty may arise in determining whether and to what extent IHRL is applicable during armed conflicts; that too for the protection of environment.

The US and Israel have at times claimed that IHRL is irrelevant during war. However, the prevailing view is that human rights law continues to apply during armed conflict. For instance, the IHL instruments affirm support for the application of other applicable rules of international law relating to the protection of fundamental human rights during armed conflict. The Commentary to AP I stipulates that these "other applicable rules of international law" refer to IHRL conventions. A similar paragraph in the ICRC's Commentary to Additional Protocols refers to "international instruments relating to human rights."[166] Further, the application of human rights norms during armed conflict is also consistent with human rights conventions, which preclude derogation of certain fundamental norms, such as the right to life, even during a public emergency or armed conflict.[167] The ICJ has also repeatedly affirmed that both IHL and IHRL apply during armed conflict. [168] The application of IHRL during armed conflict is also consistent with the rules of treaty interpretation. For instance, Article 31(3) (a) of the Vienna Convention on the Law of Treaties provides that State Parties shall take into consideration "any relevant rules of international law applicable in the relations between the parties".

Some believe that during armed conflict, IHRL is superseded by IHL,

---

166 Sandoz, Yves; Swinarski, Christophe; and Zimmerman, Bruno, (eds.). 1987. *Commentary on the Additional Protocols of 8 June 1977 to the Geneva Conventions of 1949,* paragraph 4428-29, at p. 1339-1440, Geneva: ICRC. Preamble to AP II also states that international instruments relating to human rights offer a basic protection to the human persons.

167 International Covenant on Civil and Political Rights, 1966, Article 4.

168 The International Court of Justice (ICJ) has emphasized in its Advisory Opinion on the *Construction of the Wall in the Occupied Palestinian Territory* (9 July 2004) and *DRC v. Uganda* (19 December 2005), that human rights treaties together with humanitarian law continue to apply in wartime.

which is specifically designed for armed conflict. While IHL and IHRL coincide and may mutually reinforce each other on some issues, under different circumstances, the two legal constructs conflict with one another. For example, during war, the use of deadly force is authorized. Outside of war, deadly force is permissible only in rare instances. Therefore, there has been doubt over the applicability of IHRL for the protection of environment during IAC or NIAC.[169] There has been significant difficulty in resolving this perceived incompatibility,[170] particularly during NIAC, when it is unclear whether armed conflict is actually taking place. The UN Report on the situation of the detainees in Guantanamo emphasizes the complementarity of human rights law and humanitarian law, especially with reference to the applicability of human rights in war.[171]

There are a number of human rights treaties which establish the link between IHRL and environmental protection, but very few contain provisions on their application in times of armed conflict. The 1948 UDHR, a soft-law, does not contain any provision relating to the protection of the environment during armed conflict; though it provides for the 'right to life', 'adequate standard of living', and 'do no harm' principles. Certain provisions of the 1966 ICCPR could be considered as providing indirect protection to the environment during an armed conflict. Article 27, of the ICCPR provides for the right of minority groups to protect of their culture and traditional practices.[172] This provision has been held to support self-determination and the utilization of natural resource access.[173] It indicates that during armed conflict, occupying States could be required to let local groups exploit natural resources, when those resources are not considered a legitimate military objective.[174] In addition, Article 17 of the

---

169 The fundamental question of applicability of IHRL during internal conflicts is contentious. *Protecting the Environment During Armed Conflict: An Inventory and Analysis of International Law*, November 2009, UNEP, p. 50.

170 *Protecting the Environment During Armed Conflict: An Inventory and Analysis of International Law*, November 2009, UNEP, p. 48.

171 Situation of detainees at Guantanamo Bay, E/CN.4/2006/120.

172 Article 27 ICCPR: In those States in which ethnic, religious or linguistic minorities exist, persons belonging to such minorities shall not be denied the right, in community with the other members of their group, to enjoy their own culture, to profess and practice their own religion, or to use their own language.

173 The UN Human Rights Committee decisions in *Lubicon Band v. Canada* 1994; *Ilmari Lansman v. Finland* 1992/1996; and *Apirana Mauika v. New Zealand* 1992/2000.

174 *Protecting the Environment During Armed Conflict: An Inventory and Analysis of*

ICCPR could also be considered as prohibiting environmental damage, because it may negatively affect family and home life.[175] Article 1 of the ICESCR[176] establishes a link between human rights and the protection of natural resources that are essential to the survival of a people. The regional agreements and judicial bodies do provide environmental protection like the right to a healthy environment and the right to a generally satisfactory environment.

The protection of the environment is increasingly becoming one of the foremost concerns of the world community. Developments in international environmental law reflect this sense of urgency in the broader international community. The right to a healthy environment has been officially recognized in most constitutions adopted after the Rio Conference (1992). The enforcement of these provisions has grown significantly in most of the countries in recent years. This could supplement international jurisdictions. For instance, the constitutions of India, Korea, and the EU address the responsibilities of governments without necessarily creating justiciable environmental rights. This may influence the interpretation and application of other constitutional rights.

However, regional human rights treaties such as the European Convention on Human Rights, either make no explicit reference to the environment, or they do so only in relatively narrow terms focused on human health. It is doubtful whether these agreements add anything to the case law derived from the right to life. Only the 1981 African Charter on Human and Peoples' Rights (ACHPR) proclaims environmental rights in broadly qualitative terms. Articles 16 and 24 of ACHPR protect both the right of peoples to the "best attainable standard of health" and their right to "a general satisfactory environment favourable to their development".[177]

---

*International Law*, November 2009, UNEP, p. 48.

175 Article 17, ICCPR: 1. No one shall be subjected to arbitrary or unlawful interference with his privacy, family, home or correspondence, nor to unlawful attacks on his honour and reputation. 2. Everyone has the right to the protection of the law against such interference or attacks.

176 Article 1, ICESCR: (2) All people may, for their own ends, freely dispose of their natural wealth and resources....in no case may a people be deprived of its own means of substance.

177 The main regional instruments are the European Convention for the Protection of Human Rights and Fundamental Freedoms (1950), the American Declaration of the Rights and Duties of Man (1948) and Convention on Human Rights (1969), and the African Charter on Human and Peoples' Rights (1981).

The issue could be resolved by creating an instrument that effectively places obligations on States as well as non-state actors related to environmental damage. Such an instrument must give due regard to preventing environmental damage during IAC as well as NIAC.

# CHAPTER 6

# The Way Ahead

The environmental devastation caused during international and non-international armed conflicts, as well as during the military preparations and post-conflict periods has been discussed in the preceding chapters of this book. It should be evident from these discussions that the potential of military and non-state actors to inflict serious environmental damage during conflicts is a potent threat. It is well-accepted general rule of IHL that the means and methods of warfare are limited to activities which prevent superfluous injury, are proportionate and respect the rules of international law on neutrality.[1] As a general rule, the destruction of property is prohibited unless it is rendered absolutely necessary by military operations. However, as technology develops, and the means and methods of warfare become more advanced, military commanders may be tempted to manipulate or attack the environment of enemies in new ways to achieve military advantages and efficient outcomes[2]. Besides, there is evidence that some States have not got rid of biological and chemical weapons, and rogue States or non-state actors use these or nuclear weapons[3] to cause extreme environmental harm. Conventional weapons too can cause more widespread destruction than they have in previous wars.

---

1  Philippe Sands and Jacqueline Peel. 2012. *Principles of International Environmental Law*, Cambridge: Cambridge University Press, p. 793.

2  Military commanders tend to accumulate and use all the firepower they can, both to accomplish their assigned missions and to protect their troops from harm. Sometimes they use more force than necessary, or miss their targets because of human error, flawed intelligence, enemy deception, computer glitches, or other equipment failure.

3  Iraq has recently notified the United Nations that militants have seized about 90 pounds of uranium compound that had been kept for research purposes at the Mosul University, which could be used for manufacturing weapon of mass destruction. Cowell Alan, Low-grade Nuclear Material seized by Rebels in Iraq, United Nations says, *The New York Times*, 10 July 2014.

The contention that the present environmental law of war is adequate is not reasonable. It is an imprecise law that is full of gaps and open to different interpretations.[4] Let us consider the conventions passed in the wake of the Vietnam War. They were intended to deter environmental damage, but not only did they not deter the environmental devastation of the 1990-91 Gulf War, they also did not provide any guidance on punishing the offender or redressing the damage. It is apparent from this example that international systems to deter and redress wartime environmental damage remain ad hoc.[5] In the light of the rapid development of international law, particularly IEL and international criminal law (ICL), the international community now has an opportunity to examine the existing international legal regime regarding the environmental consequences of armed conflict.[6] The importance of the environment has been established by the highest judicial authority in international law, the International Court of Justice (ICJ), which has stated in its *Advisory Opinion on the Legality of the Threat or Use of Nuclear Weapons*, "The environment is not an abstraction but represents the living space, the quality of life and the very health of human beings, including generations unborn."[7]

---

4   Schmitt Michael N., Green War: An Assessment of the Environmental Law of International Armed Conflict, Vol. 22 (1), *Yale Journal of International Law*, (1997), p. 1-107;

5   There are presently 171 parties to AP I, but these do not include the US, India, Israel, Iraq, and Iran; while the ENMOD Convention has only been ratified/acceded to by only 74 states, not including France and most Middle Eastern states. Most major incidents of post-1980 wartime environmental damage were therefore committed by states not party to these international agreements, including the Iraqi use of oil installations in the Iran–Iraq and Persian Gulf wars, the US-led NATO bombings in Kosovo in 1999, and the Israeli actions in Lebanon and Gaza. Neither Iraq nor Israel, nor the US was subject to an international law treaty that could have rendered them in breach of an international obligation not to damage the environment in IAC. Further, ENMOD is neither a Convention that prosecutes wartime environmental damage as such nor a Convention that bans the use of certain weapons, but rather an effort to restrict the use of certain techniques in armed conflict such as those that had been employed by the US military in Vietnam. Wyatt Julian, Law-making at the Intersection of International Environmental, humanitarian and criminal Law: The Issue of Damage to the Environment in International Armed Conflict, Vol. 92, No. 879, *International Review of the Red Cross*, September 2010, p. 611.

6   *Addressing Environmental Consequences of War*, Background Paper for the First International Conference on Addressing Environmental Consequences of War: Legal, Economic, and Scientific Perspectives, 10-12 June 1998, Washington DC, Environmental Law Research Institute.

7   *Advisory Opinion on Legality of the Threat or Use of Nuclear Weapons*, 1996, International Court of Justice, (ICJ), 8 July 1996, p. 226, 241.

The analysis presented in the preceding chapter shows that the existing legal framework is altogether inadequate and ineffective. Treaties like AP I and ENMOD, which are meant to prevent environmental destruction during international armed conflict, lack the detail, clarity, and authority to restrict ecological damage. Further, since the terms of these treaties are ambiguous, they can be manipulated easily to protect the interests of concerned parties.[8] Dinstein (2001) cautions that the threshold set by AP I is too high and that the ENMOD Convention lends itself to a rather restrictive interpretation.[9] Besides, some intentional and direct damage to the environment is not covered by either the ENMOD or AP I and, therefore, such damage is still, at least in so far as these two instruments are concerned, permissible. Also, these provisions do not deal with environmental protection during peacetime preparations, pre-conflict mobilizations of militaries and post-conflict periods.

The International Criminal Court (ICC) was established under the Rome Statute to end impunity for the most serious international crimes. However, the reach of the ICC in relation to prosecution for environmental crimes is seriously limited. If law is to be of useful service to the global community, it must lend itself to a consistent, uniform, and practical application. Unfortunately, the part of IHL which operates to safeguard the environment exhibits overall vagueness and inconsistency.[10] Modern militaries, in fact, do not give any importance to environmental damage caused by them in other States. For example, a recent 600 page analysis titled "The War in Afghanistan: A Legal Analysis" by the US Naval War College fails to mention the environmental harm caused in Afghanistan during the last two decades of armed conflict.[11] The question thus arises as to how the discrepancies inherent in AP I, the ENMOD, and the Rome Statute can be rectified. However, before these options are discussed, it would be worthwhile to look at the efforts made by the UNEP in this regard.

8   Barnaby Frank, The Environmental Impact of the Gulf War, Vol. 21, *The Ecologist*, (1991), p. 172.

9   Dinstein Yoram. 2001. 'Protection of the Environment in International Armed Conflict', In Frowein J.A. and R Wolfrum (ed.), *Max Planck Yearbook of the United Nations Law*, Vol. 5, p. 523-549.

10  Richards Peter J. and Schmitt Michael N., Mars Meets Mother Nature: Protecting the Environment During Armed Conflict, Vol. 28, No. 4, *Stetson Law Review*, (1999), p. 1047-1092.

11  Michael N. Schmitt, *The War in Afghanistan: A Legal Analysis*, The US Naval War College, Newport, Rhode Island, International Legal Study: Vol. 85, 2009.

## I. The United Nations Environment Programme

The United Nations Environment Programme (UNEP) has conducted nearly twenty-five post-conflict assessments since 1999, to determine the environmental impact of armed conflict. [12] These studies have identified the following principal issues associated with armed conflict: land degradation, extreme deforestation, ecosystem degradation, loss of biodiversity, loss of wildlife and marine resources, landmines, environmental impact of refugees and IDPs, use of depleted uranium weaponry (Bosnia and Herzegovina, Iraq, Afghanistan, Serbia and Montenegro), military hazardous waste and unexploded ordnance.[13] The studies have in general emphasized the magnitude of the threat to the environment posed by armed conflicts. A growing body of literature indicates that the failure to respond to the environmental needs of a conflict-ridden society may greatly complicate the difficult task of peace building. In the short run, it can deepen human suffering and increase vulnerability to natural disaster. In the long run, it may threaten the effective functioning of the governmental, economic, and societal institutions necessary for sustained peace.[14]

The recent UNEP's report[15] states that the existing international legal

---

12  The United Nations Environment Programme (UNEP) has conducted over twenty post-conflict assessments since 1999, using state-of-the-art science to determine the environmental impacts of war.These include Afghanistan, Albania, Bosnia and Herzegovina, Democratic republic of Congo (DRC), Iraq, Kosovo, Lebanon, Liberia, Macedonia, Nigeria, Rwanda, Serbia, Somalia, Sudan, and occupied Palestinian territories. UNEP has found that armed conflict causes significant harm to the environment and the communities that depend on natural resources. Direct and indirect environmental damage, coupled with the collapse of institutions, leads to environmental risks that can threaten people's health, livelihoods and security, and ultimately undermine post-conflict peace-building. With a view to identifying the current gaps and weaknesses within the existing legal framework the report reviews the provisions within the four main bodies of international law that provide protection for environment during armed conflict. These include international humanitarian law (IHL), international criminal law (ICL), international environmental law (IEL), and international human rights law (HRL). UNEP, Post-Conflict and Disaster Management Branch (PCDMB). Reports available at: http://www.unep.org/disastersandconflicts/Publications/tabid/54718/Default.aspx, accessed 27 March 2014.

13  Conca Ken and Jennifer Wallace, Environment and Peace-building in War-torn Societies: Lessons from the UN Environment Programme's Experience with Post-conflict Assessment, Vol. 15, *Global Governance*, (2009), p. 485-490.

14  Ibid, p. 493-504.

15  *Protecting the Environment During Armed Conflict: An Inventory and Analysis of International Law*, November 2009, The United Nations Environment Programme (UNEP), p. 4.

framework contains many provisions that either directly or indirectly protect the environment during armed conflict. However, except in the case of Iraq, these provisions have not been effectively implemented or enforced. The key findings of the report are: (i) Articles 35 and 55 of Additional Protocol I do not effectively protect the environment during armed conflict due to the stringent and imprecise threshold required to demonstrate damage; (ii) IHL provisions that regulate the means and methods of warfare or protect civilian property and objects provide only indirect protection of the environment; (iii) The majority of international legal provisions protecting the environment during armed conflict were designed for IAC and do not necessarily apply to NIAC; (iv) There is a lack of case law on protecting the environment during armed conflict because of the limited number of cases brought before the courts; (v) There is no permanent international mechanism to monitor legal infringements and address compensation claims for environmental damage sustained during international armed conflicts; (vi) The general humanitarian principles of distinction, necessity, and proportionality may not be sufficient to limit damage to the environment; (vii) Environmental damage that amounts to war crime, crime against humanity or genocide is a criminal offence under international law; (viii) Unless otherwise stated, IEL continues to apply during armed conflicts and could be used as a basis for protection; (ix) Human rights law, commissions and tribunals can be used to investigate and sanction environmental damage caused during IAC and NIAC; and (x) There is no standard UN definition of what constitutes a "conflict resource" and when sanctions should be applied to stop illegal exploitation and trade of such resources.[16]

Based on these findings, the Report made 12 recommendations. The important recommendations are: (i) the terms widespread, long-term and severe within Articles 35 and 55 of Additional Protocol 1 to the 1949 Geneva Conventions should be clearly defined; (ii) the ICRC's Guidelines on the Protection of the Environment during Armed Conflict (1994) needs to be updated and considered by the UN General Assembly for adoption; (iii) a permanent UN body should be created to monitor violations and

---

16  Considering the frequent role of high-value natural resources, such as diamonds, oil and timber, in providing revenue streams for the purchase of weapons and hiring of combatants, a standard definition by the UN is required for identifying "conflict resources." Such a definition would facilitate a more consistent and effective international approach to sanctions. *Protecting the Environment During Armed Conflict: An Inventory and Analysis of International Law*, November 2009, The United Nations Environment Programme (UNEP), p. 51-52.

address compensation for environmental damage. The report called for a legal instrument for the place-based protection of critical natural resources and areas of ecological importance during armed conflicts. It also recommended that the ILC, as "the leading body with expertise in international law", should "examine the existing international law for protecting the environment during armed conflict and recommend how it can be clarified, codified and expanded".[17]

International law has, unfortunately, failed to keep pace with the increasing environmental destruction during armed conflict. The international agreements that regulate environmental destruction during armed conflict are mainly anthropocentric,[18] and prohibit only such attacks on the non-human environment that harm human interests. The agreements that are eco-centric do not place any responsibility on the States for environmental damage and leave the decision to impose individual criminal responsibility to the States themselves.[19] These limitations undermine the ability of such agreements to prevent environmental destruction during armed conflict.

## II. Proposals

There have been a few proposals to correct the environmental deficiencies in IHL. The suggestions are: (i) a new convention to deal exclusively with

---

17 *Protecting the Environment During Armed Conflict: An Inventory and Analysis of International Law*, November 2009, UNEP, p. 52-54.

18 Motivations for protecting the non-human environment are generally divided into two categories: anthropocentric and ecocentric. The anthropocentric perspective values the environment for what it offers humankind, for example food, shelter, fuel, and clothing and focuses on the environment's ability to make life possible. The ecocentric perspective does not deny the environment's importance to human survival, but it insists that the value of protecting the non-human environment is independent of the uses for which human beings may exploit it. In the ecocentric view, the entire environment deserves protection, even those elements that play no role in human survival, because non-human species and entire ecosystems exist not merely as elements in an anthropocentric utilitarian calculus or as extensions of human moral characteristics, but as entities with moral value in their own right. Schmitt Michael N., Green War: An Assessment of the Environmental Law of International Armed Conflict, Vol. 22 (1), *Yale Journal of International Law*, (1997), p. 1-107; Lawrence Jessica C. and Heller Kevin Jon, The First Eco-centric Environmental War Crime: The Limits of Article 8(2)(b)(iv) of the Rome Statute, Vol. 20 (1), *Georgetown International Environmental Law Review*, Fall 2007, p. 61-96.

19 Lawrence Jessica C. and Heller Kevin Jon, The First Eco-centric Environmental War Crime: The Limits of Article 8(2)(b)(iv) of the Rome Statute, Vol. 20 (1), *Georgetown International Environmental Law Review*, Fall 2007, p. 61-96.

environmental harm in armed conflict;[20] (ii) amending Article 8(2)(b)(iv) of the Rome Statute; (iii) the establishing an International Environmental Criminal Court; (iv) creating a new crime of 'ecocide' or 'geocide'[21] within the jurisdiction of the ICC; and (v) better application and respect for the existing rules of IHL. All these five options are discussed below.

## A. New Convention

The Vietnam War and the 1991 Gulf War have highlighted the incongruity between the environmental accountability of a vanquished and a victorious State. The former, already devastated by war is diplomatically isolated in the post-war period, while the later is exempted from any accountability. The United State was never held accountable for the environmental devastation caused during the Vietnam War; and no one was found guilty of the environmental consequences of the NATO bombing in the former Yugoslavia.[22] While Iraq was held accountable during the Gulf

---

20 The London Conference, convened in June 1991, sought to establish a "Fifth Geneva" Convention on the Protection of the Environment in Time of Armed Conflict. The general premise behind this new Convention was due to the deliberate environmental damage that occurred in the Persian Gulf War. This new framework was to restate and consolidate the relevant rules of customary law concerning state responsibility by updating the current IHL, as well as improving the language of the conventional sources of Geneva and Hague laws. Although the term "environment" was not defined, it was suggested that the new Convention would deal with "damage to the marine environment as a whole and marine wildlife and habitats in particular, pollution of the atmosphere, destructive climate modification, enhanced global warming and degradation of the ozone layer, and the destruction or degradation of terrestrial fauna and flora and their habitats." It was proposed that the Convention must also clearly define the types of weapon it will ban. Since environmental modification may be brought about using several types of weaponry (conventional or of a type causing mass destruction, including biological and chemical weapons), a clear restriction on the use of these armaments is necessary. In summary, a Fifth Geneva Convention may be able to address some ambiguities contained in the current set of IHL; however, the Convention must be wary of the infirmities that have plagued its predecessors, such as ambiguity in terms, divergence in interpretations, and lack of enforcement. Only when the Convention explicitly defines the terms, prohibits specific methods employed, and provides objective criteria for military targets, can States eliminate destruction. Until States establish a new legal regime on warfare, however, environmental protection in times of armed conflict remains limited. Plant, Glen. 1992. *Environmental Protection and the Law of War: a fifth Geneva Convention on the protection of the environment in the time of armed conflict.* London; New York: Belhaven, Press.

21 Ecocide is sometimes also referred to as 'geocide' – a killing of the earth. Lynn Berat, Defending the Right to a Healthy Environment: Toward a Crime of Geocide in International Law, Vol. 11, *Boston University International Law Journal,* (1993), p. 327.

22 Operation Allied Force, the United States-led NATO bombing campaign against

War, the US and the UK were never even questioned for the use of DU and cluster bombs.[23] Iraq was held "liable for environmental restitution due to its unlawful invasion and occupation of Kuwait", but this principle was not applied universally to other conflicts. NATO's bombardment of Kosovo was internationally viewed as "an intervention that did not result in occupation, and therefore was not subject to the same legal liability."[24]

Hypothetically, if a US general who had directed the spraying of chemicals (defoliants) over vast tracts of Vietnamese territory was tried under Article 8(2)(b)(iv) of the Rome Statute, he would defend his actions as a 'military necessity' to remove the forest cover exploited by Vietcong fighters. A court would not be in a position to determine that the damage caused to the foliage, most of which subsequently grew back, was clearly excessive to the military advantage obtained by pursuing this objective. Similarly, it would

---

the Former Republic of Yugoslavia (FRY) on behalf of Kosovo, was initiated on 24 March 1999. The US/NATO forces targeted an aircraft production factory, multiple fuel storage facilities, oil refineries, pharmaceutical plants, fertilizer production facilities, and petrochemical plants. The impact of the release of the chemicals into the environment was devastating to humans and other elements of the ecosystem. The US military activities in Kosovo could be considered a violation of one or more international treaties or norms. However, jurisdictional issues will prevent the US from ever being hailed in front of an international tribunal. Further, the doctrine of "military necessity" in combination with the "widespread, long-term, and severe" requirements indicate that there is little chance that any military activity in the nature of that conducted by the US in Kosovo will reach the level of a prosecutable action in either a criminal or a reparations context. Alexander Nicholas G., Airstrikes and Environmental Damage: Can the United States be Held Liable for Operation Allied Force?, Vol. 11, No. 2, *Colorado Journal of International Environmental Law and Policy*, 2000, p. 471-498, at p. 491.

23 The UN response to the Vietnam War was in radical variance with its response to the tactics of environmental destruction relied upon by Iraq in the Gulf War. With strong geopolitical backing, the UN Security Council in Resolution 687 condemned Iraq's action and imposed liability including a legal obligation to compensate for damages caused by deliberate dumping of barrels of oil into the Gulf and setting fire some 700 oil wells. The Security Council failed measurably in taking similar action against the US military for the use of chemicals in the Vietnam War. It has been estimated by Human Rights Watch that, during the course of the 2003 invasion of Iraq, the United States and British forces used almost 13,000 cluster bombs –containing almost two million munitions that killed or wounded more than 1,000 civilians and caused very significant environmental damage. Human Rights Watch report, *Off Target: The Conduct of the War and Civilian Casualties in Iraq*, 2003, Available at: http://www.hrw.org/en/reports/2003/12/11/target-0, accessed 18 June 2014.

24 Tu Chelsea H., From Norm to Practice: Comparative Case Studies on International Mechanisms for Wartime Environmental Restitution, 12 May 2008, available at: http://nature.berkeley.edu/classes/es196/projects/2008final/Tu_2008.pdf, accessed 15 May 2014.

be difficult to determine whether the action of Iraqi forces in igniting oil wells to create a smoke cover against US aircraft and jettisoning millions of barrels of oil into the Persian Gulf to obstruct US naval movements, was excessive in relation to the military objectives, given that the environmental consequences of these actions were not catastrophic. Thus, it seems difficult to imagine a situation in which a court would definitely deem the environmental damage caused as clearly excessive to the overall military advantage anticipated.[25]

Falk (2000:153) is of the view that the existing standards of international law seem arbitrary and inconsistent in application.[26] Birnie (2009), support this view and holds that IHL is one of the "least sophisticated" branches of "contemporary international law" in that it lacks an "institutional structure for supervision of compliance", and that it thus "relies mainly on the good faith of the parties to a conflict for implementation and application".[27]

The degree of protection afforded to the environment is limited under the existing IHL. In many instances, military necessity and the preoccupation with ameliorating human suffering have outweighed environmental concerns. This shortcoming can be overcome by adopting a new convention with clear and enforceable legal standards. While the liability for the wrong should, depending on the circumstances of the case, relate to compensation, repatriation and restitution, criminal responsibility of individuals, which is already an established feature under some existing IHL instruments, should be preserved. The new convention should provide redress for both individual and group claimants for damage caused to the natural environment during armed conflict. Redress should be in the form of either restitution or compensation.[28] The new convention should expressly

---

25 Wyatt Julian, Law-making at the Intersection of International Environmental, humanitarian and criminal Law: The Issue of Damage to the Environment in International Armed Conflict, Vol. 92, No. 879, *International Review of the Red Cross*, September 2010, p. 635-636.

26 Falk, Richard. 2000. 'The Inadequacy of the Existing Legal Approach to Environmental Protection in Wartime', In Austin, Jay E., and Bruch, Carl E., (ed.), *The Environmental Consequences of War: Legal, Economic and Scientific Perspectives*, Cambridge: Cambridge University Press, p. 154.

27 Birnie, P., Boyle, A., & Redgwell, C. 2009. *International law and the environment* (3rd ed.), Oxford, England: Oxford University Press, p. 207. In 1992, a proposal on the drafting of a "Fifth Geneva Convention on the protection of the environment in time of armed conflict" was discussed at a conference in London.

28 As provided for expressly by Article 36(2) of the Statute of the ICJ, which states: "The states parties to the Statute may at any time declare that they recognize as compulsory

demilitarize protected forests and call for sensitizing the military through revised, environmentally sensitive manuals issued by their governments.[29]

The adoption of a new convention[30] is preferable to the mere drafting of an additional protocol [31] to the four Geneva Conventions. A new convention would have the additional advantage of allowing for the correction of errors and omissions and the addition of supplementary provisions in a subsequent protocol. Westing (1997: 548) has suggested that a new treaty be adopted to prohibit the use in war of nuclear weapons, and designate natural heritage

---

*ipso facto* and without special agreement, in relation to other States accepting the same obligation, the jurisdiction of the Court in all legal disputes concerning: (a) the interpretation of a treaty; (b) any question of international law; (c) the existence of any fact which, if established, would constitute a breach of an international obligation; (d) the nature or extent of the reparation to be made for the breach of an international obligation". Article 36(3) stipulates that such declarations "may be made unconditionally or on condition of reciprocity on the part of several or certain states, or for a certain time". Declarations are to be deposited, in terms of Article 36(4), with the Secretary-General of the UN. For the purpose of group or individual claims, states need not make a declaration to submit to the jurisdiction of the proposed court or tribunal, as jurisdiction should be compulsory.

29  Falk, Richard. 2000. 'The Inadequacy of the Existing Legal Approach to Environmental Protection in Wartime', In Austin, Jay E., and Bruch, Carl E., (ed.), *The Environmental Consequences of War: Legal, Economic and Scientific Perspectives*, Cambridge: Cambridge University Press, p. 139.

30  Glen Plant (1991), proposed a new convention on the protection of environment in time of armed conflict, which should include liability to make restitution pursuant to criminal prosecution. Elements of a 'Fifth Geneva' Convention on the Protection of Environment in Time of Armed Conflict, in Plant G., (ed.), *Environmental Protection and the Law of War: A 'Fifth Geneva' Convention on the Protection of the Environment in Armed Conflict.* London and New York: Belhaven Press. The environmentalist group Greenpeace International announced in London conference in March, 1991, that the Persian Gulf War demonstrates a need for a "Fifth Geneva Convention on the Protection of the Environment in the Time of Armed Conflict". It was proposed that the new framework would restate and consolidate the relevant rules of customary law concerning state responsibility by updating the current laws of war, as well as improving the language of the conventional sources of Geneva and Hague laws. The new Convention was to deal with "damage to the marine environment as a whole and marine wildlife and habitats in particular, pollution of the atmosphere, destructive climate modification, enhanced global warming and degradation of the ozone layer, and the destruction or degradation of terrestrial fauna and flora and their habitats."

31  There are three existing additional protocols to the four Geneva Conventions of 1949 include: (a) Additional Protocol I of 1977 on the protection of victims of international armed conflicts; (b) Additional Protocol II of 1977 on the protection of victims of non-international armed conflicts; and (c) Additional Protocol III of 2005 on the use of the emblems (the red cross, red crescent and red crystal) of the ICRC during armed conflict.

sites of outstanding universal value as demilitarized zones.[32] Falk (1984) has proposed the drafting a new convention on the crime of ecocide. In the long run, it may be desirable to formulate a special treaty explicitly to protect the environment in wartime. Such an instrument should be designed to gain rapid acceptance by as many militarily significant States as possible, by minimizing any avoidable political controversies, such as those which burden AP I.[33] The convention should contain rules for criminal responsibility and investigation by a commission established by the United Nations.[34] It would afford an opportunity to clarify and develop existing law, lowering the threshold of harm, defining with precision what is to be protected; clearly limiting the permissible classes of weapons; settling any ambiguities regarding the priority to be given to military necessity over environmental protection; establishing an effective institutional framework; and importing relevant norms from IEL.[35]

In the case of States which do not ratify the new convention, the rules and principles of customary international law, would always remain applicable. That damage to the natural environment in armed conflict is prohibited

---

32 Westing Arthur H. 1997. 'Environmental Protection form Wartime Damage: The Role of International Law', in Gleditsch NP et. al., (eds.), *Conflict and the Environment*, Netherlands: Kluwer Academic Publishers, p. 535-553.

33 Szasz Paul C. International Law Applicable to the Gulf War, Vol. XV, No. 2, *Disarmament*, (1992), p. 101-161. The proposed treaty might include: (i) general provisions contained Articles 35 (3) and 55 of AP I, and paragraphs 5 and 20 of the World Charter for Nature; (ii) specific humanitarian provisions applicable to environmental protection such as those contained in Article 56 of AP I and in Article II, paragraph 4, of Protocol III to CCW; (iii) Provisions relating to explosive remnants of war contained in CCW; (iv) peacetime anti-pollution provisions contained in Part XII of the 1982 UNCLOS, 1954 Oil Pollution Convention and MARPOL Convention; (v) obligations for environment impact evaluation of new weapons; (vi) financial liability of belligerent towards damage done in a neutral territory or to international commons; and (vii) criminal liability of State and individuals for wanton destruction of environment under the guise of military operations.

34 Falk, Richard A.,1984. 'Proposed Convention on the Crime of Ecocide', in Westing Arthur H., (ed.), *Environmental Warfare: A Technical, Legal and Policy Appraisal*, London: Taylor & Francis, p. 45-49. The definition of ecocide includes any of a number of acts committed with intent to disrupt or destroy, in whole or in part, a human ecosystem, including use of nuclear, biological or chemical or other weapons of mass destruction, chemical herbicides to defoliate and destroy natural forests for military purposes, and extreme use of bombs and artillery.

35 Tarasofsky Richard G, Legal Protection of the Environment During International Armed Conflict, Vol. XXIV, *Netherlands Yearbook of International Law*, (1993), p. 78-79.

under customary international law[36] is clearly manifest in the fundamental principles of IHL,[37] including even the United Nations General Assembly Resolution 47/37 of 1992,[38] which states that the "destruction of the environment not justified by military necessity and carried out wantonly, is clearly contrary to existing international Law".

However, if one wants to effectively protect the environment during armed conflict, the only option available[39] is to draft the proposed 'Fifth Geneva Convention', with more rigorous standards.[40] In 1991, a draft Covenant on Environmental Conservation and Sustainable Use of Natural Resources was prepared by the Group of Legal Experts. Article 9 of the draft Covenant reads as follows:

Military and Hostile Activities

1.  States shall not engage in military activities resulting in widespread, long-lasting or severe damage to the environment.

2.  States shall not engage in any military or other hostile use of the environment as a direct means of destruction, damage or injury.

3.  States shall take special measures to protect resources, sites and installations from acts of terrorism or sabotage which may result in damage to the environment.

4.  States whose military activities contravene the provisions of paragraphs 1 and 2 shall be held responsible for the subsequent

36  In contemporary times evidence of custom can be deduced from statements by the UN General Assembly without regard to state practice: see, in particular, James T, Customary law and ad hoc international criminal courts, available at: http://www.allacademic.com//meta/p_mla_apa_research_citation/3/1/4/1/4pages314148/p314148-11.php, accessed 23 March 2014.

37  A guide to the legal review of new weapons, means and methods of warfare: Measures to implement Article 36 of Additional Protocol I of 1977, No 864 *International Review of the Red Cross*, p. 938-945. Recheck

38  Protection of the environment in times of armed conflict, UN General Assembly Resolution 47/37, 47 UN GAOR Supp (No 49) 290, UN Doc A/47/49 (1992).

39  Verwey Wil D., Observations on the Legal Protection of the Environment in Times of International Armed Conflict, Vol. 7, *Hague Yearbook of International Law*, (1994), p. 35-52.

40  Alexander Nicholas G., Airstrikes and Environmental Damage: Can the United States be Held Liable for Operation Allied Force?, Vol. 11, No. 2, *Colorado Journal of International Environmental Law and Policy*, 2000, p. 498; also see Indre Lechtimiakyte, Preservation of Environment in Times of Non-International Armed Conflict: Legal Framework, Its Sufficiency and Suggestions, Volume 20 (2), *Jurisprudence*, 2013, p. 569–590.

environmental restoration.

5.  States shall avoid or minimize, as far as possible, all military activities harmful to the environment when not engaged in armed conflict.

Such drafts, prepared by experts in their individual capacities and in non-governmental settings, could provide a useful basis for the work of governmental experts who may be called upon to consider a specific legal instrument for the protection of the environment in times of armed conflict.[41]

## B. Amendments to the Rome Statute

The ICC has a mandate to try individuals and to hold them accountable for the most serious crimes of concern to the international community - genocide, crimes against humanity, and war crimes.[42] A few scholars have analysed the feasibility of prosecuting perpetrators of environmental crimes during armed conflict as 'genocide'[43] and 'crime against humanity'[44]

---

41  Draft of the Working Group of Legal Experts on Environmental Law convened by the International Council of Environmental Law (ICEL) of the International Union for Conservation of Nature and Natural Resources (IUCN), Bonn, draft of April 29, 1991 submitted to UNCED and circulated as UN Doc. A/CONF.151/AG/WG.III/4.

42  These crimes have been described as the most serious crimes of concern to the international community as a whole, and as unimaginable atrocities that deeply shock the conscience of humanity. Articles 6, 7 and 8 of the Rome Statute define the crimes of genocide, crimes against humanity, and war crimes. These definitions also contain a list of acts that can amount to the said crimes when the threshold test for each crime is met. These crimes are of recent origin and their recognition and subsequent development is closely associated with the human rights movements after the World War II. Jha U.C. 2011. *International Humanitarian Law: The Laws of War*, New Delhi: Vij Books India Pvt. Ltd., p. 285.

43  The crime of genocide is defined in Article 6 of the Rome Statute. It mirrors the definition contained in the 1948 Convention on the Prevention and Punishment of the Crime of Genocide (Genocide Convention), as well as the Statutes for both the ICTY and the ICTR. Genocide has been referred to as the 'crime of crimes' and requires a very high threshold of intent before a conviction can be upheld – an 'intent to destroy, in whole or in part' a particular group. The characterization of a relevant group is restricted to one based on 'national, ethnical, racial or religious' criteria. Freeland Steven, 'Crime Against the Environment – A Role for the International Criminal Court?' in Alberto Costi and Yves-Louis (eds.), *Environmental Law in the Pacific: International and Comparative Perspectives*, p. 361. Available at: http://www.upf.pf/IMG/pdf/16-freeland.pdf, accessed 20 June 2014.

44  The term "crimes against humanity" was first used to describe the Turkish massacre of the Armenian population in 1915. It was also used in the 1919 Report of the Commission on the Responsibilities of the Authors of War and Enforcement of

under the Statue of the ICC. Though the term 'genocide' does not relate directly to the protection of the environment, a careful analysis reveals that the various acts of genocide defined in Article 6 of the Rome Statute permit an interpretation that protects groups whose existence is threatened by environmental degradation. However, the application of Article 6 to extreme cases of environmental destruction presents two main problems: (i) Environmental degradation may not physically destroy a group, but instead may destroy its cultural identity by, for instance, forcing an indigenous community to resettle from its sacred lands or to integrate into the dominant society, and (ii) The law requires direct intent or motive to commit the crime of genocide, reinforcing the general requirement of knowledge and intent for a criminal conviction. [45] It is very unlikely that the destruction of a natural habitat would per se be prosecuted as an act of genocide.[46] Having to wait for environmental degradation to approach the level of genocide before prosecuting, raises the threshold far too high and limits criminal law's effectiveness to deter such crimes.[47]

According to Peterson (2009: 325), under Article 8 (2)(b)(iv), the natural environment has been included into the category of goods that generally need preservation in times of armed conflict, an injury to which amounts to one of them most serious crimes of international concern. The incorporation of offence into the ICC statute appears to be a great achievement, as it is the first time that such conduct has expressly been declared to entail individual criminal responsibility under an international treaty.[48]

However, a number of problems substantially limit the Article 8(2)(b)(iv)'s ability to punish wartime environmental damage. Its *actus reus* is excessively

---

Penalties for Violations of the Laws and Customs of War. Kai Ambos, Current Issues in International Criminal Law, Vol. 14, *Crim L F*, (2003), p. 225-228.

45 Orellana Marcos A. Criminal Prosecution for Environmental Damage: Individual and State Responsibility at a Crossroad, Vol. 17, *The Georgetown International Environmental Law Review*, (2004-05), p. 692.

46 Freeland Steven, Crime Against the Environment – A Role for the International Criminal Court? in Alberto Costi and Yves-Louis (eds.), *Environmental Law in the Pacific: International and Comparative Perspectives*, p. 366-67. Available at: http://www.upf.pf/IMG/pdf/16-freeland.pdf, accessed 24 June 2014.

47 Megret Frederic, The Problem of an International Criminal Law of the Environment, Vol. 36, No. 2, *Columbia Journal of Environmental Law*, 2011, p. 195-257.

48 Peterson Ines, The Natural Environment in Times of Armed Conflict: A Concern for International War Crimes Law? Vol. 22 (2), *Leiden Journal of International Law*, (2009), p. 325-343.

vague, particularly the requirement that damage be "widespread, long-term, and severe". Its proportionality standard is heavily weighted against finding an attack disproportionate. Its *mens rea* is purely subjective, making it nearly impossible to find that a perpetrator "knew" that the attack would be disproportionate. Also, it does not apply to NIACs.[49] Drumbl (1998) has argued that because of these limitations of Article (8)(2)(b)(iv), the ICC "might not be the most effective way to sanction" environmental war crimes.[50]

Some of the proposals for removing inadequacies in Article 8(2)(b)(iv) would require comprehensive changes to the Article, while others would require terminological clarity. Lawrence and Heller have proposed[51] that Article (8)(2)(b)(iv) be redrafted to provide real protection against wartime environmental damage. In particular, (i) it should be supplemented with a clear definition of what qualifies as "widespread, long-term, and severe damage"; (ii) its standard for finding an attack disproportionate should be lowered; (iii) the *mens rea* requirement should be made more objective; and (iv) it should be made applicable to NIAC[52]. There are view that it may not be necessary to make the environmental damage provision of Article 8(2)(b)(iv) applicable to NIAC, because limits on environmental damage could be read into Article 8(2)(c) and Article 8(2)(e), which contain war crimes that do apply in internal situations. For example, that many of the war crimes in Article 8(2)(e)--intentionally attacking civilians or historic monuments and culturally-significant buildings; pillaging; ordering the displacement of civilian populations; or destroying property unless it is a military necessity--could be used to impose criminal liability for environmentally-destructive tactics. In NIAC, commander and troops could be held liable under article 8(2)(c)for the use of weapons and practices with environmental impacts—such as landmines and scorched

---

49  Lawrence C. Jessica & Kevin Jon Heller, The First Eco-centric Environmental War Crime: The Limits of Article 8(2)(b)(iv) of the Rome Statute, Vol. 20 (1), *Georgetown International Environmental Law Review*, Fall 2007, p. 61-96.

50  Drumbl, Mark A., Waging War Against the World: The Need to Move from War Crimes to Environmental Crimes, Vol. 22 (1), *Fordham International Law Journal*, (1998), p.122-153.

51  Lawrence C. Jessica & Kevin Jon Heller, The First Eco-centric Environmental War Crime: The Limits of Article 8(2)(b)(iv) of the Rome Statute, Vol. 20 (1), *Georgetown International Environmental Law Review*, Fall 2007, p. 61-96.

52  Brusch Carl E., The Environmental Law of War: All's Not Fair in (Civil) War: Criminal Liability for Environmental Damage in Internal Armed Conflict, Vol. 25, No. 3, *Vermont Law Review*, (2000-2001), p. 695-752.

earth tactics—that cause 'violence to life and person'. In addition, Article 8(2)(b)(iv) should be divided into two sets of provisions, one addressing civilian damage and the other addressing environmental damage.

## C. International Environmental Criminal Court

Megret (2011) has argued that we can conceive of an international criminal law (ICL) of the environment that will be a complement to IEL.[53] Though IEL focuses on protection of the environment during peace time,[54] and environmental protection during armed conflict has developed through the laws of war, the two regimes interact. As a result, developments in one regime contribute to developments in the other. Therefore, it is necessary that IEL should be considered in any process of interpretation of the laws of armed conflict.[55]

An international criminal law of the environment has been proposed for the prosecution of individuals accused of deliberate environmental harm during armed conflict. Proposals have also been made for supranational jurisdiction[56] for grave harms to the environment, as well as for the jurisdiction of the ICC itself. The arguments are fundamentally the same as for universal jurisdiction, although there are several additional institutional implications. Prosecuting certain environmental offences before an international criminal tribunal may prove necessary when States conduct sham proceedings to protect an offender. Under the principle of

---

53  Megret Frederic, The Problem of an International Criminal Law of the Environment, Vol. 36 (2), *Columbia Journal of Environmental Law*, 2011, p. 195-257.

54  International environmental law was not meant to be applied during armed conflict because its creation was a response to accidental events that occurred during peace time. Leibler Anthony, Deliberate Wartime Environmental Destruction: New Challenges for International Law, Vol. 23, *Cal. W. Int'l L. J.*, (1992), p. 67-71.

55  Eifan, Meshari K., *Head of State Criminal Responsibility for Environmental War Crimes: Case Study: The Arabian Gulf Armed Conflict 1990-1991*, (2007), unpublished thesis, p. 31. Available at: http://digitalcommons.pace.edu/lawdissertations/2, accessed 11 June 2014.

56  Kenneth F. McCallion & Sharma H. Rajan, Environmental Justice Without Borders: The Need for an International Court of the Environment to Protect Fundamental Environmental Rights, Vol. 32, *Geo. Wash. J. Int'l L. & Econ.* (2000), p. 351-358; Antonino Abrami, Proposal of Two Historical Reforms: An International Environmental Criminal Court (IECC), A European Environmental Criminal Court (EECC), International Academy of Environmental Sciences, Venice, 2010. Available at: http://www.europarl.europa.eu/document/activities/cont/201007/20100714ATT78992/2010 0714ATT78992EN.pdf, accessed 24 May 2014.

complementarity,[57] in situations where States are "unable or unwilling" to prosecute an offender, the crimes against the environment could be prosecuted supra-nationally. Having a provision for the international prosecution of environmental crimes would illustrate the willingness of the international community to stand as one against such behaviour. The rationale for universal jurisdiction is that environmental crimes affect the whole international community, such that each state has an interest in repressing them even if they were not committed in its territory or by its nationals.[58]

There are proposals to introduce a new international judicial body, an International Environmental Court (IEC), to the existing international courts and tribunals.[59] Advocates of the IEC cite uncertain environmental jurisdiction in existing courts and tribunals to address serious international environmental harm, and a deficiency in the environmental expertise of judges in the existing courts as reasons for establishing such a court. However, the institution of an IEC may prove more difficult than ensuring the proper functioning of the current courts and tribunals.[60] While existing courts and tribunals may not deal effectively with serious international environmental problems, the establishment of a new court may lead to

---

57 An important element of the principles guiding the International Criminal Court (ICC) is that the national criminal justice processes should be used if they are adequate to ensure the investigation, prosecution and punishment related to a crime. This principle, called 'complementarity', is dealt with in the Preamble and in Articles 1 and 17 of the Rome Statute. Preamble paragraph 11 states that the ICC shall be complementary to national criminal jurisdictions. The Statute is clear that national courts have the first right and duty to prosecute perpetrators of international crimes. However, the ICC is empowered to intervene not only where the existing national judicial machinery is insufficient to allow a successful prosecution, but also where national governments are unwilling or unable to fulfil their responsibility to prosecute. Though the principle of complementarity preserves national criminal jurisdiction as primary, it allows the ICC to step in when States fail to act and allow a person accused of genocide, war crimes or crimes against humanity from escaping justice altogether.

58 Megret Frederic, The Problem of an International Criminal Law of the Environment, Vol. 36 (2), *Columbia Journal of Environmental Law*, 2011, p. 195-257.

59 Hinde Susan M., International Environmental Court: Its Broad Jurisdiction as a Possible Fatal Flaw, Vol. 32, *Hofstra Law Review*, (2003), p. 727-757; Audra E. Dehan, An International Environmental Court: Should There Be One?, Vol. 3, *Touro J. Transnational Law*, (1992), p. 31; Postiglione Hon. Amedeo, A More Efficient International Law on the Environment and Setting Up an International Court for the Environment Within the United Nations, Vol. 20, *Environmental Law*, (1990), p. 321-323.

60 Hinde Susan M., International Environmental Court: Its Broad Jurisdiction as a Possible Fatal Flaw, Vol. 32, *Hofstra Law Review*, (2003), p. 728.

inconsistent judgments among the many courts able to adjudicate the same environmental problems, as well as a fragmentation of international environmental law.[61]

The deliberate destruction of the environment in an armed conflict may fall within the jurisdiction of the ICC in one of two ways – either by the inclusion of 'crimes against the environment',[62] as a new crime within the jurisdictional competence of the ICC or by interpreting the existing provisions of the Rome Statute to apply to actions intended to cause significant environmental harm. The need to promote environmental justice and strengthen the reach of ICL necessitates that a specific crime, i.e., crimes against the environment, be considered for inclusion within the jurisdiction of the ICC.[63] However, creation of a new crime under the Statute of ICC could be a difficult exercise, though strong arguments exist both for the criminalization, and the international criminalization of grave harm to the environment.

## D. Crime of Ecocide

The term 'ecocide' refers to the deliberate and large-scale destruction of the environment in conflict.[64] There has been a strong demand for the inclusion of the crime of ecocide under international criminal law.[65] It has been

---

61  Hinde Susan M., International Environmental Court: Its Broad Jurisdiction as a Possible Fatal Flaw, Vol. 32, *Hofstra Law Review*, (2003), p. 755

62  Stephen C McCaffrey, Crimes Against the Environment, Vol. 1, *Int Crim L J.*, (1986), p. 541.

63  Freeland has suggested that the starting point for a definition of "crimes against the environment", the breach of which would potentially give rise to international criminal responsibility, could in broad terms be as follows: "A deliberate action committed with intent to cause significant harm to the environment, including ecological, biological and natural resource systems, in order to promote a particular military, strategic, political or other aim, and which does in fact cause such damage." Freeland Steven, Crime Against the Environment – A Role for the International Criminal Court? in Alberto Costi and Yves-Louis (eds.), *Environmental Law in the Pacific: International and Comparative Perspectives*, p. 358, available at: http://www.upf.pf/IMG/pdf/16-freeland.pdf, accessed 24 June 2014.

64  Commission on Human Security, *Human Security Now* (New York, 2003) p. 16-18; Ludwik A Teclaff, Beyond Restoration – the Case of Ecocide, Vol. 34, *Nat Res J*, (1994), p. 933.

65  While environmental damage may sometimes fall within the reaches of existing international criminal law (ICL) proscriptions, it will always be the human cost of the actions that attach it to the crimes of genocide, crimes against humanity or war crimes. Pure environmental damage does not fall within the existing international crimes. In order to overcome this lacuna, it is proposed that a new crime against the environment-

suggested that a new international crime of environmental degradation, ecocide, or geocide be created as the fifth core crime under the jurisdiction of the ICC;[66] and the offence should carry heavy penalties.[67] A few authors have even argued in favour of considering cases of deliberate destruction of a part of the global ecosystem involving the killing of members of a particular animal or plant species under the crime of genocide.[68] The crime of ecocide, literally a killing of the earth, is the environmental counterpart of genocide, and could be enshrined in a single international convention.[69]

A global conference on environmental protection in armed conflict should be followed by the drafting of a new convention dedicated to the prevention and punishment of deliberate, incidental, and negligent environmental harm, specifying the main types of harm, degrees of liability of governments and individuals, and institutional mechanisms for verifying violations and assessing responsibility. It must incorporate ecocide as a crime complementing the crime of genocide.[70] The concept of

-'ecocide' be created. Mark Halsey, Against 'Green' Criminology, Vol. 44, *British Journal of Criminology*, (2004), p. 833-53.

66  Juliette Jowit, British Campaigner Urges UN to Accept 'Ecocide' as International Crime, *The Guardian*, 9 April 2010; Sills Joe, Jerome C. Glenn, Elizabeth Florescu and Theodore J. Gordon, *Environmental Crimes in Military Actions and the International Criminal Court -- United Nations Perspectives*, April 2001, Army Environmental Policy Institute, Atlanta. Available at: http://www.aepi.army.mil/publications/overseas-international/docs/env-crime-icc-printer.pdf, accessed 11 March 2014.

67  Christopher H. Lytton, Environmental Human Rights: Emerging Trends in International Law and Ecocide, Vol. 13, *Envtl. Claims J.*, (2000), p. 73-74; Lynn Berat, Defending the Right to a Healthy Environment: Toward a Crime of Geocide in International Law, Vol. 11, *B.U. Int'l L.J.*, (1993), p. 327-29; Gray Mark Allan, The International Crime of Ecocide, Vol. 26, *Cal. W. Int'l L.J.*, (1995), p. 215-217; Juliette Jowit, British Campaigner Urges UN to Accept 'Ecocide' as International Crime, *The Guardian*, 9 April 2010; J Sebastien, Crimes Against Future Generations, World Future Council, A WFC & CISDL Legal Working Paper, 15 August 2010. In its Draft Code on State Responsibility, the International Law Commission equated 'serious acts of environmental degradation with crimes such as aggression...slavery, genocide and apartheid.' See: Smith Tara, Creating a Framework for the Prosecution of Environmental Crimes in International Criminal Law, available at: http://ssrn.com/abstract=1957644, accessed 24 April 2014.

68  Lynn Berat, Defending the Right to a Healthy Environment: Toward a Crime of Genocide in International Law, Vol. 11, *Bos U Int LJ*, (1993), p. 327.

69  Drumbl, Mark A., Waging War Against the World: The Need to Move from War Crimes to Environmental Crimes, Vol. 22, Issue 1, *Fordham International Law Journal*, (1998), p.143.

70  Falk, Richard. 2000. 'The Inadequacy of the Existing Legal Approach to Environmental Protection in Wartime', In Austin, Jay E., and Bruch, Carl E., (ed.), *The Environmental Consequences of War: Legal, Economic and Scientific Perspectives*, Cambridge:

ecocide[71] ought not to be restricted to actual war; it could also apply to the pre-deployment and post-deployment phases of armed activity.

## E. Better Application and Respect for the Existing Rules of IHL

The existing legal norms and standards for the protection of the environment during armed conflict have been considered adequate by a few researchers e.g., Sharp (1992: 65).[72] This conviction is based on: (i) the existing norms and standards establish a workable balance in combat settings between environmental protection and military necessity; (ii) any further weighting of this legal balance in favour of environmental protection would be politically futile and may not get the support of governments, in particular the US; (iii) any attempt to produce a more coherent and comprehensive legal framework would result in an unwieldy and time-consuming process and may take several decades to finish; and (iv) more efforts should be made towards implementing the existing norms.[73] Essentially, this is the view the US holds.

The Parliamentary Assembly, Council of Europe, while acknowledging certain problems with the application of the rules of IHL for environmental protection during armed conflict, holds the view that if the existing rules are respected and applied correctly, they would offer adequate protection. The Assembly has drawn the conclusion that there is no need for a new convention and that the time and effort required to draft such a document could be devoted to the more important task of persuading armed forces and governments to respect and implement the existing legislation.[74]

A few recommendations made by the Assembly to the member and

---

Cambridge University Press, p. 154-55.

71  Ecocide could also apply in times of peace. Environmental crime, most notably trade in endangered species, hazardous wastes, and ozone-depleting substances, constitutes an underground market estimated at US$20 billion annually. Drumbl, Mark A., Waging War Against the World: The Need to Move from War Crimes to Environmental Crimes, Vol. 22, Issue 1, *Fordham International Law Journal*, (1998), p.152.

72  Sharp Walter G., The Effective Deterrence of Environmental Damage During Armed Conflict: A Case Analysis of the Persian Gulf War, Vol. 137, *Military Law Review*, (1992), p.1-66.

73  Roach J. Ashley, The Laws of War and the Protection of Environment, Vol. I, No. 2, *Environment and Security*, (1997), p. 53-67.

74  Parliamentary Assembly, Council of Europe Doc. 12774, 17 October 2011, available at: http://assembly.coe.int/Documents/WorkingDocs/Doc11/EDOC12774.pdf, accessed 15 September 2013.

non-member States for better application of and respect for the rules of IHL are: (i) ensuring the training of civilian and military personnel on environmental issues in times of armed conflict; (ii) exchanging information on environmental management during armed conflict; (iii) appointing a sustainable development correspondent in the European Defence Agency; (iv) re-launching the ENMOD Convention to restrict military climate control programmes; (v) integrating eco-design into arms programmes; (v) assessing the risks to the environment posed by military exercises; (vi) encouraging NGOs to undertake pre-conflict assessments where possible, to improve the humanitarian planning of conflicts and, in particular, the siting of refugee camps; (vii) releasing funds so that international organizations such as the UNEP can carry out pre-conflict environmental assessments; (viii) ratifying the treaty banning cluster munitions; and (ix) supporting the drafting of a treaty to ban phosphorus weapons.

The ICRC too was initially of the view that the existing rules of IHL could considerably limit environmental damage in warfare, provided they were correctly applied and fully respected. Therefore, rather than initiating a new codification process, a special effort should be made to ensure that these rules are adopted by as many States as possible.[75] However, it has now changed its stance and holds the view the international rules protecting the environment during armed conflicts are either lacking or insufficient.[76]

---

75 *Protection of the Environment in Time of Armed Conflict*, Report Submitted by the ICRC to the 48th Session of the UN General Assembly, 17 November 1993. Part IV, Position of the ICRC: ... the institution believes that, if several aspects of the existing law were elaborated on and if the law were more fully implemented, it would provide adequate protection of the environment in time of armed conflict. The ICRC therefore wishes to see a special effort made to increase compliance with existing rules and to improve their implementation. This naturally requires the greatest possible number of States to become party to IHL treaties and to use the specific means of implementation provided for by these instruments and by other treaties and resolutions. Available at: www.icrc. org/eng/resources/documents/misc/5deesv.htm,accessed 22 September 2012. Also see: Bouvier Antoine, Protection of the natural environment in time of armed conflict, No. 285, *International Review of the Red Cross*, December 1991, p. 567-578.

76 The International Committee of the Red Cross, Geneva, October 2011, the principal conclusions of the ICRC study on 'Strengthening legal protection for victims of armed conflicts' contained:.....the ICRC study showed that IHL, in its current state, was not perfect in every respect and should be developed in some areas. More precisely, it must be strengthened in four main areas....The third area of concern in which, in the ICRC's view, humanitarian law has to be reinforced is *protection of the natural environment*. The serious harm done to the natural environment during numerous armed conflicts has only added to the vulnerability of those affected by the fighting. Human beings depend on the environment for their livelihood and well-being, in some cases even their

About two decades back, the general consensus among researchers was that the prospect of a new IHL convention specifically devoted to the issue of environmental damage was bleak, as the international community would hesitate to take on the task of crafting a new treaty.[77] They felt that it would be more fruitful to identify common purposes and pursue them in a constructive and systematic fashion to lay the foundation for a true and meaningful international consensus. In the last two decades enough research has been undertaken towards scientific understanding of the relevant issues of environmental damage during IAC and NIAC. International institutions like the ICRC and the UNEP have focused their attention on environmental protection as a separate category of damage. It is now felt that a durable answer to the problem of environmental destruction can be found in the adoption of a new convention.[78]

The new convention should set a lower threshold for damage caused to the natural environment and establish a redress mechanism for states. There is also a need to establish an effective judicial system under such a convention to consider issues of liability and redress. This would ensure impartiality at the level of international adjudication.[79] Under such a convention the Security Council could serve as the enforcer of judgments as it is already equipped to exercise this duty in terms of Article 94(2) of the Charter.[80] The new convention should extend its regime of liability to

---

survival. However, international rules protecting the environment in armed conflicts are either lacking or insufficient. Available at: http://www.icrc.org/eng/assets/files/red-cross-crescent-movement/31st-international-conference/31-int-conference-5-1-1-report-strength-ihl-en.pdf, accessed 12 September 2013. The subject was, however, not included in the Resolutions 1-9 adopted at the conclusion of 31st Annual Conference on 2 December 2011.

77 Richards Peter J. and Schmitt Michael N., Mars Meets Mother Nature: Protecting the Environment During Armed Conflict, Vol. 28, No. 4, *Stetson Law Review*, (1999), p. 1047-1092.

78 The adoption of the Fifth Geneva Convention on the Environment can support the curtailing of deliberate environmental modification and the strengthening of an environmentally protective regime. Such a Convention would ameliorate the infirmities of the current set of laws of armed conflict by pronouncing clear standards for military operations and defining quanta of proof of environmental damage. Yuzon Ensign Florencio J., Deliberate Environmental Modification Through the Use of Chemical and Biological Weapons: "Greening" the International Laws of Armed Conflict to Establish an Environmentally Protective Regime, Vol. 11 (5), *AM. U. INT'L L. & POL'Y*, (1996), p. 845-46.

79 Ibid, at p. 258.

80 Art 94(2) of the UN Charter reads: "2. If any party to a case fails to perform the obligations incumbent upon it under a judgment rendered by the [International] Court

both the States and individuals, thereby ensuring accountability of non-state actors under international law. The UNCC can be used as a model for the administration of future post-conflict reparations, however, similar compensation schemes would be limited by the economic circumstances of the post-conflict situation.[81]

## III. Drafting of New Convention

The drafting of a new convention should preferably be a joint exercise undertaken by the ICRC and UNEP, as both have expertise and experience in the sphere of protection of the environment in armed conflict. The new convention may be adopted under the auspices of the ICRC, keeping in view its ethos of neutrality for greater acceptance by the international community.[82] Some related aspects that must be given due consideration are: (i) Investigations related to environmental destruction; (ii) Fixing accountability for environmental destruction; (iii) Reparations for the damages through compensation commission; (iv) Responsibility of a military superior; (v) Environmental management by militaries during the peacetime; and (vi) Environmental protection in UN Peacekeeping missions

## A. Investigation of Environmental Destruction

The duty of the States to investigate and punish wilful destruction of the natural environment during an armed conflict is contained in IHL. The four Geneva Conventions of 1949 cast a duty upon the State Party to

---

[of Justice], the other party may have recourse to the Security Council, which may, if it deems necessary, make recommendations or decide upon measures to be taken to give effect to the judgment".

81  The UN's ability to establish similar compensation schemes is limited by two important factors: the economic circumstances of the post-conflict situation and the UN's degree of authority to sanction either unlawful acts within an armed conflict or impermissible acts of aggression. Libera, R. E., Divide, Conquer and Pay: Civil Compensation for Wartime Damages, Vol. 24, *BCICLR*, (2001) p. 291 at p. 301.

82  Although states displayed some reservation in the early 1990s for such a "dramatic metamorphosis of the *lex scripta*" and governments were generally reluctant to accept significant new obligations in this field, global concern about the natural environment has gained considerable momentum in the last decade. It need not be argued that the natural environment is under increased threat and this reality may well encourage the international community to reconsider its former position on the adoption of a new convention. Also see Dinstein Yoram. 2001. 'Protection of the Environment in International Armed Conflict', In Frowein J.A. and R Wolfrum (ed.), *Max Planck Yearbook of the United Nations Law*, Vol. 5, p. 523-549.

actively pursue prosecution for grave violations of their provisions during armed conflicts.[83] These provisions require that States Parties should shoulder three fundamental obligations: (i) to enact domestic legislation necessary to prosecute potential offenders; (ii) to search for those accused of violating the Conventions; and (iii) to either prosecute such individuals or turn them over to another State for trial. The grave breaches are set forth in other articles of the Conventions.[84] The 1977 Additional Protocol I (AP I) to the Geneva Conventions of 1949, casts a duty on State Parties to investigate and prosecute for grave breaches set forth in the Conventions, and requires States to cooperate in criminal investigations.[85] Article 87 provides:

1.  The High Contracting Parties and the Parties to the conflict shall require military commanders, with respect to members of the armed forces under their command and other persons under their control, to prevent and, where necessary, to suppress and to report to competent authorities breaches of the Conventions and of this Protocol.

2.  In order to prevent and suppress breaches, High Contracting Parties and Parties to the conflict shall require that, commensurate with their level of responsibility, commanders ensure that members of the armed forces under their command are aware of their obligations under the Conventions and this Protocol.

3.  The High Contracting Parties and Parties to the conflict shall require any commander who is aware that subordinates or other persons under his control are going to commit or have committed a breach of the Conventions or of this Protocol, to initiate such steps

---

83   The relevant articles in each Geneva Convention are nearly identical. Article 49, Geneva Convention for the Amelioration of the Condition of the Wounded and Sick in Armed Forces in the Field (Geneva Convention I); Article 50, Geneva Convention for the Amelioration of the Condition of the Wounded, Sick and Shipwrecked Members of Armed Forces at Sea (Geneva Convention II); Article 129, Geneva Convention Relative to the Treatment of Prisoners of War (Geneva Convention III); and Article 146, Geneva Convention Relative to the Protection of Civilian Persons in Time of War (Geneva Convention IV).

84   Article 50, GC I; Article 51, GC II; Article 130, GC III; and Article 147, GC IV.

85   Articles 85 of AP I deals with the repression of breaches of the Protocol; Article 86 with failure to repression of breaches; Article 87-duty of commanders to prevent, suppress and where appropriate initiate disciplinary or penal actions; Article 88-mutual assistance in criminal matters; and Article 89 deals with cooperation in the investigation and prosecution in situations of serious violations.

as are necessary to prevent such violations of the Conventions or this Protocol, and, where appropriate, to initiate disciplinary or penal action against violators thereof.

Article 87 of AP I, thus imposes a duty on members of the armed forces to act proactively in the face of potential or possible IHL violations. They need not be formally designated as commanders according to the regulations of their armed forces; the obligations attach as soon as they assume a command function.[86] Commanders are also responsible for the actions of other persons under their control, as in the case of the civilian population in occupied territory or troops of other units operating in their sector of occupation. The State must take measures to impose these duties upon commanders and ensure that they implement them. The responsibilities are complementary, with commanders expected to exercise whatever authority has been vested in them within the implementation, enforcement, and disciplinary structure of their armed forces and government.[87] Military manuals of all states generally impose a duty on their armed forces to investigate and prosecute possible war crimes.

The principles contained in the Geneva Conventions of 1949 and AP I regarding investigations and prosecutions have customary status of IHL. Rule 158 of Customary IHL, provides that "States must investigate war crimes allegedly committed by their nationals or armed forces, or on their territory, and, if appropriate, prosecute the suspects. They must also investigate other war crimes over which they have jurisdiction and, if appropriate, prosecute the suspects." There are a number of international treaties which articulate the obligation to investigate possible war crimes and to prosecute those responsible for them. For example, the 1948 Genocide Convention, the 1954 Hague Cultural Property Convention and its Second Protocol of 1999, the 1984 Torture Convention, the 1993 Chemical Weapons Convention, the 1996 Amended Landmines Protocol, the 1997 Ottawa Convention on Landmines, the Statute of the International Criminal Court, and the 2008 Convention on Cluster Munitions.

The Basic Principles and Guidelines on the Right to a Remedy and Reparation for Victims of Gross Violations of International Human Rights

---

86  Schmitt Michael N., Investigating Violations of International Law in Armed Conflict, Vol. 2, *Harvard National Security Journal*, (2011), p. 41.

87  Sandoz Yves, Chrisotphe Swinarski and Bruno Zimmermann (eds.). 1987. *Commentary on the Additional Protocols of 8 June 1977 to the Geneva Conventions of 12 August 1949*, International Committee of the Red Cross, Geneva: Martinus Nijhoff Publishers, paragraphs 3553-62.

Law and Serious Violations of International Humanitarian Law, adopted by the General Assembly in 2005 also provide: "The obligation to respect, ensure respect for and implement international human rights law and international humanitarian law as provided for under the respective bodies of law, includes, inter alia, the duty to....investigate violations effectively, promptly, thoroughly and impartially and, where appropriate, take action against those allegedly responsible in accordance with domestic and international law."[88]

The duty to investigate and prosecute has been the subject of agreements between belligerents. For instance, in 1991 Croatia and Yugoslavia agreed that "each party undertakes, when it is officially informed of (an allegation of violations of IHL) made or forwarded by the ICRC, to open an inquiry promptly and pursue it conscientiously, and to take the necessary steps to put an end to the alleged violations or prevent their recurrence and to punish those responsible in accordance with the law in force."[89] A similar agreement was executed by the parties to the conflict in Bosnia and Herzegovina the following year.[90]

Though Common Article 3 of the Geneva Conventions and AP II contains no reference to investigations or prosecution during a NIAC; Rule 158 of the Customary IHL extends the norm to NIAC. Also, the Commentary to the Geneva Conventions of 1949 confirms that the duty to suppress applies to any breach of the conventions, which would encompass violations of Common Article 3.[91] Besides, the Statute of the ICC does not make any distinction between categories of armed conflict in either its Preamble (which asserts that war crimes and other offences "must not go unpunished and that their effective prosecution must be ensured by taking measures at the national level"), or in the article on command responsibility (which discusses situations in which a commander has failed to "submit the

---

88  G.A. Res. 60/147, Annex, A/RES/60/147, 16 December 2005, Paragraph 3.

89  Memorandum of Understanding on the Application of International Humanitarian Law between Croatia and the Socialist Federal Republic of Yugoslavia, Article 11, 27 November 1991.

90  Agreement between Representatives of President of the Republic of Bosnia and Herzegovina and President of the Party of Democratic Action, Representatives of President of the Serbian Democratic Party, and Representative of President of the Croatian Democratic Community, Article 5, 22 May 1992.

91  Pictet Jean (ed.). 1958. Commentary: Geneva Convention for the Amelioration of the Condition of the Wounded and Sick in Armed Forces in the Field (GC I), p. 367; Commentary: Geneva Convention Relative to the Protection of Civilian Persons in Time of War (GC IV), p. 594, Geneva: ICRC.

matter to the competent authorities for investigation and prosecution").[92] Therefore, the requirement to investigate and prosecute crimes relating to wilful environmental damage attaches in both IAC and NIAC. The jurisprudence of the ICTY also supports the extension of the obligation to investigate and prosecute during NIAC.[93]

## B. Accountability for Environmental Damage

Despite the recent developments in holding individuals criminally liable for war crimes, genocide and crime against humanity, there remains a distinct lack of practice and mandate to prosecute environmental crimes.[94] There is a need for norms and institutions that can impose criminal liability on offenders in IAC and NIAC.[95] The norms may be developed along the lines of those of international criminal law (ICL),[96] international environmental law (IEL) applicable during the peacetime, and domestic criminal and environmental law. International law has seen the emergence of a generalized right to a healthy environment, through detailed treaties,

---

92 ICC Statute, Preamble and Article 28.

93 *Prosecutor v. Tadic*, Case No. IT-94-1-I, Decision on Defence Motion for Interlocutory Appeal on Jurisdiction, para 111–27, International Criminal Tribunal for the Former Yugoslavia, 2 October 1995.

94 Bruch Carl E., All's Not Fair in (Civil) War: Criminal Liability for Environmental Damage in Internal Armed Conflict, Vol. 25 (3), *Vermont Law Review*, (2000-2001), p. 695-752.

95 In an era where morality, ethics and international law now recognize the rights of individuals, and notions of environmental or ecological rights are becoming increasingly accepted, it is only natural that the deliberate destruction of the environment should give rise to individual criminal responsibility at the international level. Further, if such destruction is carried out in a manner as to cause severe destruction and consequent human suffering, there is every reason to assert that such offending act is brought within the definition of a new international crime. The 'individual criminal responsibility' and the 'responsibility of commanders and other superiors' have been explicitly clarified in the Rome Statute of the International Criminal Court (Articles 25 and 28) to ensure that the superiors and subordinates cannot get away with the excuses of following orders. Similar provisions could be created under the proposed convention.

96 International criminal law (ICL) refers to the law, procedures, and institutions connected with the trials of persons accused of the most serious crimes of concern to the international community. Past-trials focused on serious episodes of criminality in Rwanda, Sierra Leone, the ex-Yugoslavia, Cambodia, and East Timor. Various institutions have applied ICL over the last two decades, beginning with the International Criminal Tribunal for the former Yugoslavia (ICTY) and the International Criminal Tribunal for Rwanda (ICTR) in 1990s, following on with the creation of the International Criminal Court (ICC) in 1998, and the recent establishment of the Special Tribunal for Lebanon.

protocols and state practices. There is also a large body of law regarding the human right to a healthy environment. A number of IEL treaties concern species of flora and fauna, the seas, and the atmosphere and require States to criminalize damage to these. The Nuremberg Principles that continue to guide international criminal justice could also be considered for holding an individual accountable for environmental crimes in an armed conflict:

- Principles 1 and 2: Any person who commits an act which constitutes a crime under international law is responsible therefor and liable to punishment, regardless of whether the act is prohibited under local law.

- Principles 3 and 4: The fact that a person who committed an act which constitutes a crime under international law acted as Head of State or responsible government official does not relieve him from responsibility under international law, and the individual is not protected from criminal punishment simply because he or she was carrying out orders.

- Principles 6 and 7: Describing punishable international crimes as including crimes against peace, war crimes, crimes against humanity, and complicity in any of the above.

## C. Reparations

Under the general principle of public international law any wrongful act (or violation of an obligation), gives rise to an obligation to make reparation. Historically, war reparations have been a combination of (i) compensation for damage incurred, (ii) punitive damages, and (iii) preventing the paying nation from regaining its former economic and political strength. [97] The aim of reparation is to eliminate, as far as possible, the consequences of the illegal act and to restore the situation that would have existed if the act had not been committed. Reparation can take various forms, including

---

97 The 1927 *Chorzow Factory (Indemnity) Case* expresses the basis of compensation in international law for the damages suffered as a result of wrongful acts. In this case, Germany sought reparations for factories seized by the Polish government. The Permanent Court of International Justice ruled that the principles governing restoration include restoration in kind, a monetary sum equivalent to the value of in-kind restoration, and additional payments as necessary to fully compensate for the damages. The Court stated: "reparation must, as far as possible, wipe out all the consequences of the illegal act and re-establish the situation which would, in all probability have existed if that act had not been committed". However, the court did not address the methodologies for assessing the damages. Chorzow Factory (Indemnity) (*Germany v. Poland*), 1927 PCIJ (Ser. A), No. 17, p. 47.

restitution, compensation or satisfaction. These remedies can be applied either singly or in combination in response to a particular violation. IHL treaties contain some specific rules that also lay down a State obligation of reparation in favour of individual victims of treaty breaches;[98] however, these rules can be invoked only by the States and not by individuals. This interpretation should not be adhered to for several reasons: (i) the preparatory work of Article 3 of the Hague Convention shows that its goal was to provide for reparation to injured individuals; (ii) the use of the term 'compensation' confirms the intention to grant reparation to individuals only; (iii) the Hague Convention and AP I and other rules of the law have created a series of obligation not only for the States, but also for individuals, and aim to prosecute individuals who violate these obligations; and (iv) a number of existing norms of IHL, are similar to function and nature of IHRL. [99]

The UN General Assembly resolution containing the Basic Principles and Guidelines on the Right to Reparation[100] affirms the importance of

---

98 For example, Article 3 of the 1907 Hague Convention IV provides that a belligerent State that commits a breach of the provisions of the Regulations annexed to the Convention must pay compensation for those breaches, and it further establishes that states are responsible for all the acts committed by their armed forces. This rule has been further taken up in Article 91 of AP I, which lays down the obligation to pay compensation for states that breach the provisions of the four Geneva Conventions of 1949 or of the Protocol itself. Additionally, a common article of the four Geneva Conventions of 1949 (Article 51 of the first and second Geneva Convention, Article 131 of the third Convention, and Article 148 of the fourth Convention) establishes the responsibility of the conflicting States for grave breaches of the Conventions. Article 3 of The Hague Convention and Article 91 of AP I regulate only interstate relationship, and lay down an obligation of reparation of the responsible State towards the other contracting State and not towards the injured individuals.

99 Mazzeschi Riccardo Pisillo, Reparation Claim by Individuals for State Breaches of Humanitarian Law and Human Rights: An Overview, Vol. 1, *Journal of International Criminal Justice*, (2003), p. 339-347.

100 The full title of the Resolution: "The Basic Principles and Guidelines on the Right to a Remedy and Reparation for Victims of Gross Violations of International Human Rights Law and Serious Violations of International Humanitarian Law", adopted and proclaimed by the UN General Assembly resolution 60/147 of 16 December 2005. The resolutions refers the right to a remedy for victims of violations contained in article 8 of the Universal Declaration of Human Rights, 1 article 2 of the International Covenant on Civil and Political Rights, 2 article 6 of the International Convention on the Elimination of All Forms of Racial Discrimination, article 14 of the Convention against Torture and Other Cruel, Inhuman or Degrading Treatment or Punishment, and article 39 of the Convention on the Rights of the Child, and of international humanitarian law as found in article 3 of the Hague Convention respecting the Laws and Customs of War on Land of 18 October 1907 (Convention IV), article 91 of AP I, and articles 68 and 75 of the

addressing the question of remedies and reparation for victims of gross violations of IHRL and serious violations of IHL in a systematic and thorough way at national and international levels. The resolution provides:

Para 4: In cases of gross violations of IHRL and serious violations of international humanitarian law IHL constituting crimes under international law, States have the duty to investigate and, if there is sufficient evidence, the duty to submit to prosecution the person allegedly responsible for the violations and, if found guilty, the duty to punish her or him. Moreover, in these cases, States should, in accordance with international law, cooperate with one another and assist international judicial organs competent in the investigation and prosecution of these violations.

Para 8: For purposes of the present document, victims are persons who individually or collectively suffered harm, including physical or mental injury, emotional suffering, economic loss or substantial impairment of their fundamental rights, through acts or omissions that constitute gross violations of IHRL, or serious violations of IHL. Where appropriate, and in accordance with domestic law, the term "victim" also includes the immediate family or dependants of the direct victim and persons who have suffered harm in intervening to assist victims in distress or to prevent victimization.

Para 11: Remedies for gross violations of IHRL and serious violations of IHL include the victim's right to the following as provided for under international law: (a) Equal and effective access to justice; (b) Adequate, effective and prompt reparation for harm suffered; and (c) Access to relevant information concerning violations and reparation mechanisms.

Para 15: Adequate, effective and prompt reparation is intended to promote justice by redressing gross violations of international human rights law or serious violations of international humanitarian law. Reparation should be proportional to the gravity of the violations and the harm suffered. In accordance with its domestic laws and international legal obligations, a State shall provide reparation to victims for acts or omissions which can be attributed to the State and constitute gross violations of international human rights law or serious violations of international humanitarian law. In cases where a person,

---

Rome Statute of the International Criminal Court.

a legal person, or other entity is found liable for reparation to a victim, such party should provide reparation to the victim or compensate the State if the State has already provided reparation to the victim.

Para 17: States shall, with respect to claims by victims, enforce domestic judgments for reparation against individuals or entities liable for the harm suffered and endeavour to enforce valid foreign legal judgments for reparation in accordance with domestic law and international legal obligations. To that end, States should provide under their domestic laws effective mechanisms for the enforcement of reparation judgments.

Para 18: In accordance with domestic law and international law, and taking account of individual circumstances, victims of gross violations of IHRL and serious violations of IHL should, as appropriate and proportional to the gravity of the violation and the circumstances of each case, be provided with full and effective reparation, which include the following forms: restitution, compensation, rehabilitation, satisfaction and guarantees of non-repetition.

Para 19: Restitution should, whenever possible, restore the victim to the original situation before the gross violations of IHRL or serious violations of IHL occurred. Restitution includes, as appropriate: restoration of liberty, enjoyment of human rights, identity, family life and citizenship, return to one's place of residence, restoration of employment and return of property.

Para 20: Compensation should be provided for any economically assessable damage, as appropriate and proportional to the gravity of the violation and the circumstances of each case, resulting from gross violations of IHRL and serious violations of IHL, such as: (a) Physical or mental harm; (b) Lost opportunities, including employment, education and social benefits; (c) Material damages and loss of earnings, including loss of earning potential; (d) Moral damage; and (e) Costs required for legal or expert assistance, medicine and medical services, and psychological and social services.

Para 21: Rehabilitation should include medical and psychological care as well as legal and social services.

Para 22: Satisfaction should include, where applicable, any or all of the following:

(a) Effective measures aimed at the cessation of continuing violations;

(b) Verification of the facts and full and public disclosure of the truth to the extent that such disclosure does not cause further harm or threaten the safety and interests of the victim, the victim's relatives, witnesses, or persons who have intervened to assist the victim or prevent the occurrence of further violations;

(c) The search for the whereabouts of the disappeared, for the identities of the children abducted, and for the bodies of those killed, and assistance in the recovery, identification and reburial of the bodies in accordance with the expressed or presumed wish of the victims, or the cultural practices of the families and communities;

(d) An official declaration or a judicial decision restoring the dignity, the reputation and the rights of the victim and of persons closely connected with the victim;

(e) Public apology, including acknowledgement of the facts and acceptance of responsibility;

(f) Judicial and administrative sanctions against persons liable for the violations;

(g) Commemorations and tributes to the victims;

(h) Inclusion of an accurate account of the violations that occurred in IHRL and IHL training and in educational material at all levels.

Para 23: **Guarantees of non-repetition** should include, where applicable, any or all of the following measures, which will also contribute to prevention:

(a) Ensuring effective civilian control of military and security forces;

(b) Ensuring that all civilian and military proceedings abide by international standards of due process, fairness and impartiality;

(c) Strengthening the independence of the judiciary;

(d) Protecting persons in the legal, medical and health-care professions, the media and other related professions, and human rights defenders;

(e) Providing, on a priority and continued basis, human rights and IHL education to all sectors of society and training for law enforcement officials as well as military and security forces;

(f) Promoting the observance of codes of conduct and ethical norms, in particular international standards, by public servants, including law enforcement, correctional, media, medical, psychological, social service and military personnel, as well as by economic enterprises;

(g) Promoting mechanisms for preventing and monitoring social conflicts and their resolution;

(h) Reviewing and reforming laws contributing to or allowing gross violations of IHRL and serious violations of IHL.

In the light of the preceding discussions possible compensable environmental damages could include: (i) reasonable incurred costs of removing pollution and mitigating environmental harm; (ii) reasonable incurred and future costs of restoring the environment to its pre-injury state (could be related to removal and prevention); (iii) reasonable costs of monitoring and assessing environmental injury and determining appropriate remedial measures; (iv) compensation for the loss of consumptive and non-consumptive environmental uses, such as fishing, recreation, and aesthetic enjoyment; (v) compensation for depletion of or damage to natural resources; (vi) compensation for loss of passive use values, such as existence value, option value, bequest value, and stewardship value; and (vii) compensation for the interim loss of direct and passive environmental use values for the period from injury to restoration.[101]

## United Nations Compensation Commission

The UN Compensation Commission (UNCC) was established to adjudicate claims of compensation relating to the 1990-1991 Gulf War. [102] The UNCC, by Resolution 692 (2001), was mandated to examine claims resulting from the invasion and occupation and also to administer the fund. The circumstances leading to creation of UNCC were, however,

---

101 Addressing Environmental Consequences of War, Background Paper for the First International Conference on Addressing Environmental Consequences of War: Legal, Economic, and Scientific Perspectives, June 10-12, 1998, Washington DC: Environmental Law Research Institute, p.12.

102 The UN Security Council considered the difficulty in criminally prosecuting Iraqi military officers responsible for the environmental harm during 1990-1991Gulf War; and eventually established the UN Compensation Commission (UNCC), instead of criminal tribunals, to punish the environmental war criminals.

unique. Iraq had admitted its responsibility for the consequences of the aggression, including its liability under international law 'for any direct loss, damage, including environmental damage and depletion of natural resources'. Furthermore, the enforcement procedure had the full backing of the Security Council's Chapter VII powers. The compensation regime was, therefore, clearly grounded on the illegality of Iraq's conduct under *jus ad bellum*, rather than the law of war. It left open the question whether a state using force in self-defence or on the authority of the Security Council could ever be made liable for consequential damage including environmental damage. The UNCC did not concern itself with claims by Iraqi nationals or losses and damage incurred on account of the coalition forces' own conduct, of which the most significant was damage allegedly caused by the use of DU weapons.

The UNCC became the first international body to deal with compensations for deliberate damage to the environment during an armed conflict.[103] It administered the claims process and made payments to claimants from a fund that was capitalized through a 30 per cent levy on Iraqi oil exports. The UNCC received more than 2.6 million claims, corresponding to an amount of approximately US$ 368 billion. The Governing Council had identified six categories of claims (Category A to F). [104] Category "F" claims were claims filed by governments and international organizations for losses incurred in evacuating citizens; providing relief to citizens; damage to diplomatic premises and loss of, and damage to, other government property; and damage to the environment.[105] All environmental compensation claims

---

103 A partisan application of responsibility significantly undermines the legitimacy of the system in so far as it is seen as a particular application of victor's justice. It is significant that the Iraqi precedent has not been followed in other conflicts. Okowa Phoebe. 2009. 'Environmental Justice in Situations of Armed Conflict', in Ebbesson Johan and Phoebe Okawa (eds.), *Environmental Law and Justice in Context*, Cambridge: Cambridge University Press, p. 246-47. Also see: Juni Robin L. and Elliot Eder, Ecosystem Management and Damage Recovery in International Conflict, Vol. 14, Number 3, *Natural Resources & Environment*, (Winter 2000), p. 193- 197.

104 The Governing Council is a policy-making organ of the UNCC and its membership is the same as that of the Security Council, of which the Commission is a subsidiary body. The six categories of claims comprise four categories of claims of individuals (Category A, B C and D), one for corporations (Category E) and one for Governments and international organizations, which also includes claims for environmental damage (Category F). Available at: http://www.uncc.ch/theclaims.htm, visited 20 June 2014.

105 The Commission has received approximately 300 category F claims, submitted by forty-three Governments and six international organizations, seeking a total of approximately US$210 billion in compensation. The category F claims were organized into four subcategories. Among the 19 panels set up for six categories of claims, one

were processed by 2005 and were related to risks from: (i) laying and clearance of mines, (ii) mines, unexploded ordnance and other remnants of war, (iii) oil lakes formed by oil released from damaged wells in Kuwait, (iv) oil spills in the Persian Gulf caused by oil released from pipelines, offshore terminals and tankers, (v) pollutants released from oil-well fires and fire-fighting activities in Kuwait, (vi) exposure of the populations of the claimants to pollutants from the oil-well fires and oil spills in Kuwait and to hostilities and various acts of violence, (vii) movement of military equipments, vehicles and personnel, and military operations, (viii) construction of military fortifications, encampments and roads, (ix) oil-filled trenches, (x) movement and presence of refugees who departed from Iraq and Kuwait, and (xi) influx of refugees into the territories of some of the claimants[106]

The claims relating to environmental damage and depletion of natural resources fell into two broad groups under Category F4: (i) claims for environmental damage and the depletion of natural resources in the Persian Gulf region, including those resulting from oil-well fires and the discharge of oil into the sea; and (ii) claims for costs incurred by governments outside of the region in providing assistance to countries that were directly affected by the environmental damage. This assistance included the alleviation of the damage caused by the oil-well fires, the prevention and clean-up of pollution, and the provision of manpower and supplies. The compensation sought included compensation for loss of use of the resources during the period between the occurrence of the damage and the full restoration of the resources, either through natural recovery or as a result of remediation or restoration measures undertaken by a claimant.

Several non-regional States (Germany, Australia, Canada, The United States, the Netherlands and the UK) were also compensated for expenses incurred in the effort "to respond to the oil spills, oil fires and other environmental damage or threats of environmental damage resulting

---

panel (F4) was specifically mandated to investigate the 168 environmental claims. The F4 panel concluded that Iraq's liability for environmental damage "is comprehensive and extends to all damage and losses related to environmental and any consequences of such damage that can reasonably be attributed directly to Iraq's invasion and occupation of Iraq". Available at: http://www.uncc.ch/theclaims.htm, visited 20 June 2014.

106 The F4 panel submitted five Reports: First Report S/AC.26/2001/16, 22 June 2001; Second Report S/AC.26/2002/26, 3 October 2002; Third Report S/AC.26/2003/31, 18 December 2003; Fourth Report S/AC.26/2004/16, 9 December 2004 (Part 1); S/AC.26/2004/17, 9 December 2004 (Part 2); and Fifth Report S/AC.26/2005/10, 30 June 2005.

from the invasion and occupation, including monitoring and assessment of the impacts of the oil spills and oil fires."[107] Following a request from the UN, the right to bring claims before the Commission was extended to States which had incurred economic losses for supportive assistance to environmental protection in the Gulf region. The F4 Panel justified these expenses recalling that, "specific appeals for assistance in dealing with the environmental damage caused by Iraq's invasion and occupation of Kuwait were made by the General Assembly and by other organizations and bodies of the UN system as well as by the countries affected by environmental damage or threat of such damage resulting from Iraq's invasion and occupation of Kuwait."[108]

The decisions taken by the UNCC are significant for interpreting and applying international law to protect the environment during armed conflict. The extensive environmental damage caused by Iraq was widely condemned by the international community. In addition, the damage caused outside the territory of Iraq was declared to have violated Article 23(g) of the Hague Regulations regarding the destruction of enemy property. As a result, UNSC Resolution 687 stated in Paragraph 16 that "Iraq is liable under international law for any....damage, including environmental damage and the depletion of natural resources....as a result of Iraq's unlawful invasion and occupation of Kuwait."

There was a general consensus that Iraq's obligation to pay reparations as an invader was justified under established customary international law, specifically Article 23 of The Hague Convention and Article 53 of the fourth Geneva Convention of 1949.[109] Article 23 of the Hague Convention "prohibits the destruction of enemy property in wartime," and Article 53 of the fourth Geneva Convention restricts the destruction of an occupied place by occupying forces. Iraq's violation of its legal obligations under Resolution 687, based on customary law, therefore resulted in its liability to pay Kuwait and other countries for environmental damage occurred. The

---

107 Report 2, Paragraph 211.

108 Report 2, Paragraph 34.

109 Many experts have debated the issue of the legality of the UNCC using both customary and conventional international laws that have either a direct or indirect relevance to wartime environmental damage. International laws that contain language that directly address wartime environmental damage are AP I to the Geneva Conventions and ENMOD Convention. However, Iraq cannot be held responsible under these laws because neither AP I nor ENMOD has been accepted as customary law, nor they have not been ratified by Iraq.

specific methodologies and standards that the UNCC adopted in analysing, assessing, evaluating and deciding whether to award compensation provide a baseline for future forums tasked with similar responsibilities.

Depending on the complexity of the damages and the causation chain that connects particular damages to events during the crisis, an interdisciplinary team would be necessary to identify and quantify damages and to present a persuasive claim for damage recovery. The team should include specialists, such as lawyers, resource economists, physicians, hydrologists, geochemists, epidemiologists, marine biologists, agronomists, or eco-toxicologists. In addition, future definitions of compensable environmental damage should include reasonable geographical limitations to ensure that sanctioned nations are not held responsible for unrelated environmental problems in remote regions, where there is a tenuous chain of causation.[110] There must also be a deadline so that the sanctioned nation need not fear the filing of claims indefinitely.

## D. Responsibilities of Military Superiors

Military commanders have a heavy responsibility during peace and war. In peacetime, they must train their soldiers and maintain military equipments. They also have the responsibility to protect their subordinates and to ensure that their subordinates do not violate military manuals; and if they do so, punish them for the violations. The question then arises as to why a military commander should be concerned with protecting a forest, wetland, a water body, wildlife, or threatened and endangered species while his subordinates are fighting for the survival of their unit or the nation?[111] The military ethos is likely to be dominated by considerations of patriotism and the desire to win the battle.

At the time of active hostilities, military commanders tend to accumulate and use all the military resources they can, both to accomplish their assigned missions and to protect their troops from harm. Decision-making in combat situations involves a continuous effort to adjust to and accommodate on the spot developments in the battlefield. Sometimes a commander may use more force than necessary, or cause excessive collateral damage because of poor planning, flawed intelligence, enemy

---

110 Andrea Gattini, The UN Compensation Commission: Old Rules, New Procedures on War Reparations, Vol. 13, *Eur. J. Int'l L.* (2002), p. 177.

111 Drucker Major Merrit P., The Military Commander's Responsibility for the Environment, Vol. 11 (2), *Environmental Ethics*, (1989), p. 135-152.

deception, or equipment failure. In such a situation, it is unlikely that the protection of the environment as a part of military operation would be a consideration in the mind of the commander.

Hazardous wastes produced during military operations can also pose a risk to soldiers and local inhabitants. Improper handling of hazardous wastes can also create significant costs and liabilities for the Army. The volumes of waste that can be generated in military operations can be staggering. For instance, in one year during Operation Joint Endeavour (OJE) in Bosnia-Herzegovina, the US military with a few thousands of soldiers generated more than 1.8 million kg of hazardous waste.[112] The overseas military commanders have little to be concerned about environmental damage as compared to comparable environmental planning requirements within the US.[113] The drawbacks of the overseas requirement are that they lack clear standards to ensure that minimum environmental protections are put into place and there is no enforcement authority.[114]

In view of the growing importance of environmental considerations in military operations, the US Army Environmental Policy Institute (AEPI) had asked the RAND Arroyo Centre to assess how the Army should

---

112 Mosher David E., Beth E. Lachman, Michael D. Greenberg, Tiffany Nichols, Brian Rosen, Henry H. Willis. 2008. *Green Warriors: Army Environmental Considerations for Contingency Operations from Planning Through Post-Conflict*, RAND Corporation, p. 24; Though in the US military bases, the focus has been on four environmental pillars—prevention, conservation, compliance and restoration--- the US military do not apply them in overseas contingency operations. Mosher David E., Beth E. Lachman, Michael D. Greenberg, Tiffany Nichols, Brian Rosen, Henry H. Willis. 2008. *Green Warriors: Army Environmental Considerations for Contingency Operations from Planning Through Post-Conflict*, RAND Corporation, p. 26.

113 In the early 1990s the US naval base at Subic Bay was formally handed over to the Philippine Government. The departure of the American military, however, left behind a substantial quantity of toxic waste. It was found that untreated chemical and heavy metal wastes were discharged into the air, the ground, and Subic Bay, from Subic Bay Naval and Clark Air Force Bases; and the cleanup would cost approximately US$12-15 million for each site. An on-site investigation by Filipino scientists and the Philippine Centre for Investigative Journalism reported that, for over forty years, the US Navy and Air Force had stored and improperly disposed of tons of military and industrial wastes, including asbestos and polychlorinated biphenyls (PCBs), in and around Subic Bay and Clark Air Force Bases. The US activities at these bases failed to comply with environmental regulations and standards. Bayoneto M. Victoria, The Former US Bases in the Philippines: An Argument for the Application of US Environmental Standards to Overseas Military Bases, Vol. VI, *Fordham Environmental Law Journal*, (1994), p. 111-155.

114 William A.Wilcox, Jr. 2007. *The Modern Military and the Environment: The Laws of Peace and War*, Maryland: The Scarecrow Press, Inc., p. 38.

approach environmental considerations in overseas operations, including planning and training. The report prepared by the RAND concludes that environmental considerations, including clean water, sanitation, hazardous-waste management, can be important for achieving overall US objectives during reconstruction and post-conflict operations, including both short- and long-term stability. If not properly addressed in planning or operations, environmental considerations can increase the costs of an operation and make it more difficult for the Army to sustain the mission. The RAND Corporation has identified existing problems and gaps in the environmental policy and doctrine of the US military and made certain recommendation. The major findings, which could be applicable to militaries world over, are: [115]

- Environmental issues can have a significant impact on military operations. They can have far-reaching impacts across operations, military organizations, and the world.

- Environmental considerations can be particularly important for success in the post-conflict phase of operations.

- Inadequate environmental practices in military operations can increase current and future costs, liabilities, diplomatic problems, and risks to soldier health.

- The Army could improve its understanding of environmental considerations and could incorporate them more effectively into plans and operations.

- The Army has no comprehensive approach to environmental considerations in the post-conflict phase.

In light of these findings, the report recommended that the army needs to: (i) improve its policy and guidance for environmental considerations in military operations; (ii) bring about a cultural change regarding the ways environmental issues are viewed and includes changes in doctrine, training, and equipment; (iii) improve the incorporation of environmental considerations into planning; (iv) improve pre-deployment and field environmental training; and (v) invest more in environmental resources and good environmental practices in military operations.

---

115 Mosher David E., Beth E. Lachman, Michael D. Greenberg, Tiffany Nichols, Brian Rosen, and Henry H. Willis. 2008. *Green Warriors: Army environmental considerations for contingency operations from planning through post-conflict*, USA: Rand Corporation.

## E. Environmental Management System

The environmental management of military activities is of growing concern for defence forces worldwide. At present, there are many environmental management tools employed to manage environmental performance, such as environmental impact assessment; environmental auditing; substance flow analysis; life cycle assessment; and environmental management system. Among these, environmental management system (EMS) is the most commonly used. Recent research has focused on estimating the effectiveness and environmental performance of EMS, rather than on its adoption and development in an organization.[116]

According to the International Organization for Standardization (ISO), an environmental management system (EMS) is part of the management system of an organization used to develop and implement its environmental policy and manage its environmental aspects (i.e. the elements of the activities or products or services of an organization that can interact with the environment).[117]

Implementation of EMS can lead to: (i) Conservation of resources, (ii) Effective resource allocation, (iii) Enhanced confidence within the chain of command, (iv) Enhanced public and community relations, (v) Compliance with environmental legislation (vi) Management of environmental risks and prevention of incidents/accidents, (vii) Reduced liability, (viii) Enhanced efficiency of environmental training through standardization and integration, (ix) Ease of regulatory burden, (x) Lesser cleanup cost of military assets used by civilians at a later stage, (xi) Conservation of environmental resources, (xii) Reduction in staff, (xiii) Substantial cost saving, and (xiv) Improved cooperation with foreign militaries. Governments have to ensure that environmental considerations are integrated into (i) domestic policies, (ii) military doctrines, (iii) strategic planning process, (iv) planning of military exercises and operations, (v) general military training, (vi) functional training of the armed forces, and (vii) utilization of facilities.

---

116 Ramos, T.B., Alves, I., Subtil, R. & de Melo, J.J., Environmental performance policy indicators for the public sector: The case of the Defence Sector, Vol. 82, *Journal of Environmental Management*, (2007), p. 410-432.

117 Formal certification to ISO 14001 can be achieved either by third party audit or self-declaration of conformance with the standard. It is possible to implement ISO 14001 without seeking formal certification. *International Standard ISO 14001*, Environmental management systems - Requirements with guidance for use, Second edition, 2004, p. 2.

Increased pressure from environmental legislation and public opinion has resulted in a general increase in environmental awareness amongst militaries of the world. A recent joint project of between the Swedish military and the US Department of Defence led to the publication of the first Environmental Guidelines for the military. NATO has also instituted a pilot study on EMS in the Military Sector. South Africa has adopted Military Integrated Environmental Management (MIEM) or Green Soldiering, which aims to ensure environmentally sustainable management of military facilities and activities. The US Army has now adopted the ISO 14001 for some of its bases.[118]

## F. UN Peacekeeping Missions

The UN peacekeeping personnel and their supporting infrastructure contribute to the recovery and security of countries emerging from conflict, but also place considerable demands on the local environment, including natural resources. In 2008, an inventory conducted by the UN Environment Management Group calculated that peacekeeping operations alone represent over 56 percent of the UN system's total climate footprint of approximately 1.75 million tons of $CO_2$ equivalent per year.[119]

Often the countries in which peacekeeping personnel operate have very little infrastructure and the UN people produce liquid and solid waste[120]

---

118 The International Organization for Standardization (ISO) developed the ISO 14001 standard to provide a set of internationally recognized criteria for EMS. The US Army Environmental Command (USAEC) has prepared the following documents to assist commanders and other installation personnel understand and implement their EMS: (i) US Army EMS Commander's Guide, and (ii) US Army EMS Implementer's Guide, version 3.0, October 2005. Available at: http://www.sustainability.army.mil, accessed 12 June 2014.

119 *Greening the Blue Helmets: Environment, Natural Resources and UN Peacekeeping Operations*, United Nations Environment Programme (UNEP), Nairobi, 2012, p.8.

120 Solid waste can include office refuse, construction debris, scrap metal and food refuse. Hazardous waste encompasses medical products, used oil, tires, batteries, electronic waste, stocks of chemicals, explosives and ammunition. Disposal of hazardous waste – such as pesticides, oil products, hazardous chemicals, batteries, tires, ammunition, ozone-depleting substances and electronic equipment – is a significant challenge for UN peacekeeping operations. Mission waste can also contain heavy metals that require long-term environmental management, including proper storage prior to disposal. Furthermore, the increasing use of IT equipment has resulted in electronic waste becoming one of the most significant parts of the hazardous waste stream. There have been a few instances where the governments have been asked to pay for the environmental degradation caused by their forces while functioning as part of UN peacekeeping force. For example, the Canadian government was forced to pay

which, if not treated and disposed properly, can have serious impact on the local environment. Peacekeeping missions that are deployed in remote areas often generate their own power and use aircraft that consume a lot of fuel, emit greenhouse gases and may also cause soil pollution. Waste disposal is often sub-contracted and carried out by local contractors, who may lack the capacity to do so in a responsible manner. Waste management infrastructure in the majority of post-conflict countries could be either non-existent or inadequate. Therefore, the reliance on local capacities and infrastructure to manage and dispose of waste in a safe manner can have unwanted consequences for the health and safety of both the peacekeepers and local communities.[121]

The disposal of waste to poorly constructed and managed landfill sites can lead to the pollution of local water bodies as well as direct exposure of the local population to contaminated waste during salvage activities. Improper treatment of liquid waste or wastewater may cause environmental as well as health problems for the UN staff and local communities.[122] UN missions can threaten local ecosystems, including plant and animal species, in various ways that may have a detrimental impact on the livelihoods of nearby communities. Peacekeepers have significant buying power and are attractive targets for vendors selling endangered fauna or flora. While peacekeepers are rarely involved in the illegal wildlife trade, there have

USD 1 million for the remediation of 2800 sqm of petroleum-contaminated soil to the Government of Bosnia and Herzegovina following its contribution to the UN Protection Force (UNPROFOR). *Greening the Blue Helmets: Environment, Natural Resources and UN Peacekeeping Operations*, United Nations Environment Programme (UNEP), Nairobi (2012), p.21

121 Awareness of and compliance with international legislation, such as the Basel Convention, is of paramount importance when dealing with hazardous waste. The Convention governs the trans-boundary movement of hazardous waste. It applies to UN waste when operating in signatory countries. It requires the disposal of hazardous waste to be undertaken as close as possible to their source of generation in accordance with environmental guidelines.

122 The cholera epidemic that broke out in Haiti in October 2010, has killed more than 8,000 people and infected more than 700,000 was believed to have been caused by a disease strain originating from a UN peacekeeping camp. The disease was allegedly introduced by Nepalese UN peacekeepers sent in the wake of devastating January 2010 earthquake. The source was tracked to a river that runs next to a UN camp in the central town of Mirebalais, where Nepalese troops had been based. The strain of cholera is the same as one endemic in Nepal. 'UN Has 'moral responsibility' to tackle Haiti cholera', says Ban Ki-moon, The Hindu, 15 July 2014. This created a negative perception of UN peacekeeping troops within the local population and led to violent demonstrations against them. *Greening the Blue Helmets: Environment, Natural Resources and UN Peacekeeping Operations*, 2012, UNEP.

been a few cases of their being involved in illegal activities.[123]

In 2009, with a view to minimizing the environmental impacts of peacekeeping missions, the UN Department of Peacekeeping Organization (DPKO) and the Department of Field Support (DFS) adopted an Environmental Policy for UN Field Missions.[124] The objective of the policy is to decrease the overall consumption of natural resources[125] and the production of waste, protect the local environmental and public health and establish UN peacekeeping as a role model for sustainable practices.[126] The policy provides a series of minimum operating standards and requires each mission to adopt environmental objectives and control measures through all phases of the mission. It focuses on a range of issues, including water, energy, solid and hazardous wastes, wastewater, wildlife and the management of cultural and historical sites. It requires the Director of Mission Support to issue instructions to prohibit the hunting, logging, harvesting, collecting, purchasing or acquiring of wildlife, live or dead, or

---

123 A high ranking officer was arrested in 2001 for allegedly trying to smuggle elephant tusks and animal skins out of Kenya. An investigation uncovered the involvement of three other UN soldiers.

124 In June 2009, Alain Le Roy, Under-Secretary-General for Peacekeeping, promulgated an *Environmental Policy for UN Field Missions* to develop baselines and objectives for missions on environmental issues. According to Policy Objective "Each mission will take actions to integrate environmental measures into its planning and operations in order to avoid and minimize the impact of activities carried out by the mission and its staff on the environment and to protect human health from such environmental impact."

125 For instance, during UN peace operations, water use is estimated at 84 litres per person per day. This can be contrasted with the UN High Commissioner for Refugees (UNHCR) recommendation for water in refugee situations of 15 litres per person per day, and an absolute survival minimum of 7 litres. Thus, in areas like Darfur or Chad, where water is a scarce resource, the local community may see the UN mission as a resource competitor, so even small efficiency gains in mission use of water may have a large impact on human needs in water-scarce situations. The Operational Support Manual (Provisional), 1996, UN Department of Field Support (DFS): New York; and *Water Manual for Refugee Situations,* 1992, Office of the UN High Commissioner for Refugees (UNHCR), Geneva.

126 In 1991, an international Commission headed by former IPB President Maj-Britt Theorin proposed the creation of a 'Green Beret' corps of military forces assigned to the UN for rapid response to ecological disasters, including war. The resulting UN-sponsored Study "*Charting Potential Uses of Resources Allocated to Military Activities for Civilian Endeavours to Protect the Environment,*" detailed a whole series of proposals which, if implemented, would have significantly changed the role of the military in many countries. *The Military's Impact on the Environment: A Neglected Aspect of the Sustainable Development Debate,* A Briefing Paper for States and NGOs, International Peace Bureau, August 2002, p. 11. Available at: http://www.ipb.org/i/pdf-files/The_Militarys_Impact_on_the_Environment.pdf, accessed 21 June 2014.

any parts and derivatives. Fishing is only permitted as a recreational activity when it does not interfere with the needs of the local population. The mission must also respect the norms of the Convention on International Trade in Endangered Species of Wild Fauna and Flora (CITES), which aims to ensure that the international trade in wildlife does not threaten their survival.

The 2009 Environmental Policy provides the chain of command (green hierarchy) for environmental responsibility in UN peacekeeping missions:[127]

1. The DPKO and DFS Under-Secretary-Generals for Peacekeeping Operations and Field Support are responsible for taking measures to ensure that all field missions integrate environmental considerations into their respective operations and endeavour to secure resources required for this purpose.

2. The Head of Mission, which could be either the Special Representative of the Secretary-General or the Force Commander, is responsible for promulgating the environmental policy objectives of the field mission and issuing annual mission environmental statements.

3. The Director/Chief of Mission Support is responsible for the mission's compliance with the environmental policy, including formulating instructions and operating procedures to implement the mission's environmental objectives.

4. The Force Commander is responsible for instituting instructions and operating procedures to ensure that the military component complies with the environmental policy and objectives of the mission.

5. The Head of the Police Component of the mission is responsible for instituting instructions and operating procedures to ensure that the police component complies with the environmental policy and objectives of the mission.

6. The Environmental Officer is responsible for coordinating the management of actions on environmental issues in the mission. This includes establishment of the mission's EMS by supporting

---

127 *Environmental policy for UN field missions*, UN Department of Peacekeeping Operations and UN Department of Field Support (2009), UN: New York, p. 4-5.

the development and drafting of the mission's environmental policy and objectives, undertaking environmental surveys and assessments, producing an environmental baseline study (EBS) and an action plan, advising and providing information on environmental issues, establishing a list of potentially hazardous installations, liaising with local authorities, investigating claims, recommending measures to mitigate environmental problems, keeping records, regular reporting and briefing of peacekeepers during their induction.

Compliance with the 2009 Environmental Policy should be mandatory for all personnel working in UN peacekeeping operations. To date, however, the policy has not led to sufficient concrete change on the ground. It is necessary that EBS and environmental impact assessments (EIA) be conducted for each mission as a standard due diligence procedure. Training on environment and natural resource management in a post-conflict context should be made a standard component of pre-deployment and in-mission orientation.

## IV. Recommendations

Though scientists, governments and NGOs are increasingly concerned about industrial pollution, the military generally evades responsibility for polluting the environment and ecological disasters. It is time to change this practice. The recommendations that follow are addressed to the United Nations, governments and their militaries.

### The United Nations

The United Nations must initiate the process for a new convention on the protection of the environment applicable to both IAC and NIAC. The future law must have unambiguous provisions and system for the uniform imposition of justice.[128] The Security Council must consider alternatives to military action wherever possible, not only to reduce the direct human cost, but also the indirect costs through environmental degradation and use of non-renewable resources. At present, environmental issues

---

128 There have been instances in international law, where justice has been unfair and prejudiced. For instance, Germany and Japan were prosecuted for war crimes following the WW II, but not allied forces. State responsibility was imposed on Iraq for damages in Kuwait, but not on the US in Vietnam. In non-international conflicts, tribunals were established for Rwanda and Yugoslavia, but not for Russia (Chechnya) or China (Tibet).

are not integrated into the larger UN humanitarian programmes, and numerous structural and management problems reduce the effectiveness of environment-specific programmes, such as those funded by the Global Environment Facility. Improved coordination could resolve many of these problems without significantly raising overall aid expenditure. All UN relief and development projects in post-conflict situations should integrate environmental considerations in order to improve the effectiveness of the UN country programme. The UN peacekeeping contingents must have environment-restoration experts.

An international agency should be established to ensure the protection of the environment in times of armed conflict; preferably as a component of the UN. It should have the power to prosecute nations, organizations and individuals for crimes against the environment committed during armed conflict. It should also have the ability to monitor the activities of combatants, to ensure compliance with international law, and to secure compensation where there has been a breach. International law should protect States which are not parties to an armed conflict from any consequential environmental damage. Special rights of compensation should be established. A State or non-state actors guilty of unlawful aggression, including the waging of environmental warfare, or wanton destruction of the environment, not justified by military necessity, should be made responsible for any unjustified environmental damage which results.

Armed hostilities may cause disastrous consequences when they occur in zones of major ecological importance. Areas containing unique ecosystems or endangered species may be completely destroyed if they are not provided with effective and specific protection.[129] In order to avoid the consequences of hostilities, certain fragile environments or areas of major ecological importance, such as groundwater aquifers, national parks and habitats of endangered species, need to be kept away from any form of military activity. Such areas should therefore be delineated and designated as demilitarized zones before an armed conflict occurs, or when fighting breaks out.[130] The ICRC's Guidelines on the Protection of the Environment

---

129 For instance, Virunga National Park in the Democratic Republic of the Congo, which contains some of the richest biodiversity in Africa, has been affected by armed conflicts for the last 20 years. *Conservation and Conflict: A Case Study for Virunga National Park*, International Institute for Sustainable Development, MEAs, Democratic Republic of the Congo, 2008.

130 The establishment of such a system of specially protected areas could be based, for

during Armed Conflict (1994) must be updated and considered by the UN General Assembly for adoption.

## States

The increase in environmental damage during the last few decades requires that certain constraints be placed on the war-fighting decisions of the commander so far as they relate to environmental protection. Just as military commanders have a serious responsibility to minimize casualties during armed conflict, they must also show concern for the environment in military operations. Taking the cue from IEL and IHL, governments should make environmental protection during armed conflicts a centrepiece of their military doctrines. This would necessitate that commanders not only be trained on environmental concerns but also be provided the services of specialist staff with experience in environmental protection issues.

Governments must outlaw the military use of any practice or device that would have long-lasting injurious effects on people or the natural environment, for example nuclear weapons, anti-personnel land mines, poisonous and nerve gases, germ warfare and defoliants. The environment itself should not be used as a weapon. The destruction of large areas of natural habitat or the poisoning of waterways, for instance, should be prohibited. The use of environmental modification techniques, that is, any techniques for changing, through the deliberate manipulation of natural processes, the dynamics, composition or structure of the earth, including the biota, lithosphere, hydrosphere and atmosphere, or of outer space, should be prohibited.

Governments must ensure the preparation of national military manual on IHL or the law of armed conflict,[131] which should incorporate provisions

---

example, on the system of enhanced protection for cultural property. Under that system, cultural property of special significance for humanity is entered on a list and the parties concerned undertake never to use it to back up military operations. The property is thus protected from attack for as long as it is not used for military purposes. See: Second Protocol to the Hague Convention of 1954 for the Protection of Cultural Property in the Event of Armed Conflict.

131 See Articles 80, 82 and 83 of 1977 Additional Protocol I. Article 80 obligates contracting states to take all necessary measures with a view to ensuring observance of the law. From this general obligation emanate two further duties, one on the provision of legal advisers to the military (Article 82) and the other on dissemination (Article 83). Publishing national manuals is a component of dissemination. Manuals, besides clarifying legal issues, reaffirm the government's commitment to ensuring respect for the law, assisting armed forces personnel with decision making and providing

relating to environmental protection in IAC and NIAC. The national manual should not be too voluminous and must avoid technical terms and jargon, so that its provisions can be understood by those without military or legal training. Environmental considerations must be included in military training, research and development programmes.[132]

Governments administrating post-conflict areas should associate with the civil society organizations to provide basic environmental services (safe drinking water, food, sanitation services, reliable energy supplies and refuse collection) for the population on priority. They must adopt a participatory approach with populations and help the latter build their capacity to meet their basic environmental needs.

National parks, reserves and areas of special ecological significance should be declared demilitarized zones.[133] Attacks on infrastructure or installations that result in the release of poisonous substances, radioactivity or other forms of pollution must be prohibited. Such infrastructure should be clearly marked and identified in accordance with international law. Sites for storage of armaments must be selected with equal regard for the health and safety of residents and the ecology of the areas. Such sites must be restricted in number and damage must be repaired and rehabilitated.

A taskforce should be set up by the States to establish clean production standards and life cycle analyses for all military equipment, whether manufactured locally or imported. The task force should seek ways to avoid the production of toxic wastes, the dumping of wastes and the unacceptable disturbance of the environment wherever raw materials are extracted, equipment is used, or worn-out or obsolete equipment is discarded. The taskforce should include representatives of environmental agencies and

---

material for training.

132 The armed forces should, without impacting their readiness and ability to protect the country, comply with environmental laws, regulations, and policies that apply to the rest of society. Changes in manufacturing or maintenance practices, spurred by environmental considerations, can improve mission performance of the military. By acting in an environmentally responsible manner, the armed forces can have a significant influence on the rest of society to act in a similar manner. While it would be exceedingly difficult to eliminate any impacts on the environment during armed conflict, consideration of environmental implications is prudent to ensure the post-war viability of the natural environment and lessening of human strife.

133 In the proposed convention, provisions contained in Article 4 to 7 for national and international protection of the cultural and national heritage under the 1972 World Heritage Convention could be suitable modified and incorporated for the protection of national parks, reserves and areas of special ecological significance.

organizations. Areas that suffer environmental damage through their use for such military purposes as artillery ranges, armoured vehicle practice, sea and aerial bombardment, conventional weapons testing, etc, should be subject to environmental audit and environmental impact assessment. The armed forces must assist in cleaning up areas to rid them of all toxic residues and unexploded ordnance.

## Militaries

Despite the importance of environmental considerations in soldier's health, stability and reconstruction, and mission success, environmental issues are often not considered in the planning and conduct of military operations. The main reason for this is the lack of political awareness and the absence of environmental emphasis in military doctrine, training, and leadership. Leadership education on environmental issues in military operations is a rare phenomenon.

Military commanders must ensure that a proper balance is maintained between environmental protection constraints and mission accomplishment. The ever increasing vigilance by environmental organizations will demand that in future, military commanders consider the environmental impact of their operations, if they desire to avoid possible public censure. There is a need to include environment-related objectives in military operations plans and to follow [134] standard operating procedures (SOPs) for environmental protection in the field. Environmental policy for military operations should include: (i) Understanding that the environmental protection is every individual's responsibility; (ii) Compliance with applicable national and international agreements; (iii) Recognition of the importance of environmental planning; (iv) The goal of minimizing environmental damage; (v) The minimization of waste by wisely using raw materials, energy, water, etc. (vi) Effective handling and storage of hazardous substances; (vii) Timely response to environmental incidents to mitigate impacts; and (viii) Minimizing noise and other safety hazards. The armed forces must assist in cleaning up post-conflict areas to rid them of all toxic residues and unexploded ordnance. The navies must ensure that maritime areas are as environmentally benign as possible. Naval exercise held off the coast must have regard for breeding marine life

All military personnel should be educated in international and national

---

134 *Environmental Guidebook for Military Operations* (2008). Available at: http://www. phrakl.fi/en, accessed 12 June 2014.

'best environmental practice' and environmental legal requirements. Military manuals should contain clear instructions in this regard for all military activities.[135] Commanders must ensure that the forces under their command receive the appropriate levels of environmental awareness training. An officer with sufficient knowledge and experience in environmental protection should be designated by the commander as the primary point of contact for environmental issues. Peacetime military activities and training have some adverse impact on the environment. Information about such environmental damage should not be concealed, and a system of sharing information with public should be established by every State.[136]

The armed forces manage large tracts of land for military bases and training areas. They could play an important role in the protection of flora and fauna because this land remains in a relatively pristine natural condition, protected from more extensive development and encroachment.[137] Many of these areas contain valuable habitats and endangered plants and animals. The armed forces must develop environmental management

---

135 Shahi, G.S. and V.W. Sidel, 'The Impact of Military Activities on Development, Environment, and Health' in Shahi GS et. al., (eds.), *International Perspectives on Environment, Development, and Health,* New York: Springer Publishing Company, 1997, p. 283.

136 The general principles of governance that can be employed in the area of environment are greater participation, fairness, access to justice, transparency, accountability, efficiency, leadership/direction and timeliness. The Convention on Access to Information, Public Participation in Decision-making and Access to Justice in Environmental Matters (Aarhus Convention), adopted by the European Community in 2007 provides access to environmental information, public participation and access to justice. Similar legislations for sharing of information with the public can be adopted by all the States. Jha U C, 'Environmental Governance: Corruption and Access to Information', in Sinha M.K. (ed.), 2009. *Global Governance, Human Rights and Development*, New Delhi: Satyam Law International, p. 255-271.

137 The Indian army has been playing important role in the protection and preservation of the environment. Ecology and Environment Cell of the Indian Army is located at army headquarters under the quartermaster general. The army has also joined hands with the private sector to implement projects like rainwater harvesting, ground water rejuvenation, construction of check dams and water treatment/de-siltation of water bodies, new and renewable energy initiatives, etc. In addition an ecological task force (ETF) has been functioning since 1982 to undertake afforestation programmes and related projects to improve the environment. These projects are expected to enhance the biodiversity conservation potential of the Army's various establishments, such as cantonments, depots, manoeuver areas and military farms. The project also involves spreading awareness on ecology and biodiversity related concepts among school children. For details see: Gautam P.K. 2003. *Environmental Security: Internal and External Dimensions and Response*, New Delhi: Knowledge World, p. 212-227.

plans for its major facilities. These plans should address the protection and conservation of biodiversity at military bases. The forces may use the services of specialist consultants to undertake ecological surveys of the military facilities and maintain lists of the type, number and condition of vulnerable flora and fauna species at each facility.

Demilitarized equipments, weapons and munitions should be recycled. This includes anti-personnel landmines, small arms and light weapons, chemicals, cluster munitions, ammunition containing white phosphorus, depleted uranium and tungsten. Obsolete military equipment such as vehicles, ships and aircraft containing harmful elements such as asbestos, PCBs (Polychlorinated biphenyls), lead, chromates etc. must be disposed in an environmentally responsible manner. Obsolete military equipments and weapons could be recycled to extract valuable metals and chemicals, for example, steel from weapons could be turned into manhole covers, piping and reinforcing rods for the building industry; the bodies of demilitarized missiles could be turned into water tanks; demilitarized explosives could be put to commercial use; demilitarized white phosphorous could be converted into phosphoric acid for commercial use; and plastic landmine bodies could be converted into toys and plastic piping.

There is a need to create a broad-based framework for public participation in pre-conflict decisions to ensure that the conduct of belligerents in an armed conflict is sensitive to possible damage to the environment. The international community must develop the notion that total immunity for wartime environmental destruction cannot be accorded to militaries. The regime of criminality must also be extended to all forms of excessive assaults on the environment in international as well as non-international armed conflicts. According to the World Resource Institute; "Amid war's brutality, death, and deprivation, the environment may seem a minor casualty. Yet, the destruction of the environment, along with the demolition of democratic, informed decision-making, can prolong human suffering for decades, undermining the foundation for social progress and economic security."[138]

---

138 World Resources Institute, *World Resources 2002–2004: Decisions for the Earth: Balance, Voice, and Power*, p. 27. Available at: http://www.wri.org/publication/world-resources-2002-2004, accessed 1 June 2014.

# Bibliography

Abaraviciute, Dalia, *Environmental Protection Through Criminal Law: The case study of Lithuania*, Unpublished Master's Thesis, 2010.

Abdulraheem Mahmood Y. 2000. 'War-related Damage to the Marine Environment in the ROPME Sea Area, in Austin, Jay E., and Bruch, Carl E., (ed.), *The Environmental Consequences of War: Legal, Economic and Scientific Perspectives*, Cambridge: Cambridge University Press.

Addressing Environmental Consequences of War. 1998. Background Paper for the First International Conference on Addressing Environmental Consequences of War: Legal, Economic, and Scientific Perspectives, Washington, D.C., Environmental Law Institute.

Adhikari, Jay Ram and Bhim Adhikari, Political Conflicts and Community Forestry: Understanding the Impact of the Decade-Long Armed Conflicts on Environment and Livelihood Security in Rural Nepal, 2010, available at: http://www.capri.cgiar.org/pdf/CAPRi_Conflict_Adhikari.pdf.

*Afghanistan: Post-Conflict Environment Assessment*, 2003, United Nations Environment Programme (UNEP).

Afriansyah Arie, International Environmental protection During Armed Conflict; Case Study: Israel-Lebanon Conflict, *Jurnal Hukum dan Pembangunan Tahun*, Vol. 38, No. 1, January-March 2008, p. 35-57. Available at: http://isjd.pdii.lipi.go.id/admin/jurnal/381083557.pdf.

Abijola, B. 'Protection of the Environment in Times of Armed Conflict". In Al-Nauimi, N. and Meese, R. (eds.), *International Legal Issues Arising Under the United Nations Decade of International Law*, 1995, The Hague: Martinus Nijhoff Publishers.

Abouali Gamal, Natural Resources under Occupation: The Status of Palestinian Water under International Law, Vol. 10 (2), *Pace International Law Review*, 1998, p. 411-574.

Adede, Andronico O., 'Protection of the Environment in Times of Armed Conflict: Reflections on the Existing and Future Treaty Law', Vol. 1 (1), *Annual Survey of International & Comparative Law*, Article 7, (1994), p. 161-179.

Alexander Nicholas G., Airstrikes and Environmental Damage: Can the United States be Held Liable for Operation Allied Force?, Vol. 11, No. 2, *Colorado Journal of International Environmental Law and Policy*, 2000, p. 471-498.

Al-Delphi Hassan Hassoon, The Environmental Tragedies of the Wars on Iraq. Available at: http://ehealth.hbmeu.ac.ae/eHealthProceedings/PDF/Dr.%20Hassan%20Hasson%20-%20Full%20Paper.pdf.

Al-Duaij Nada. 2004. *Environmental Law of Armed Conflict*, New York: Transnational Publishers.

Alfredson Gudmundur. 2010. Human Rights and the Environment, in Leary David & Balakrishna Pisupati (eds.), *The Future of International Environmental Law*, Tokyo: United Nations University Press, p. 127-146.

Amanda Doty, Reshaping Environmental Criminal Law: How Forfeiture Statutes Can Deter Crime, Vol. 18, Issue 3, *Georgetown International Environmental Law Review*, Spring 2006, p. 521-542.

*Annual Report 2007*, Wildlife Watch Group: Nepal, Kathmandu.

Antoine Philippe, International Humanitarian Law and the Protection of the Environment in Time of Armed Conflict", No. 291, *International Review of the Red Cross*, November-December 1992, p. 517-537.

Arkin William M., Cyber Warfare and the Environment, Vol. 25 (3), *Vermont Law Review*, (2000-2001), p. 779-791.

Armed Conflict and the Environment, Report of the Committee on the Environment, Council of Europe, Doc 12774, 17 October 2011.

Assessment of the Environmental Impact of Military Activities During the Yugoslavia Conflict, Prepared by: The Regional Environmental Center for Central and Eastern Europe, June 1999. Available at: http://www.grip.org/bdg/pdf/g1691.pdf.

Asthana Vandana and Shukla AC, Environmental Consequences of Armed Conflict in South Asia, *South Asian Journal*, October-December 2008

Issue, p. 79-91.

Augst Robert M, Environmental Damage Resulting From Operation Enduring Freedom: Violations of International Law? *ELR News & Analysis*, Vol. 33, 2003, p. 10668-10681.

Austin, Jay E., and Bruch, Carl E., (ed.). 2000. *The Environmental Consequences of War: Legal, Economic and Scientific Perspectives*, Cambridge: Cambridge University Press.

Australian Defence Force: Environmental Management, Appendix 4, Defence Annual Report 2009-2010, p. 310-315.

Babcock, Hope M., The Problem with Particularized Injury: The Disjuncture Between Broad-Based Environmental Harm and Standing Jurisprudence, Vol. 25, *Journal of Land Use*, Fall 2009, p. 1-18.

Baker B., Legal Protection for the Environment in Times of Armed Conflict, Vol. 33, *Virginia Journal of International Law*, 1993, p. 352.

Baral, N. and J. T. Heinen, The Maoist People's War and Conservation in Nepal, Vol. 24, Issue 1-2, *Politics and the Life Sciences*, (2006), p. 2-11.

Batal al-Shishani, Murad, Environmental Ramifications of the Russian war on Chechnya, *Central Asia-Caucasus Analyst*, 3 May 2006, p. 10-11.

Bayoneto M. Victoria, The Former US Bases in the Philippines: An Argument for the Application of US Environmental Standards to Overseas Military Bases, Vol. VI, *Fordham Environmental Law Journal*, (1994), p. 111-155.

Benjamin Paul, Green Wars: Making Environmental Degradation a National Security Issue Puts Peace and Security at Risk, *Policy Analysis*, No. 369, April 20, 2000.

Bergstrom Margareta. 1990. The Release in War of Dangerous Forces from Hydrological Facilities, in Westing Arthur H (ed.), *Environmental Hazards of War: Releasing Dangerous Forces in an Industrialized World*, New Delhi: Sage Publications, p. 38-47.

Berhe, A.A., The Contribution of Landmines to Land Degradation, Vol. 18, *Land Degradation & Development*, 2007, p. 1-15.

Bhurtel, Jugal, & Saleem H. Ali. 2009. 'The Green Roots of Red Rebellion: Environmental Degradation and the Rise of the Maoist Movement in Nepal', in Mahendra Lawoti & Anup Pahari (eds.), *The Maoist Insurgency in Nepal: Dynamics and Growth in the 21ˢᵗ Century*. New York: Routledge.

Biringer Kent L., The Siachen Peace Park Proposal: Reconfiguring the Kashmir Conflict, available at: http://peaceparks2007.whsites.net/Papers/Biringer%20&%20Cariappa_Siachen%20Peace%20Park%20Proposal.pdf.

Biswas Asit K. 2000. 'Scientific Assessment of the Long-term Environmental Consequences of War', In Austin, Jay E., and Bruch, Carl E., (ed.), *The Environmental Consequences of War: Legal, Economic and Scientific Perspectives*, Cambridge: Cambridge University Press.

Blank Laurie and Amos Guiora, Teaching an Old Dog New Tricks: Operationalizing the Law of Armed Conflict in New Warfare, Vol. 1, *Harvard National Security Journal*, (2010), p. 45-85.

Bleise A, P.R. Danesi, W. Burkart, Properties, use and health effects of depleted uranium (DU): A general overview, Vol. 64, *Journal of Environmental Radioactivity*, (2003), p. 93-112.

Bodansky Daniel. 2003. *Legal Regulation of the Effect of Military Activity on the Environment*, Berlin, Erich Schmidt Verlag, p. 126.

Bondarenko BB and Kasyanenko, 'Military Pollution—Chemical Waste' in Taipale Ilkka, P. Helena Makela and Kati Juva (ed.). 2001. *War or Health? A Reader*, London: Zed Books, p. 426-430.

Boothby Bill, 'The Law of Weaponry—Is It Adequate'? in Schmitt Michael and Jelena Pejic. (ed.). 2007. *International Law and Armed Conflict: Exploring the Faultlines*; Essays in Honour of Yoram Dinstein, Martinus Nijhoff Publisher, p. 297-316.

Boothby William H. 2009. *Weapons and the Law of Armed Conflict*, Oxford: Oxford University Press.

Borrie John. 2009. *Unacceptable Harm: A History of How the Treaty to Ban Cluster Munition Was Won*, Geneva: United Nations Institute for Disarmament Research.

Bostian Ida L., The Environmental Consequences of the Kosovo Conflict and the NATO Bombing of Serbia, *Colorado Journal of International Environmental Law and Policy*, 1999, p. 230-240.

Bothe Michael, Carl Bruch, Jordan Diamond, and David Jensen., International Law Protecting the Environment during Armed Conflict: Gaps and Opportunities, Vol. 92, No. 879, *International Review of the Red Cross*, September 2010, p. 569-592.

Bothe Michael, The Protection of Environment in Times of Armed Conflict, Vol. 34, *German Yearbook of International Law*, 1991, p. 54.

Bothe M., Partsch, K.J. & Solf, W.A. 1982. *New Rules for Victims of Armed Conflicts*, Hague: Martinus Nijhoff, p. 746.

Bothe Michael, Environmental Destruction as a Method of Warfare, *Disarmament*, Vol. XV, (1992), No. 2, p. 101-161.

Bouvier Antoine, Protection of the natural environment in time of armed conflict, No. 285, *International Review of the Red Cross*, December 1991, p. 567-578.

Bouvier Antoine, Recent Studies on the Protection of the Environment in Time of Armed Conflict, No. 291, *International Review of the Red Cross*, November-December 1992, p. 554-566.

Brantz Dorothee, 'Environments of death: trench warfare on the western front, 1914-1918', in Closmann Charles E., (ed.). 2009. *War and the Environment: Military Destruction in the Modern Age*, USA: Texas A&M University Press, p. 68-91.

Brauer Jurgen. 2011. *War and Nature: The Environmental Consequences of War in a Globalized World*, London: AltaMira Press.

Breau Susan, 'Protection of Environment during Armed Conflict', in Shawkat Alam (ed). 2013. *Routledge Handbook of International Environmental Law*, London: Ruotledge, p. 617-632.

Briggs Chad M., et.al., Environmental health risks and vulnerability in post-conflict regions, Vol. 25, No. 2, *Medicine, Conflict and Survival*, April-June 2009, p. 122-133.

Bring O., Regulating Conventional Weapons in the Future: Humanitarian Law or Arms Control? Vol. 24, *Journal of Peace Research*, Oslo, 1987, p. 275-286.

Bring O., 'Arms Control and International Environmental Law', in Wahlgren, Peter (ed.). 2000. *International Aspects*, Stockholm Institute for Scandinavian Law, p. 397-417.

Brisman Avi, Crime-Environment Relationship and Environmental Justice, Vol. 6, Issue 2, *Seattle Journal for Social Justice*, 2008, p.727-817.

Brough Michael W., John W. Lango and Harry van der Linden (eds.). 2007. *Rethinking the Just War Tradition*, USA: State University of New York Press.

Bruch Carl E., All's Not Fair in (Civil) War: Criminal Liability for Environmental Damage in Internal Armed Conflict, Vol. 25, No. 3, *Vermont Law Review*, (2000-2001), p. 695-752.

Bruch, Carl E., et. al. 2009. 'Post-conflict Peace Building and Natural Resources', in Ole Kristian Fauchald, David Hunter, and Wang Xi (eds), *Yearbook of International Environmental Law*, Vol. 19, 2008, Oxford: Oxford University Press.

Bull John M.R., Decades of Dumping Chemical Arms Leave a Risky Legacy, Special Report, Part 1 & 2, *Daily Press*, 30 and 31 October 2005. Available at: http://www.dailypress.com/news/dp-02761sy0oct30,0,5136883,full. story.

Bunker Alice Louise, Protection of the Environment During Armed Conflict: One Gulf Two Wars, *RECIEL*, Vol. 13(2), 2004, p. 201-213.

Butler Carolyn, Journey Without End, *National Geographic*, March 2014, p. 52.

Butts Kent Hughes. 1994. 'Why Military is Good for the Environment', in Kakonen Jyrki (ed.), *Green Security or Militarized Environment*, USA: Dartmouth.

Caggiano Mark J.T., The Legality of Environmental Destruction in Modern Warfare: Customary Substance Over Conventional Form, Vol. 20, *B.C. ENVTL. AFF. L. REV.*, (1993), p. 479.

Caron David D. 2000. 'The Place of Environment in International Tribunals', In Austin, Jay E., and Bruch, Carl E., (ed.), *The Environmental Consequences of War: Legal, Economic and Scientific Perspectives*, Cambridge: Cambridge University Press.

Carr Paul, "Shock and Awe" and the Environment, Vol. 19, *Peace Review: A Journal of Social Justice*, 2007, p. 335-342.

Carus, W. Seth, *Defining "Weapons of Mass Destruction"*, Centre for the Study of Weapons of Mass Destruction, Occasional Paper, No. 8,

Washington, DC: National Defence University Press, January 2012.

Cave, Rosy. 2003. *Explosive Remnants of War in Sri Lanka*, London: Landmine Action 2003.

Chamber, W. Bradnee, Towards an Improved Understanding of Legal Effectiveness of International Environmental Treaties, Vol. 16, *Georgetown International Environmental Law Review*, Spring 2004, p. 501-530.

Chamorro Susana Pimiento and Edward Hammond, *Addressing Environmental Modification in Post-Cold War Conflict*, Occasional Paper, USA: The Edmonds Institute. Available at: http://www.edmonds-institute.org/pimiento.html.

Chartier, Robert J., Environmental Issues Associated With Operation Enduring Freedom, *Engineer*, October-December 2003, p. 24-27.

Closmann Charles E., (ed.). 2009. *War and the Environment: Military Destruction in the Modern Age*, USA: Texas A&M University Press.

Cohan John Alan, Modes of Warfare and Evolving Standards of Environmental Protection under International Law of War, Vol. 15, *Fla. J. Int'l L.* (2002-03), p. 481-539.

Coleman Kim. 2005. *A History of Chemical Warfare*, New York: Palgrave Macmillan.

Conca Ken and Jennifer Wallace, Environment and Peacebuilding in War-torn Societies: Lessons from the UN Environment Programme's Experience with Pos-tconflict Assessment, *Global Governance*, Vol. 15, (2009), p. 485-504.

CSO Report on the Application of Environmental Norms by Military Establishments *For submission to the United Nation Environment Programme,* The Sub-Committee on Military Related Environmental Concerns, Vermont Law School International Law Society, February 2008.

Daehler, Curtis C. and Majumdar SK. 1992. 'Environmental Impacts of the Persian Gulf War' in Majumdar SK, Forbes GS, Miller EW and Schmalz (ed.), *Natural and Technological Disasters: Causes, Effects and Preventive Measures*, The Pennsylvania Academy of Science, p. 329-336.

Dahl Arne Willy, Environmental Destruction in War, Vol. XV, No. 2,

*Disarmament*, (1992), p. 113-127.

DeSaussure, Major Ariane L. The Role of the Armed Conflict During the Persian Gulf War: An Overview, *The Air Force Law Review*, 1994, p. 41-68.

Desgagne Richard, The Prevention of Environment Damage in Time of Armed Conflict: Proportionality and Precautionary Measures, in Horst Fischer and Avril McDonald (eds.), *Yearbook of International Humanitarian Law*, Vol. 3, 2000, p. 109-129.

Deweerdt Sararh, War and the Environment, *World Watch*, Vol. 21 (1), Jan-Feb 2008.

Dhar Aarti, Manmohan calls for saving Himalayan Eco-system, *The Hindu*, 27 October 2009.

Dibley Arjuna & Emily Kerr, Denouncing and deterring environmental harm: An argument for the reconsideration of international crimes to protect the environment, available at: http://law.anu.edu.au/coast/events/environment/papers/dibley&kerr.pdf.

Diederich Michael, Law of War and Ecology: A Proposal for a Workable Approach to Protecting the Environment through the Law of War, Vol. 136, *Military Law Review*, Spring 1992, p.137-160.

Dinstein Yoram. 2001. 'Protection of the Environment in International Armed Conflict', In Frowein J.A. and R Wolfrum (ed.), *Max Planck Yearbook of the United Nations Law*, Vol. 5, p. 523-549.

Document A/CN.4/SR.2430, Summary record of the 2430 Meeting, Extract from the *Yearbook of the International Law Commission*, 1996, Vol. I, available at: http://untreaty.un.org/ilc/documentation/english/a_cn4_sr2430.pdf.

Dogra Bharat, How destructive can these weapons be, *The Statesman*, New Delhi, 17 December 2009.

Dominguez-Mates Rosario, 2005, 'New Weaponry technologies and International Humanitarian Law: Their Consequences on the Human Being and the Environment', in Fernandez-Sanchez Pablo Antonio (ed.), *The New Challenges of Humanitarian Law in Armed Conflicts*, Leiden: Martinus Nijhoff Publishers, p.91-119.

Dorfman Bridget, Permission to Pollute: The United States Military,

Environmental damage, and Citizen's Constitutional Claims, Vol. 6, No. 3, *Journal of Constitutional Law*, March 2004, p. 604-622.

*Draft International Covenant on Environment and Development*, International Union for Conservation of Nature and Natural Resources, Fourth Edition, 2010.

Draulans Dirk and Ellen Van Krunkelsven, The impact of war on forest areas in the Democratic Republic of Congo, Vol. 36, No. 1, *Oryx*, 2002, p. 35-40.

Drucker Major Merrit P., The Military Commander's Responsibility for the Environment, Vol. 11 (2), *Environmental Ethics, (1989), p. 135-152.*

Drumble Mark A., *Accountability for Property Crimes and Environmental War Crimes: Prosecution, Litigation, and Development*, International Centre for Transitional Justice, November 2009.

Drumbl, Mark A., Waging War Against the World: The Need to Move from War Crimes to Environmental Crimes, Vol. 22, Issue 1, *Fordham International Law Journal*, (1998), p. 122-153.

Dudley Joseph P., et. al., Effects of War and Civil Strife on Wildlife and Wildlife Habitats, Vol. 16, No. 2, *Conservation Biology*, April 2002, p. 319-329.

Dycus Stephen, Nuclear War: Still the Gravest Threat to the Environment, Vol. 25 (3), *Vermont Law Review*, (2000-2001), p. 753-771.

Dycus, Stephen, Osama's Submarine: National Security and Environmental Protection After 9/11, Vol. 30, No. 1, *WM. & MARY ENVTL. L. & POL'Y REV.*, (2005), p. 1- 54.

Eifan, Meshari K., Head of State Criminal Responsibility for Environmental War Crimes: Case Study: The Arabian Gulf Armed Conflict 1990-1991, (2007). Pace University, School of Law, Dissertation and Theses.

El-Baz Faronk and R M Makharita. 1994. *The Gulf War and Environment*, USA: Gordon & Breach Science Publishers.

Elliot L. Environment and Security: What's the Connection, Issue No. 174, *Australian Defence Force Journal*, 2007, p. 39-52.

Enduring Effects of War: Health in Iraq, 2004, London: Medact.

Enemark Christian. 2003. *Biological Weapons: An Overview of Threats and*

*Responses*, Working Paper No. 379, Canberra: Strategic and Defence Studies Centre.

Environmental Assessment of the Gaza Strip following the Escalation of Hostilities in December 2008 – January 2009, United Nations Environment Programme, (2009).

Environmental Contaminants from War Remnants in Iraq, NGO Coordination Committee for Iraq, June 2011, available at: http://reliefweb.int/sites/reliefweb.int/files/resources/images... unitionsHumanHealthinIraq.pdf.

Etten Jacob van, Joost Jongerden, Hugo J. de Vos, Annemarie Klaasse, Esther C.E. van Hoeve, Environmental destruction as a counterinsurgency strategy in the Kurdistan region of Turkey, *Geoforum*, Vol. XXX (2008), p. 1-12.

Evans Gareth, *The Responsibility to Protect in Environmental Emergencies*, American Society of International Law, Proceedings of the 103rd Annual Meeting, March 25-28, 2009, Washington, DC, p. 27-32.

Falk, Richard. 2000. 'The Inadequacy of the Existing Legal Approach to Environmental Protection in Wartime', In Austin, Jay E., and Bruch, Carl E., (ed.), *The Environmental Consequences of War: Legal, Economic and Scientific Perspectives*, Cambridge: Cambridge University Press.

Feinstein Barry A., The Applicability of the Regime of Human Rights in Times of Armed Conflict and Particularly to Occupied Territories: The Case of Israel's Security Barrier, Vol. 4, Issue 2, *Northwestern Journal of International Human Rights*, Fall 2005, p. 238-302.

Fidler David P. 2000. 'War and Infectious Diseases: International Law and the Public Health Consequences of Armed Conflict', In Austin, Jay E., and Bruch, Carl E., (ed.), *The Environmental Consequences of War: Legal, Economic and Scientific Perspectives*, Cambridge: Cambridge University Press.

Finger Matthias. 1994. 'Global Environmental Degradation and the Military', in Kakonen Jyrki (ed.), *Green Security or Militarized Environment*, USA: Dartmouth.

Fleck Dieter (ed.). 2008. *The Handbook of International Humanitarian Law*, Oxford: Oxford University Press.

Forces for Sustainability: Report of the first Peace and Sustainability Session, Peace Palace, The Hague, 14-15 March 2007, Netherlands, The Hague: Institute for Environmental Security.

Fort Timothy L. and Cindy A. Schipani, Ecology and Violence: The Environmental Dimensions of War, William Davidson Institute Working Paper Number 698, May 2004.

Freeland Steven, 'Crime Against the Environment – A Role for the International Criminal Court', in Alberto Costi and Yves-Louis (eds.), *Environmental Law in the Pacific: International and Comparative Perspectives*, p. 335-372. Available at: http://www.upf.pf/IMG/pdf/16-freeland.pdf.

Freeland Steven, Human Rights, the Environment and Conflict: Addressing Crimes Against the Environment, *The International Journal of Human Rights*, Vol. 2, No. 2, (2005), p. 112-139.

Freeland Steven, Human Security and the Environment: Prosecuting Environmental Crimes in the International Criminal Court, Available at:http://law.anu.edu.au/anzsil/conferences/2004/proceedings/freeland.pdf.

Furitsu Kastumi, *Hazard of Uranium Weapons to Health and Environment*, Report to the Workshop Towards a Ban of DU, Organized by the International Coalition to Ban Uranium Weapons (ICBUW) in cooperation with the International Peace Bureau (IPB), Geneva, 9 November 2005.

Gander T.J. 1987. *Nuclear, Biological and Chemical Warfare*, London: Ian Allan Ltd.

Gangwar Abdhesh, Impact of War and Landmines on Environment, Centre for Environmental Education, Available at: http://archive.mtnforum.org/rs/ol/counter_docdown.cfm?fID=1409.pdf.

Garrett Benjamin C. and John Hart. 2010. *Historical Dictionary of Nuclear, Biological and Chemical Warfare*, USA, Maryland: The Scarecrow Press.

Gasser Hans-Peter, For Better Protection of the Natural Environment in Armed Conflict: A Proposal for Action, Vol. 89 (3), *American Journal of International Law*, (1995), p. 637-645.

Gasser, Hans-Peter, Guidelines for Military Manuals and Instructions on the

Protection of the Environment in Times of Armed Conflict, *International Review of the Red Cross*, No. 311, (1993), p. 230-237.

Gattini Andrea, The UN Compensation Commission: Old Rules, New Procedures on War Reparations, Vol. 13, *European Journal of International Law*, (2002), p. 161-181.

Geib Robin, Poison, 'Gas and Expanding Bullets: The Extension of the List of Prohibited Weapons at the Review Conference of the International Criminal Court in Kampala', in Schmitt M.N. (eds.), Volume 13, *Yearbook of International Humanitarian Law*, 2010, p. 337-352.

Gibbons Owen Thomas, Uses and Effects of Depleted Uranium Munitions: Towards a Moratorium on Use, *Yearbook of International Humanitarian Law*, Vol. 7 (2004), p. 191-232.

Gibson Sarah, Polluters as Perpetrators of Person Crimes: Charging Homicide, Assault, and Reckless Endangerment in the Face of Environmental Crime Vol. 25, *Journal of Environmental Law and Litigation*, (2010), p. 511-558.

Gill Terry D. and Dieter Fleck (ed.). 2010. *The Handbook of the International Law of Military Operations*, Oxford: Oxford University Press.

Gillet Matthew, Prosecuting Environmental Damage Under International Criminal Law, p. 1-11, available at: http://www.esil-en.law.cam.ac.uk/Media/Draft_Papers/Agora/Gillett.pdf.

Gilman Ryan, Expanding Environmental Justice after War: The Need for Universal Jurisdiction over Environmental War Crimes, Vol. 22, No. 3, *Colo. J. Int'l Envtl. L. & Pol'y*, (2011), p. 447-471. S-256.

Gleditsch Nils Petter, Armed Conflict and The Environment: A Critique of the Literature, Vol. 35, No. 3, *Journal of Peace Research*, 1998, p. 381-400.

Godschalk Seakle K.B., Green Soldiering – Integrated Environmental management as a Major Contribution towards Military Mission Achievement, available at: http://www.dfac.mil.za/publications/presentations/papers/Article%20MIEM.pdf.

Goldblat, Jozef, Laws of Armed Conflict: An Overview of the Restrictions and Limitations on the Methods and Means of Warfare, Vol. 13, *Bulletin of Peace Proposals*, Oslo, 1982, p. 127-133.

Goldblat Jozef. 1990. The Mitigation of Environmental Disruption by War: Legal Approaches, in Westing Arthur H. (ed.), *Environmental Hazards of War: Releasing Dangerous Forces in an Industrialized World*, New Delhi: Sage. p. 48-60.

Gopal Sriram and Nicole Deller, *Precision Bombing, Widespread Harm; Two Case Studies of the Bombings of Industrial Facilities at Pancevo and Kragujevac During Operation Allied Force, Yugoslavia 1999*, Institute for Energy and Environmental Research November 2002. Available at: http://www.ieer.org/reports/bombing/pbwh.pdf.

Grace Charles S. 1994. *Nuclear Weapons: Principles, Effects and Survivability*, London: Brassey's.

Granoff Jonathan, Nuclear Weapons, Ethics, Morals, and Law, Vol. 4, *Brigham Young University Law Review*,(2000), p. 1413-1442.

*Greening the Blue Helmets: Environment, Natural Resources and UN Peacekeeping Operations*, United Nations Environment Programme (UNEP), Nairobi, 2012.

Grunawalt Richard J., King John E. and McClain Ronald S. (eds). 1996. *Protection of the Environment During Armed Conflict*, Newport, Naval War College, International Law Studies, Vol. 69, pp. 720.

Guidelines for Military Manuals and Instructions on the Protection of the Environment in Times of Armed Conflict, No. 311, *International Review of the Red Cross*, March-April 1996, p. 230-237.

Guruswamy Lakshman D. and Grillot Suzette R. 2001. *Arms Control and the Environment*, New York: Transnational Publishers Inc. Ardsley.

Haavisto Pekka, 'Kosovo War: First Environmental Impact Assessment', in Taipale Ilkka, P. Helena Makela and Kati Juva (ed.). 2001. *War or Health? A Reader*, London: Zed Books, p. 447-451.

Halle Silja (ed.). 2009. *From Conflict to Peace-building: The Role of Natural Resources and the Environment*, The United Nations Environment Programme (UNEP), pp. 50.

Hamilton, A, A. Cunningham, et al., Conservation in a region of political instability: Bwindi Impenetrable Forest, Uganda, *Conservation Biology*, 14(6), (2000), p. 1722-1725.

Hancock Jan. 2003. *Environmental Human Rights: Power, Ethics and Law*,

USA: Ashgate.

Harland Christopher, Anti-Personnel Landmines: Balancing Military Utility and the Humanitarian Cost, *CLAWS Journal*, Summer 2008, p. 236-248.

Harrell Eben, Regional Nuclear War and the Environment, *Times*, January 22, 2009.

Hart, T. and A. Hart, Conservation and civil strife: two perspectives from central Africa, *Conservation Biology*, 11(2), (1997), p. 308-314.

Hay Alastair W. 2000. 'Defoliant: The Long-term Health Implications', In Austin, Jay E., and Bruch, Carl E., (ed.), *The Environmental Consequences of War: Legal, Economic and Scientific Perspectives*, Cambridge: Cambridge University Press.

Haye Eve La. 2008. *War Crimes in Internal Armed Conflicts*, Cambridge: Cambridge University Press.

Henckaerts Jean-Marie, Towards Better Protection for the Environment in Armed Conflict: Recent Developments in International Humanitarian Law, *RECIEL*, Vol. 9 (1), 2000, p. 13-19.

Henckaerts, Jean-Marie. 2000. 'International Legal Mechanism for Determining Liability for Environmental Damage under International Humanitarian Law', in Austin, Jay E., and Bruch, Carl E., (ed.). *The Environmental Consequences of War: Legal, Economic and Scientific Perspectives*, Cambridge: Cambridge University Press, p. 602-619.

Henckaerts, Jean-Marie and Louise Doswald-Beck. 2005. *Customary International Humanitarian Law*, Vol. I, International Committee of the Red Cross and Cambridge: Cambridge University Press.

Hinde Susan M., International Environmental Court: Its Broad Jurisdiction as a Possible Fatal Flaw, Vol. 32, *Hofstra Law Review*, (2003), p. 727-757.

Hiskes R. P., The Right to a Green Future: Human Rights, Environmentalism, and Intergenerational Justice, Vol. 27, No. 4, *Human Rights Quarterly*, (2005), p.1346–1364.

Homer-Dixon, Thomas F., On the Threshold: Environmental Changes as Causes of Acute Conflict, Vol. 16 (2), *International Security*, (1991), p. 76-116.

Hosmer Alicia Watts, Colby E. Stanton, and Julie L. Beane, Intent to Spill: Environmental Effects of Oil Spills Caused by War, Terrorism, Vandalism, and Theft, Paper presented at International Oil Spill Conference, 1997. Available at: http://www.iosc.org/papers/01058.pdf.

Hourcle Laurent R., Environmental Law of War, Vol. 25 (3), *Vermont Law Review*, (2000-2001), p. 653-693.

Hulme Karen. 2010. A Darker Shade of Green: Is it time to Ecocentrise the Laws of War, in Quenivet Noelle and Shilan Shah-Davis (ed.), *International Law and Armed Conflict: Challenges in the 21ˢᵗ Century*, TMC Asser Press, p. 142-160.

Hulme Karen, Environmental Security: Implications for International Law, Vol. 19, *Yearbook of International Environmental Law*, 2008, p. 3-36.

Hulme Karen, Taking Care to Protect the Environment against Damage: A Meaningless Obligation, *International Review of the Red Cross*, Vol. 92, No. 879, September 2010, p. 675-69.

Hulme Karen. 2004. *War Torn Environment: Interpreting the Legal Threshold*, Leiden: Martinus Nijhoff Publishers.

Humphreys, M., Natural resources, conflict and conflict resolution: uncovering the mechanisms, Vol. 49, No. 4, *Journal of Conflict Resolution*, August 2005, p. 508-537.

Hupy, Joseph, The Environmental Footprint of War, Vol. 14, No. 3, *Environment and History*, (August 2008), p. 405-21.

Huston Meredith DuBarry, Wartime Environmental Damage: Financing the Cleanup, Vol. 23, *U. Pa. J. Int'l Econ. L.*, (2000), p. 899-929.

Ignatavicius Gytautas and Vytautas Oskinis, Some aspects of interaction between military activities and environmental protection on Lithuanian military grounds, Vol. 53, *Ekologija*, Supplement, 2007, p.16–21.

Insurgents Don't Spare Tigers too, *The Times of India*, 1 June 2010.

International Committee of the Red Cross (ICRC), Guidelines for Military Manuals and Instructions on the Protection of the Environment in Times of Armed Conflict. Available at: http://www.icrc.org/eng/resources/documents/misc/57jn38.htm.

Jabbari-Gharabagh Mansour, Type of State Responsibility for Environmental

Matters in International Law, Vol. 33, *RJT*, (1999), p. 59-121.

Jacobsson, Marie G., *Protection of the environment in relation to armed conflicts*, Annex E, Report of the International Law Commission, Sixty-third session, (26 April–3 June and 4 July–12 August 2011), to General Assembly, Supplement No. 10 (A/66/10), p. 358.

Jensen Eric Talbot, The International Law of Environmental Warfare: Active and Passive Damage During Armed Conflict, Vol. 38 (1), *Vanderbilt Journal of Transnational Law* (2005), p. 145-185.

Jensen Eric Talbot and James J. Teixeira, Prosecuting Members of the US Military for Wartime Environmental Crimes, Vo. 17, *The Georgetown International Environmental Law Review*, (2004-05), p. 651-671.

Jones Carol A. 2000. 'Restoration-based Approach to Compensation for Natural Resource Damage: Moving Towards Convergence in US and International Law', In Austin, Jay E., and Bruch, Carl E., (ed.), *The Environmental Consequences of War: Legal, Economic and Scientific Perspectives*, Cambridge: Cambridge University Press.

Jongerden, Joost, et.al., Forest burning as a counterinsurgency strategy, 2006, available at: http://www.joostjongerden.info/ForestBurning_website.pdf.

Jorgensen Nikolai, The Protection of Freshwater in Armed Conflict, Vol. 3 (2), *Journal of International Law and International Relations*, 2007, p. 57-96.

Joyner Christopher C. and James T. Kirkhope, The Persian Gulf War Oil Spill: Reassessing the Law of Environmental Protection and the Law of Armed Conflict, Vol. 24, No. 1, *Case Western Reserve Journal of International Law*, Winter 1992, p. 29-62.

Kanyamibwa Samuel, Impact of War on Conservation: Rwandan Environment and Wildlife in Agony, Vol. 7, *Biodiversity and Conservation*, 1998, p. 1399-1406.

Kellman Barry. 2000. 'The Chemical Weapons Convention: A Verification and Enforcement Model for Determining Legal Responsibility for Environmental Harm Caused by War', in Austin, Jay E., and Bruch, Carl E., (ed.), *The Environmental Consequences of War: Legal, Economic and Scientific Perspectives*, Cambridge: Cambridge University Press.

Kelly Katherine M., Declaring War on the Environment: The Failure of International Environmental Treaties During the Persian Gulf War, Vol. 7, *American University Journal of International Law and Policy*, (1992), p. 921-950.

Kemkar Neal A, Environmental Peacemaking: Ending Conflict between India and Pakistan on the Siachin Glacier through the Creation of a Trans-boundary Peace Park, *Stanford Environmental Law Journal*, Vol. 25 (1), (2006), p. 1-56.

Kerbrat Yann and Sandrine Maljean-Dubosos (eds.). 2011. *The Transformation of International Environmental Law*, Oxford UK: Hart Publishing Ltd.

Kerr Glenn and Barry Snushall. 2005. *Future Environmental Policy Trend to 2020: Impact on Ship Design and Operation*, Centre for Maritime Policy, University of Wollongong, Commonwealth of Australia.

Khan Imtiyaz Gul, Afghanistan: Human Cost of Armed Conflict since Soviet Invasion, Vol. XVII, No. 4, *Perceptions*, Winter 2012, p. 209-224.

Kirby Alex, World 'Needs Green Geneva Convention', 10 February 2003, available at http://news.bbc.co.uk/1/hi/sci/tech/2744359.stm.

Kirk Talbott & Melissa Brown, Forest Plunder in Southeast Asia: An Environmental Security Nexus in Burma and Cambodia, Environmental Change & Security Project Rep., Spring 1998.

Kiss Alexandre, International Humanitarian Law and the Environment, *Environmental policy and Law*, Vol. 31/4-5, (2001), p. 223-231.

Kiss Alexandre, State Responsibility and Liability for Nuclear Damage, Vol. 35 (a), *Denv. J. Int'l L.& Pol'y*, (2006), p. 67-83.

Kolesnikov Sergei and Aleksander Yemelyanenkov, 'Nuclear Pollution in the Former USSR, in Taipale Ilkka, P. Helena Makela and Kati Juva (ed.). 2001. *War or Health? A Reader*, London: Zed Books, p. 420-425.

Koplow David A. 2001. 'Green Chemistry: Dismantling Chemical Weapons While Protecting the Environment', in Guruswamy Lakshman D (ed.) *Arms Control and the Environment*, New York: Transnational Publishers, Inc, p. 143-157.

Koppe Erik. 2008. *The Use of Nuclear weapons and the Protection of Environment During International Armed Conflict*, USA, Oregon:

Oxford and Portland.

Krass Allan S. 1990. 'The Release in War of Dangerous Forces from Nuclear Facilities', in Westing Arthur H (ed.), *Environmental Hazards of War: Releasing Dangerous Forces in an Industrialized World*, New Delhi: Sage, p. 10-29.

Kritsiotis, Dino, The fate of nuclear weapons after the 1996 advisory opinions of the world court, *Journal of Armed Conflict Law*, 1996, p. 95-119.

Kumar Manoj, Challenges for the Indian Military: Managing Ozone Depleting Substances, Vol. 5 (2), *Air Power Journal*, Summer 2010, p. 117-131.

Lamm Vada, Protection of Civilian Nuclear Installations in Time of Armed Conflict, p. 1-10. Available at: http://www.oecd-nea.org/law/nlb/nlb-72/029_038.pdf.

Landel Morgane, Are Aerial Fumigations in the Context of the War in Colombia a Violation of the Rules of International Humanitarian Law? Vol. 19, *Transnational Law & Contemporary Problems*, Spring 2010, p. 491-513.

Lanier-Graham Susan D. 1993. *The Ecology of War: Environmental Impacts of Weaponry and Warfare*, New York: Walker and Company.

Larsson Marie-Louise, Legal Definitions of the Environment and of Environmental Damage, Stockholm Institute for Scandinavian Law, Available at: http://www.scandinavianlaw.se/pdf/38-7.pdf.

Lawrence C. Jessica and Heller Kevin Jon, The First Eco-centric Environmental War Crime: The Limits of Article 8(2)(b)(iv) of the Rome Statute, Vol. 20 (1), *Georgetown International Environmental Law Review*, Fall 2007, p. 61-96.

Leaning Jennifer, Environment and health: Impact of war, *Canadian Medical Association Journal*, October 31, 2000, 163(9): 1157-1161.

Le Billon Philippe, The Political Ecology of War: Natural Resources and Armed Conflicts, Vol. 20, *Political Geography*, 2001, p. 561–584.

Leibler Anthony, Deliberate Wartime Environmental Damage: New Challenges for International Law, *California Western International Law Journal*, Vol. 23, No. 1, 1992-1993, p. 67-137.

Lewis Jeff, Unexploded Ordnance and the Environment – a Legacy of Past Practices, Vol. 10. No. 4, *Canadian Military Journal*, (2009), p. 46-52.

Lijiang Zhu. 2011. 'A Test of International Humanitarian Law on Landmines in recent Conflicts: Problems and Possible Solutions', in Matheson M.J. and D. Momtaz (ed.), *Rules and Institutions on International Humanitarian Law Put to the test of recent Armed Conflicts*, Leiden/Boston: Martinus Nijhoff Publishers, p. 653-693.

Lind Jeremy and Kathryn Sturman. 2002. *Scarcity and Surfeit: The Ecology of Africa's Conflict*, South Africa: Institute for Security Studies.

Linda Nowlan. 2001. *Arctic Legal Regime for Environmental Protection*. IUCN, Gland, Switzerland and Cambridge, UK and ICEL, Bonn, Germany, p. 70.

Littlewood, Jez. 2005. *The Biological Weapons Convention: A Failed Revolution*, England: Ashgate.

Livingstone Ann and Kristine St-Pierre (eds.). 2009. *Environmental Considerations for Building Peace*, The Pearson Papers, Vol. 12, Canada: Pearson Peacekeeping Centre.

Loets Adrian, An Old Debate Revisited: Applicability of Environmental Treaties in Times of International Armed Conflict Pursuant to the International Law Commission's 'Draft Articles on the Effects of Armed Conflict on Treaties', Vol. 21 (2), *RECIEL*, 2012, p. 127-136.

Lopez Aurelie, The Protection of Environmentally-Displaced Persons in International Law, Vol. 37, *Environmental Law*, (2007), p. 365-409.

Lopez Aurelie, Criminal Liability for Environmental Damage Occurring in Time of Non-International Armed Conflict: Rights and Remedies, Vol. 18, *Fordham Environmental Law Review*, (2006-2007), p. 247-248.

Lorenz Frederick M, *The Protection of Water Facilities under International Law*, A Research Project Sponsored by the International Water Academy, Oslo, Norway. Available at: http://webworld.unesco.org/water/wwap/pccp/cd/pdf/legal_tools/protection_of_water_facilities_2.pdf.

Loretz John, The Animal Victims of the Gulf War, The PSR Quarterly, December 1991, Vol. 1, No. 4, p. 221-225. Available at: http://www.ippnw.org/pdf/mgs/psr-1-4-loretz.pdf.

Low Luan and David Hodgkinson, Compensation for Wartime

Environmental Damage: Challenges to International Law After the Gulf War, Vol. 35, No. 2, *Virginia Journal of International Law*, (1995), p. 405-483.

Luck Edward C, *Environmental Emergencies and the Responsibility to Protect: A Bridge Too Far*, American Society of International Law, Proceedings of the 103rd Annual Meeting, March 25-28, 2009, Washington, DC, p. 32-38.

Lujala, Paivi, The Spoils of Nature: Armed civil Conflict and Rebel Access to Natural resources, Vol. 47 (1), *Journal of Peace Research*, (2010), p. 15-28.

Lundberg Michael A. The Plunder of Natural Resources during War: A War Crime, Vol. 39 (3), *Georgetown Journal of International Law*, (2008), p. 495-525.

MacKenzie Catherine P., Barking Up the Wrong Tree: Current Challenges in International Environmental Law, Vol. 58, *Virginia Lawyer*, February 2010, p. 44-49.

McCallion K.F., Sharma R.H., Environmental justice without borders: The need for an international court of the environment to protect fundamental environmental rights, Vol. 32, No. 3, *The George Washington Journal of International Law and Economics*, (2000), p. 351-365.

McLaughlin Kathryn and Kathryn Nixdorff (ed.), *Biological Weapons Reader*, The Bio-Weapons Prevention Project (BWPP), Geneva, 2009.

McNaught L.W. 1984. *Nuclear Weapons and Their Effects*, London: Brassey's Defence Publishers.

Machlis Gary E. and Thor Hanson, Warfare Ecology, Vol. 58, No. 8, *BioScience*, September 2008, p. 729-736.

Majeed Abeer. 2004. *The Impact of Militarism on the Environment: An Overview of Direct & Indirect Effects*, 2004, Canada: Physicians for Global Survival.

Malone Linda A, *Green Helmets: Eco-Intervention in the Twenty-first Century*, American Society of International Law, Proceedings of the 103rd Annual Meeting, 2009, Washington, DC, p. 19-27.

Malone Linda A, Green Helmets: A Conceptual Framework for Security

Council Authority in Environmental Matters, Vol. 17, *Michigan Journal of International Law*, 1996, p. 515-536.

Mannion A.M., 2003, T*he Environmental Impact of War and Terrorism*, Geographical Paper No 169, Department of Geography, University of Reading, Whiteknights, UK.

*Manual on International Law Applicable to Air and Missile Warfare.* 2009. Harvard University, Program on Humanitarian Policy and Conflict Research (HPCR), Bern.

Marauhn Thilo, Environmental damage in times of armed conflict not really a matter of criminal responsibility? *International Review of the Red Cross*, No. 840, (2000), p. 1029-1036.

Marauhn Thilo, Georg Nolte, and Andreas Paulus, Possible Future Trends in International Humanitarian Law, Vol. 28, No. 3-6, *Human Rights Journal*, August 31, 2007, p. 65-75.

Marsh Jeremy J., *Lex Lata* or *Lex Ferenda?*: Rule 45 of the ICRC Study on Customary International Humanitarian Law, Vol. 198, *Military Law Review*, 2008, p. 116-164.

Martin Jean-Christophe. 2011. 'The United Nations Compensation Commission Practice with Regards to Environmental Claims', in Kerbrat Yann and Sandrine Maljean-Dubosos (ed.), *The Transformation of International Environmental Law*, Oxford UK: Hart Publishing Ltd, p. 253-55.

Mason, Michael, 'The application of warfare ecology to belligerent Occupations', in Machlis, Gary and Hanson, Thorand Spiric, Zdravko and McKendry, J. E., (eds.). 2011. *Warfare Ecology: a new synthesis for peace and security*, Germany: Springer, Dordrecht.

Matheson Michael J., The Environmental Effects of Nuclear Weapons and the 1996 World Court Opinion, Vol. 25 (3), *Vermont Law Review*, (2000-2001), p. 773-777.

Mason, Simon A., and Adrian Muller. 2008. *Linking Environment and Conflict Prevention: The Role of the United Nations*, Centre for Security Studies (CSS), ETH Zurich.

Mathien Timothy R., Environmental Protection and the Law of Armed Conflict: A Study of Current Provisions and a Recommendation for the

Future, Vol. VIII, *The Bowdoin Forum: Journal of International Affairs*, Spring 2005, p. 37-65.

Matousek Jiri. 1990. The Release in War of Dangerous Forces from Chemical Facilities, in Westing Arthur H (ed.), *Environmental Hazards of War: Releasing Dangerous Forces in an Industrialized World*, New Delhi: Sage. p. 30-37.

McDonald Avril, Jann K. Kleffner and Brigit Toebes (eds). 2008. *Depleted Uranium Weapons and International Law: A Precautionary Approach*, T.M.C. Asser Press.

McEwan A.C. 1988. 'Environmental Effects of Underground Nuclear Explosions', in Goldblat Jozef and David Cox (ed.), *Nuclear Weapon Tests: Prohibition or Limitation*, SIPRI, Oxford: Oxford University Press.

McKay Catriona L. and Donald K Anton, *Protecting the Silent Victim from Irregular Actors: Improving Non-State Compliance with the International Law of Environmental Protection in Armed Conflict*, ANU College of Law Research Paper No. 12-18.

McManus Keith P., Civil Liability for Wartime Environmental Damage: Adapting the United Nations Compensation Commission for the Iraq War, Vol. 33, No. 2, *Boston College Environmental Affairs Law Review*, (2006), p. 417-448.

McNeely Jeffery A. and Susan A. Mainka, Conservation for a New Era: Conservation and Armed Conflict, International Union for Conservation of Nature (2009), Switzerland: IUCN.

McNeely Jeffery A. 2001. 'Environmental Impacts of Arms and War', in Guruswamy Lakshman D (ed.) *Arms Control and the Environment*, New York: Transnational Publishers, Inc, p. 41-58.

McNeely Jeffrey A., Conserving Forest Biodiversity in times of Violent Conflict, *Oryx*, Vol. 37, No.2, April 2003, p. 142-152.

McNeely Jeffery A. 2000. 'War and Biodiversity: An Assessment of Impacts, In Austin, Jay E., and Bruch, Carl E., (ed.), *The Environmental Consequences of War: Legal, Economic and Scientific Perspectives*, Cambridge: Cambridge University Press.

McNeill J.R., 'The Global Environmental Footprint of the US Military', in Closmann Charles E., (ed.). 2009. *War and the Environment: Military*

*Destruction in the Modern Age*, USA: Texas A&M University Press, p.10-31.

Megret Frederic, The Problem of an International Criminal Law of the Environment, Vol. 36 (2), *Columbia Journal of Environmental Law*, (2011), p. 195-257.

Mensah Thomas A. 2000. 'Environmental Damage Under the Law of Sea Convention', In Austin, Jay E., and Bruch, Carl E., (ed.), *The Environmental Consequences of War: Legal, Economic and Scientific Perspectives*, Cambridge: Cambridge University Press.

Miguel Edward and Gerard Roland, The Long-run Impact of Bombing Vietnam, Vol. 96, *Journal of Development Economics*, 2011, p. 1-15.

Miller Jeferey G. 2000. 'Civil Liability for War-caused Environmental damage: Model from United States Law', In Austin, Jay E., and Bruch, Carl E., (ed.), *The Environmental Consequences of War: Legal, Economic and Scientific Perspectives*, Cambridge: Cambridge University Press.

Mishra Charudutt and Anthony Fitzherbert, War and wildlife: a post-conflict assessment of Afghanistan's Wakhan Corridor, Vol. 38, No. 1, *Oryx*, January 2004, p. 102-105.

Moret Leuren, Depleted Uranium: The Trojan Horse of Nuclear War, Vol. 8, No. 2, *World Affairs*, p. 110-135.

Mosher David E., Beth E. Lachman, Michael D. Greenberg, Tiffany Nichols, Brian Rosen, Henry H. Willis. 2008. *Green Warriors: Army Environmental Considerations for Contingency Operations from Planning Through Post-Conflict*, RAND Corporation.

Mossalanejad A., International Security through Environmental Challenges, *Int. J. Environ. Res.*, Vol. 3 (3), Summer 2009, p. 429-434.

Moxley, Charles J., John Burroughs, and Jonathan Granoff, Nuclear Weapons and Compliance with International Humanitarian Law and the Nuclear Non-Proliferation Treaty, Vol. 34, *Fordham International Law Journal*, (2011), p. 595-697.

Murphy Mark, Krishna Prasad Oli, & Steve Gorzula. 2005. *Conservation in conflict: The impact of the Maoist-government conflict on conservation and biodiversity in Nepal*. Winnipeg: International Institute for Sustainable Development.

Murray Richard R. & Kellye L. Fabian, Compensating the World's Landmine victims: Legal Liability and Anti-Personnel Landmine Producers, Vol. 33, *Seton Hall Law Review*, (2003), p. 303-369.

Nagle Luz E., Placing Blame Where Blame is Due: The Culpability of Illegal Armed Groups in Narco-traffickers in Colombia's Environmental and Human Rights Catastrophes, Vol. 29, *William & Marry Environmental Law and Policy Review*, (2004), p.1-106.

Nair Pavan, The Siachin War: Twenty-five Years On, *Economic & Political Weekly*, March 14, 2009, Vol XLIV, No. 11, p. 35-40.

Nanda, Ved P., International Environmental Norms Applicable to Nuclear Activities, With Particular Focus on Decisions of International Tribunals and International Settlements, Vol. 35 (1), *Denv. J. Int'l L & Policy*, (2006), p. 47-65.

Nasr, D, et. al., Environmental Impacts of Reconstruction Activities: A Case of Lebanon, Vol. 3, No. 2, *Int. J. Environ. Res.*, Spring 2009, p.301-308.

Naxal Threat Affects Tigers too, *The Hindu*, 20 December 2010.

Nicolson Garth L and Marawn Nasralla, 'Gulf War Illnesses', in Taipale Ilkka, P. Helena Makela and Kati Juva (ed.) 2001. *War or Health? A Reader*, London: Zed Books, p. 431-46.

Okowa Phoebe. 2009. 'Environmental Justice in Situations of Armed Conflict', in Ebbesson Johan and Phoebe Okawa (eds.), *Environmental Law and Justice in Context*, Cambridge: Cambridge University Press, p. 246-47.

Okowa Phoebe N., Natural Resources in Situations of Armed Conflict: Is There a Coherent Framework for Protection? Vol. 9, No. 3, *International Community Law Review*, 2007, p. 237-262.

Omar, Samira A., E. Briskey, R. Misak, and Adel Asem. 2000. "The Gulf War Impact on the Terrestrial Environment of Kuwait: An Overview." In *The Environmental Consequences of War: Legal, Economic, and Scientific Perspectives*. J. Austin and C. Bruch, (eds.), Cambridge: Cambridge University Press, p. 316–337.

Orellana Marcos A. Criminal Prosecution for Environmental Damage: Individual and State Responsibility at a Crossroad, Vol. 17 (2004-2005), *The Georgetown International Environmental Law Review*, p. 673-696.

Page Edward, Theorizing the Link Between Environmental Change and Security, *RECIEL*, Vol. 9 (1), 2000, p. 33-43.

Parsons, Rymn James, The fight to save the planet: US Armed Forces, 'Greenkeeping', and Enforcement of the law pertaining to environmental protection during armed conflict, Vol. 10, No. 2, *Georgetown International Environmental Law Review*, 1998, p. 482.

Partow Hassan, Environmental Impact of Wars and Conflicts, available at: http://www.afedonline.org/afedreport/english/book12.pdf.

Percival Robert V., Liability for Environmental Harm and Emerging Global Environmental Law, Vol. 25, *Maryland Journal of International Law*, (2010), p. 37-63.

Peterson Ines, The Natural Environment in Times of Armed Conflict: A Concern for International War Crimes Law? *Leiden Journal of International Law*, Vol. 22, issue 2, (2009), p. 325-343.

Peytrignet Gerard, Protection of the Natural Environment in Time of Conflict: Overview of the State of International Humanitarian Law and the Position of the International Committee of the Red Cross (ICRC), available at: http://www.bibliojuridica.org/libros/4/1985/15.pdf.

Plant Glen. 1993. 'Environmental Damage and the Laws of War: Points Addressed to Military Lawyers', in Fox Hazel & Meyer Michael A. (eds.), *Armed Conflict and the New Law, Volume II – Effecting Compliance*, p. 159-174.

Plant, Glen. 1992. *Environmental Protection and the Law of War: a fifth Geneva convention on the protection of the environment in the time of armed conflict*. London; New York: Belhaven, Press.

Polkinghorne Michael and James Cockayne, Dealing with the Risks and Responsibilities of Landmines and their Clearance, Vol. 25, Issue 5, *Fordham International Law Journal*, (2001), p.1187-1204.

Poll Letetia van der and Ashraf Booley, In Our Common Interest: Liability and Redress for Damage Caused to the Natural Environment During Armed Conflict, Vol. 15, *Law, Democracy & Development*, (2011), p. 1-43.

Popovsky Mark, Nanotechnology and Environmental Insurance, Vol. 36, No. 1, *Columbia Journal of Environmental Law*, 2011, p.125-161.

*Protecting the Environment During Armed Conflict: An Inventory and Analysis of International Law*, November 2009, UNEP, pp.79.

Price, S. V. (ed.). (2003). *War and Tropical Forests: Conservation in Areas of Armed Conflicts*, New York: Food Products Press.

Puleo Lt. Col. Louis J., Conservation Issues on Military Land: Some Thoughts on a Framework for Successful Mission Integration, Vol. 17 (2), *Journal of Land Use and Environmental Law*, (Spring 2002), p. 413-439.

Quinn John P., Richard T. Evans and Michael J. Boock. 2000. 'United States Navy Dvelopment of Operational Environmental Doctrine', In Austin, Jay E., and Bruch, Carl E., (ed.), *The Environmental Consequences of War: Legal, Economic and Scientific Perspectives*, Cambridge: Cambridge University Press, p.156-170.

Rahman Chris and Robert J. Davitt. 2006. *ADF Training in Australia's Maritime Environment*, Papers in Australian Maritime Affairs, No. 18, Australia: University of Wollongong, p. 72.

Rao, N.H., Environmental management: Relevance and implications for management of defence installations for sustainability, *Current Science*, Vol. 88, No. 11, 10 June 2005, p. 1753-1758.

Rappert Brian. 2006. *Controlling the Weapons of War: Politics, Persuasion and the Prohibition of Inhumanity*, London: Routledge.

Rawcliffe, Maj John (ed.), *Operational Law Handbook-JA 422, International and Operational Law*, The Judge Advocate General's Legal Centre and School, US Army, Virginia, 2007.

Reichberg Gregory & Syse Henrik, Protecting the Natural Environment in Wartime: Ethical Considerations from the Just War Tradition, Vol. 37, No. 4 *Journal of Peace Research*, 2000, p. 449-468.

Rest Alfred, Enhanced Implementation of International Environmental Treaties by Judiciary-Access to Justice in International Environmental Law for Individuals and NGOs: Efficacious Enforcement by the Permanent Court of Arbitration, Vol. 1, *MqJICL*, p. 1028,

Reyhani Roman O., The Protection of the Environment During Armed Conflict, Vol. 14, No. 2, *Missouri Environmental Law and Policy Review*, 2007, p. 323-338.

Richards Peter J. & Schmitt Michael N., Mars Meets Mother Nature: Protecting the Environment During Armed Conflict, Vol. 28, No. 4, *Stetson Law Review*, (1999), p. 1047-1092.

Richter Elihu, et. al., Ecocide: A Crime Against Humanity, available at: http://beta.genocidepreventionnow.org/Portals/0/docs/Ecocide_Collegium%20Ramazzini_Richter.pdf.

Riordan Kevin, Protecting Fundamental Human Rights in Times of War—The Means and Methods of Warfare, Human Rights Research, available at: http://www.victoria.ac.nz/nzcpl/HRRJ/vol3/Riordan.pdf.

Roberts Adam. 2000. 'The Law of War and Environmental Damage', In Austin, Jay E., and Bruch, Carl E., (ed.), *The Environmental Consequences of War: Legal, Economic and Scientific Perspectives*, Cambridge: Cambridge University Press.

Roberts Adam, 'Failure in Protecting the Environment in the 1990-1991 Gulf War, in Rowe Peter (ed.). 1993. *The Gulf War 1990-1991 in International and English Law*, London: Sweet and Maxwell, p.111-154.

Roberts Adam, Environmental Destruction in the Gulf War", No. 291, *International Review of the Red Cross*, November-December 1992, p. 538-553.

Roberts Michael, Oil War II: The Environmental Consequences, available at: http://www.ecu.edu.au/chs/cem/research/reviews%20&%20articles/articles/M_Roberts_art.pdf.

Robinson J.P. Perry, Difficulties facing the Chemical Weapons Convention, Vol. 84, No. 2, *International Affairs*, (2008), p. 223-239.

Robyn Eckersley, Ecological Intervention: Prospects and Limits, available at: http://www.redorbit.com/news/science/1101311/ecological_intervention_prospects_and_limits/index.html.

Roka Krishna B., Armed Conflict and its Impact on Community Forestry in Nepal, Vol. 26, *Tropical Resources Bulletin*, Spring 2007, Yale Tropical Resource Institute, Yale School of Forestry and Environmental Studies, p. 55-62.

Roscini Marco. 2009. Protection of the Natural Environment in the Time of Armed Conflict, in Bhuiyan Md. J. H., Louise Doswald-Beck, and A.R. Chowdhury (eds.) *International Humanitarian Law – An Anthology*,

Nagpur: LexisNexis Butterworths, p. 155-179.

Ross, Marc A., Environmental warfare and the Persian Gulf War: possible remedies to combat intentional destruction of the environment', Vol. 10, *Dickinson Journal of Environmental Law and Policy*, 1992, p. 534.

Rubenson David, Jerry Aroesty and Charles Thompsen, Two Shades of Green: Environmental Protection and Combat Training, RAND's Army Research Division for United States Army.

Sadik M. and McCain J.C. 1993. *The Gulf War Aftermath: An Environmental Tragedy*, Springer.

Saillan Charles de, Disposal of Spent Nuclear Fuel in the United Sates and Europe: A Persistent Environmental Problem, Vol. 34, *Harvard Environmental Law Review*, (2010), p. 461-519.

Saleem Farrukh, Strategic Dialogue is the only answer, *The Times of India*, 17 January 2010.

Sand Peter H., International Environmental Law After Rio, Vo. 4, *EJIL*, (1993), p. 377-389.

Sandoz Yves, Chrisotphe Swinarski and Bruno Zimmermann (eds.). 1987. *Commentary on the Additional Protocols of 8 June 1977 to the Geneva Conventions of 12 August 1949*, International Committee of the Red Cross, Geneva: Martinus Nijhoff Publishers.

Sands Philippe. 2003. *Principles of International Environmental Law*, New York: Cambridge University Press, p. 219-316.

Santiapillai Charles and S. Wijeyamohan, The Impact of Civil War on Wildlife in Sri Lanka, *Current Science*, Vol. 84, No. 9, 10 May 2003.

Sassoli, Marco, State responsibility for violations of international humanitarian law, *International Review of the Red Cross*, Vol. 84, No. 846, June 2002, p. 401-433.

Sassoli Marco, Antoine A. Bouvier and Anne Quintin, 2011. *How Does Law Protect in War?* Volume II, Part II: Cases and Documents, Geneva: International Committee of the Red Cross, p. 621-622.

Scheetz Lori, Infusing Environmental Ethics into the Space Weapons Dialogue, Vol. 19, No. 1, *Georgetown International Environmental Law Review*, Fall 2006, p. 57-82.

Schmitt Michael N., Investigating Violations of International Law in Armed Conflict, Vol. 2, *Harvard National Security Journal*, (2011), p. 31-84.

Schmitt Michael N., Humanitarian Law and the Environment, Vol. 28 (3), *Denv. J. International Law & Policy*, (2000), p. 265-323.

Schmitt Michael N. 2000. 'War and the Environment: Fault Line in the Perspective and Landscape', In Austin, Jay E., and Bruch, Carl E., (ed.), *The Environmental Consequences of War: Legal, Economic and Scientific Perspectives*, Cambridge: Cambridge University Press.

Schmitt Michal N., Green War: An Assessment of the Environmental law of International Armed Conflict, Vol. 22, No.1, *Yale Journal of International Law*, Winter 1997, p. 1-109.

Schmitt Michael N., The Environmental Law of War: An Invitation to Critical Re-examination, Vol. 6, *Journal of Legal Studies*, 1995-96, p. 237-271.

Schofield Timothy, The Environment as an Ideological Weapon: A Proposal to Criminalize Environmental Terrorism, Vol. 26, Issue 3, *Boston College Environmental Affairs Law Review*, (1999), p. 619-647.

Schwabach Aaron, Law Regarding Protection of the Environment During Wartime, International Law and Institutions, p. 1-7. Available at: http://www.eolss.net/Sample-Chapters/C14/E1-36-02-04.pdf.

Schwabach Aaron, Ecocide and Genocide in Iraq: International Law, the Marsh Arabs and Environmental Damage in Non-international Conflicts, (2004), The Berkeley Electronic Press.

Schwabach Aaron, Humanitarian Intervention and Environmental Protection: The Effect of the Kosovo War on the Law of War, Vol. 6, *Columbia Journal of Eastern European Law*, (2001), p. 405.

Schwabach Aaron, Environmental Damage Resulting From the NATO Military Action Against Yugoslavia, Vol. 25, No. 1, *Columbia Journal of Environmental Law*, (2000), p. 117-140.

Schwartz, Daniel M., Environmental Terrorism: Analyzing the Concept, Vol, 35, No. 4, *Journal of Peace Research*, (July 1998), p. 483-496.

Scott Karen N. International Environmental Governance: Managing Fragmentation through Institutional Connection, Vol. 12, Issue 1,

*Melbourne Journal of International Law*, June 2011, p. 177-216.

Scovazzi Tullio, State Responsibility for Environmental Harm, Ulfstein Geir and Jacob Werksman (ed.), *Yearbook of International Environmental Law*, Vol. 12 (2001), p. 43-67.

Seacor Jesica E., Environmental Terrorism: Lessons from the Oil Fires of Kuwait, Vol. 10, *AM U. J. INT'L L. & POL'Y*, 1994, p. 481-523.

Shakya, M. M. and A. Chitrakar (ed.). 2006. *Cost of Conflict on Nepal's Conservation Efforts*, Nepal, Kathmandu: Wildlife Watch Group.

Shambaugh, J., J. Oglethorpe, and R. Ham with contributions from S. Tognetti. 2001. *The Trampled Grass: Mitigating the Impacts of Armed Conflict on the Environment*. Washington, DC: Biodiversity Support Program.

Shapiro, Judith. 2001. *Mao's War Against Nature*. Cambridge: Cambridge University Press.

Sharp Peter, Prospects for Environmental Liability in the International Criminal Court, Vol. 18, No. 2, *Virginia Environmental Law Journal*, 1999, p. 217-243.

Sharp Walter G., The Effective Deterrence of Environmental Damage During Armed Conflict: A Case Analysis of the Persian Gulf War, Vol. 137, Military Law Review, (1992), p.1-66.

Shelton Dinah and Kiss Alexandre, Martens Clause for Environmental Protection, Vol. 30, No. 6, *Environmental Policy and Law*, (2000), p. 285-86.

Sherman Wesley, The Economics of Enforcing Environmental Laws: A Case for Limiting the Use of Criminal Sanctions, Vol. 23 (1), *Journal of Land Use*, Fall-2007, p-87-110.

Shrestha, R. B. and S. Suvedi. 2006. 'Impact of insurgency on community forestry program in Nepal', in Shakya M.M. and A. Chitrakar, *Cost of Conflict on Nepal's Conservation Efforts*, Kathmandu, Nepal, Wildlife Watch Group, p. 209-221.

Sidel Victor W. 2000. 'The Impact of Military Preparedness and Militarism on Health and Environment', In Austin, Jay E., and Bruch, Carl E., (ed.), *The Environmental Consequences of War: Legal, Economic and Scientific Perspectives*, Cambridge: Cambridge University Press, p. 426-443.

Sidel Victor W., Barry S. Levy, and Jonathan E. Slutzman, Prevention of War and Its Environmental Consequences, *Hdb Env Chem*, 2009, p. 21-39.

Sieg Richard, A Call to Minimize the Use of Nuclear Power in the Twenty-first Century, Vol. 9, *Vermont Journal of Environmental Law*, (2008), p. 305-373.

*Sierra Leone: Environment, Conflict and Peace-building Assessment*, Technical Report, 2010, United Nations Environment Programme, Nairobi.

Sills Joe, Jerome C. Glenn, Elizabeth Florescu and Theodore J. Gordon, *Environmental Crimes in Military Actions and the International Criminal Court -- United Nations Perspectives*, April 2001, Army Environmental Policy Institute, Atlanta.

Simonds S.N., Conventional warfare and Environmental damage Vol. 29, *Stanford Journal of International Law*, (1992), p. 165.

Sinha Manoj Kumar, Protection of the Environment During Armed Conflict: A Case Study of Kosovo, Paper presented at All India Law Teachers Conference held at Indian Society of International Law, New Delhi on 6-7 December 2008.

Sinha Uttam Kumar, Environmental Stresses and their security Implications for South Asia, Vol. 30, No. 3, *Strategic Analysis*, July-Sep 2006, p. 599-618.

Singh Shubha, Step out of dangerous terrain, *Hindustan Times*, New Delhi, 19 May 2003.

Skons, Elisabeth, *The Costs of Armed Conflict*, Stockholm International Peace Research Institute Project on Military Expenditure and Arms Production, p. 169-190.

Smith, D. 2001. *Trends and Causes of Armed Conflicts,* Berlin: Berghof Research Center for Constructive Conflict Management.

Smith Tara, Creating a Framework for the Prosecution of Environmental Crimes in International Criminal Law, available at: http://ssrn.com/ abstract=1957644.

Smith Tara. 2010. Criminal Accountability or Civil Liability: Which Approach Most Effectively Redresses the Negative Environmental

Consequences or Armed Conflict? in Quenivet Noelle and Shilan Shah-Davis (ed.), *International Law and Armed Conflict: Challenges in the 21st Century*, TMC Asser Press, p. 95-120.

Solf Waldemar A., Protection of Civilians Against the Effects of Hostilities under Customary International Law and under Protocol I, Vo. 1, No. 1, *AM. U.J. INT'L L. & POL'Y*, 1986, p. 117-135.

Solf, Waldemar A., 'Article 55: Protection of the Natural Environment', in Bothe Michael, Karl Josef Partsch, and Waldemar A. Solf. 1982. *New Rules for Victims of Armed Conflict: Commentaries on the Two 1977 Protocols Additional to the Geneva Conventions of 1949*, Nijhoff, The Hague, p. 347.

Sprinz Detlef F, Modeling Environmental Conflict, p. 1-12, available at: http://www.uni-potsdam.de/u/sprinz/doc/model.pdf.

Stenhouse M.J. and V.I. Kirko.1998. *Defence Nuclear Waste Disposal in Russia: International Perspective*, NATO ASI Series, Disarmament Technologies Vol. 18, London: Kluwer Academic Publishers.

Stephen Dale, Human Rights and Armed Conflict—The Advisory Opinion of the International Court of Justice in the Nuclear Weapons Case, Vol. 4, *Yale Human Rights & Development L.J.*, 2001, p. 1-24.

Stewart James G., Corporate War Crime: Prosecuting the Pillage of Natural Resources, New York: Open Society Institute, available at: http://www.pillageconference.org/wp-content/themes/pillage-2010/pillage-manual-10-16-2010.pdf.

Stone Christopher D. 2000. 'The Environment in Wartime: An Overview', In Austin, Jay E., and Bruch, Carl E., (ed.), *The Environmental Consequences of War: Legal, Economic and Scientific Perspectives*, Cambridge: Cambridge University Press.

Stubblefield Cynthia H. and Mahendra Shrestha, Status of Asiatic Black Bears in protected areas of Nepal and the effects of political turmoil, Vol. 18, No. 1, *Ursus*, (2007), p. 101–108.

Suba Chandran D and J Jeganaathan (Ed.). 2011. *Energy and Environmental Security: A Cooperative Approach in South Asia*, New Delhi: Institute of Peace and Conflict Studies.

Sundaram Vinothine, Fighting a Chemical War: The Environmental

Impact of War on Iraq and Its Neighboring Regions, Available at: http://www.cwru.edu/med/epidbio/mphp439/Chemical_War.pdf.

Symposium: The Environmental Law of War, A Note from the Editors, Vol. 25 (3), *Vermont Law Review*, (2000-2001), p. 649-651.

Szasz Paul C. International Law Applicable to the Gulf War, Vol. XV, No. 2, *Disarmament*, (1992), p. 101-161.

Tarasofsky Richard G, Legal Protection of the Environment During International Armed Conflict, Vol. XXIV, *Netherlands Yearbook of International Law*, (1993), p. 17-79.

Tarlock, A. Dan, In There a There There in Environmental Law? Vol. 19 (2), *Journal of Land Use*, (Spring 2004), p. 213-254.

Taylor Linda A. 2009. 'The United Nations Compensation Commission', in Ferstman Carla et. at., (Eds.), *Reparations for Victims of Genocide, War Crimes and Crimes Against Humanity: Systems in Place and Systems in Making*, Leiden: Martinus Nijhoff Publishers, p. 197-216.

Teclaff Ludwik A., Beyond Restitution—The Case of Ecocide, Vol. 34, *Natural Resources Journal*, Fall 1994, p. 933-956.

The Continuing Environmental Threat of Nuclear Weapons: Integrated Policy Responses, Vol. 88, No.21, *EOS*, 22 May 2007, p. 228-231.

The Environmental Effects of the Gulf War, Gulf War Environmental Information Service: Impact on the Land and Atmosphere, The World Conservation Monitoring Centre, UK: Cambridge.

*The Manual of the Law of Armed Conflict*, 2004, UK Ministry of Defence, Oxford: Oxford University Press.

*The Military Impact on the Human Environment*, SIPRI Yearbook, 1978, p. 43-68.

The Military's Impact on the Environment: A Neglected Aspect of Sustainable Development Debate, A Briefing Paper for States and Non-Governmental Organizations, International Peace Bureau, Geneva, August 2002.

Theisen Ole Magnus, Blood and Soil? Resource Scarcity and Internal Armed Conflict Revisited, Vol. 45, No. 6, *Journal of Peace Research*, 2008, p. 801-818.

Themner Lotta & Peter Wallensteen, Armed Conflicts, 1946-2011, Vol. 49 (4), *Journal of Peace Research*, p. 565-575.

Thompson Robert, Radioactive Warfare: Depleted Uranium Weapons, the Environment, and International Law, Vol. 36, *Environmental Law Reporter*, 2006, p.10474-10486.

Threat of modern warfare to man and his environment: An Annotated Bibliography, UNESCO Publication No. 40, UNESCO, 1979.

Thurer Daniel. 2011. *International Humanitarian Law: Theory, Practice and Context*, Hague Academy of International Law.

Tignino Mara, Reflections on the Legal Regime of Water during Armed Conflicts, available at: http://www.afes-press.de/pdf/Hague/Tignino_LegalRegime_Water.pdf.

Tomuschat Christian, Draft Code of Crimes Against the Peace and Security of Mankind, Extract from the Yearbook of the International Law Commission, 1996.

Toon Owen B., Alan Robock, and Richard P. Turco, Environmental Consequences of Nuclear War, *Physics Today*, December 2008, p. 37-42.

Trail Smelter Case (*United States v. Canada*), 16 April 1938 and 11 March 1941, Reports of International Arbitral Awards (R.I.A.A.), Vol. III, p. 1905.

Tranquillo Nicoletta, 2007. *Green Casualties of War: The need for international protection of the environment during armed conflicts and the case of the war between Israel and Lebanon in 2006*, Sweden: Lund University.

Tu Chelsea H., From Norm to Practice: Comparative Case Studies on International Mechanisms for Wartime Environmental Restitution, 12 May 2008, available at: http://nature.berkeley.edu/classes/es196/projects/2008final/Tu_2008.pdf.

Tucker Matthew L, Mitigating Collateral Damage to Natural Environment in Naval Warfare: An Examination of the Israeli Naval Blockade of 2006, Vol. 57 *NAVAL L. REV.* (2009), p. 161-201.

UNEP Report of the international meeting on environmental norms and military activities, UNEP/Env.Law/Mil/IG/1/2, 10 December 2009.

UN General Assembly Resolution 47/37, 9 February 1993, Protection of the Environment in Times of Armed Conflict, UN Doc. A/RES/47/37.

United Nations Environment Programme, Yearbook 2010, UNEP.

United Nations Environment Programme (UNEP), and United Nations Centre for Human Settlements (UNCHS). 1999. *The Kosovo Conflict: Consequences for the Environment and Human Settlements.* Geneva, Switzerland: UNEP and UNCHS.

Upreti B.C. 2011. 'Conflict in Nepal: Impact on Nepal and its Cross-border Consequences', in Raghavan V.R. (ed.) *Internal Conflict in Nepal: Transnational Consequences*, New Delhi: Vij Books India Pvt. Ltd. p. 100-118.

Upreti Bishnu Raj. 2004. *The Price of Neglect: From Resource Conflict to Maoist Insurgency in the Himalayan Kingdom,* Nepal: Bhrikuti Academic Publications, Kathmandu.

Ur-Rehman Ejaz, Impact of Armed Conflict on Environment in the State of Jammu and Kashmir: An Overview, April 2009, available at: http://www.scribd.com/doc/14892353/Impact-of-Armed-Conflict-on-Environment-in-the-State-of-Jammu-and-Kashmir.

Vanasselt Wendy, Armed Conflict, Refugees, and the Environment, *World Resources Institute 2002-2004*, June 2003, p. 25-27.

Vander Vyver Johan D., The Environment: State Sovereignty, Human Rights, and Armed Conflict, Vol. 23, No.1, *Emory International Law Review*, 2009, p. 85-112.

Varisco Andrea Edoardo, A Study of the Inter-Relation between Armed Conflict and natural resources and its Implications for Conflict resolution and Peace-building, *Journal of Peace, Conflict and Development*, Issue 15, March 2010.

Vermeer Arjen , The Laws of War in Outer Space: Some Legal Implications for the *Jus ad Bellum* and the *Jus in Bello* of the Militarisation and Weaponisation of Outer Space, p. 1-18.

Verwey Wil D., Observations on the Legal Protection of the Environment in Times of International Armed Conflict, *Hague Yearbook of International Law*, Vol. 7 (1994), p. 35-52.

Verwey Wil D., Protection of the Environment in Times of Armed Conflict:

In Search of a New Legal Perspective, Vol. 8 (1), *Leiden Journal of International Law*, 1995. p. 7-40.

Vietnam and US in joint venture to clean up Agent Orange damage, 17 June 2011, available at: http://www.guardian.co.uk/world/2011/jun/17/vietnam-us-agent-orange-damage.

Vinuales, Dr Jorge E., The Contribution of the International Court of Justice to the Development of International Environmental Law: A Contemporary Assessment, Vol. 32 (1), *Fordham International Law Journal*, (2008), p. 232-258.

Voneky Silja, A New Shield for the Environment: Peacetime Treaties as Legal Restraints of Wartime Damage, *RECIEL*, Vol. 9 (1), 2000, p. 20-32.

Vonkey Silja. 2000. Peacetime Environmental Law as a Basis of State Responsibility for Environmental Damage Caused by War', In Austin, Jay E., and Bruch, Carl E., (ed.), *The Environmental Consequences of War: Legal, Economic and Scientific Perspectives*, Cambridge: Cambridge University Press.

Vyver Johan D van der, The Environment: State Sovereignty, Human Rights and Armed Conflict, Vol. 23, No. 1, *Emory International Law Review*, (2009), p. 85-112.

Wall Andru E. 2002. *Legal and Ethical Lessons of NATO's Kosovo Campaign*, International Law Studies, Vol. 78, Newport: Naval War College, pp. 602.

Walsh Nicolas E. & Wendy S. Walsh, Rehabilitation of landmine victims — the ultimate challenge, *Bulletin of the World Health Organization*, 2003, 81 (9), p. 665-670.

Wantuck Marnie, Broken Arrows: Movement Towards Complete Prohibition of Nuclear Weapons through International Environmental Law, Editorial, *Vermont Journal of Environmental Law*, 2005.

War and the Environment, *World Watch Magazine*, January/February 2008, Volume 21, No. 1.

War Impact on Forest resources and Olive Groves in South Lebanon, Association for Forests, Development and Conservation and UNDP, Final Report, May 2007.

*Water and War: ICRC Response*, Geneva: ICRC, July 2009.

Waters Christopher and Ashley Barnes, The Arctic Environment and the Law of Armed Conflict, Vol. 6, No. 4, *Canadian Naval Review*, Winter 2011, p. 16-21.

*Weapons of Mass Destruction and the Environment*, Stockholm International Peace Research Institute (SIPRI), (1977), London: Taylor & Francis Ltd.

Weisberg Barry. 1970. *Ecocide in Indochina: The Ecology of War*, San Francisco: Canfield Press.

Weistein Tara, Prosecuting Attacks that Destroy the Environment: Environmental Crimes or Humanitarian Atrocities, Vol. 17 (2004-2005), *The Georgetown International Environmental Law Review*, p. 697-722.

Westing, Arthur H., Warwick Fox and Michael Renner, *Environmental Degradation as both Consequence and Cause of Armed Conflict*, Working Paper for Nobel Peace Laureate Forum participants by PREPCOM subcommittee on Environmental Degradation, June 2001.

Westing Arthur H. 2000. 'In Furtherance of Environmental Guidelines for Armed Forces During Peace and War', In Austin, Jay E., and Bruch, Carl E., (ed.), *The Environmental Consequences of War: Legal, Economic and Scientific Perspectives*, Cambridge: Cambridge University Press.

Westing Arthur H. 1997. 'Environmental Protection form Wartime Damage: The Role of International Law', In Gleditsch N.P. et al, (eds.), *Conflict and Environment*, Netherlands: Kluwer Academic Publishers, p. 535-553.

Westing Arthur H (ed.). 1990. *Environmental Hazards of War: Releasing Dangerous Forces in an Industrialized World*, New Delhi: Sage.

Westing Arthur H. 1984. *Herbicides in War: The Long-term Ecological and Human Consequences*, London: Taylor & Francis.

Westing Arthur H. (ed.). 1984. *Environmental Warfare: A Technical, Legal and Policy Appraisal*, SIPRI, London: Taylor & Francis.

Westing Arthur H, 'Conventional Warfare and the Human Environment', in Taipale Ilkka, P. Helena Makela and Kati Juva (ed.). 2001. *War or Health? A Reader*, London: Zed Books, p. 407-415.

Westing Arthur H, Environmental and Ecological Consequences of War, Conflict Resolution-Vol. II, available at: http://www.eolss.net/Sample-

Chapters/C14/E1-40-05-01.pdf.

Westra Laura, Ecological Integrity and Biological Integrity: The Right to Life and the Right to Health in Law, Vol. 18, No. 3, *Transnational Law & Contemporary Problems*, p. 3-44.

Wexler Lesley, Limiting the Precautionary Principle: Weapons Regulation in the Face of Scientific Uncertainty, Vol. 39, *University of California, Davis*, (2006), p. 459-529.

*What Rights for Mine Victims? Reparation, Compensation: From Legal Analysis to Political Perspectives.* France: Handicap International, April 2005.

White, Ronald H., et.al., Premature Mortality in the Kingdom of Saudi Arabia Associated with Particulate Matter Air Pollution from the 1991 Gulf War, Vol. 14, No. 4, *Hum. Ecol. Risk Assess*, 2008, p. 645-664.

Wilson Robert, 'Birds on the Home Front: Wildlife Conservation in the Western United States during World War II', in Closmann Charles E., (ed.). 2009. *War and the Environment: Military Destruction in the Modern Age*, USA: Texas A&M University Press, p. 132-149.

Winnefeld James A. and Mary E. Morris, Where Environmental Concerns and Security Strategies Meet: Green Conflict in Asia and the Middle East, RAND, 1994, p. 133.

Woods Mark, Some Worries about Ecological-Humanitarian Intervention and Ecological Defence, Vol. 21.3, *Ethics & International Affairs*, Fall 2007.

*Worldwide Emerging Environmental Security Issues Affecting the US Military.* The Millennium Project for the US Army Research Office Scientific Services Program Administered by Battelle, 30 June 2010.

Wyatt Julian, Law-making at the Intersection of International Environmental, humanitarian and criminal Law: The Issue of Damage to the Environment in International Armed Conflict, *International Review of the Red Cross*, Vol. 92, No. 879, September 2010, p. 593-646.

Yemelyanenkov Aleksander and Andrei, 'Military Pollution—Nuclear Waste', in Taipale Ilkka, P. Helena Makela and Kati Juva (ed.). 2001. *War or Health? A Reader*, London: Zed Books, p. 416-419.

York Christopher, International Law and the Collateral Effects of War on the Environment: The Persian Gulf, Vol. 7, *South Africa Journal of Human Rights*, 1991, p. 269-290.

Yves Sandoz, Christophe Swinarski, and Bruno Zimmermann (eds), 1987. *Commentary on the Additional Protocols of 8 June 1977 to the Geneva Conventions of 12 August 1949*, ICRC, Geneva/Martinus Nijhoff Publishers.

Yuzon Ensign Florencio J., Deliberate Environmental Modification Through the Use of Chemical and Biological Weapons: "Greening" the International Laws of Armed Conflict to Establish an Environmentally Protective Regime, Vol. 11, No, 5, *AM. U. INT'L L. & POL'Y*, (1996), p. 793-846.

Zemmali Ameur, The Protection of Water in Times of Armed Conflicts, No. 308, *International Review of the Red Cross*, September-October 1995, p. 550-564.

Zemmali Ameur. 2004. The Right to Water in Times of Armed Conflict, in Lijnazaad Liesbeth, Van Sambeek Johanna & Tahziblie Bahia (eds), *Making the Voice of Humanity Heard*, Leiden/Boston, M. Nijhoff, p. 307-318.

Zirojevic Mina, Markovic Milos and Pocuca Milan, Nuclear and Biological terrorism Implication on Environment, Vol. LXII, No. 1144, *The Review of International Affairs*, 2011, p. 97-108.

# Index